GOVERNMENT WORKS:

PROFILES OF PEOPLE
MAKING A DIFFERENCE

GOVERNMENT WORKS:

PROFILES OF PEOPLE MAKING A DIFFERENCE

James P. Troxel, General Editor

AN ANTHOLOGY OF READINGS
ON PARTICIPATION
IN VARIOUS LEVELS OF GOVERNMENT

Miles River Press

1009 Duke Street, Alexandria, Virginia 22314

Published by:
Miles River Press
1009 Duke Street
Alexandria, VA 22314
(703) 683-1500, Fax: (703) 683-0827
(800) 767-1501

Miles River Press Team
Peg Paul, Publisher
Elizabeth Katz, Project Editor
Libby Schroeder, Marketing Coordinator
Coda Graphics, Design and Production

Editorial Note:
* *The editors express appreciation to the government employees who gave permission to share their stories for this book.*
* *Graphics appear in the form supplied from each profile contributor.*
* *Copy editing was styled using the Chicago Manual of Style; certain contributors requested deviation from that format for their chapters.*

Library of Congress Cataloging-in-Publication Data:
Government works : profiles of people making a difference / James P.
  Troxel, General Editor.
        p.   cm.
    "An anthology on particpation on various levels of
government."
    Includes bibliographical references.
    ISBN 0-917917-04-9 (alk. paper)
    1. Political participation—United States—Case studies. 2. Local
government—United States—Citizen participation—Case studies.
3. State governments—United States—Citizen participation—Case
studies. 4. Federal government—United States—Citizen
participation—Case studies. I. Troxel, James P., 1948-
JK1784.G68 1995
323'.42'0973—dc20   94-41769
                                                              CIP

10 9 8 7 6 5 4 3 2

DEDICATION

*To my mother
and father*

ACKNOWLEDGEMENTS

Thanks to my colleagues with the Institute of Cultural Affairs in Chicago for providing the professional environment in which I decided to undertake this project. They have been very supportive and I appreciate that support.

The opportunity to serve as General Editor of this collection allowed me to meet some wonderful people working at various levels of government to transform it. They inspired me greatly and I want to single them out for their encouragement: Barbara Dyer, Neil Johnson and William Wolf of the Alliance for Redesigning government, Ronald Redmond, Joseph Slye, and Frank Lewis of the Federal Quality Institute, and various staff members of the National Performance Review, especially Mike Serlin.

Many people reviewed various outlines and drafts of the case studies and provided valuable insight that enhanced the final publication. I especially want to thank Alderman Don Richards of Milwaukee and Bill Potapchuk of the Program for Community Problem Solving.

I particularly want to take this opportunity to thank my colleague John Burbidge for his assistance in the preparation of the case studies. John had a chance to review nearly all the draft manuscripts during a critical phase

This publication was a family project with my wife, Karen, making sure I was clear about what I was trying to say, improving each draft, and proof-reading at the later stages of the process. My son, Jonathan, did yeoman's work in some critical production phases of the project.

Also, a great big "thank you" to the professional staff of Miles River Press who had to cope with the unique problems publishing an anthology always brings — organizing multiple authors' styles, and recasting them into an integrated whole. Thanks to Peg, Betty, Libby and all their colleagues.

TABLE OF CONTENTS

Contributors

James P. Troxel is senior consultant for The Institute of Cultural Affairs in Chicago and has 25 years' experience in community and organizational development and leadership training. Jim is one of the founders of that group's participative strategic planning process now installed in organizations worldwide. He has conducted over 100 seminars in 30 states and 10 nations. He has facilitated training and planning sessions with private companies, national associations, local civic groups, and public agencies around the country. Recent clients include Household International, KPMG Peat-Marwick, the American Public Health Association, the Chicago Community Trust, Chicago Departments of Housing, Human Services, and Planning and Development.

Institute of Cultural Affairs, 4750 North Sheridan Road, Chicago, IL 60640

Tammy Bosse was administrator for the Phoenix Futures Forum/The Community Forum for six years. As a result of the Futures Forum process, Phoenix received the 1989 All American City award and the 1993 Bertelsman Best Managed City Award. Tammy has 15 years experience in participatory process management, communications, marketing, and community problem solving. She currently has her own consulting business.

3417 N. 60th Street, Scottsdale, AZ 85251

Michelle Bressler is currently working with the Breastfeeding Program of the Women Infants and Children Supplementary Feeding program (WIC) in Greenwood, Mississippi. She was first a research assistant at Partners in Nutrition and Health (PINAH), then program director for its Community Health Advisor Network after graduating from University of North Carolina's School of Public Health. She also served as a health educator in the Philippines with the Peace Corps.

311 Maclemore Street, Greenwood, MS 38930

John Burbidge is presently communication director for ICA West, the Institute of Cultural Affairs' division serving the western United States. Since 1971 his work experiences have taken him from sites as varied as villages in India and the European capital, Brussels. His articles have been published in magazines and journals in Australia, Canada, and the United States. He is the editor of the book Approaches That Work in Rural Development and the newsletter Initiatives.

Institute of Cultural Affairs, 1504 25th Avenue, Seattle, WA 98122

Donald O. Bushman, Jr. helps leadership teams change and improve their organizational systems. He trains and facilitates teams, and assists in organizational change efforts by designing and facilitating planning and implementation events that include broad participation. Since 1966 he has worked with the Institute of Cultural Affairs, primarily in Chicago.

The Institute of Cultural Affairs, 4750 North Sheridan Road,
Chicago, IL 60640

Kirk Cheramie is the chief administrative officer of the Bayou Lafourche Fresh Water District in Thibodaux, Louisiana, where he has been involved with the Barataria-Terrebonne National Estuary Program since its inception. His work experience includes 13 years as a licensed marine captain in the estuaries of the Gulf Coast. His family has lived in coastal Louisiana since the late 1600s.

311 Hale Drive, Thibodaux, LA 70301

Carol R. Coles is the assistant director of the Gloucester Prevention Network. Her background includes three years with VISTA on the Fort Apache Indian Reservation. Other work experience includes grant writing and marketing, as well as her current prevention practice.

Gloucester Prevention Network, 96 Main Street, Gloucester, MA 01930

David Dunn is a process consultant and writer who divides his time between Denver, Colorado, and Moscow. From a background in hospital management development and community organization, he has designed and led citizen participation events and participatory management workshops with government departments, not-for-profit social service organizations, and city agencies in the United States, India, Australia, and Egypt.

Whitney, Jones & Dunn, 1741 Gaylord Street, Denver, CO 80206

Kim Alire Epley currently oversees the Council of Energy Resource Tribes' Facilitation Services program offering facilitation and training in planning and problem solving with consensus-building methodologies. In her four years with CERT she has conducted over 110 workshops with more than 55 Tribes, Indian organizations, and agencies that serve Tribes. Kim has over 18 years of experience in facilitation and training in the United States and Latin America.

Council on Energy Resource Tribes, 1999 Broadway, Suite 2600, Denver, CO 80202

Janis Sabin Elliot has been involved in community-based decision making since the mid-60s. A social worker with an emphasis in community organizing and human services administration, Janis believes that the content of her work has changed, but the process remains the same: giving people information and access to decision making brings about fundamental change.

3216 N.E. 14th Avenue, Portland, OR 97212

Beret E. Griffith, an organization development consultant, has over 24 years of experience as a program designer and developer, seminar facilitator, and trainer, using the technologies of participation developed by the Institute of Cultural Affairs. She has facilitated seminars and delivered programs in over twenty states, Portugal, Canada, Europe, and the Philippines.

10 Buttercup Lane, San Carlos, CA 94070

Mirja P. Hanson most recently served as director of transition for the Metropolitan Council in Minnesota to refocus the mission of the Twin Cities' regional government. For six years she was senior consultant with the Management Analysis Division of the Minnesota state government, directing the quality improvement program (STEP) and working with over 100 clients in 25 state agencies, including the governor's cabinet.

Management Consultant, 5510 Edgewater Boulevard, Minneapolis, MN 55417

Ellie Haydock joined the city of Miami as its first labor-management coordinator and facilitator in 1991. Since the "total quality management" concept is fairly new to Miami, she uses creative strategies to adapt TQM principles and builds new approaches with the help of other trainers and guest speakers she brings to Miami. She currently coordinates the city's training programs and attends Barry University.

City Manager's Office, 3500 Pan American Drive, Miami, FL 33133

Shirley I. Heckman, Ph.D., is the coordinator of member services for the ICA West, the Institute of Cultural Affairs division serving the western United States. From 1989 through 1992, she was interim administrator for the Nigerian Integrated Rural Accelerated Development Organization (NIRADO).

The Institute of Cultural Affairs, 4220 North 25th Street, #7,
Phoenix, AZ 85016

Nancy S. Hewison has been planning librarian for Purdue University Libraries in West Lafayette, Indiana since 1991. As an internal consultant for the Libraries, she facilitates strategic and action planning efforts in various units and teams. Nancy provides facilitation and training for library, student, and community organizations. She has worked with the Institute of Cultural Affairs to train health sciences librarians in leadership skills.

Purdue University Libraries, 1250 Potter Engineering Center,
West Lafayette, IN 47907

Elizabeth L. Hollander is executive director of the Government Assistance Project (GAP) program and director of the Msgr. John J. Egan Urban Center of DePaul University in Chicago. From 1983 to 1989, Liz was commissioner of planning for the city of Chicago; prior to that she was the director of the Metropolitan Planning Council. She serves on the National Commission for the Board of Trustees of the Illinois Institute of Technology, Government Assistance Project.

Egan Urban Center, DePaul University, 243 S. Wabash, Chicago, IL 60601

Elizabeth W. Katz has over 20 years of experience in all phases of writing, editing and publishing in both international and U.S. agencies and companies. As Miles River Press' senior editor, she is responsible for overseeing the entire publication process. She also teaches advanced scientific editing courses at a large training and publications center in Alexandria, Virginia.

Miles River Press, 1009 Duke Street, Alexandria, VA 22314

Heidi Kolbe has over 20 years of public and private sector experience serving clients in organizational development, training, and team building. She is an adjunct professor of organizational development, strategic planning, and training at Golden Gate University and also trains mediators for community mediation centers. Her former work includes department manager and administrator positions with Sacramento County.

The Kolbe Company, 2443 Fair Oaks Blvd., #157, Sacramento, CA 95825

Edward Knight, Ph.D., is director of the Recipient Empowerment Program of the Mental Health Association in New York State, Inc. Dr. Knight was associated with the Institute of Cultural Affairs "Town Meeting Campaign," and uses ICA's methods in his Town Meetings for Empowerment across New York State.

Mental Health Association in New York State, Inc.

169 Central Avenue, Albany, NY 12208

Sue Laxdal is a senior management consultant for an internal consulting group within Minnesota's state government's, Management Analysis Division. Here she consults with state and local government units and serves as a facilitator of change processes for agencies and divisions within agencies. Her work covers transitions or major systems change, but also involves interaction with government's customers, the citizenry.

Management Analysis Division., Department of Administration,

State of Minnesota, 203 Administration Building, St. Paul, MN 55155

Teresa Lingafelter served as program coordinator of Partners for Improved Nutrition and Health (PINAH) in the Mississippi Delta from 1988 to 1991. Her work as student and practitioner of local empowerment and community development has taken her from Chicago to Southeast Asia, Australia, Jamaica, and Brussels, Belgium. She is currently working on a graduate degree in neighborhood planning and empowerment.

60 N. Buena Vista, Redlands, CA 92373

Carolyn J. Lukensmeyer Ph.D., former consultant to the White House office of the Chief of Staff, was previously deputy project director for management of the National Performance Review (NPR), Vice-President Al Gore's reinventing government taskforce. From 1986 to 1991, Lukensmeyer served as Chief of Staff to Governor Richard F. Celeste of Ohio. Currently on leave from Lukensmeyer Associates, Inc., the organization consulting firm she founded in Cleveland in 1974, Lukensmeyer's consulting projects have included private/public partnerships and education reform, as well as the transformation and revitalization of bureaucratic systems and planning processes to integrate corporate strategy, structure, and human resources.

1969 Biltmore Street, N.W., Washington, D.C. 20009

Jackie Weeks Miller has served as Tribal operations officer since 1991, to assist the chairman of the Ft. Peck Tribes in implementation of new initiatives such as gaming and taxation. An enrolled member of the Assiniboine Tribe, Jackie also serves as the appointed secretary/accountant for the Tribe. Born and raised on the Ft. Peck Reservation, she received a graduate degree in regional and community planning at North Dakota State University in 1982, after ten years of service on the Ft. Peck Reservation.

Council of Energy Resource Tribes,
1999 Broadway, Suite 2600, Denver, CO 80202

Kenneth O'Hare is principal of Kenneth O'Hare and Associates, a management consulting firm in Chicago specializing in strategic planning as well as program development and evaluation. Before starting his firm, Ken served in federal, state and local government for over 20 years in the U.S. Department of Labor, the Illinois governor's office, and Chicago's city government.

Kenneth O'Hare Associates, 3833 N. Hoyne, Chicago, IL 60618

Ike G. Powell is a community organizer and group facilitator. He currently works as a consultant to the New York State Office of Mental Health and Mental Health Association in New York State, Inc. Prior to creating his own consulting business, he worked for 20 years for the Institute of Cultural Affairs in India, Egypt, and the United States.

Innovative Group Processes, P.O. Box 209, Cairo, GA 31728

Helen Peddle, O.P., is a Dominican sister, a librarian by profession, and member of the Racine 2000 project from the start. She has edited its newsletters and documented information, recording progress and reminding Racine of its history as a community. She is a member of the Strengthening Families Task Force and spearheaded the Children's art project celebrating the United Nations Year of the Family in 1994.

The Dominican Sisters of Racine, Siena Center,
5635 Erie Street, Racine, WI 53402

Catherine A. Rategan, principal of Writer, Inc., has been an independent writer and consultant for over 15 years. She specializes in scriptwriting, public relations, advertising and corporate communications, and has worked with over a hundred Chicago area corporations and associations. Catherine is the recipient of a number of awards for her work in advertising and corporate television.

Writer, Inc., 1355 N. Sandburg Terrace, Suite 303, Chicago, IL 60610

Kathyrn Roberts is community prevention organizer for the Gloucester Prevention Network and a Gloucester native. She has worked primarily with five groups within the community: religious leaders, parents, men who serve as mentors to young boys, and women and adolescent girls.

The Gloucester Prevention Network,
96 Main Street, Gloucester, MA 01930

Philip L. Salzman is the director of the Gloucester Prevention Network and chair of Massachusetts Communities in Partnership, a statewide network of community partnership grantees. He has been involved in community-based prevention for the past 20 years as a community activist/educator, and also serves as an independent community prevention consultant.

The Gloucester Prevention Network, 96 Main Street,
Gloucester, MA 01930

Sandra A. True is currently principal of True Associates, a process consultant and training firm. For the past 10 years she has served as a health care and social program coordinator and trainer for Institute of Cultural Affairs in India, Egypt, the Philippines, and Korea. She also conducted training and planning seminars with social service agencies in Arizona, New Mexico, Oregon, Minnesota, and the Hopi and Navajo nations.

17 E. 16th Street, 3rd floor, New York, NY 10003

Brenda Walsh, O.P., is a Dominican sister involved in local community development in Racine, Wisconsin, for over 25 years. She speaks to numerous groups, writes articles on local development, and works with local citizens to help them articulate and implement vision goals. She has also worked in India and Thailand where she assisted with local development.

The Dominican Sisters of Racine, Siena Center, 5635 Erie Street,
Racine, WI 53402

Jean Watts is currently director of the New Orleans office of the Institute of Cultural Affairs, where she conducts training and research programs on employee participation and facilitates structured planning sessions for private, public, and not-for-profit organizations and associations. She has worked with the ICA in Chicago, Atlanta, Boston, Hong Kong, Paris, Brussels, and Vienna since 1964.

The Institute of Cultural Affairs, 1629 Pine Street, New Orleans, LA 70118

Douglas A. Wilson, Ph.D., is president of the Wilson Consulting Group in Newport Beach, CA. He has been working with the Fieldstone Company for the past seven years teaching them how to implement their company values as a base for dealing with day-to-day business and management issues.

Wilson Consulting Group,
1701 Port Westbourne, Newport Beach, CA 92660

Chapter 1
A New Vision of Public Service

ELIZABETH L. HOLLANDER

*In the spring of 1992, a distinguished monthly magazine
published by the* Congressional Quarterly *changed its
name from* The Bureaucrat *to* The Public Manager.
*"Bureaucrat" had become a dirty word. In 1990, the
Illinois Commission on the Future of Public Service held
focus groups of State of Illinois public managers. When
asked why they worked for the state, their overwhelming
response was, "Because I can make a difference." When
these same public managers were asked how they felt
when people said, "And what do you do?" they groaned
and put their heads down on their desks. Managers
responsible for the lives of children, the condition of the
environment, and the safety of roads felt embarrassed
that they held these jobs.*

These examples reflect the plummeting regard of many U.S. citizens
for their public servants. In fact, it was concern over this falling
esteem that led Paul Volcker, the former chairman of the federal
reserve board, to address the "quiet crisis'" in the federal government, namely, the crisis of keeping and recruiting first class
managers. His report, *Leadership for America, Rebuilding the
Public Service*[1], argues that the lack of public trust in government, the
need for higher standards of accountability, inadequate pay scales, as well
as cumbersome recruitment and hiring procedures have created this crisis
of confidence. In fact, this seminal Volcker report set off an avalanche of
special commissions and books on the need to "reinvent government."
As a result of this movement, widespread interest in finding better ways
to deliver government service is growing.

At the same time, alarms about American political life are also being sounded. The popular political writer E. J. Dionne and the Kettering Foundation of Dayton, Ohio, long concerned about citizen engagement, are among the influential voices articulating the public's frustration about its ability to influence public policy. Congress, these voices said, is dominated by large and well-funded political action committees and advancing special interests. These critics see efforts to get public input, such as public hearings, as shams, occurring only after the real decisions are made. Political campaigns are hugely expensive media events focused on personalities. Little time or effort is put into engaging voters in substantive policy discourse or debate. Politics, it is argued, has lost all sense of "the public good." Robert Bellah, sociologist and author of *Habits of the Heart,* a widely read exploration of the contradictions between individualism and community in American society, argues for reestablishment of a sense of the common good of the civil society[2].

Dionne notes furthermore that the American middle class sees government as failing to deliver on such basics as education, health care, road building, and crime fighting. As a consequence, "The broad American middle gave up on government, misread by conservatives as a demand for less government when, in fact, it was a demand for better government"[3]. The extent to which the "broad American middle" has given up on government has created a crisis of confidence in both the politics and public administration of government in the United States. This crisis of confidence requires us to paint a new vision of public service that can inspire private citizens as well as those who serve in government. At least the beginning elements of a new vision are driving the efforts to "redesign" government and to reengage citizens in the enterprise of government.

A New Vision

A question posed to me by David Rosenbloom, editor of the *Public Administration Review,* awakened me to the importance of a new vision. "What is your vision of the public servant?" he asked, at a meeting of the National Academy of Public Administration in 1991, where I was reporting on the work of the Illinois Commission on the Future of Public Service. It was a defining moment for me because I had no ready answer. How, I thought, can we citizens "reinvent" the public service if we do not have a clear vision that guides us? Is there, I wondered, some central idea about public service that is pushing the ever-increasing demand for change? How have our notions of public service changed and why?

Can we paint a new vision for the public servant that fits our times, hard times, in which we are not clear that the American dream of upward mobility for each new generation will hold? Fundamental changes in the role of the U.S. in a global economy have changed the nature of work, as the dramatic reduction of blue collar jobs that pay a "middle class" wage indicates. Huge federal deficits have curtailed the U.S. ability to invest in domestic needs. The gap between the very rich and very poor has widened dramatically and the middle class has shrunk. All of these economic realities create a governmental climate in which the pressures to "do more with less" are unrelenting. A new vision for the public service needs to confront these realities.

The new vision of public service also needs to be one uniquely American, one that requires us to acknowledge a deep distrust for government, yet still maintains a deep respect for the general public's role in carrying out the responsibilities of government. The 19th century commentator on American life, Alexis de Tocqueville, expressed the following insight into American democracy:

> [The] duties of private citizens are not supposed to have lapsed because the state has come into action; but every one is ready, on the contrary, to guide and support it. This action of individuals, joined to that of the public authorities, frequently accomplishes what the most energetic centralized administration would be unable to do[4].

American present-day discontent with both political systems and public agencies seems to reflect a feeling that citizens are no longer in a position to "guide and support" the actions of their public authorities. The idealism de Tocqueville saw in his vision of American democracy seems to have completely vanished.

Is there some way that a new vision of the public servant could help reestablish these relationships with the citizenry, the relationships that are a centerpiece of the case studies in this book? Several ideas underlying both the government reinvention and citizen involvement movements can help us paint a new vision of the public servant as the "collaborator," in the best sense of the word, as one who according to a dictionary definition "works jointly with others for a common goal." Working jointly with others for a common goal applies both to how government workers relate to each other and how they relate to their constituents.

Notions of Bureaucracy

Our traditional notions of how government should be organized have been governed by traditional Weberian notions of bureaucracy formed in the 1890s. According to Max Weber, "Ideally bureaucracy is characterized by hierarchical authority relations, defined spheres of competence subject to impersonal rules, recruitment by competence, and fixed salaries. Its goal is to be rational, efficient, and professional." This ideal of public service was a compelling alternative in the late nineteenth century days of the free-wheeling political bosses of the big city halls. Pursuit of this ideal in the 1890s was evident in the founding of the National Civic League and the city management movement.

Now, however, the fundamental assumptions underlying this way of organizing government bureaucracy are being seriously challenged. Civil service systems have not accomplished the task of preventing patronage appointments. One example was the startling evidence presented in a U.S. Supreme Court case, *Rutan v. the State of Illinois.* It showed that obtaining a low-level state job often required a signed statement from the political committeeman documenting how the job applicant had voted in the last three elections. If he or she were too young, the applicant's parents voting record was reviewed. This case addressed only one of the failures of the civil service system. Even internally the systems have not provided enough sense of protection to workers to reduce their interest in union membership. In fact, union membership in government is rising at the same time that it is declining in the private sector. This reality leaves government managers with the constraints of two systems designed to protect the interests of workers.

Impersonal rules have not ensured the fairness they promised either; instead they have become a substitute for reasoned judgment. For example, case workers in the Illinois Department of Children and Family Services are governed by a 2,400 page manual with multiple changes to the document issued every month. At the federal level, Vice President Gore has compiled extensive evidence of such rules including the 100,000 pages of personnel rules on how to hire, promote, or fire federal employees [6].

Examples of this kind of bureaucratic excess are all too easy to uncover. Even the *Columbia Desk Encyclopedia* gives this definition of bureaucracy:

> ...because of the shortcomings that have in practice afflicted...large administrative structures, the terms bureaucracy and bureaucrat in popular usage usually carry a suggestion of reprobation and imply incompetence, a narrow outlook, duplication of effort, and application of a rigid rule without due consideration of specific cases[7].

Let the Record Show

Beyond encyclopedia entries, historical evidence shows that the ideal of the fair-minded, rule-driven bureaucrat has failed us. So has another compelling vision of the public servant fostered during the 1930s. In the era of the New Deal, we had faith in the idea of the government worker as a social engineer who both formulated and implemented public policies. We had great optimism that the New Deal programs would bring substantial change and that public intervention to reduce poverty and increase job opportunities was both appropriate and workable. This vision reappeared during the 1960s in such initiatives as the "War on Poverty." This Johnson Administration program put much greater emphasis on the involvement of citizens in solutions, and a high level of suspicion about the ability of professionals to engineer solutions. This was the era in which federal legislation carried such mandates as "maximum feasible participation" by the public.

That vision of the 1960s failed us, too. The 1970s reflected a very deep disappointment in the ability of government to bring effective social change, and marked the time when we began to lose faith as a nation in the American dream of upward mobility. For many Americans, it was not clear that the next generation was going to do better than their own. Alice Rivlin, in her 1992 book, *Reviving the American Dream,* makes the case that it is this loss of faith in the American economy and its ability to sustain an increase in the quality of American life that is at the root of the disillusionment with government[8].

For whatever reasons, the late 1970s through the 1980s evolved into the era of government bashing. Starting with President Carter and reaching a zenith under President Reagan, government bureaucracy was cited as "the problem." Bloated, inefficient bureaucracies were blamed for soaking up resources at a time when deficits were growing, and with them, resource constraints on social programs. Major scandals in federal agencies like the Department of Housing and Urban Development and the Environmental Protection Agency added to public disillusionment. Public polls conducted by the Institute for Social Research at the University of Michigan, the *Washington Post,* and ABC News showed that the number of citizens who trusted the government in Washington to do what is "right only some of the time" rose from 22% in 1964, to 73% in 1980, and leveled at 60% in 1985 and 1986[9].

Politicians joined the bandwagon in bashing government's ability to do its job well, and many did an about-face and ran against their own bureaucracies at the federal, state, and local levels. At the same time, legislatures continued to pass mandates to address public concerns about such matters as environmental conditions. The city of Chicago, in conjunction with Roosevelt University's Institute for Metropolitan Affairs, conducted an in-depth study of problems posed by unfunded federal mandates and overregulation. Released in 1992, the study cited one finding estimating that between the years 1996 to 2000, "environmental compliance" with federal and state regulation will cost the city of Chicago an average of $135 million annually, or 23 percent of the total municipal budget[10]. Moreover, on the environment and other issues, politicians across the nation have promised that services could be maintained without tax increases if waste and inefficiencies were rooted out.

During the 1980s business practice was increasingly held up as the model of efficiency and government was urged to adopt more businesslike practices. At the federal level, President Reagan in 1984 established the Grace Commission as a group of big-business leaders led by J. Peter Grace, chief executive officer of W. R. Grace & Co. In 1984, the Grace Commission made news by recommending 2, 478 ways to reduce federal spending and save $424 billion over three years. At the state level, Governor Arne Carlson of Minnesota in 1991 formed the Commission on Reform and Efficiency (CORE) to address problems in the state bureaucracy. The charge was given to make deep changes in state services and programs. Both of these government reform efforts engaged leading business leaders in the enterprise of helping government increase its efficiency. Privatization became another popular strategy for introducing the discipline of business practice in delivering government services.

Total Quality Management

As government was looking to business practice as an alternative model, business itself was going through a major self-examination. Japan's extraordinary success in competing in American markets for such goods as automobiles was calling into question the ability of major American companies to produce competitive quality products efficiently. Business, too, was finding the traditional hierarchical corporate organization insufficient to the task of global competition. American business "discovered" the power of the total quality management principles that Edward Deming had taught the Japanese after World War II. Dr. Deming urged that instead of trying to achieve quality through a hierarchy of "inspectors," it would be far more effective to allow front line workers to be engaged in the enterprise of producing what customers want. Teams of front-line workers were trained to reexamine and redesign the systems in which they worked; their managers were trained to be coaches in this enterprise, rather than "controllers," and top management was assigned the task of creating a vision of producing a consistently high-quality product that met or, better yet, exceeded the desires of their customers.

The Deming approach to the organization of a company and the roles and responsibilities of the people in it was a revolution in the U.S. way of thinking about how to organize a large enterprise. It is a revolution that is, in its own unique form, being adopted increasingly by government because it contains at least two powerful ideas that address the quandary facing government administration in the United States today. The first principle is that the quality of products should be driven by the needs of the customer. The second tenet is that traditional hierarchical systems should be replaced with systems redesigned by those who actually produce the product, i.e. front-line workers should be trusted and empowered. These ideas are the basis for helping to sketch a new vision of the public servant.

Focus on the Customer

Let's first examine the Deming focus on the customer as the one who defines the quality of the product. We do not ordinarily think of American citizens as "customers" of government. They do not have the alternative of shopping elsewhere for most of what government provides. Nevertheless, there is a powerful effect when large organizations turn their attention to those for whom they are providing service. Large organizations, in whatever sector, have a tendency to fall into patterns of serving their own needs and doing things they way they have "always done them." For example, private companies like Sears Roebuck lost touch with the change in their customers' lifestyles, and continued to produce catalogues aimed at a mythical four-person middle class family. Other organizations that fail to focus on customers include museums that clear their galleries at 4:45 p.m. so the guards can go home at the 5:00 p.m. posted closing time, or city health clinics that are not open evenings or weekends.

Government can be much more effective when it turns to its users (Deming would call them "external customers."), as Cook County, Illinois, did in trying to extend information about contract opportunities for minorities. In that instance a team of government employees in the Cook County Contract Compliance division asked a minority business vendor to join them in devising new ways of getting the word out about job opportunities. He was able to help identify the kind of information minority contractors needed, and the right timeframe to compete effectively for county contracts. Many more examples of this kind of outreach can be found in Chapter 8 on the Chicago Models of Excellence.

Staff functions of government — budget, comptroller, purchasing, law, personnel — similarly forget their users or "internal customers," the other government agencies. Centralization of the above functions was designed to provide uniformity and efficiency. While staff agencies may provide a modicum of uniformity, they are often the least efficient in getting the job done. In Minnesota, when the Department of Administration sought to treat other government agencies as their customers, it transformed the way they did business (Chapter 7). For example, the consulting and training division became a competitive consultant and raised all of its costs through selling its services to state and other government agencies[11].

Citizen Involvement

For government, involving the citizen requires more than focus groups or opinion surveys. In the words of Ernie Cortez, organizer for the Industrial Areas Foundation in the Southwest, "Does my opinion really matter, or is what matters my judgment?...Judgment is a public process of discussion and debate"[12]. The implication is that time should be taken to teach citizens their choices and involve them in policy development. In that way, they can become a powerful force in "supporting and guiding it," and achieving more than any centralized administration. Just one example, from my time in Mayor Harold Washington's administration of Chicago government, was a 1983 taskforce created to develop policy for homeless shelters. The group involved many city agencies and shelter providers, as well as state and federal agencies. Because all of these groups shared power, they were able to get new laws enacted to provide for homeless shelters. Coordinated funding of new shelters across the city was also achieved within a year.

Citizen involvement is, of course, not a strategy of Democrats alone. Jack Kemp, President Reagan's Secretary of Housing and Urban Development, touted the advantages of tenant management in transforming public housing. In fact, the 1980s was a time when both liberals and conservatives promoted similar strategies for citizen involvement, although not always clothed in the same rhetoric.

In the late 1980s and early 1990s, at all levels of government, federal, state, and local, it became obvious that citizen initiatives were finding their places. The 1992 federal elections were marked by attempts to reengage citizens in the political process. During the campaign Bill Clinton reached out to the voters through town meetings, bus trips, and appearances on popular TV shows. As President, he continued this trend in such undertakings as the Economic Summit, in which citizens' varying points of view were debated.

The recent federal Empowerment Zone legislation is a powerful example of the assertion that citizens need to engage in their own community rebuilding. This legislation requires the involvement of all sectors of urban and rural communities in the strategic planning of neighborhood rebuilding strategies. Engaging citizens and community groups effectively requires that government employees develop a whole set of skills that are not regularly a part of their training. Before exploring this situation further, let's examine the dynamic idea of worker empowerment.

What a Picture is Worth

Imagine a chart with a stick figure at the top, representing the CEO. Several lines emanate from below the feet to another row of stick figures, representing middle management. Below the feet of each of these managers is another series of lines pointing to stick figures representing the front-line workers. There is one big difference in this last line of figures, however; they have no heads. One quality management consultant uses this diagram to describe the traditional bureaucracy.

Today, however, a new vision of organization is emerging that has front-line workers depicted at the top of the page; they are represented as whole people (with heads) grouped into teams and supported from below by both middle managers and the CEO. The assumption in the second chart is that front-line workers have a profound knowledge of their own work. When they are free to use that knowledge, they can change the delivery systems in which they work to produce a better quality product or improved service for the citizen. Experiments in Chicago, and in other places in the U.S. like naval bases and IRS offices, as well as local government agencies in Austin, Texas, and Madison, Wisconsin, have demonstrated the power of this approach to government bureaucracies.

The report of the National Commission on the State and Local Public Service[13] describes the essence of this approach as "trust and lead," instead of "command and control." Can it really be that we can reform government practice on the basis of trusting government employees to want to do their jobs and to deliver quality services? Isn't government filled with patronage workers who got their jobs for the wrong reasons and are unlikely to do a day's work for a day's pay without elaborate systems of control?

Workers Redesigning Systems

Once again, we have to look at the actual impact of our rule-driven, hierarchical systems with their defined spheres of competence. In reality we have not prevented poor performance with our command and control systems, but instead have reduced productivity by focusing on what Deming calls the 5% of the workforce who are malingering. Examples in government abound of such practices as requiring multiple sign-offs on documents. Perhaps even more serious, government blames individual workers for failing even when they are asked to perform within impossible systems. One example that comes to mind is the situation facing childcare workers in states like Illinois; they have impossibly large caseloads. If a child comes to harm and there is publicity about it, the caseworker is likely to be blamed and fired. Such cases perpetuate impossible situations when another approach, that of redesigning the assignment of cases to make child protection a feasible enterprise, would alleviate these problems.

When workers are asked to redesign systems, based on consumer needs, there is a powerful shift in responsibility, away from managers, to the workers themselves. With such shifts comes a powerful sense of engagement with the enterprise. For example a 20-year veteran in a Cook County, Illinois, hospital reports a new excitement about coming to work because "someone listened to what I had to say"[14].

At the same time that teams of workers are trained to redesign their work systems, they can also learn to measure their own productivity and take ownership of accountability systems. The upshot of this approach is a reduction in the number of middle managers. Also inherent in this design is a vision of organizations that honor the day-to-day work of their employees, whether it's the teacher in the classroom, the income maintenance worker, or a beat patrol officer. Traditionally, rewards for doing these jobs well have resulted in promotion away from the front line to middle-management positions. Under the new organizational structures implicit in this approach, rewards for good work will not necessarily mean promotion away from the front line. Instead, employees will receive increased remuneration, as well as gainsharing and team awards, for increased experience and wisdom in carrying out the "real work" of the organization.

What does this new approach imply about a new vision for public service? How can such redesigning help us to reestablish the American tradition that the government is not "them" but "us?" First, shot through all of the government reform initiatives of the 1990s is a fundamental respect for public management, whether it's the 1989 Volcker Report, Osborne and Gaebler's book *Reinventing Government,* the National Commission on the State and Local Public Service (the Winter Commission), or the National Performance Review. Each of these reports wants to reestablish a sense of "higher calling" in doing the public's business. What better way than to devise organizations that are built on employee trust and respect? Many surveys of government workers show that the desire to "make a difference" is a number one motivator for doing their work; in fact, it is listed ahead of salary and security. Doesn't it make sense to reinforce this desire "to make a difference?" This redirection does not mean that we have to give up on eliminating waste and inefficiency. Instead, the workers themselves become engaged in the enterprise of stopping wasteful practices and assume responsibility for increased productivity.

Citizens as Customers

If we keep our focus on the public as the customer for whom we have established public services, we can meet people's needs, and also seek to reengage citizens in the hard work of government, sharing difficult decisions and real responsibilities. To achieve the new vision of public service, we will need public servants who are capable of collaborating with each other and with the public. They will not be social engineers, arrogant about their abilities to improve the lives of citizens, but will understand instead that every public service is a joint enterprise that includes citizens, their own fellow workers, and other agencies. The role of beat patrol officers in community policing is a good example of this new ideal. The officer's task is to form with the neighborhood a relationship that will lead to citizen assistance in crime control and maintenance of community safety and harmony. These patrol officers must also come to be seen in the neighborhood as a valuable source of assistance and protection. To be effective, they need to engage increasingly in developing partnerships with community groups and with their own bureaucracy. These partnerships allow them to gain valuable information on crime patterns from community residents. They also become welcomed community partners, for example, when they arrange towing of abandoned automobiles and improve neighborhood conditions.

However, for beat patrol officers to succeed at these tasks, their managers and department top brass will need to shift attention from counting the number of arrests or responses to 911 calls to supporting these officers in their collaborative work and rewarding them for it. Central offices will need to make resources as ordinary as copying paper available at the local level. These are examples of a fundamental shift in perspective required by the bureaucracies themselves to create government organizations that can work with local citizens.

The Ideal Public Servant

What else will be essential for this new vision to succeed? Embedded in this vision is the idea of the "learning" government. Government employees will need to acquire and sharpen their skills at teamwork, analyzing their own work systems, devising accountability standards, and learning how to work more closely with citizens. Models, such as those from Chicago, show that investment in the right kind of training can pay off. Government leaders will need to hone their skills in motivating and coaching their employees, as well as in engaging citizens and others in effective dialogue about the mission of their organizations. The Winter Commission report suggests that we will need to encourage movement in and out of government by supporting portable pensions, thereby fostering a capacity for government administrators to work with other sectors[15]. A recent Government Assistance Project survey in Chicago of government leaders, known to be successful in collaborating with their communities, found that the vast majority had spent time in the nonprofit sector as well as government[16].

On the citizen side, we must continue to seek effective ways to engage citizens in the public debate and in the actual provision of service. Government and citizens need to work together to reweave the social fabric in our dysfunctional communities. The more citizens become engaged in the difficult process of creating the public good, the more they will understand its complexities. In this way they can achieve another goal: reducing the attractiveness of easy but unrealistic political rhetoric. This means that government needs to take the time to involve citizens in decision making at every level, whether in neighborhood plans, city-wide capital investment programs, or state and federal welfare policy. Government leaders and managers must recognize that citizens, in some cases, can and will provide complementary services that are more effective than their own. Neighborhood block watches, tenant management committees, or docent programs in historic structures have proved this point in many communities. Government also needs to share real information about the limited resources available to meet public needs and face the tough choices about what to buy with those limited resources.

The ideal public servant who emerges from the description above is one who can work with others to achieve the public good, a collaborator who recognizes that public administration in an American democracy requires that public servants encourage citizens to support the public enterprise. Such an employee will have a profound respect for democratic decision making, and the patience to engage in it. In addition, the ideal public servant is a collaborator within his or her own bureaucracy, seeking the engagement of workers, working on teams, and crossing turf lines to provide sensible services to customers.

If there is concern that this profile is not an achievable vision, and a vision is, after all, a picture of something that can't yet be seen, the case studies that follow in this book will allay that concern. This volume is rich in various examples of citizens and government workers who have found ways to collaborate to enhance the public good, which after all is the *raison d'etre* of government. In the words of the Chicago community policing strategic plan, "Together we can."

References

[1] Volcker, Paul A. *Leadership for America, Rebuilding the Public Service, The Report of the National Commission on the Public Service* (Albany: The Nelson A. Rockfeller Institute of Government and SUNY, 1989).

[2] Bellah, Robert. *Habits of the Heart, Individualism and Commitment in American Life* (New York: Harper & Row, 1985).

[3] *Utne Reader* (Nov./Dec., 1991).

[4] De Tocquevelle, Alexis. *Democracy in America,* ed. and abr. Richard D. Heffner (Canada: Penguin Books, 1956).

[5] Harris, William H. and Judith S. Levey, eds., *The New Columbia Encyclopedia* (New York: Columbia University Press, New York, 1975).

[6] *National Performance Review. From Red Tape to Results: Creating a Government that Works Better and Costs Less* (Washington: GPO, 1993).

[7] Harris, William H. and Judith S. Levey, ed. *The New Columbia Encyclopedia* (New York: Columbia University Press, New York, 1975).

[8] Rivlin, Alice. *Reviving the American Dream, the Economy, the States and the Federal Government* (Washington: The Brookings Institute, 1992).

[9] Sussman, Barry. *What Americans Really Think: And Why Our Politicians Pay No Attention.* (New York: Pantheon Books, 1988).

[10] City of Chicago and Roosevelt University Institute for Metropolitan Affairs. *Putting Federalism to Work for America: Tackling the Problems of Unfunded Federal Mandates and Burdensome Regulations* (Chicago: City of Chicago and Roosevelt University, 1992).

[11] Barzelay, Michael and Babak J. Armajani. *Breaking through Bureaucracy* (Berkley: University of California Press, 1992).

[12] Winter, William F. *Hard Truths/Tough Choices, An Agenda for State and Local Reform, The First Report of the National Commission on the State and Local Public Service* (Albany: The Nelson A. Rockefeller Institute of Government and SUNY, 1993).

[13] Ibid.

[14] The Chicago Community Trust, *Models of Excellence Special Report, Government Assistance Project* (Chicago: The Chicago Community Trust, 1993).

[15] Osborne, David and Ted Gaebler. *Reinventing Government: How the Entrepreneurial Spirit is Transforming the Public Sector* (Reading, MA: Addison-Wesley,1992).

[16] McDonough, William. *Excellence in Public Service: Illinois' Challenge for the 90s, Preliminary Report of the Illinois Commission on the Future of Public Service* (Chicago: Community Trust/Government Assistance Project, 1991).

Chapter 2
Making Government Work:
A View from the Inside
Interview with Carolyn J. Lukensmeyer

JAMES P. TROXEL

Carolyn J. Lukensmeyer, Ph.D., certified organizational development consultant, gives a view of the inside of politics from an organizational management perspective. She spent four years as the Chief of Staff for Governor Richard Celeste of Ohio during his second term in office (1986-1990). From December, 1992 until July, 1994 she worked for the Clinton-Gore Administration; first on the management team that led Vice-President Gore's National Performance Review, then in the office of the White House Chief of Staff. James Troxel, General Editor, conducted this interview during the summer of 1994, just after Dr. Lukensmeyer left the White House.

Working Inside on Governance

Troxel: *I'd like to understand how your work on governance has developed. How did you as an OD consultant find your way into public service?*

Lukensmeyer: Twenty years ago I completed my Ph.D. in organizational development, and began consulting with a variety of organizations in the fields of manufacturing, energy, health, education, and government.

Whether my work was private sector or public sector, I was always fascinated with the issues of public policy and who is accountable for the "common good." For example, considering the water rights of the Quirajan Indians adjacent to the coal deposits being developed by an Exxon joint venture in Colombia, or the "Chemical Facts of Life" program developed as part of the Corporate Social Responsibility function I helped create at Monsanto in the early 1970s. Looking back I see it is obvious that there always has been a public service aspect to my work.

However, it was in December, 1982 that I was first offered an opportunity to have a direct impact at the senior level of government. Then recently-elected Governor Richard F. Celeste of Ohio asked me to facilitate a retreat to organize his Cabinet and senior staff. During this first term I continued to do retreats and to consult to the administration. At the beginning of Governor Celeste's second term, I moved into the position of Chief of Staff. Although it was quite a jump from being an organizational consultant to managing a state government, I knew the governor had an excellent vision for what could happen in Ohio. I also knew his top team well and knew that collectively they were people who could make his vision a reality.

Troxel: *Was there any kind of professional motivation for the move?*

Lukensmeyer: As an OD professional, I was dedicated to the question of learning about organizations as systems. Early in my career three questions about how we organize human efforts challenged me to compare and contrast three kinds of differences in our society. One was the difference between big and small organizations; another, the difference between public and private organizations. The third was the difference between those organizations that were created and fashioned out of male consciousness and run by men, and those created by female consciousness and run by women (which incidentally, in the '70s were hard to find). I had followed these questions through a ten year learning path trying to better understand how companies and organizations worked.

When I had come to a point at which I was not learning more in the consultant role to corporations, I was mostly working with joint ventures in Europe and South America. I was burned out on traveling and tired of having no managerial clout. As a consultant you can influence management in the short term, but in the end someone else holds the position with the power to follow through or not. I think Governor Celeste sensed my desire to "come inside" and asked, "Wouldn't you like to be chief operating officer of a 55,000 person entity?" and I said, "Yes, I would," even though it scared me.

Changing Access and Decision Making

Troxel: *What were some of the challenges you encountered when you went to work full time for the governor?*

Lukensmeyer: At the time I became Chief of Staff, one of the criticisms of the governor was that he was indecisive. The perception was that the last person the governor talked to got the decision he or she wanted. From my experience I knew that wasn't true; if anything, the governor was like a lot of private sector leaders in that he moved too quickly to action. To me, it was a management problem reflecting how decision options were brought to him, not on his skills as a decision maker.

I believed we could change that perception by changing the way staff people presented their ideas to the governor. We instituted meetings in which all the opposing points of view were present in one meeting at the same time. Once those meetings were set up, the governor could quickly make decisions. Sometimes he needed more data, or identified other people he wanted to consult. But his capacity to assimilate data from many people in a meeting was extraordinary. In a few weeks we changed the staffing pattern. We also changed the access to the governor's office, so that the pattern of people just walking in at will was stopped. By the end of the first six months, the criticism of the governor as a poor decision maker was gone. As a result, the media stopped focusing on it. I gained confidence because of how quickly and easily we did it.

Working with the Media on Factual Reporting

Another challenge was dealing with the media. The media people had decided during Celeste's first term that he had an ethics problem. I knew that Celeste was clean ethically; otherwise I would not have taken the job. However, we never changed the media's perception. I think we are watching a similar media/ethics issue in Washington now. Part of what is wrong with the media today is that a reporter develops a stake in the outcome of a story. Once a reporter gets an investment in a position or outcome, he or she becomes a player in the story rather than covering it objectively. Most are not aware of this day-to-day investment, which often distorts coverage.

The following incident illustrates my point. I met with an editor of a major Ohio newspaper at the end of Governor Celeste's second term. I raised the question of the newspaper's coverage on Celeste's ethics. I said, "Yes, you are right about some of the administration's personnel choices early in the first term. But, name one person hired after 1985 [third year of first term] who made the same kind of mistakes." He couldn't. "Name me one contract that had any link to campaign financing." He couldn't. "How can you not acknowledge that there has been a change from the first term to the second term?" He looked me straight in the eye and said, "Carolyn, all I know is my job is to report, as best I can, the truth. I know the truth about the governor, and the truth is that he is weak on ethics." This is an editorial page editor of a major Ohio newspaper. Some media people know they are distorting information because of investment in a position and some do not. What concerns me most is the level of arrogance and self-righteousness reflected in their use of power. It is very disturbing. To whom are the media accountable when they misuse their power?

A Case Study in Citizen Involvement

Troxel: *One of the things I heard about Governor Celeste's time in Ohio was that he tried to improve opportunities for constituents to participate. What were some of the things you did to get citizens involved in government?*

Lukensmeyer: The best example was the work we did with the mental health system. When we took office, Ohio was 46th or 47th in dollar aid to the mental health system. Actually Ohio had little credibility across the country in this field. We found that there was very little professional integrity in the system in terms of how treatment was delivered.

Governor Celeste's commitment to doing this differently was clear from day one. Mental health was the last Cabinet position that he filled because it took him some time to find the right person. He interviewed all the obvious prospects and he could tell that none of them really saw it the way he saw it and he would have to bring someone along. He finally interviewed Pam Hyde, a brilliant 33-year-old lawyer, who had been executive director of Ohio Legal Rights Service, an advocacy organization. Celeste had a vision for mental health and she understood how to make it a reality.

Her leadership focused on a very sophisticated stakeholder input process. First, she worked inside the department to get all the right top people together. As a consultant for the Department of Mental Health, I had helped develop strategy and led planning retreats for her team. While most people think of including from 18 to 25 people in this kind of work, Director Hyde included 50 to 80 because she understood that maximum commitment was necessary to make change within the bureaucracy happen. Support for change must be broad.

The mental health division was the second largest employer in the state government. In her first 18 months, we undertook a very sophisticated, full analysis of the system. We understood that to make the vision a reality would take major legislation, and the only way we could get that major legislation was to convince the legislative committee members who monitored the mental health system. We knew we would have to have a "citizen's voice" from consumers and their family network. Pam used several other states that had model financing systems based on community support to begin to build the Ohio model. Community-based mental health was what we wanted to promote. The dollar following the client into the community was our primary goal.

Pam started giving discretionary grants to the community mental health boards in the state to help them develop citizen advocacy groups on the local level. She also funded a statewide consumer network and a statewide family advocacy group. We helped create the family network because family members had to be heard in the public policy debate. It is not government's role to make public policy without citizen input. Of course you can do it without the citizens, but it will only hold for the short term; it does not last.

That system is still in place. Most of the local groups now have seats on the county level mental health boards. One of the groups eventually took the state government to court. There was a period when Pam and I and a lot of her people used to ponder and say, "Why did we ever create this system for feedback? These people are giving us such a hard time, too." No matter how much we as a state agency did, it never seemed to be enough. But we knew that the local citizen advisory boards were the people who had to bring the county boards and the state into accountability. There had to be some way of organizing citizens all over the state who would go to

Columbus and look the legislators straight in the eye and say, "You have to do this and this is why."

By the time we left office, in January of 1990, Director Hyde and her top management team had given speeches in 38 states and several foreign countries about the mental health program in which dollars follow clients. Ohio was one of the models for allowing the consumer to have a voice in the system. The institutional change spanned seven years culminating in the passage of legislation with a five-year implementation time frame.

Creating a Risk-Taking Culture

Troxel: *How would you describe the kind of organizational culture you wanted to create inside the governor's office and with the Cabinet?*

Lukensmeyer: The culture we set out to create was one of higher support for speaking your own truth, whatever that might be. In my experience, women make this transition more easily than men. I know that is a sweeping generalization, but it is my experience. By the time I became Chief of Staff, the governor believed it was not possible to hold an honest discussion at the Cabinet meetings. I said, "Give me a chance; let me try to set a new norm." At first it was the women whom I could count on to get the discussion going at a serious level; once the new approach became more familiar, everybody who had a stake in the issue spoke.

A powerful way to change an organization's culture is by increasing the amount of diversity in it. More women and minorities are essential to the culture change we are trying to make in organizations. Of the 30 people in the governor's Cabinet, it was a core of women who provided the leadership for the culture change we created. This does not downplay the contributions of men; but the real up-front risk takers in the culture change tended to be women. The women seemed to be naturally attuned to creating new visions with other team members.

The culture we created was more participatory, more truth-telling, and more power-sharing rather than power-holding, which in politics is a very dramatic change in culture. I set a few norms when I went into the governor's office. One of the strongest was regarding truth-telling. If you lie to me, you're out of here. The first time it happened, I fired the person; so, that norm was highly respected.

A game when I arrived in the governor's office was to withhold information so that a particular staff member could look more competent in front of the governor. I changed that: if you did that, you were closed out of the meetings. So the norm became "share information about our jobs." There were about twelve people involved in this. Each of us had access to all of the other's information as we developed positions to present to the governor, thereby facilitating the decision-making process.

Government cultures are risk averse to a highly dysfunctional level. So I always want to create systems that reward people who take risks. Here are some examples from my experience of simple day-to-day reminders being useful. In several federal agencies in the Clinton administration, some Cabinet members authorized little pocket cards. These listed five simple conditions for personal risk taking and action:

Reinvention Permission Slip

Ask yourself...

1. Is it good for my customers?
2. Is it legal and ethical?
3. Is it something I am willing to be accountable for?
4. Is it consistent with my agency's mission?
5. Am I using my time wisely?
6. If the answer to all of these questions is yes...don't ask permission. You already have it. JUST DO IT!

This tackles the notion that a decision has to go through seven or more steps up and down the bureaucratic chain before a person can take action.

Dan Beard, commissioner of the Bureau of Reclamation, went even further and other managers emulated him. To encourage his senior managers to take risks, Beard gave them "forgiveness coupons" that they were able to cash in upon making a mistake. ("It's easier to get forgiveness...than permission," the coupon said.) He put this into people's performance reviews; if you did not use your coupons, you had to explain why.

To increase staff input, Beard distributed what he calls "How Am I Doing?" cards. On one side is a series of questions about intrabureau communication, cooperation, empowerment, and recognition and rewards. The other side, under the heading "Make A Difference — Talk Back to Dan," asks staffers for their ideas and suggestions.

Reducing the Gap Between
Appointed and Career Officials

Troxel: *These examples sound good, but what happens when a new leader comes in? How do you ever really inculcate this new culture in government with some permanence? It seems to me that's the hardest place to do it.*

Lukensmeyer: It's a much more serious problem in the federal government. In Washington, it was surprising to me to learn about the distance between political appointees and career bureaucrats that manage programs. You can operate for years in the federal bureaucracy in some pretty significant program area and not even experience a slight impact from the political process. In state government, there is a raw edge between the political appointees and the career people. It's dynamic. You either connect or you don't connect. In the federal government, unless you really work at it at the Cabinet level, connection just doesn't happen. Again, from the Clinton administration, Secretary of the Interior Bruce Babbitt spent his first few months visiting the office of every program department head. This had not been done in the recorded history of the department. This was a first, and the easiest step in making a meaningful connection with the career bureaucrats at Interior.

To really change culture in four to eight years, the politically appointed level has to link quickly with the bureaucracy in an authentic, healthy way to solve problems and develop public policy. You have to create diagonal slices and/or networks between the two. You have to end up — as fast as you are capable — with people in the bureaucracy believing in the vision that you believe in, and knowing and feeling that they are part of your team. If, as a political appointee, you can make that happen, they can carry the vision and change strategy throughout the agency and give it life beyond your tenure.

Spreading Accountability

Troxel: *How did you go about reorganizing patterns of participation and cooperation?*

Lukensmeyer: In Ohio we became known for the "cluster system." This reorganization was done at both the Cabinet level and working levels. For example, if the goal were to export more agriculture products, which were the agencies in Ohio that had something to contribute? We picked a person from every one of those agencies to join a cluster, and then chartered that group to be responsible for increasing the volume of exports of agriculture products from the state. The governor then held this cluster of Cabinet officials accountable for increasing agriculture exports, not just the secretary of agriculture. And the Cabinet officials were in turn holding a cluster of working-level technical, professional people accountable.

When we first started doing the clusters, there was a lot of resistance to it from people all over state government. Here is where my OD background was helpful because I knew how to integrate substance and process. Many excellent managers of programs don't know enough about process to manage and lead organization change. Because I represented the governor, when I called a meeting of 18 people from different agencies, everyone came and listened to the absolute best of their ability. When people played "games" that stood in the way of making the cluster process work, they were at a very sophisticated level so that when we broke up the "games," we broke the back of the resistance to the whole process.

And of course there were games being played that went beyond individuals. They were at the program level, for instance with Medicaid funding. Negotiating with the "feds" about Medicaid funding was a nightmare for every state in this country at that time. Our numbers in Ohio showed that if we stayed on the straight-line growth path that we were on in 1989, the state would be bankrupt by 1998 because of unfunded mandates. We decided to put together a team that would negotiate with the "feds" in a different way. The game that the federal bureaucracy played with the state bureaucracy was to get the human services people to fight with the mental health people to fight with the health people, and so on. The result was that all the states were fighting within themselves and against each other; this enabled the "feds" to maintain their position because it appeared the states could not get their acts together.

So we changed the process. We said, "Nobody in this room is going to talk to a representative of the federal government until we've all done our figures, and until we're all absolutely clear about our talking points. Every time somebody from a federal agency talks to somebody from Ohio, they are going to hear exactly the same story." We won the first suit that had ever been won against the federal government in a certain payment category for mental retardation and developmental disabilities. Once we won one, people's attitude about clusters shifted immediately. My favorite memory about the shift from initially taking a lot of guff about forcing people to work this way to embracing the cluster system instead was the time, between the November election and when we left office, that some of the same people in the state agencies most adamantly against this kind of working structure were in my office saying, "Isn't there some way you can pass a law requiring clusters to continue operation after you leave office?"

President Clinton's First Cabinet Retreat

Troxel: *How did you find yourself working for the federal government in Washington?*

Lukensmeyer: In October of 1992, I gave a speech at the Organizational Development Network (ODN) meeting in Toronto on challenging OD professionals to consider working in government and politics. After the speech I had dinner with Jane Hopkins, who was working as a consultant with then-Senator Gore. During dinner she asked excellent questions about how we organized the Cabinet in Ohio and took notes on my responses. When I asked what this was all about she said, "I'll call you after the election." She did and that is how I came to co-facilitate the President's first Cabinet retreat.

Troxel: *What did you do at that retreat?*

Lukensmeyer: It was a very substantive two-day retreat. The President and Cabinet set the six priorities for 1993, all of which were accomplished (except welfare reform which, upon review, was shifted to a later timetable). Leon Panetta and Alice Rivlin, then director and deputy of the Office of Management and Budget, did a presentation on the budget that became the focus of the Cabinet's discussion of the budget. It was a significant accomplishment.

In helping to design the retreat, I relied on my state experience. I recommended that we join the politics of the campaign with the Cabinet's mandate to govern. President Clinton understood the importance of this immediately and the focus of the first two-and-a-half hours of the retreat was, "Why did we win, and what is our mandate?" The message of the American people was the basis for setting the direction of the new administration's work agenda.

Let me digress for just a second to say a word about spirit that may surprise you. As a nation and as a culture we have gone so far in valuing materialism that we often obliterate our conscious connection to the world of spirit in most of what we do. Given the history of our country's founding and our deep concerns about the separation of church and state, this is particularly true in the political realm. As a culture we are finally learning to acknowledge the difference between religion as an institution and one's personal connection with spirit. This connection is part of the quality present when people are in genuine dialogue.

In all of my work I look for ways to connect myself and others with "spirit," "energy," or "universal reality and vitality." I paid close attention to this dimension both in the design process and in the working environment for this Cabinet retreat. There were 45 Cabinet members and key staff for the first evening and day. People's energy, vitality, and open-heartedness were clearly available for each other. To generate those qualities in a group that size is not that unusual. But the next morning we were joined by 65 more people for a total of 110. Yet we managed to create the same level of openness, candor, and real dialogue on the second day as we did on the first. I guess we were blessed. I would have almost said that it could not happen, but it did.

Troxel: *Did you continue to work with Cabinet members?*

Lukensmeyer: Not right away. After the retreat I continued my consulting practice. In late March, Vice-President Gore tracked me down while I was working on the West Coast. He asked me to work for him on the "reinventing government" initiative and I went to Washington immediately, and worked on those efforts until I went to work for the White House Chief of Staff in November, 1993.

Initiating Guidelines for a Changing Bureaucracy

Troxel: *How did the National Performance Review come into being?*

Lukensmeyer: Well, here's a good example of how a new administration struggles to make the transition from campaign mode to governing. It was a typical, political event on March 3, 1993, when the President stood at a press conference with the Vice-President, and congressional leaders, and announced the formation of the National Performance Review (NPR). They set a deadline of September 7th of that year for its report to the President. When the podium and microphones were cleared away, there was no staff, no budget, no office, no plan. It was incredible to anyone who is knowledgeable about management. And so typical of our political system. In a flash a campaign promise was transformed into a governing imperative with no infrastructure to support it.

Three aspects of the staffing and methodology of the NPR made it unique from previous similar efforts to reform the federal government such as the Grace Commission and the Ash Council. First, the clear majority of the staff of NPR were career federal employees — people who knew the details of how things operated, knew the problems, and knew the solutions; second, NPR identified success stories, enabling people to transfer learning in addition to identifying problems; third, all estimates of cost savings had to be agreed to by both the agency and the Office of Management and Budget *before* publication.

Another key strategic decision made by the Vice-President early on was *not* to create a lot of new structures or a separate bureaucracy to manage implementation of the report's recommendations. He understood that federal employees had to be committed to the change process and own the implementation. We did not want to foster yet another layer of organization so we created only five cross-agency mechanisms staffed by people who were on loan from their agencies. This group kept the President and Vice-President linked to implementation: (1) the President's Management Council, (2) the National Partnership Council working with the labor unions, (3) the Community Enterprise Board, which is the link between the federal, state, and local governments, (4) the Government Information Technology Group, and (5) the Ecosystem Management Group.

By the way, we did meet the September 7, 1993 deadline. And a year later, the first status report was presented to the President at a White House South Lawn ceremony. All of us who were involved, as well as many internal and external critics, were amazed at how much was accomplished in that first year. We all knew that the next challenge would be to imbed the movement for change in the bureaucracy itself.

Reinventing Government

Troxel: *What have you learned, Carolyn, in your time at the state and federal government, about what reinventing government entails?*

Lukensmeyer: I think that the American people, whether they work in government or out of government, have got to reestablish clarity about what is unique in their governmental systems. Government bureaucracies exist only to serve the citizens of the United States of America. Those bureaucracies have to be deeply committed to and focused by mission and purpose on the "common good." They exist to help us all figure out how to live together.

As a result, government systems cannot be meaningfully changed from the inside out without some link with the citizens. There must be a constant commitment from the public to pay attention, to be engaged, to care, and to voice real concerns. Broad citizen participation has to be linked with public interest and public policy issues. Citizens must assume responsibility for the political electoral process.

Bridging the Gap Between Policy and Management

I was beginning to get an inkling of this in Columbus, but I saw it more clearly in Washington. We know that the public policy think tanks have evolved in Washington, D.C., and have multiplied. Also the numbers of all the lobbyists in oil, business, agriculture, and every other field have increased. One of the unintended negative consequences of all this activity is that in fact there is a mentality that separates public policy from public management. In most cases, there is an insidious value structure that makes the policy part important and the management part unimportant. In other words, to be engaged in the work of public policy development is seen as superior to being engaged in the work of public administration. Many of the people who are in those policy think tanks are people who have the highest and best purposes and values about how government should serve its people. But their work is disconnected from the management systems which turn policy into action.

Also, we have politicians who are not particularly savvy or connected to these management systems. We have public policy gurus who are not particularly connected to public management. And we have a political system full of good ideas, which is not linking good management with good government. Back in Ohio, Governor Celeste, Pam Hyde, myself, and other Cabinet members and staff used to discuss this a lot. One of the things we saw was that there are three factors that must be put back together to make a working triangle: good management is good politics is good government. It does not matter where you start, but there's got to be a comprehension that managerial leadership is one of the essential elements to making government responsive and accountable again.

The Citizen's Role

Citizens are not going to have a meaningful role unless they stand up and say that they want it. Starting with Proposition 13 in California, citizens got angry about the way government was disconnected from the amount of money it was taking out of their pockets. It has taken a full 15 years for citizens to be as vocal and angry about poor service as they were about paying too much money for taxes. I also have seen this trend of citizens connecting money and service, first in Ohio and now in Washington.

Troxel: *What do you think accounts for this burst of citizen interest and involvement?*

Lukensmeyer: I would attribute it to the consumer revolution in this country. People have learned they can demand cars that don't need repairs every three months. So they ask, "Why should I have to call the Social Security Administration and be left on hold for 30 minutes and never get an answer to my questions about my mother's monthly disability payments?" The ethos has changed in this country; people are beginning to demand that government work better, not just cost less.

The point is that people have got to reexperience both conceptually and behaviorally the link between how they participate in the political system and the end-result. Citizens need to ask themselves if they are getting what they want or not. They need to ask if the government serves them. This is one thing that is unique about our government.

Hope versus Cynicism

When, with some successes under my belt, I went to Washington, D.C., I found that everybody in Washington tends toward cynicism. It is unbelievable the way that cynicism dominates; it is a stunning experience for an outsider. For example, here we were at NPR, working our hearts out to create real change in government and Capitol Hill told us this is a joke: it's dead on arrival. The lobbyists were all laughing. But, we were a bunch of true believers, so we got down and worked even harder on the report. We hired a professional to write it rather than government bureaucrats. We presented the report on September 7, 1993, on deadline. The President's approval rating went up 11 points in 48 hours and all of a sudden everybody in Washington was listening. Laughing stopped for a time.

Troxel: *So, what do you see in the future now?*

Lukensmeyer: Well, I think this is an extraordinary moment in history for public service. I think that to whatever extent the reinventing government movement might fail, its failure means that it didn't take hold sufficiently in the bureaucracy itself to go forward. At the federal level, that will be true even if Clinton and Gore are reelected. For some, it will be one more piece of data to substantiate people's cynicism. It will kill hope and breed cynicism. I happen to be a person who believes that for our nation the balance between cynicism and hope is very precarious. And if we let ourselves slip more into the cynical side and lose energy on the hope side, we don't have a prayer in the long run.

I am staying in Washington because there is a critical mass of key individuals in key positions who are aligned and working in the same direction. And there is enough citizen activism nationwide to provide support for real changes in how government works. If we can link good politics, good government, and good management in these key policy areas Americans care deeply about, we can take the kinds of risks and create collaborative efforts that will move us forward and give us hope. This is the kind of work I find most challenging and meaningful.

SECTION I
Citizens Taking Initiative

Rebuilding from the Bottom Up

One of my fondest memories as a boy growing up was the summer I spent with my grandparents in Sayre, Oklahoma. It was the mid-1950s and I was about 10 years old. Sayre is a county seat in the western part of the state on old Route 66. It is famous for its red clay soil, reminiscent of the 1930s Dustbowl era, a time of hardship still fresh in the memory of some people.

One event stands out in my mind from that summer. One morning my grandmother received a phone call revealing that something unfortunate had happened to her friend, Mrs. Gardner, who lived a couple of streets away. I don't think I ever knew what the particulars were, but I do remember that after a brief conference with my grandfather and my great-aunt Ada, Grandmother swung into action. She spent the remainder of the day in the kitchen cooking. Then toward the end of the afternoon I accompanied my grandparents as we walked up to Mrs. Gardner's carrying the food Grandmother had prepared.

When we arrived I was astonished to find a lot of other people, many of whom also had brought prepared food. Great-Aunt Ada seemed to be supervising things in Mrs. Gardner's kitchen and after a while all the guests were invited to partake of the bounty, though most did not. It seemed as if the whole community had mobilized itself to assist Mrs. Gardner in her misfortune, which was still very mysterious to me. On the front porch swing that night sitting between my grandparents, I asked them how everyone knew what to do. How did Grandmother know to fix the fried chicken? Why was Great-Aunt Ada supervising in the kitchen? Why did all those people show up for something so unusual? Before I received an answer, a chain link snapped and we three pummeled to the ground. And the unanswered question has been one that has driven my curiosity for nearly 40 years.

All of us have witnessed similar stressful situations in which family and friends mobilized to come to the aid of someone. Sayre, Oklahoma, didn't have a Department of Human Services, a state office for social services, or a federal program for distraught people. The *community mobilized itself* in its care for Mrs. Gardner. Section I of this book spotlights how government works best when allied with the spirit of citizen responsibility. These are stories of local communities leading the way. Government is the form and structure that houses the political process usually establishing programs to serve its *polis*. Though the term politics usually refers to the activities of politicians within governments, as we use it here, "politics" stays close to its original meaning. It refers to all of those activities required to sustain a *polis* or community.

Politics and Community Action

A neighborhood association revitalizing its community is political. A citizen coalition working for a better education system is political. Politics, and therefore governing, includes all our common efforts to solve common problems. Gradually over time, however, in assigning this kind of social responsibility to the plethora of public agencies, we have deluded ourselves in thinking that we have been excused or exempted from the basic care of community. Now, obviously we are simply asking more from our public institutions than they possibly can supply.

For example, perhaps you will remember the unfortunate story that came out of Chicago during the winter of 1994 when 19 children were found living in squalor in a two-bedroom apartment. A tragedy to be sure, but what struck me was how quickly the media turned its attention on the negligent social worker from the state's Department of Children and

Family Services. Apparently this one case worker was being chastised for not reporting that he or she had been unable to enter the apartment on earlier visits. The police, in fact, had found the kids during a drug raid on the apartment. Our society in the last several years has often been placing responsibility and accountability at the wrong feet. In the case of the Chicago social worker, who is holding the parents accountable? Who is asking why the other apartment residents didn't report this outrageous situation? Why do we think this is only a failure of a civil employee of a public institution? Aren't we expecting too much of government?

Resurging Citizen Initiatives

People are beginning to understand that government cannot do everything a community needs. Slowly, local groups are unifying, rebuilding, and renewing themselves. Scores of little-known, small-scale success stories are building into a major force for political and social change. And the change agenda that brings these attempts together is basic social responsibility.

The Kettering Foundation conducted a study of community initiatives across the country and concluded that:

> There are certain things that our governments, schools, experts, professionals, and officials — even at their best — can never do. A community has certain undelegable responsibilities. Only the public can define the purposes of the community, choose the directions in which it should move, create common interests, build common ground, and generate the political will to act together[1].

The Chicago Tribune ran a series of articles in the fall of 1993 about the numbers of people moving out of the city into the suburbs and cited all the negative reasons why this was taking place. Ted Wysocki of the Chicago Association of Neighborhood Development Organizations (CANDO) in his rebuttal to the story simply indicated that "People moving out of the city is an old story. People fighting to save their neighborhoods *is news* (italics added) [2].

Wysocki and his organization, CANDO, representing 70 neighborhood organizations in Chicago, illustrate a major but oftentimes hidden movement that has swept across the country in the last 25 years or so. It is the movement of grassroots community based organizations — many in low income areas—working and recovering one of the fundamental principles upon which our nation is built, a government by the people. It is the story of local citizens who have banded themselves together in various forms to alleviate some felt need. They go by such names as community development corporations (CDCs), neighborhood development organizations (NDOs), or community-based organizations (CBOs). Whatever their title, they have become one of the most critical influences in fostering the self-help approach. Over 5,000 such organizations have sprung up in the past quarter of a century.

The New Community Corporation of Newark, N..J., which began in 1968 in a riot-torn area of the inner city, is now one of the largest CDCs in the nation with a staff of 152 and an operating budget of over $6 million. They have rehabilitated or built 2500 units of housing for 6000 residents using a blended management approach that includes social services along with building maintenance. They have over 1000 graduates of their job training program, operate eight businesses, and have a federal credit union for 1300 individuals. .By keeping this earning power in the local community, the group has fostered the spirit of empowerment and self-help, and is building up the local economy as well.

Another successful CDC is The Northwest Side Community Development Corporation of Milwaukee, which has been working since 1983 to revitalize its neighborhood. The people have improved the commercial street of Villard Avenue, enhanced the industrial area around them, opened a small business incubator, and launched education and job training programs. "We're an example of what can happen if you stay at it long enough and don't get worn down by things that can't be done," says Executive Director Howard Snyder.

These are just three among thousands of such groups operating across the country. Not all these initiatives are found in the cities. Small towns also know the importance of framing a vision for the future. Ponca City, Oklahoma, a town of 26,000 in the northern part of the state, began a highly participative approach to involve every member of the town in shaping its vision for the future. Launched through the efforts of the town's Chamber of Commerce, what began as a novel idea has evolved into an independent, nonprofit foundation called Ponca City Tomorrow. Its mission is to improve upon the quality of community life continuously for all the citizens of Ponca City, and to create and maintain an ongoing community dialogue that will encourage citizens of Ponca City to become involved and proactive in creating and building the future. An additional purpose of the foundation is to recognize and respect each other for their individual and collective differences, and to become better informed on the issues and challenges confronting the community.

The group decided that the issues that will guide their future actions include exemplary educational systems, a diversified industrial and retail base, outstanding tourism and recreation opportunities, responsive, responsible local government; effective public transportation, quality retirement living, environmental awareness, and city beauty." It's just community planning," says Cheryl Fletcher, chair of Ponca City Tomorrow. "The idea is to empower our community residents with the sense that they can create and control their future and the future of the community."

A boost from the federal government that supports programs like Ponca City Tomorrow is the Empowerment Zone Act. Enacted in 1994, this piece of legislation gives Washington a chance to respond to locally based partnerships of government, business, and community institutions. The legislation mandates that before a local community can be designated as an empowerment zone, a strategic planning process within the community must bring together all the elements of an area to analyze the locally available assets.

If all of these local experiences and lessons could be summarized in one statement, it would be that effective communities make use of political capacities not normally called into play in politics as usual. Effective communities go beyond conventional wisdom. The difference is reflected in the way they define and respond to their problems, and in the types of actions that flow from a resurgence of political will. A community's citizens are more likely to support programs, initiatives, and decisions they understand and in which they have participated in creating. It can take the responsibility off government and put it back where it belongs—with the citizens themselves. "Right now most people view government as a vending machine," says Rick Cole, mayor of Pasadena, California. "You put in your 25 cents and you want back 50 cents' worth of services. But what government really ought to be is a barn raising," a community effort in which everyone works together for an end that benefits all[3].

One of America's best-kept secrets is that in many places, local democracy is alive and well, in fact thriving through creative experiments and fresh initiatives[4]:

- Birmingham, Alabama, with a population of 180,000, has some 95 neighborhoods electing leaders by open ballot. City-funded mailings communicate monthly to every resident. Some of the 22 community coalitions serving to represent the neighborhoods in a citywide Citizens Advisory Board have created tool-lending libraries and neighborhood-painting programs as well as extensive neighborhood festivals and street fairs.

- Dayton, Ohio, boasts seven priority boards and 74 neighborhoods intricately linked with a model of performance-oriented public administration. All city agencies work under a detailed set of goals; a key measure of agency success is whether the public likes the results. They had better, because every five years the city has had to face an all-or-nothing public vote on the local income tax.

One of the nation's leading practitioners of citizen-based government is Anne Dosher, an organizational development consultant based in San Diego. In responding to an interviewer's question about how a local community can be assured of its right to citizen initiatives, she responded:

> The individualism, consumerism, and materialism of our society are antagonistic to the creation of community. This is why we have to create community over and over again....Individualism and property rights, the basis of our society, created a desouled, despirited reality by design. People are becoming more and more disenchanted with it. Community is the opposite of that. It's about connectedness, bondedness, wholeness, and spirit. If community isn't an ensouled, spirited reality, then it becomes meaningless[5].

The case studies in this book embody this spirit of basic social responsibility. They tell us that government works best when it works with local communities. Some of these lessons include:

- Increased participation in community planning fosters increased responsibility;

- Participation by individuals enhances their self-image and moves them from victimization to empowerment;
- With participation, the group determines the issues; the more broad-based the group, the more comprehensive the list of issues and solutions;
- Increased participation can turn the table on adversarial relationships;
- In identifying problems, people need to see how they participate in perpetuating the problem;
- Increased participation in community planning offers the possibility of the practical recovery of democracy.

References

[1] *Community Politics,* by David Mathews and Noelle McAfee. David Mathews, executive director of the Kettering Foundations, has written another book detailing many of the same themes, *Politics for People: Finding a Responsible Public Voice,* 1994, Urbana, IL, University of Illinois Press.

[2] Letter to Editor, *Chicago Tribune,* December 19, 1993.

[3] *Governing,* February, 1994, page 56.

[4] Taken from information provided by the Lincoln Filene Center, Tufts University, Medford, MA.

[5] Burbidge, John. "Guarding Community in America," *Edges,* Vol. 4, No. 2, Institute of Cultural Affairs, Toronto, Ontario, Canada, pp.31-35.

Chapter 3
Winds of Change in the Valley of the Sun

SHIRLEY HECKMAN, PH.D. AND TAMMY BOSSE

*Finally, the winds of change are blowing in the Valley of
the Sun. Institutions and individuals are waking up to
realize the importance of the neighborhoods. You can
feel it in the air. It feels as if wildflower seeds have been
spread across the land and spring is here. Many things
contributed to this phenomenon, but the open,
participatory, comprehensive process of the Futures
Forum enabled the dialogue that created the vision and
plan that unleashed the magic of the human spirit.
Suddenly people had ways to share their hopes, dreams,
vision, concerns, and solutions with others—and
someone was listening. When the city of Phoenix
created the Futures Forum, it had no idea of the impact
to be realized in the years since then.*

—Tammy Bosse

I n fall 1993, the city of Phoenix, Arizona, won the Carl Bertelsmann
Prize, tying for first place with Christchurch, New Zealand, as the best-
run city in the world. Bertelsmann A.G., a German-based major media
organization owning RCA, Bantam/Doubleday, and Arista Records
supports through its foundation a different future-oriented project
each year. The Bertelsmann representatives asked organizations of
city managers, city planners, and other professionals working with cities
to nominate the U.S. entry. Phoenix was the only city listed by every one
of those organizations. Not surprisingly, the selection group chose
Phoenix as the national representative.

The German-based Bertelsmann Foundation visited the city to check how Phoenix measured up in its cooperation among departments, balance between innovation and evolution, and its orientation toward its customers, the citizens of the city. During their examination visit to the city, the Bertelsmann people praised the city's:

- Strong social structure,
- Residents who take action when signs of deterioration appear in their areas,
- Focus on teamwork with the community,
- Council-manager form of government, and
- Committed team of employees.

Even as recently as 1987, it would have been surprising for Phoenix to receive such an award. The populated area around Phoenix, the state capital of Arizona, is called the Valley of the Sun. It stretches about 30 miles from Avondale in the west to Apache Junction in the east, and about 30 miles from the south edge of Chandler to the north edge of Sun City. In an incredible 936 square miles, the population as of 1994 was about 2.1 million. In 1940, only 65,000 people lived on 9.6 square miles. If the growth had come gradually this would have been an average annual increase over the last 50 years of about 40,000 people and 18 square miles. But in the peak growth years of the 1980s, 120,000 to 130,000 people arrived annually. Problems inevitably developed with this sudden increase in population. New freeways could not handle the increased traffic. Air pollution increased. Speculators proposed converting whole neighborhoods to commercial use. Schools became overcrowded and social agencies could not keep up with the demand for services. By 1986-87, growth began to slow. For every four people moving in, three moved away.

Phoenix had before it the examples of Detroit, St. Louis, Houston, Denver, and Newark, N. J., which in the 1980s were struggling to survive after experiencing population or economic growth in similar short periods of time only a few years before. In late 1986, conditions in Phoenix stimulated Pat Murphy, publisher of the major daily newspaper, *Arizona Republic and Gazette*, to commission the nationally syndicated columnist on state and local government, Neal Peirce, and three associates to "provide a fresh and untainted view of our problems and opportunities." Published in February, 1987, the Peirce Report was very positive about many aspects of the area, "but we also found the Valley lacking in some of the critical capacities that enable cities or regions to 'get their act together' and move in timely, assertive fashion. These capacities include:

- Broad and cooperative agreement of citizens, business, and government;
- An expectation that interests will differ, and a willingness to negotiate to find common ground for dealing with the differences;
- An openness to experimentation and risk taking, with local corporations and foundations providing some of the seed money; and
- Local media as committed to covering constructive partnership building as they are committed to exposing wrongdoing."

It is difficult to identify what caused the shift from Phoenix's being a "developer-driven city" unable to keep up with increasing problems to the point of receiving an award for "the best-run city in the world." Many people agree that the Phoenix Futures Forum contributed greatly to that change. One indication of the significance of the Futures Forum is that primarily because of its work, Phoenix received the All-America City Award in 1989.

The Phoenix Futures Forum
Creating and Carrying Out a Community Agenda

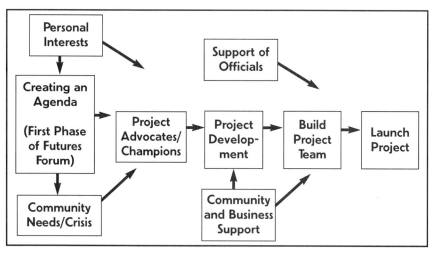

Tammy Bosse, as staff for the Futures Forum, describes the effect of Phoenix's experience with citizen participation in government, with these words:

> Finally, the winds of change are blowing in the Valley of the Sun. Institutions and individuals are waking up to realize the importance of the neighborhoods. You can feel it in the air. It feels as if wildflower seeds have been spread across the land and spring is here. Many things contributed to this phenomenon, but the open, participatory, comprehensive process of the Futures Forum enabled the dialogue that created the vision and plan that unleashed the magic of the human spirit. Suddenly people had ways to share their hopes, dreams, visions, concerns, and solutions with others—and someone was listening. When the city of Phoenix created the Futures Forum, it had no idea of the impact to be realized in the years since then.

In a speech given in February, 1992, Neal Peirce attested to this same impact when he said, "The Phoenix Futures Forum has been one of the most heartening demonstrations of civic growth—sparked by far-sighted political leadership, energized by citizens, given solid financial backing,

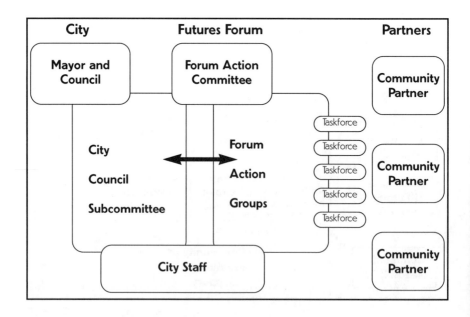

and viewed as a real national model." He said that those associated with the 1987 report could try to take credit for catalyzing the developments, but "one cannot catalyze something not ready to happen anyway." He reminded the listeners that thoughtful people in the community were ready to think and act more cooperatively, that they were ready "to emerge from the innocence of unplanned, *laissez-faire* growth."

Terry Goddard became mayor of Phoenix in 1986, after launching a successful campaign built on activism around freeway construction. Before his administration, all city council members were elected at large. He led the successful drive to elect the city council members by district so they would feel responsibility for their home areas. He strengthened the city's citizen-based committee system through which he encouraged increased citizen involvement. Before Goddard, citizens with concerns had to go to the weekly city council meeting and wait until the end of the meeting for the time for citizen input. He created the Citizens' District Forum, held regularly in different parts of the city, through which citizens had direct access to the city council. He also created hundreds of new seats on city boards and commissions, giving these groups more real authority.

At the beginning of his second term in his May, 1988 State of the City address, Mayor Goddard proposed the Futures Forum as a way of involving citizens in shaping the city's future. He asked the city council for $100,000 for the first year with the understanding that this amount would be matched by private contributions. He also pledged $28,450 from his personal pension fund. The mayor wanted to help the community realize the need for social, economic, and environmental change, and hoped that the Forum would produce a vision of the future that the community would support.

Some ideas for the Futures Forum came to Goddard from his conversations with representatives of the National Civic League and the National League of Cities. He learned what had not worked well from results of a ten-year project sponsored by the Ford Foundation to stimulate citizen involvement in New York City. Goddard felt that the New York project had failed because it was "top-down and had no real constituency." He knew that the Phoenix group needed to have enough framework and structure to be productive, but also needed to be broad-based and energized from citizen participation.

An important factor in the success of the Futures Forum was the passion and vision of the volunteer leaders who contributed many hours to it. With his belief in citizen participation, Terry Goddard trusted the citizens appointed to carry major responsibility. He appointed Rod Engelen, who was at that time assistant to the mayor, to be director of the Futures Forum. Other city staff members were assigned to work and report directly to Engelen. In addition, the mayor recruited strong, effective citizens to provide needed leadership. For instance, citizen members included the owner of a computer wholesale outlet, several attorneys, a psychiatrist, a manager of public affairs for a large corporation, and a Sierra Club leader.

Also significant at this stage of the Forum's development was the response of the city council and Honeywell Corporation. The committee received an unsolicited grant from the Honeywell Corporation of $50,000 to help fund the Forum. The active participation of Honeywell personnel in the Futures Forum gave it an immediate boost and created wide credibility in the community.

At the mayor's request, the city council allocated the requested funds and appointed the first Futures Forum planning committee of 14 people from widely varied backgrounds. The planning committee recruited a steering committee of nearly 100 people who were representative of various sectors in the city. The steering committee hired a public relations firm to disseminate information about the process and issue progress reports. City, state, and private agencies compiled facts and projections to be used as input. Several major gatherings called forums provided occasions for citizen participation. The first forum was held in October, 1988. Neal Peirce, the journalist whose specialty was writing about cities, was the

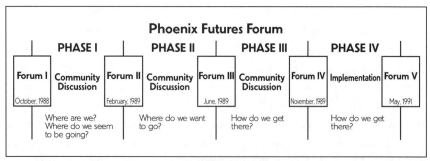

The Futures Forum process is graphically represented in the chart below. Because of its dynamic nature, the process is subject to revisions. Any changes or additional opportunities for participation will be announced.

principal speaker while dozens of experts made presentations in smaller workshops. In this first meeting, the speakers used up all the time, leaving no time for questions and discussion. At Forums II, III, and IV in February, June, and November, 1989, citizens worked to draft a vision statement and create and present taskforce reports from nine taskforces that met biweekly throughout that summer.

Right from the beginning of the Forum experiences, people were excited. In the last few days before Forum I, registrations skyrocketed, threatening to exceed facility and program capacities. To avoid overcrowding, city department personnel were asked to limit their participation. Unfortunately some of them interpreted this request to mean that they were unwelcome. This misperception by government staff later caused some unexpected negative challenges to implementing Futures Forum recommendations. As a result, Futures Forum personnel tried hard to overcome this staff attitude after the first forum so they would feel welcome to participate. Forum participants included a CEO of USWest, policy makers from arts organizations, a community revitalization corporation, Arizona State University professors

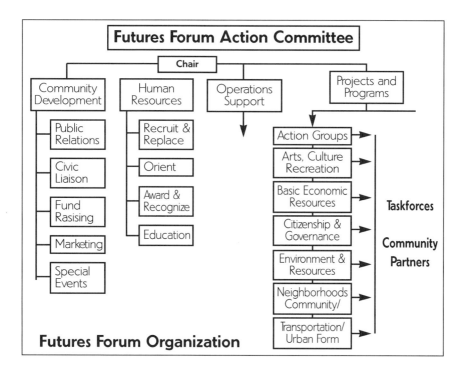

Futures Forum Organization

The Vision Statement

The Preamble

We, the people of Phoenix, having embarked upon a continuing, community-wide dialogue to reach a shared vision of our future, find that we hold these values in common:

- We have a duty to create and maintain an effective community. We are committed to each other and to an ethic that requires each individual, family, and institution to act responsibly to meet our shared needs, dreams and aspirations.
- We believe that each person has an equal right to opportunities that allow full realization of that individual's potential.
- We acknowledge our responsibility to and dependence upon the healthy, natural world environment, and affirm that we must sustain and protect our Sonoran Desert.
- We have the obligation to learn from the past, to take responsibility for creating the future of Phoenix, and to affirm our role in the world community.

Being from diverse backgrounds and bound together by these shared values, we are committed to achieving the following vision of the future of Phoenix:

Our Vision

"OUR VISION is of ..."

These words are followed by one-paragraph descriptions of 1) community, 2) education, 3) economy, 4) basic human needs, 5) natural environment and resources, 6) urban form, 7) transportation and communication, 8) art, culture, and recreation and 9) governance.

Our Vision

AS PROUD CITIZENS OF PHOENIX, WE COMMIT our individual and collective effort to create a future for our city that reflects this vision. To this end, we dedicate our time, our resources, and our talents, and we invite our neighboring communities to join us in this endeavor.

and staff, the Urban Forum, landscape architects, the head of the Greater Economic Development Council, transportation experts, human service agencies, and a homeless man.

As follow-ups to the first forum, six "mini-forums," one youth forum, and other city events occurred between November, 1988 and February, 1989. The results of these gatherings formed the basis for the initial drafts of the Forum's vision statement. Participatory methods helped everyone involved to share ideas about the most critical problems or opportunities to be faced in the next 25 years. Initially, many people mistrusted the intent of the Forum, thinking it was just another empty gesture by the city asking for their input. As they participated, however, they realized that their ideas did receive genuine attention. Frank Fiore, project director of a hardware/software distributor and present director of Micro Age, chaired the vision drafting committee and coordinated some of the implementation taskforces. He commended the dedication of the 300 people who worked to create the vision statement and implementation strategies through the summer of 1989 "when it was so hot in Phoenix that it was hard to get anything done."

Futures Forum Vision Becomes Phoenix City Goals

In January, 1990, the city council adopted this vision statement as a set of goals for Phoenix and set up structures to work on the recommended initiatives. The printed report published early in 1990 reported on the work of "thousands of citizens who dedicated over a year to visualizing Phoenix in 2015 and beyond."

Implementation Following the Futures Forum

After this vision was accepted by the city council, the challenge to the city and to citizens was to implement the recommendations. The Futures Forum staff shared the report with people in city departments, various city-associated boards, committees and commissions, as well as citizen, business, and nonprofit organizations. They requested that recommendations be incorporated into ongoing programs. Arizona State University was among those who responded.

In early 1990, Dr. Lattie Coor, new president of Arizona State University in Tempe. President Coor wanted to forge stronger links between the city and the university, so he responded positively to initiatives from Herb

Ely and Jim Howard, Futures Forum leaders who were encouraging multi-sector involvement in the implementation of the Futures Forum recommendations. President Coor decided to lend a full-time faculty member from ASU to work with the Futures Forum. The first of these "loaned executives" appointed by ASU in mid-1990 was Professor of Public Affairs in the School of Public Affairs at ASU, Dr. Louis Weschler, who had participated as a citizen from the first 18 months of the Futures Forum.

As part of the Futures Forum staff, Dr. Weschler worked with citizen groups, providing professional support for the movement into the implementation phase and helping them to understand the city's operation. He trained local people to be better advocates for their own positions and was a liaison between the university and the city. He describes his role, "I was sort of a midwife between crises or needs in the city and resources of ASU." Dr. Weschler says that the Futures Forum changed the agenda of the city to include a focus on neighborhoods.

When Dr. Weschler completed his term in 1991, ASU decided to continue its "loaned executive" idea and assigned Dr. Robert Stout of the College of Education to the Forum. In 1992, when ASU appointed Joochul Kim from the School of Planning to this post, the city assigned Charles Hill of the Strategic Planning Department as its "loaned executive" to ASU. This reciprocal relationship continues with the ASU representative working through the offices of the mayor and the city manager.

The Futures Forum 21 Initiatives

At the core of what ASU and other organizations were working to implement were the Forum's *21 Initiatives for the 21st Century*. These 21 Initiatives represented significant changes in direction, resource allocation and/or levels of effort. Some of the recommendations in these Forum initiatives responded to particular needs of specific groups, like putting bike racks on the city buses. The September 1992 issue of *The Transportation Exchange Update* devoted all four of its pages to this action as a model to be emulated.

Some effects of these initiatives are widespread. Recommendations from the Futures Forum were incorporated into the city's Corporate Strategic Plan and into its General Plan, the city's primary planning documents. The Corporate Strategic Plan guides longer-range planning, while the General

Plan is used daily for decision making. As strategic planner for the city from 1987-1993, Lance Decker prepared a 1991 document reporting that 15% of the Futures Forum recommendations had been completed; 32% were in process; 47% needed further study; the remaining had not yet been catalogued. He recommended that a process similar to the Futures Forum should happen in every community.

Access to Information

One Forum recommendation was that people deserved more access to information. The city responded with three specific actions:

1. Initiating "Phone Phoenix" as a hotline for information about city services with one number for English language and another for Spanish; they also distributed widely a brochure describing this service;
2. Negotiating with area newspapers to include a weekly "city page" listing city programs, regulations, and issues;
3. Creating kiosks in accessible locations. For example, in the main public library in Phoenix, a video invites people to "touch the screen" to get information about the city. Touch one of the eight choices marked "about the city" and another screen of choices appears. Touch "Futures Forum" and the following on-screen message appears:

> A premier desert city in tune with its environment, an ethical people coexisting responsibly—too good to be true. Not to the thousands who participated in the Futures Forum in 1988-89, when 3,500 citizens and city employees working together built a consensus for the future of the area. If you would like a copy of the report of that work or would like to help implement some of their recommendations, please call 262-4838.

Call the number and a pleasant voice tells you that it is the Neighborhood Services Department.

Neighborhood Development

A significant result of the Futures Forum was the city's picking up on its emphasis on neighborhood development. This focus was evident in other recommendations fed into the ongoing framework of the city.

These included:

Refining and implementing a neighborhood concept;
Actively coordinating and integrating community services;
Creating a good neighborhood network and program;
Establishing a housing and neighborhood investment fund.

Some concerns raised by Futures Forum participants were:

- The increase in crime,
- Deterioration of both public and private property,
- Pervasive sense of isolation,
- Delinquency,
- Inadequate support network for families,
- Insufficient youth programs and play areas,
- Graffiti, and
- Inability of neighborhoods to cooperate with one another.

People who wanted to take action to improve their neighborhoods had no way to link with each other or with city services, and the city had no way to connect with the neighborhoods. To deal with that concern, the city created a new Neighborhood Notification Office in 1990 to register neighborhood organizations and communicate regularly with them. The focus of this office was expanded when, in 1992, the city combined the Neighborhood Notification Department and other neighborhood-oriented city programs into a new Neighborhood Services Department (NSD). This expansion and coordination of neighborhood development came in response to a series of Futures Forum studies and taskforce activities. Previously, services to neighborhoods had been scattered with no coordination and were a low priority for budget and time allocation. The coordinated NSD allows the city to be proactive and comprehensive rather than reactive and dispersed. The three divisions of NSD are Advocacy, Neighborhood Preservation, and Neighborhood Development; by 1994, there was an NSD staff of 180 people.

The following vignettes give some insights into the work of the NSD.

Story #1: By spring of 1994, about 350 neighborhood associations were registered with the Neighborhood Notification office. One of the associations, Maryvale UNITE, uses juveniles from the court system to paint out graffiti and clean up its area. The Juvenile Court Probation system expanded this program to all Block Watch and neighborhood associations. First- and second-time juvenile minor offenders receiving sentences of "community service" can work out their owed hours in supervised graffiti paintouts and neighborhood cleanups. Parents provide transportation and one adult supervises every 8-10 youths. The court carries insurance to cover the young people.

Story #2: Another NSD program is Neighborhood Maintenance and Zoning Enforcement (NMZE). The NMZE staff responds to concerns like: "The vacant lot next door has dry weeds three feet high and I'm afraid they're going to catch on fire and burn my place down." The staff also inspects the city's assisted housing programs and reviews requests for regulatory licenses. By emphasizing customer service and citizen education, the staff obtains voluntary compliance with 95% of its cases.

Story #3: Several weekends a year, NSD employees and their family members show up on a Saturday in their work clothes, with tools and supplies to put neglected yards back into shape. They work with homeowners with financial problems to clean up properties and correct code violations. Nonprofit organizations provide names of elderly and disabled homeowners who need this help. A pizza party caps off the end of the day of work. "As employees of NSD, we feel it is important to take this extra step to participate in helping preserve our neighborhoods," said one city staff member.

Story #4: The Neighborhood Fight Back Program is another part of NSD. It provides a one-time allocation or grant as a temporary increase in city services to reduce crime, pick up uncontained trash, paint over graffiti, install street lighting, and help citizens participate actively in upkeep and stabilization efforts. Ten neighborhoods participated in the program during 1993. More than 8,000 people participated in the annual Red Ribbon Parade and Rally.

Model Municipal Environmental Ordinance

Positive results other than the new Neighborhood Services Department are not always so easily linked to the Futures Forum. One of the Futures Forum 21 Initiatives was to design a comprehensive model of a municipal environmental ordinance. As the Forum Action Group for this initiative began work, they expanded to a taskforce composed of city staff and members of the city's Environmental Quality Commission, people from ASU, outside environmental experts, law firms, and environmental group members. The taskforce wanted a regulatory ordinance mandating action, but the senior city staff and members of the council subcommittee preferred an environmental policy to be used as a guideline. The proposed ordinance is still stuck in that impasse.

Recycling and Waste Disposal

Another initiative was to establish more effective structures for recycling and waste disposal. People from this taskforce developed the Recycling Hotline that operates like this:

> Suppose you are concerned about recycling. You have items to take somewhere or you want to find out what is happening about recycling. Dial 1-800-94-REUSE or local C-L-E-A-N-U-P. Decide if you want the messages in English or Spanish. Give your zip code. Make your choices. #1 gets you an Earth Watch tip. One message is about garage sales being recycling and how secondhand is not second rate. #1 is also the number for discovering the nearest site for recycling 16 different items. #2 lets you leave a message for the Arizona Department of Environmental Quality or gives you phone numbers to reach ten environmental agencies. #3 lists community environmental events for the current month. #4 provides general information on the 3Rs—Reduce, Reuse, Recycle. #5 encourages you to leave a message for one of the sponsors of this program in Arizona: America West, NBC Channel 12, KTAR 620AM and the Outdoor Systems advertising company.

This recycle hotline is funded privately and costs the taxpayers no money. In mid-1994, it had spread to 5 states using the same 800 number. Environmental Protection Agency personnel and other concerned people want this service to become nationwide.

Housing and Neighborhood Investment Fund

Response to Forum Initiative 11 to create a housing and neighborhood investment fund is evident in the experience of David Yniguez, a Futures Forum participant in its early years. In 1988 he moved to Washington, D.C., but in June, 1992, David returned to Phoenix to open an office of Local Initiatives Support Corporation (LISC). One factor in the LISC decision to open an office in Phoenix was the Futures Forum emphasis on the need for affordable housing and support for neighborhood groups. LISC's mission is to build the capacity of neighborhood groups by providing support and resources to community development corporations engaged in transforming distressed neighborhoods into more livable places.

Negative and Positive Forum Effects

The LISC experience reflects a very supportive attitude toward the Forum's effectiveness. Not everyone reacted to the Phoenix experience so positively. One active participant said that a negative result of the Futures Forum was that "the city became paranoid and hostile about direct citizen participation." He went on to say that municipal bureaucracies are designed to have experts make expert decisions. Because the Futures Forum left out the opinions of experts and worked directly with citizens, some city experts felt slighted. Others, however, embraced the recommendations and worked to implement them.

A positive influence was that the Futures Forum mobilized a new set of people in communicating with elected and appointed people. It energized more people to become involved in the reconstruction of the city. Some people active in the Futures Forum ran for offices—some won and some lost. People became more concerned not only with Phoenix but with the extended intergovernmental and intermunicipal linkages. Alan Hald, who chaired the Futures Forum from May, 1990 to November, 1992, went on to chair the Arizona Strategic Plan for Economic Development.

One point on which most observers of the Forum agree is that the Futures Forum was expensive. By the third year, $265,000 had come to the project from city funds, with $250,000 in private contributions. In 1990-1991, ASU contributed more than $110,000 in-kind with its "loaned executive"; others contributed an estimated 10,000 hours of planning and 20,000 hours of implementation.

Training in Practical Civics

Despite the price, Dr. Weschler, the executive loaned by ASU to the Futures Forum, saw a very practical Forum result: "Through the Futures Forum, a lot of people were trained in practical civics. There is no question in my mind that it was massively successful, more as a training device than as a mobilization device."

One person who attests to the effectiveness of this training is Catherine Osborn, a fourth generation Arizonan who is a research and development specialist with Maricopa Community Colleges. She describes her Forum experience:

> It was just by chance that I was able to participate in the Futures Forum. My boss was not able to go and asked if I'd like to go. Generally in meetings, I did not talk because when I did I stammered and stuttered. They put us into small groups with a specific task to do. All of a sudden I started talking and people listened. Then I saw my ideas go up on the board. They were good ideas and other people thought they were good. Where I am today is because of my experience with that participatory process. I went for training as a facilitator. I learned how to interact with people. I learned how to make decisions. I learned how to participate with other people.

> I use the methods in my work as well as working as a volunteer in other settings. I'm trying to get strategic planning started in my hometown of Gilbert by facilitating a town hall meeting there.

Dwindling Support From the City and Business

Just after the city council adopted the vision statement in early 1990, several changes occurred that seriously affected the implementation phase of the Futures Forum recommendations. Mayor Goddard, a primary moving force in the Futures Forum, resigned in 1990 to run for governor of Arizona. Paul Johnson, the new mayor, had other priorities. The operation of the Futures Forum was moved from the mayor's office into the budget and research office. City council members supporting the Futures Forum moved on to other pursuits.

Another obstacle to the Forum's growth occurred in 1991, when the city experienced a substantial budget crunch. It was obvious that another $250,000 was not going to be available to implement further the recommendations of the Futures Forum. Because they could no longer count on financial and administrative support to continue to implement as they had for four years, the enthusiasm of citizens for Futures Forum activity was dwindling. Several people expressed disappointment that direct support from the city stopped. One person said that the Futures Forum was an unprecedented involvement of citizens that could well be emulated in other places, but that with the shift in city leadership, the Futures Forum was not institutionalized with public or private structures that could continue implementation.

When asked what changes he would recommend to others trying this process, Rod Engelen, director of the Futures Forum, stressed the importance of getting business leadership involved. "When it comes time to implement, you can't do it without the participation of business leaders because the big stuff really requires that kind of muscle."

Many businesses were directly involved with the design and planning stage of the Futures Forum. Two regional utilities, Salt River Project and Arizona Public Service, gave money and allowed their people to participate. Phillips-Ramsey, a large public relations firm, did the massive public relations job required by the Futures Forum and donated $2 for every $1 they billed. Part of the implementation phase centered around negotiations among local neighborhood groups and a variety of other groups and agencies. This kind of activity is not as clear a field for participation by large regional businesses.

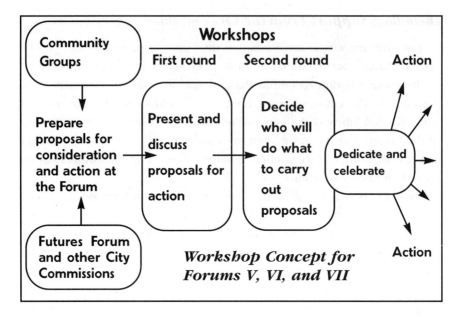

Workshop Concept for Forums V, VI, and VII

Emergence of the Community Forum

Although Forum implementation slowed down with the cutoff of city funds and support as well as the diminished participation of big business, the momentum of the Futures Forum continued, with its vision and recommendations of promising new possibilities. By 1991, Futures Forum volunteers and staff began to devote attention to how the operation could continue outside the structure of the city government. They decided that it needed to be spun off into a private organization, preferably one already existing that had a similar mission.

At this same time, a 51-year-old United Way human services planning agency, the Community Council, was questioning its own future. Founded in March, 1941 by the Phoenix Business and Professional Women's Club, the Community Council was incorporated in 1947. The founders recognized a need in the community to coordinate responses to social problems. Community leaders offered their expertise and perspectives in problem definition and finding solutions. One person interviewed said that the Community Council was "the social conscience of the Phoenix 40," the economic power brokers of the Phoenix area called the Valley of the Sun. The Peirce report published for Phoenix newspapers in 1987 stated, "In days past, the old lions of the Phoenix business establishment...constituted a small club that could call the shots—or at least appeared to....(This) Phoenix 40...is widely resented as too elitist." The group was later called the Greater Phoenix Leadership and members were the powerful yea- and nay-sayers regarding city development for years.

The president of the Community Council at this time was Jerri Pastor. She was born in Phoenix into a Mexican-American family living in Arizona for five generations. When she became leader of the Community Council, Jerri and her colleagues spent a difficult year struggling with what the future of the Community Council should actually be. Finally they decided that they had only two alternatives: either dissolve the organization or find some new way of living out the mission of its founders. During their considerations, they recognized that they did some things very well that were still needed. For instance, they explored and assessed a given situation and called people to action to meet the identified need.

The leadership of the Community Council approached Mayor Johnson to discuss its future. During this conversation, the idea of possible merger with the Futures Forum evolved, and they set up a meeting with the Forum volunteers and staff. Jerri Pastor comments on the two groups' decision to

 **MISSION STATEMENT**

The Community Forum focuses appropriate human and financial resources on community concerns by bringing together all sectors of the community to work toward short and long term solutions. We:

- help communities identify their own needs,
- facilitate coordination and communication among members of the community,
- stimulate partnerships among those with common goals to help generate and focus resources,
- motivate individuals to take action and assume responsibility for fundamental change, and
- initiate projects to demonstrate solutions to community problems.

Adopted 7/24/92

merge and become the Community Forum, "When we merged, we were a natural marriage. But the bad news was we had no courtship and no formal engagement party. We had to act as a married couple overnight. And we were very different." The Community Council was a human services-delivery agency. The Futures Forum was a citizen-participation process. Created by corporate business, the Community Council brought big business people to their planning table, so the council had already leveraged their resources in the past.

The Futures Forum, on the other hand, brought out a population of entrepreneurs. Lots of good, willing 1960s people had a commitment to advocacy. So the Futures Forum was part of their own ethic. They found a home. They had great energy that government had never used, never tapped before. The Futures Forum people did not deal with large organizational charts, bureaucracy, public funding, and entitlement programs. But they were genuinely interested in the issues and knew how to put together events that elicited participation and feelings of belonging and contributing.

The management styles of these two groups differed dramatically. Futures Forum was funded directly by the city. The Community Council was a nonprofit operating out of contributions, with no certain financial backing. The Community Council knew all the social service acronyms and how to write proposals to be paid for specific service. The Futures Forum just ordered things they needed and had access to city support services and funding. Together they had to create a new culture. To do this they brought in populations who had not been exposed to either group. From her perspective as Community Council president, Jerri Pastor spoke of the faithful attendance by both Community Council and Futures Forum people during this time. She said that every meeting was charged with energy and conflict. Everyone at the table had to convince each other while at the same time learning to give up pet behaviors and models. She felt that their experience was an example of the kinds of communicating that is going on these days in neighborhoods, communities, states, and even the nation:

> Energy and anger and fear keep people from moving away from the table. The good news is that we are all participating even though we don't participate in the same way or for the same reasons. The merger is very exciting. It is still in a critical stage.

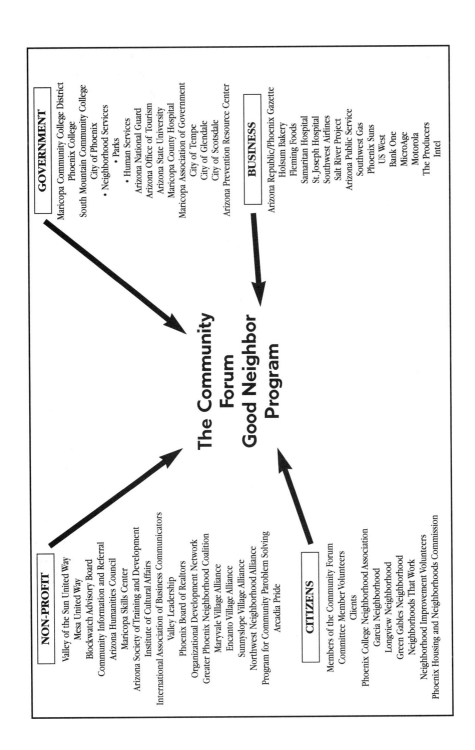

GOVERNMENT

Maricopa Community College District
Phoenix College
South Mountain Community College
City of Phoenix
• Neighborhood Services
  • Parks
  • Human Services
Arizona National Guard
Arizona Office of Tourism
Arizona State University
Maricopa County Hospital
Maricopa Association of Government
City of Tempe
City of Glendale
City of Scotsdale
Arizona Prevention Resource Center

BUSINESS

Arizona Republic/Phoenix Gazette
Holsum Bakery
Fleming Foods
Samaritan Hospital
St. Joseph Hospital
Southwest Airlines
Salt River Project
Arizona Public Service
Southwest Gas
Phoenix Suns
US West
Bank One
MicroAge
Motorola
The Producers
Intel

The Community Forum Good Neighbor Program

NON-PROFIT

Valley of the Sun United Way
Mesa United Way
Blockwatch Advisory Board
Community Information and Referral
Arizona Humanities Council
Maricopa Skills Center
Arizona Society of Training and Development
Institute of Cultural Affairs
International Association of Business Communicators
Valley Leadership
Phoenix Board of Realtors
Organizational Development Network
Greater Phoenix Neighborhood Coalition
Maryvale Village Alliance
Encanto Village Alliance
Sunnyslope Village Alliance
Northwest Neighborhood Alliance
Program for Community Paroblem Solving
Arcadia Pride

CITIZENS

Members of the Community Forum
Committee Member Volunteers
Clients
Phoenix College Neighborhood Association
Garcia Neighborhood
Longview Neighborhood
Green Gables Neighborhood
Neighborhoods That Work
Neighborhood Improvement Volunteers
Phoenix Housing and Neighborhoods Commission

Activities of the Community Forum

The Community Forum is the successor to both the Futures Forum and the Community Council. Like the Community Council, it is a nonprofit agency focusing appropriate human and financial resources on community concerns by bringing together all sectors of the community to work toward short- and long-term solutions. It is implementing the Futures Forum goal to create a sense of community, beginning at the neighborhood level.

The Good Neighbor Program works on this last goal. Director of Communication with the Samaritan Foundation, Marie Simington, contributes many hours to chair this program. About 150 people are volunteering to carry out the goals of the Good Neighbor Program. Marie says that funding operations and maintaining the infrastructure are issues essential to the continuing existence of the organization. When they talk with potential funders about their work, they find that possible funders respond favorably when they hear that the Good Neighbor Program is based on the input from 3,500 people during the Futures Forum. One difficulty, though, is getting funds for training programs and other "human" activities instead of "brick and mortar" projects preferred by many funders.

As is the usual case with participation-based operations, the unfolding development changes during the process. The leaders of the Good Neighbor Program are experiencing a bit of schizophrenia these days because they have to change the timing of some of their goals. Originally, they planned a media campaign to stimulate people's participation in neighborhood activities. Then they discovered that more supportive infrastructure was needed before launching that campaign. Support in the form of training in methods of working with people was a need identified by leaders of neighborhood groups. So they sought partners with whom to fulfill this need.

In July, 1993, the Maricopa Community College District Governing Board adopted a resolution making them partners with the Community Forum. They agreed to work together to:

- Develop a "Building Community" curriculum,
- Establish a neighborhood organization support function,
- Provide facilities for meetings and cosponsor events,
- Help with local visioning processes, and
- Encourage the community colleges to integrate the "building communities" theme into their programs and activities.

It became evident that the support most wanted by local group leaders was training in how to get neighborhood people to participate and how to sustain a volunteer organization. In November, 1993, the first in a series of "Help for Neighborhood Leaders" classes took place at Phoenix College, a 75-year-old community college. This is a joint effort of the Community Forum, the Maricopa Community College District, the City of Phoenix Neighborhood Services Department, the recently created Phoenix College Neighborhood Association, and Phoenix College. A panel of representatives from neighborhood associations presented ideas for finding and keeping people involved in an organization. A strategic planner gave information about running a good meeting, and a faculty member furnished images of participative leadership. In May, 1994, another class in this series, "Tools for Turning Your Ideas Into Action," took place.

The Community Forum Good Neighbor Program and the City of Phoenix Neighborhood Services Department co-sponsor an annual two-day public gathering to share information and to provide simple training. The forum, "Neighborhoods: Everyone's Business," ties in with National Good Neighbor Day. The focus for the first day is on building partnerships among businesses, schools, and nonprofit organizations to get more involvement in neighborhood activities. The second day centers on building skills and sharing solutions.

In early 1994, the Community Forum office received a call from Ed Eisele, chief executive officer of Holsum Bakery, a private family-owned company doing business in Arizona, New Mexico, and California. He is a member of the Greater Phoenix Leadership, successor to the Phoenix 40. Sparked by Eisele's initiative, the Greater Phoenix Leadership is now interested in getting involved with the neighborhoods, but they are not yet sure how they can best serve the community. They asked the Community Forum for input and assistance.

Eisele said that he did not want problems to continue escalating in the neighborhood in which his plant is located. The riots in Los Angeles prompted him to action. Eisele formed a coalition of businesses in Phoenix's Garcia neighborhood that included Holsum Bakery, manufacturing companies, building industry and wholesale firms, a convenience store regional office, and other food creation and distribution businesses. He and his colleagues want neighborhood leaders to know that resources are available to them, that meeting places can be arranged, that paint or other materials can be found, that help is available to organize block watches or many other community activities the neighborhood wants. The Garcia Business Coalition now works directly with the Garcia Neighborhood Partnership in a mutually helpful partnership. The Community Forum facilitates the continuing dialogue that led to holding a one-half day planning event in the Garcia neighborhood on a Saturday in May, 1994.

Gathered that day in the elementary school were Garcia residents and members of the business coalition. They worked together on stating their problems and planning for ways to solve them. The master of ceremonies was a popular TV personality who also translated between Spanish and English as needed. Speakers in the opening session included the Phoenix Chief of Police as well as Ed Eisele, who spoke on behalf of the business coalition. Cooperation among business, government, and neighborhood people, one of the original vision elements of the Phoenix Futures Forum, was obviously still in evidence at this neighborhood gathering.

A Final Note

In the Garcia neighborhood, the local group continues its efforts to improve life in its neighborhood, supported by active involvement of the business coalition, city staff, and workers from nonprofit organizations. The enlivening and enriching of neighborhood life in Garcia is an appropriate story with which to end this report of the Futures Forum, which had as its original goal the intention to generate just this kind of response by citizens. Other similar multisector partnerships have emerged in the city of Phoenix and more are still emerging. The power generated by the Phoenix Futures Forum continues to energize citizen participation. It is obvious that the winds of change stirred up by the fierce activity of the few years of existence of the Futures Forum still blow and reflect a true commitment to community participation in this Valley of the Sun.

References

Phoenix 2015, Phoenix Futures Forum Report, January 1990, published
by the Office of the Futures Forum, Municipal Building,
251 W. Washington Street, Phoenix AZ 85003.

Phoenix 2015, Technical Supplement, A Summary of Task Force
Recommendations, January 1990, published by the Office of the
Futures Forum, Municipal Building, 251 W. Washington Street,
Phoenix AZ 85003.

Urban Challenges: A Vision for the Future. Highlights of the Neal Peirce
study commissioned by *The Arizona Republic, The Phoenix
Gazette,* 120 East Van Buren Street, Phoenix AZ 85004.

Engelen, Rod., 'Phoenix Futures Forum,' "Customer-Satisfying Citizen
Participation Programs," in *Customer Service in Local Government:
Challenges for Planners and Managers,* Bruce W. McClendon,
1991, Chicago IL, Planners Press, American Planning Association,
pp. 155-168.

Hall, John Stuart and Louis F. Weschler, "The Phoenix Futures Forum:
Creating Vision, Implanting Community", *National Civic Review,*
Spring 1991, pp. 135-157.

Economics Civics for the '90s: Multiple Roads to a Stronger Economy,
Remarks by Neal R. Peirce, unpublished document, February 20,
1992.

Neighborhood News, Summer, Fall 1993, City of Phoenix Neighborhood
Services Department, 251 W. Washington Street, First Floor, Phoenix
AZ 85003

Transportation Exchange Update, September 1992, 1930 18th Street NW,
Suite 24, Washington D.C. 20009

Chapter 4
The Young Men of Dulie's Dory

PHILIP L. SALZMAN, CAROL R. COLES,
AND KATHRYN ROBERTS

Located less than 45 minutes by car from Boston,
Gloucester, Massachusetts, is an historic fishing port
with a remarkably stable population base of 28,000.
Still quite remote and provincial, Gloucester possesses
the characteristics of an island community. Its
population is ethnically diverse with Italian-Americans
of Sicilian descent comprising almost one-third of the
total. Gloucester's variety of separate and distinct
ethnic neighborhoods all hug the coastline.
The commercial waterfront's residential area, called
"The Fort," is centered on a hill located on a peninsula
jutting out into Gloucester's working harbor.
Many years ago it was the actual site of a fort that
guarded the inner harbor.

At the entrance to The Fort neighborhood in Gloucester, Massachusetts is Dulie's Dory coffee shop, the center and beginning point of this remarkable yet simple story. Shop owner and manager, Joe Palmisano, was raised in the neighborhood; the young men who gather regularly at this little restaurant, now in their late twenties and early thirties, also grew up together in this neighborhood. Over the years while some have left for college, for out-of-state-jobs, or to enter the armed services, many have stayed in Gloucester because of family ties. Others have returned home after college or the service, have married, and are now building their own small businesses through persistence and hard work. These Dulie Dory regulars share Gloucester roots, childhood friendships, and a profound respect for their Sicilian-American heritage. These young men have watched as Gloucester has changed into a different community from the one they knew as boys. Concerned about how many young boys now living in The Fort are being raised by single mothers, these old friends began to discuss how they could be positive male role models for these young boys. What began as a casual conversation over coffee mugs in the fall of 1991, grew into an organized community porgram that spread beyond The Fort.

More aware than most adults in the greater Gloucester commmunity, these men knew how pervasive alcohol, tobacco, and drug use had become over the years since they were teenagers. The square across the street from Dulie's Dory coffee shop was the place where junkies came during the '70s and '80s to make their local deals. Today, as the neighborhood's boys come of age, get their first jobs, and buy their first cars, they still congregate in this square to talk, laugh, and watch the action. This downtown corner and its nearby parking lot have become a compelling and popular location to both see and be seen. It has also become a center of local concern.

Neighborhood Norms Affect Young Lives

The men of Dulie's Dory had seen some of their own classmates and friends die from heroin overdoses during a major heroin epidemic in Gloucester in the mid-1980s. While many themselves had moved through and beyond a brief period of substance abuse, some of their friends were still addicted to alcohol and other drugs. They understood first hand the impact of substance abuse on their friends' families, spouses, and children, as well as on their community as a whole. From their tables at the coffee shop they watched young boys congregating around the square and discussed how neighborhood "norms" (or what everyone considers normal) can affect how young people live their lives. When they were teenagers, the norm for them had been to get high and hang out, just as in all of the other neighborhoods in the city. Now, during their discussions the men began to look at their own attitudes and values regarding the use and abuse of alcohol and other drugs. They began to assess how their behaviors could and would affect the parade of impressionable young boys who spent just a bit too much time hanging out in the square.

Clearly the boys needed some older, male help to both inspire and challenge them, but how to really sustain a project in the limited spare time the men had available seemed almost impossible. These young men had never had any prior experience as community activists and were never "joiners." They had no formal experience in community service, community organizing, or even in formal meetings, but they had a deep desire to give something back to the community.

One of the Dulie's Dory crowd, a third generation Italian-American young man in his twenties, had heard about the Gloucester Prevention Network, a local project dedicated to preventing substance abuse, and thought it might provide the framework for this group to put its concern for young boys into action. This young man, who had been raised in Gloucester, had just returned from a job assignment in Italy and was actively seeking ways to enhance the local cultural traditions in his home community. The Dulie's Dory idea was just what he was seeking, so off he went to the Gloucester Prevention Network in 1991, and met with a community organizer, Kathy Roberts. During two meetings with Kathy he discussed his ideas and began a networking process that paved the way for his friends at the coffee shop to get their plan moving.

Working Toward a Healthier Community

In September of 1990, in direct response to the high number of heroin overdose deaths in Gloucester during the 1980s the community applied for and received a federal grant through the local nonprofit drug intervention and treatment agency, NUVA, Inc. to create the Gloucester Prevention Network. As one of 250 such Community Partnerships, five-year demonstration projects, funded by the Center for Substance Abuse Prevention, the Gloucester Prevention Network reflected the new awareness that prevention works most effectively if it includes the energy and commitment of all parts of the community. Schools, athletic organizations, parents, as well as businesses, and city and state government are all systems that need to be working together to create lasting change. The work can be creative, in fact it must be creative, as each system sets in place a strategy of working toward a healthier community.

Forming the Young Men's Coalition

Aligning themselves formally with the Gloucester Prevention Network in the winter of 1991-92, the Dulie's Dory group called themselves the Young Men's Coalition and began to meet to plan fun activities for local boys. The Gloucester Prevention Network employs an integrated approach that makes good use of the existing systems in the community's daily life. The coalitions are simply groups of people with similar interests working together to plan training sessions, educational programs, and prevention activities. Coalitions link formal groups (agencies, organizations, etc.) with informal groups (individuals, families, and neighborhoods) to enhance the resources already working within the community.

By early spring of 1992, the Young Men's Coalition had found a project they thought would contribute to their community's health. They decided to focus on ways that they could make more "fun" things happen for the neighborhood boys during Gloucester's Saint Peter's Fiesta. Held annually since 1929 in Gloucester, the Saint Peter's Fiesta has always been celebrated near the harbor in The Fort neighborhood. It takes place in late June and honors Saint Peter, the patron saint of fishermen. The fiesta began when Salvatore Favazza, a local fisherman, encountered an especially rough storm at sea and prayed to Saint Peter, pledging that if he made it back to port safely, he would begin a novena in St. Peter's name (nine days of prayer) for the safety of all fisherman. Over the years, this novena preceded a weekend-long family celebration and eventually a procession in honor of Saint Peter. An annual Blessing of the Fleet by the archbishop of Boston also became part of the celebration and followed an outdoor Mass on Sunday. As the years went on, financial contributions grew, and more community involvement emerged to produce a family event weaving together religion, Sicilian traditions and food, sporting events, music, and community life.

During St. Peter's Fiesta, the entire Gloucester fishing fleet stays in home port to bring together family and friends to celebrate and to strengthen the bonds that are so highly valued in this harbor community. A cornerstone of their lives, St. Peter's Fiesta has been a vital link for the Young Men's Coalition members as they were growing up. In fact, two of the men are the great-grandson and the great-nephew, respectively, of the fiesta's co-founder.

As the community organizer assigned to help out the development of the Young Men's Coalition, Kathy Roberts was herself the great-granddaughter of Salvatore Favazza, the founder of the fiesta and the man responsible for buying and bringing a statue of St. Peter from Italy to Gloucester. The very same statue is used in the fiesta celebrations today. Kathy remembers:

> As a child, a teen, and an adult, I have always been involved
> in the traditions of the fiesta. I marched beside the statue
> in Sunday's parade first next to my great-grandmother,
> then later next to my grandmother, and finally next to my
> mother. Some years I posed as an angel or saint on the
> floats on the ornately decorated flatbed trucks; I was
> always involved in the fiesta.

The St. Peter's Novena's nine days of song and prayer have always been an integral part of Kathy's life and the enduring traditions have been handed down from her great-grandfather and great-grandmother to her two young girls, over a timespan of 65 years.

Although her connections to the Italian community as well as to the fiestas' family traditions were a positive factor, Kathy knew that, as a woman, working with the all men's coalition would pose many challenges. At the time, both of the Gloucester Prevention Network's community organizers were women, so assigning a male facilitator was not an option. Kathy says:

> I had known some of these men since they were kids and
> am cousins of two of them. There was some resistance by a
> couple of men to working with a woman since this was a
> 'for males only club' that was being organized by a female,
> but generally most of them were cooperative. We all realized
> that we needed each other to make this project successful.
> I needed their skills and talents and they needed mine.

Together Kathy and the Dulie's Dory group agreed it was a good idea to focus their initial efforts on the St. Peter's Fiesta. They analyzed how the original spirit of the fiesta had changed. They were clear about with their own connections with a lifetime of fiestas, but were so afraid that the spirit that they understood was not as clear to the boys. What was changing? Why their fear? As a group they were worried that the imported carnival rides, the midway, and the commercial food vendors who were traveling in from Florida and other far flung places didn't reflect the historic and special role the fiesta played in the city of Gloucester. Instead, increasing public drinking, drunkenness, and other indications of substance abuse had become the contemporary fiesta traditions.

Losing Treasured Traditions

Among the Fort neighborhood's young people, the norm had slowly begun to be one of getting high to celebrate the fiesta. The coalition agreed that they wanted St. Peter's Fiesta to be what it was intended to be: a source of joy and pride that would remind community members of their bonds of religious faith, family, friends, and fishing.

While working with the boys came easy to the coalition, the thought of seeking change in the structure of the fiesta seemed a huge task. They were intimidated by the fiesta's power structure, The Fiesta Committee, which is nearly as old as the fiesta itself. Composed of mostly fishermen, the committee had recently concentrated on hiring the carnival workers and services, setting fees, and collecting funds to defray costs. They had traditionally set all policy and approved all activities: booths, foods, music, etc. for the entire fiesta. Would they support the intervention of this new group?

Before the young men took on the committee, they needed to clarify exactly what they wanted to change. The next step was to identify how the fiesta itself had taken on a different face over the years. On the surface, the event looked the same. In their shared stories they told about their huge family reunions, hanging out with their friends, the temporary and very ornate altar constructed on the square at The Fort's entrance, and the ever-expanding carnival.

They told about the archbishop of Boston coming to bless the fishing boats. They talked about the open houses and especially about the sporting events reliving past seine boat races and greasy pole walks. The seine boats are hand-built long wooden boats shaped from spruce planks, with oak ribs. They are fashioned after the lines of a fishing dory. Rowed by ten-man crews with a coxswain/captain setting the pace, while a co-captain/scuttler holds the rudder to stay the heavy boat's course, the seine boats race an out-and-back course around a race buoy. Seine boat crews are loyal, training together and hoping to make it to the finals held on Fiesta Sunday.

Another important fiesta event is the "greasy pole," an even more unusual sporting event than the seine boat races. The greasy pole itself is a heavily greased wooden telephone pole that is fixed at one end to a platform set one-quarter mile in the sea offshore from Gloucester's Pavilion Beach. The pole extends horizontally over the water and has a flag on a short pole affixed to its very tip. Young men try to walk or run to the end of the slippery pole and grab the flag. Hundreds of boats tie up nearby, rafted to each other to watch and cheer, along with the hundreds of spectators watching from the beach. It is fun and serious at the same time, a true ethnic and cultural tradition that endures in the modern world.

The Young Men's Coalition had no intention of changing the seine or pole activities. But they were searching for ways to incorporate new activities into the 1992 fiesta that would appeal to the boys they were trying to reach. Their ideas began to float freely and quickly in the small coffee shop. The men had already finalized their plans to expand some of the children's games and activities like the kid's pie-eating contest, but they knew that the boys they had begun to work with did not usually take part in the festivities, at least not the way they had as kids. The young men began to talk about their own feelings about the fiesta as it used to be. They began to share stories, perceptions and concerns about losing the familiar version of the fiesta that had been so pivotal in their lives. As they brainstormed, they became more and more aware of how significant the fiesta was and continued to be in their lives.

Their ongoing discussions initially focused on tackling the event head on by confronting the power structure, existing leadership, and membership of the St. Peter's Fiesta Committee directly. First, they thought of trying to become members of the committee itself. Next they focused on trying to confront them about including more local food vendors. They recognized that running up against the current St. Peter's Fiesta Committee could polarize the community and create a battle without a positive outcome. Such a move could be risky. It could even be be dangerous, to go up against their fathers, uncles, and other family members who still considered them to be "children."

Focusing on the Heart of the Fiesta

In consulting with Kathy Roberts about how to plan their "attack," they told endless stories about who is really in charge of the fiesta, how the power was distributed, and how they might gain control of some of the power.

They shared the experiences of trying unsuccessfully to make changes to promote a more local event through additional local food vendor booths. They allowed themselves to feel the conflict and to look at the community structure that had taken on the management of the event. Kathy's role became especially pivotal here as she helped the young men listen creatively to focus on what they were really saying. She encouraged them to take a fresh look together at the fiesta. They began by trying to focus on the heart of the event. At first they were truly dismayed and believed that the old fiesta spirit might be totally gone. Over the years as the older men died off or became ill, the spirit of the founders seemed to have gotten lost. The novena was still being held by the women, but not many younger girls were attending anymore. The St. Peter's Fiesta Committee seemed very closed and did not appear to welcome new members or new blood. In fact, the committee ran the fiesta easily and honestly by raising funds from the same businesses and the city each year. They had it down to a science, a well-oiled machine but something important was missing. Where, they asked in frustration, was the excitement for the young people?

After a series of meetings at Dulie's Dory, the young men were able to get past their anger and focus on pleasant fiesta memories. As the men sat together one evening, someone suggested collecting old photographs and putting together a table or a small museum-like exhibit of photos of past fiestas. It would remind everyone of the fiesta's traditions and illustrate the huge number of people the event has touched over the years. The idea was doable and appealing. It involved no struggles or confrontations. Latching on happily to this positive approach, they quickly and naturally began to share resources. Between them, they represented almost every family connected to the event; they drew up a list of things to do and names to contact and, of course, more questions.

Finding the Coalition's Focus

Their overriding question was whether the St. Peter's Fiesta Committee would approve. Could they find a good photographer who could help with the technical end? Would the local families trust them with the loan of valued family photos? Where could they hold the exhibit? Would there be enough time with fiesta only a few months away?

Now that they had found the central focus, Kathy worked with the Young Men's Coalition members, constantly reminding them of their ability to access community resources (Who they know, what they know, and how their enthusiasm could be contagious, etc.). As they acquired more information and developed more leads to sources of photographs, Kathy slowly began helping them create action plans, broker needed services, and create learning/teaching opportunities.

As Kathy recalls:

> Along with the normal coalition-building tasks and problems, these men were taking on the enormous task of organizing and implementing the first fiesta photo exhibit. During the first stage of development, the young men needed to start building their coalition first by forming a vision, or mission statement, with goals and objectives which they did after a few months. Throughout this process many conflicts arose. During the first year of the coalition's development, a concern of mine was the kind of structure and leadership style they wanted for their group. They were perfectly comfortable having me write their agenda, do their mailings, and facilitate their meetings. None of the 12 men wanted to take on a position either as a chairperson, co-chair, or president. Natural leaders began to emerge from the group but a formalized structure did not crystalize until months later, at a special meeting called, 'Looking at Structure and Leadership,' when they decided to have a six-member revolving chairperson team that would be responsible for chairing the coalition for two months at a time. This seemed to work out pretty well, and gave each member a chance to learn new skills.

Later another form of conflict emerged when a couple of the men voiced their concern about the Young Men's Coalition putting all their energies into the Fiesta Photo Exhibit. They felt it was important to continue organizing activities for the kids. Angry that one event, a kid's cookout, had been cancelled because of a coalition meeting, one member went so far as to give an ultimatum — if kids' activities didn't resume soon, he would leave the coalition. Some members supported him and wanted to resume activities with kids for the summer, while others felt all their energies needed to be centered around the exhibit in order for it to be successful. Out of this lengthy discussion and conflict came a positive outcome. A three-man subcommittee for kid's activities was formed to come up with a plan of action by the next coalition meeting.

As the group continued to work together, a division of labor quite naturally occured; debates remained intense and occasionally noisy, but they were working together now and really listening to each other. The Young Men's Coalition had arrived at the edge of an attempt to significantly influence an event that had initially seemed, to quote their words, "bigger than all of us." The Gloucester Prevention Network and its community organizer had bonded with the Young Men's Coalition to help them create, by their own efforts, a new organization that they continued to make their own. In that process, they put into concrete action their new knowledge of community dynamics and conflict resolution.

Tapping Community Energy

Still they knew that the practical aspects of the planned photo exhibit would require enormous energy, resources, and time commitments. Luck and strong connections existing in a small community began to help to pull the show together. A local professional photographer agreed to work on the exhibit and offered the services of his store at the cost of materials only. His background and interest in historic photographic work, coupled with his technical ability in the lab, resulted in high quality enlargements and good advice on mounting and display methods. After seeing a few small ads requesting photo donations in the local daily newspaper, the community members came forward with over 600 old photographs, old 16 mm film strips, slides, and newspaper clippings. The materials for the exhibit were in place.

Next the group had to find a convenient location that could house a professional quality photo exhibit. The Seafarer's Union Hall, although located adjacent to the temporary altar erected each year for the festival Mass, had never been opened during the fiesta. Once a vibrant and dynamic union, the Seafarer's function in the life of the fishing community had begun to erode. Hard economic times and additional regulation forced many fishermen to fish out of other ports like New Bedford, Massachusetts, and Portland, Maine. While its location was ideal for the exhibit, the grounds and the interior of the building had become shabby. Though monies to refurbish it were not available, the young men began to look for donated services through their extensive network of local businesses. Soon sign painters, professional cleaners, carpenters, and electricians were working in their off hours to pull the show together. The leadership of Union Hall while initially skeptical became convinced that allowing the show was a good idea, with the donation of the extensive in-kind services to the building and its environs.

This experience was very powerful for the young men as they recognized their own limitless capacity to tap into resources within their own community. So often, community members are convinced that change can only occur when it is created by elected officials, community leadership, or established organizations. The Dulie's Dory men witnessed the changes that their own excitement and vision had created. The vision was their own, but the exhibit would affect the underlying conditions and attitudes of the whole community and would ultimately change the community's vision of the fiesta.

They had to learn and constantly use conflict-resolution skills to promote their event, while making it clear to the St. Peter's Fiesta Committee that they did not wish to now turn this event over to the committee. They still had unanswered questions. Would there be ownership battles? What path should communication take to ensure communication without confrontation? Would the committee come to the photo exhibit?

The Young Men's Coalition formally and informally contacted the committee by sending letters of explanation; they engaged in a process that ultimately resulted in committee approval, with exhibit ownership still totally resting with the Young Men's Coalition. Indeed the Gloucester Fiesta was no longer business as usual. They had injected new energy into the fiesta's 1992 program, and they had done it with a real respect for the enduring traditions of the historic celebration.

Engaging an Entire Community

"St. Peter's Fiesta Through the Years: a Community's Photo Album" opened in time for the 1992 fiesta. Free admission removed all barriers to entry, and to all fiscal issues. Though extensive public outreach through almost daily newspaper coverage and some paid ads spread the word about this historic exhibit, the best advertising source was word of mouth across all the neighborhoods of Gloucester.

From the Gloucester Daily Times, *Thursday, July 23, 1992*

My View
Savoring the Memories of Fiesta

By CATHY NICASTRO

We begged her to go to the photo exhibit, but she wouldn't. Although it had been almost two years since he left us, it was still too painful to be there in the midst of Fiesta without Dad.

My brothers, my husband, and I had all seen "Fiesta. Through the Years." "Ma, you have to go, you should go; it's so beautiful," we pleaded. My mother stood firm, however, until Sunday.

Brother Joe and family, Frank and I had just finished watching the parade and went back into the Seafarers Union Hall to take a second look at the exhibit. As we strolled down memory lane, we all hoped Ma would change her mind, when suddenly, in she walked. Brother Peter had shut off the spaghetti sauce, locked the door, and said, "Ma, you're coming with me."

Accompanied by brother Frank's touching song selections softly playing in the background, Ma began a tenderly nostalgic journey back to the good old days through each magnificent photo. As she tenderly savored the moment, the sadness in her face melted away into so many happy memories of a young family — *compares and commares* — many of them no longer here. They all came alive again, however, in beautiful scenes of Fiestas long ago.

My brothers and I were kids again down the Fort as Ma pointed out our birthplace, Nony's house at 47 Commercial St. There was a young Uncle Doley and friends happily sitting on the steps at Fiesta. We saw many generations of fishermen carving the statue of St. Peter from Uncle Joe D'Amico, Uncle Stevie D'Amico, and Uncle Peter Frontiero, to handsome husband Donny Nicastro, each generation so different, yet so similar and connected in the pride shown on each beaming face as they carried their patron saint.

We savored the 1987 picture of brother Sam triumphantly smiling atop brother Peter's shoulders as he so proudly clutched the greasy pole flag, a coveted prize that had eluded him for 14 long years. Sam took his place of honor beside the many spectacular shots of all time greats Salvi Benson, cousin Peter Frontiero, and all the other gutsy greasy pole walkers slithering and sliding their way to victory. The seineboat pictures were nothing short of spectacular as we savored brother-in-law Paul rowing and brother Frank scuttling his way to glory that very same year as he, too, tasted the sweet Sunday seineboat victory 17 years in the making. An especially memorable picture of a young curly-haired son Joey and his beautiful cousin Lisa looking so innocently angelic atop Nina Conti's float warmed our hearts.

The most special and heartwarming photograph of all, of course, was the beautiful picture of Sam "Boogie" Frontiero, our Dad. There he stood in all his youthful splendor proudly posing with his *compares* after marching in the St. Peter's Fiesta parade so many years ago. "Wasn't he handsome," Ma joyfully reminisced. Yes, he was, and for one fleeting moment, Dad seemed to be with us again.

"Fiesta Through The Years" is the greatest tribute to the St. Peter's Fiesta I have ever had the pleasure to experience. May I express my most sincere and heartfelt thanks to all of those special people involved in this project for their great vision and very hard work in making it such a phenomenal success.

May the masterpieces of magnificent nostalgia displayed this year and for years to come continue as an endearing tribute to the St. Peter's Fiesta and to the very special people of Gloucester.

**Cathy Nicastro lives in Gloucester
with her husband and children.**

The exhibit was a true gift from the Young Men's Coalition to their own community. It was a collective expression of their love for the culture and the people of their community, as well as their need to remind people that treasured values could easily slip away if not attended to.

Open during set hours during all four days of the fiesta and fully handicapped accessible, the exhibit drew over 5,000 people of all ages who waited in line for the chance to view the exhibit. Over 450 beautifully enlarged and mounted photographs of family, friends, and long-ago scenes hung on large display boards at eye level. Moving through the exhibit to taped music, families and friends gathered before large group photographs identifying family members and finding photos of themselves. There were tears, smiles, and shouts of glee as viewers recognized familiar faces and places. Tourists who had never visited here before became misty eyed as they watched whole families reminisce in Italian and English. "Look, Maria...it's your grandfather when he rowed in 1951!...Look how good he looks! He was such a handsome man!" "Oh my God! Its Uncle Sal!" " Look Dad, That's you!"

Bringing Back the Heart of Gloucester

The photographs had evoked emotion and connection beyond everyone's expectations. As the young men stood by at the opening, tired from the hard last minute work to hang the show, they began to recognize just what they had accomplished. They had brought back the heart to the city. They had influenced the fiesta in a very positive way. Older citizens who had stopped attending the fiesta because of its more carnival atmosphere were encouraged to come down and see the pictures. Slowly the Young Men's Coalition began to realize that their role in this amazing change was being recognized and they began to admit how proud they were.

Massachusetts State Representative, Bruce Tarr, also noted the young men's efforts and presented them with a citation of recognition. He said that their legacy is a renewed St. Peter's Fiesta that incorporates a deep cultural and spiritual integrity. Gloucester Mayor William "Bill" Rafter came by to recognize the contribution that the coalition had made and express his view that this was a perfect example of how much community members can accomplish when they contribute their support. The most meaningful recognition that the coalition received was the gratitude and excitement of local residents as they reacted in a personal and positive way. The community recognized and applauded the men for their mission and expressed strong support for the coalition's larger concern, the desire to reduce alcohol and other drug use in the community at large.

Alcohol and Drug Use Reduced

Another positive note about the 1992 fiesta was that arrests were down, both for public drinking and for public drunkenness. The Coast Guard reported fewer arrests for incidents involving alcohol and other drugs among those operating boats. Establishments licensed to serve alcohol and the owners of bars and local restaurants sent new staffers to beverage-serving workshops to learn better intervention methods for dealing with overzealous imbibers. A more positive atmosphere was apparent during the entire fiesta weekend. These changes appear to be quite lasting and have been sustained during the 1993 and 1994 fiesta weekends.

The 1994 fiesta was the third year for the photo exhibit; since 1992 the coalition has received a Gloucester Arts Council grant providing the funds to enlarge the exhibit. The coalition is now planning its first edition of a photo book in response to community interest. The market for this book will be beyond the confines of Gloucester, since there is strong interest throughout the country for the visual history of cultural traditions such as these. Funds acquired through the proposed sale of the book can help sustain the coalition's other activities as they expand their commitment to Gloucester's youth.

Each year the Gloucester Prevention Network conducts surveys for Gloucester students in grades 5-12. Trends have begun to emerge from these surveys that show a continuous increase in the number of students who perceive the use of alcohol and tobacco as a health risk. For the second year in a row, the 1993 survey revealed a decrease in the percentage of students using three or more substances.

Assessing the Outcome

The simplicity of the Gloucester Prevention Network program design has paid off. When it was funded by the Center for Substance Abuse Prevention, the Gloucester Prevention Network was proud to be able to present the

Ten Operating Principles

In the course of the first three years of this community partnership with the Young Men's Coalition, the Gloucester Prevention Network began to recognize the following ten operating principles that were key to successful initiatives:

1. Meet community members where they are and be within their own realm of experience (i.e., use a common language without prevention-specific terminology).
2. Build and maintain real relationships with community members.
3. Give people a place within the organization and give everyone something tangible to do.
4. Realize that everyone (staff included) learns more through activity than through theory. It is vital that activities create the demand and provide the opportunity for further training, and not the other way around; it is equally important that the activities reflect sound prevention theory.
5. Create a climate of inclusion and equal full value for all participants.
6. Create a vision which is doable, based on the community's strengths and its accumulated wisdom.
7. Recognize that every person is a community resource. Every individual possesses skills/functions that the community needs. People must be valued for who they are, what they feel as well as what they know and do. All residents are critical factors in creating community norms.
8. Remind people of the contributions that they are already making, rather than stressing what still needs to be done. Additionally, small positive behavior modifications are much easier to accomplish than requiring that people dramatically change their behaviors to meet unmet needs.
9. Understand that people are motivated by their special interests (by what they already care about) as evidenced by the community activities or jobs that they are already involved in. For example, local employers in Gloucester are very interested in having drug-free employees and a drug-free workplace policy, and are not interested in community statistics on underage drinking by high-school students at high-school sponsored dances.
10. Focus on family as the most basic community system and the source for linkages/opportunities for connections and the infusion of prevention practice in daily life.

city's hard work to the nation. It was named in 1993 as the only program to receive one of the 11 Exemplary Alcohol and Other Drug Prevention Program Awards given by the National Prevention Network, the National Association of State Alcohol and Drug Abuse Directors, and the Center for Substance Abuse Prevention. Also, when the chair of the U.S. House of Representatives Select Committee on Narcotics Abuse and Control, the Honorable Charles B. Rangel, sought a Government Accounting Office (GAO) study on the efficacy of community based prevention, Gloucester Prevention Network was once again the sole Center for Substance Abuse Prevention Community Partnership Program to be examined. The study's outcomes, according to the General Accounting Office Report (GAO/GGD-93-75), showed several indicators of the program's success, including increased public awareness and changes in the community mores and attitudes toward drug use.

Gloucester Prevention Network's model is a simple technique that can sometimes sound ponderous and pedantic, but it is best explained in the words of Joe Palmisano, owner/manager of Dulie's Dory and chairperson of the Young Men's Coalition:

> Before the Gloucester Prevention Network was here the death rate from alcohol and other drugs was way up. Now it's down. That's great; we accomplished something. We've accomplished something by reaching kids who were really bummed out. Their attitudes have changed. Without The Gloucester Prevention Network, we never would have gotten a group of guys together to do something like this.

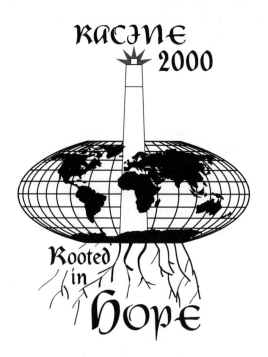

RACINE 2000

Rooted in HOPE

Chapter 5
Hope Takes Root

BRENDA WALSH, O.P. AND HELEN PEDDLE, O.P.

We dream of a Racine, the rooted community, where apathy will be unknown, where family, school, workplace, and all our social contacts will develop our human potential in service of a peaceful world. We dream of the meshing of ethnic pride and group cooperation, of lakeside festivals, of industry and art in a renewed downtown. We dream of Racine, inventor in the past, inventing again a future in which our style of community and concern will be our major export.

—One small team's vision of Racine

Racine 2000 is an umbrella under which all sorts of community groups take root, grow past early organization strains, and gradually mature into well established and accepted programs. The effort began in 1982, when a group of 200 clergy, business and government leaders, and concerned citizens gathered to discuss Racine's problems. Acknowledging the magnitude of the problems, the group worked to look deeper to find the causes of urban malaise and began to mobilize local resources. The group decided to form

"Racine in the 80s" as a community resource and empowerment project. They designed a program that was ongoing; would not have a corporate structure, but rather built-in flexibility for getting things done. Funded in part by the Roman Catholic Congregation of Racine Dominican Sisters, it has come to be called "a catalyst to help agencies and individuals organize in response to community needs and as a resource to keep them going." After 14 years, the people of Racine also characterize this catalyst, now called Racine 2000, as the place to go when a community problem requires new and innovative thinking, visioning, and creation of a hopeful future.

Sharing Community Concerns

Participating educators, business executives, high school students, concerned men and women of varied ages and races used strategic planning to create a vision that would build county-wide solutions to community needs such as a climbing crime rate, teen pregnancies, as well as drugs and gangs coming into the region from other metropolitan areas. Local people felt the need to look deeper into these critical problems to analyze their root causes, and finally address them.

Within 12 years, many changes came about: Neighborhood Watch was expanded county wide, voluntary mediation for citizen disputes was initiated, a free health care network for the medically uninsured was set up, affordable housing was organized on a model of mutuality and concern, and issues of the Hispanic and African-American communities were addressed.

Dr. Joe Holland, visiting professor of ethics and sociology at St. Thomas University in Miami, Florida, a speaker at three Racine 2000 conferences and mentor along the way, analyzes the social scars facing Racine and other communities this way:

> The cultural decay in the West is linked to the determination
> of our way of looking at life by science and the neglect of
> our spiritual roots. The accelerated pace of life has torn peo-
> ple from their past and heritage, and has left generations
> without roots and a moral framework for their lives.[1]

On the positive side, unemployment in Racine in 1993-94 was between 5 and 6%, slightly lower than the national level. Another plus is that Racine has a skilled workforce in equipment manufacturing, automotive industry,

A Quick Look at Racine

The name "Racine" comes from the French word for "root," a reference to the city's root-filled river bank. The city's ideal location on beautiful Lake Michigan and its plentiful supply of clean air have earned it the title of "Belle City of the Lakes." The county of Racine is 337 square miles, with a population of 126,400—a mix of residents of mainly European extraction as well as a growing African-American and Hispanic population, now up to 20% in the city of Racine.

The economy of the city of Racine, with a population of 84,000, made the city, until recently, one of Wisconsin's largest industrial centers. Companies such as J. I. Case, Johnson Wax, and Greene Manufacturing cover a wide range of products—agricultural and construction equipment, waxes and polishes, electrical appliances, and more. Like a number of communities in the midwest and other areas, Racine has lost many manufacturing jobs—13,000—in the past two decades, jobs that have been replaced by employment in the service sector. This means less income, more human need to be addressed, and more need for partnership and participation by the growing minority population.

Racine has a long history of creative inventions—Horlick's malted milk, Case tractors, and Johnson's worldwide home care products. More recently, Racine's Danish Kringle and the Salmon-A-Rama—a national salmon-fishing contest—have brought national, even international, attention to Racine.

and agricultural and electrical appliances. To help make the most of these advantages, partnerships involving representatives from government, churches, the religious community, labor groups, and business are already in place and have produced many positive results in health care, housing, and economic development. Results are also evident in less tangible ways, such as a growing spiritual awareness, education for peace, and positive image building. Strengthening families, a more recent focus of Racine 2000, will call for extensive mobilization of resources and the building of new partnerships for the remainder of the decade and beyond.

Health Care for the Medically Uninsured

One example of how partnerships have brought about positive results is the Racine Health Care Network, Inc. established in 1986 to serve the medically uninsured. Barb Tylenda, who now heads the Health Care Network, speaks highly of the effort and how successfully the partnership has worked. Racine, like most communities nationwide, has had about 10% of its under-65 population without health insurance and without access to medical care. Now 130 providers, including doctors, nurses, dentists, pharmacists, local hospitals and clinics are working partners with state and local governments to fill this frightening need.

The Health Care Network made 15,000 appointments for free care for the uninsured in its first eight years. In January of 1993, the program director and board president went to the White House to accept the National Points of Light Award for an innovative and successful response to the needs of the working poor. Racine's neighbor to the south, Kenosha County, has mobilized the resources of local hospitals and medical professionals to develop a small-scale health care program for the medically uninsured similar to the Racine model.

A unique feature that has made the Racine Health Care Network so successful has been passage of a bill at the state level that allows retired physicians to use their skills to serve the uninsured, with the State of Wisconsin providing their liability coverage. Says Dr. William J. Little, Medical Director for the Network: "One can only play so much golf. This way, I can use my gifts and talents for the good of the community by providing care for those locked out of the system." Everyone involved in this community endeavor believes that the model is replicable through voluntary participation by providers and the building of partnerships.

Response to Housing Needs

For decades, Racine has worked to develop a strong response to housing needs. Gradually, partnerships formed. Partners in the development of good-quality, affordable housing for Racine families now include Racine's Department of Development and Housing, Wisconsin Division of Housing, Wisconsin Housing and Economic Development Authority, local banks, Wisconsin Natural Gas, Racine County Housing Authority, the University

Extensions, and the Racine Dominican Sisters. Other groups such as Ameritech Workers and the Central American Solidarity Coalition have donated time to upgrade housing for Racine's low-income families.

Racine Mutual Housing Association was initiated in 1984 as a result of this partnering. A grant from the Wisconsin Department of Development enabled the Racine 2000 Housing Task Force to document the need and develop the plan, which has resulted in the readying of 52 units of quality, energy-efficient units. Knowing that families spend anywhere from 50 to 75% of their disposable income on housing, Racine Mutual Housing has kept the rent (known as the carrying charge) at 10-15% below market rate for the area. This lower rate is possible because of substantial grants from city and state funds, as well as from Wisconsin Natural Gas, which equips each unit with a new furnace. This way each unit is energy efficient at occupancy. Residents are urged to keep their units in good repair, which in turn results in cost containment.

Across the country, it has become evident that providing housing alone without some financial support and educational services is inadequate. For instance, Racine Mutual Housing residents get free counseling through the Family Service of Racine. They can have their concerns addressed in anonymous fashion through the "Letters to Wanda" column in the association's newsletter. Also residents receive scholarship assistance to attend the local technical college and nearby university. Ten residents have taken advantage of this benefit annually for the past two years. "Efforts are made to discourage the landlord-tenant mentality by urging residents to take pride in their own homes," said Tom Adams, director. A Skill Development Program encourages residents to develop their skills through education and job training, using local resources. Responsible behavior is being rewarded through the "Resident of the Quarter" feature in the association's newsletter as well as by gift certificates to a local grocery store. Residents also can be on the association's board of directors and on the resident council, allowing them to have a good measure of control over their local environment. The recent introduction of the Home Buyers Program has made it possible for three families to join the "rent with option to purchase" offered by Racine Mutual Housing. These families will eventually become home owners if they meet the association's requirements of fiscal responsibility, good care of property, completion of the First Time Home Buyers Course, as well as the Home Maintenance Course offered free of charge through Gateway Technical College.

While Racine Mutual Housing is not formally incorporated as a cooperative, it does embody and promote a cooperative spirit evidenced in the many ways that residents will reach and support each other. A unique expression of partnership came about when 60 volunteers sponsored by the local Central American Solidarity Coalition planned a Work-a-Thon for two weekends. Sponsored volunteers rehabilitated a house for a Racine Mutual Housing family, and the money went to provide health care for the poor in Central America. The Work-a-Thon has become an annual event each fall.

Measuring Housing Success

In the midst of all of these examples of cooperation and support, it is sometimes difficult to know how success is measured. While obvious improvements in the neighborhoods merited a civic prize, the Belle Award a couple of years ago, the residents themselves are perhaps the best judges of how well the association succeeds.

Doniele Webb, a Racine resident for eight years, recently graduated as a registered nurse from a local college and is now employed full-time as a nurse at St. Luke's Hospital. Doniele is grateful for the scholarship and the moral support she received during her years with the association. A former resident, Evelyn Sutton, who recently moved to another state, wrote: "I'll never forget the first lessons learned at Racine Mutual Housing — lessons of trust and responsibility. I will carry them with me wherever I go."

Another example of a person empowered is Kathy Jackson, a single mother of three, who came to live in Racine Mutual Housing in 1989. She needed a home, meaningful work, and the possibility of developing her skills at the local technical college. Fortunately for Kathy, she found all three. She now lives in a single family, three-bedroom home owned by the association and next year will receive an associate degree in computer and information processing. In 1993, she won the regional contest in desktop publishing and went on to the nationals in San Antonio. While she did not win a place in that competition, the event broadened her horizons, increased her self-confidence.

Kathy Jackson has spent the last three years as office manager of the Racine Mutual Housing Association. She comments: "At times, I find it hard to juggle all my responsibilities, but I can keep going when I think of my own future and that of my three school-age children." She is grateful for the support and strength she has gained through the Racine Mutual Housing Association, which is like a family. The scholarship assistance she has received has enabled her to continue her courses without interruption.

The goal of Racine Mutual Housing is not to meet all the housing needs in the community. These needs are also being filled by Habitat for Humanity and Project Pride, more recent housing initiatives. The hope is to develop a model that any community can use and to provide a stable environment for resident families. More efforts such as Racine Mutual Housing Association's work will alleviate the desperate plight of the more than five million nationwide with "worst case" housing needs.

Economic Development in Racine

Ongoing hopes and concerns about the North American Free Trade Agreement, as well as other international trade agreements, have brought job creation and economic development onto the national center stage. These same issues have been a concern at the forefront in Racine for more than a decade. To help give Racine County's sputtering economy a shot in the arm, local business people, government representatives, and the Racine 2000 Economic Development Taskforce came together to plot a course for the future of the county. "We must have a county-wide effort and get beyond issues of turf in order to have a healthy, growing community," declared former County Executive Len Ziolkowski. The result was the formation of the Racine County Economic Development Corporation (RCEDC), which has been a major force in job creation and retention for the County. Their 1994 annual report revealed that:

- Several Racine County small businesses had received loans;
- Through the Revolving Loan Fund and other public financing, the RCEDC had collected a loan portfolio which created and/or retained 650 jobs in Racine County;
- For business relocating to the county, RCEDC is able to provide guidance, demographics and other pertinent information about the community.

A follow-up summit, held in 1992 and convened by County Executive Dennis Kornwolf, became a launching pad for new endeavors in the county. The group worked together on a vision, blocks to accomplishment, strategic issues, and the development of action plans. Then the group studied an integrated model of development and charted strategic plans that considered all aspects of the community life. Elements of the model included:

- Intergovernmental cooperation,
- Infrastructure development and expansion,
- An education system to meet the needs of the community and the workforce of the future,
- A diversified, self-reliant business base,
- Adequate affordable housing stock to meet future needs,
- Promotion of a positive image by community leaders and the general public,
- Strengthening families as the core fabric of society.

Some of the more visible results of the Economic Development Corporation included the development of the Racine Harbor Marina and Festival Hall, the addition of a new hotel in downtown Racine, the attraction of companies such as Danfoss Hydraulic Fluids, expansion by Putzmeister, Inc., investment in new headquarters by J. I. Case Company, and expansion by Johnson Wax. An outside developer made a commitment to develop housing for the working low-or middle-income people in downtown Racine. The mayor, county executive and other local officials took a lead role in this development.

At the RCEDC 10th Anniversary Celebration on January 20, 1994, Governor Thompson said: "I applaud and congratulate you. Keep the prospects coming." William Nahikian, RCEDC board president, said the same spirit that began the organization ten years ago is still at work today. "We need to continue to broaden our vision and move toward greater cooperation."

The Strengthening Families Taskforce

Part of that broader mission is the recognition that economic and family issues go hand in hand. Churches, schools, and the business community highlight the need to address family issues and to join in partnership with families for positive results. At each of the small groups which participated in the 1992 Economic Summit, this issue came to the fore. Dennis Kornwolf, as county executive, commissioned Racine 2000 and Racine County Human Services to look at ways to enable them to more successfully participate in life, school, and work." A new taskforce came into being.

Taskforce members worked for months gathering information on families in Racine. The growing number of teen pregnancies and the number of children in African-American and Hispanic households living at or below the poverty level was a concern. Ten percent of the children in the Racine Unified School District were identified as having special needs, thus requiring more resources at a greater cost to the community. In this respect, Racine mirrors many other communities.

How is the Strengthening Families Taskforce responding? Partnerships are again springing into action in response to the local need:

- Families and their needs were highlighted in 1994, the United Nations "International Year of the Family" publication. Letters were sent to churches and local agencies asking them to incorporate the "International Year of the Family" information into their programs;
- Racine Area Manufacturers and Commerce (RAMAC) helped to develop a brochure listing all resources for families in Racine County, using information gathered by the taskforce;
- The taskforce sponsored a program on "Balancing Work and Family: Challenges and Solutions;"
- A home-visitation program for first-time parents was organized;
- Families organized together across racial lines for mutual support.

The United Nations logo celebrating the International Year of the Family was being used on all the Strengthening Families Taskforce literature and correspondence to heighten awareness about issues and needs of families today. The goal is not to take over family responsibilities but to enable them to carry out the important work for which they were established.

Dr. John Perkins, a nationally-known African-American minister, paid a visit to Racine in 1992. He urged strong consideration for families without fathers, not holding them up as an alternative lifestyle. He asked that this be done "without in any way degrading single parents, many of whom are doing a heroic job."

Mayor Owen Davies offered his encouragement and support. Clearly, strengthening families became a major focus of Racine 2000 that will continue to call for partnerships and mobilization of resources well into the 21st century.

Labor-Management Issues

Again the tie-in between family and economic issues came to the fore in Racine in 1992. The issue of plant closings is always a major concern because when management is considering closing a local plant, whether in Racine or elsewhere, profits and losses are not just a matter of economics or efficiency. Job loss can mean loss of population, family strife, sometimes despair or even suicide. Plant closings have long-term consequences, which Racine 2000 has tried to keep before the public.

Community leaders recognized that labor-management was an area where workable partnerships needed to be developed. Such a situation came to a head in 1992 when workers struck for six months at Rainfair, a manufacturer of protective garments. At issue was the right of striking workers to get their jobs back. Some religious leaders worked to mediate a solution. A local church offered meeting space, and the media were not invited until a settlement had been reached. The struggle and its solution brought national attention to Racine. The publication, *Christianity and Crisis*, in its June 22, 1992 issue quoted Sister Brenda Walsh, one of the mediators: "We need new models that make business more accountable to the local community. The church should be right at the heart of such developments"[4].

Meeting the Needs of the Older Population

Almost daily, calls were coming from as far away as California, New York, and Texas from worried family members concerned about their aging parents in Racine or near the Dominican Sisters, who had decades of experience in responding to this growing segment of the population. The Senior Companion Program, received national, state, and local recognition for its innovative responses to the needs of the homebound. This work for older citizens is done mainly by 130 volunteers of all ages and from various ethnic/racial backgrounds. A holistic program combines pastoral care, information, and referral services linking older adults with church and society. Listening and understanding are the key components of this program. These efforts have become a lifeline for both givers and receivers of care, as the donor-recipient attitude is replaced by one of companionship and empowerment. One recipient said, "I didn't want any agency telling me what I need until someone first hears my pain and story."

Dispute Settlement Center

The Dispute Settlement Center is another example of a Racine public-private partnership that has resolved many local conflicts, such as merchant-customer, tenant-landlord, and neighborhood disputes which might otherwise have escalated to violence. The idea of dispute resolution with trained volunteer mediators was first proposed at a Racine 2000 conference in 1983. After gaining the support of local legal and justice systems and opening an office, volunteers began to field referrals from courts and agencies. From the beginning, the Dispute Settlement Center Office has been situated in the county courthouse, emphasizing its mission to act as a community mediation and conciliation service for everyone in Racine County.

Mary Waid, program coordinator, is a warmly enthusiastic promoter in the community for settling disputes peacefully in a win-win approach. As part of the total program, she devotes quality time to training and overseeing peer mediation programs in Racine's Unified Public School System. This program has been a model for the more than 300 community mediation centers in the country. Waid credits Annette Conley, the office's first coordinator, with involving an enthusiastic principal and a teacher in Racine's Gilmore Middle School in a pilot program in 1986 to train student mediators. From that beginning, peer mediation is now in place in almost all elementary and middle schools and is beginning in Racine's public high schools. Dr. Clem Magner, crisis prevention and intervention specialist for the Milwaukee Public Schools, received his first exposure to real-life mediation at Gilmore School in Racine. He had come to see the program in action and had gone away convinced of its value in forestalling disruptive behavior. Magner brought the idea back to his own Milwaukee school system, which now employs mediation as early as the third grade. He has since gone on to convince school systems in other Wisconsin counties to employ the method he learned about in Racine and now touts it nationwide.

Recently, a group of people from the areas of business, law, government, and education spent a morning learning how the Dispute Settlement Center helps the community and how the community can lend its support to the center. At that meeting a fifth-grade boy told the participants that what he had learned in school had even helped him make peace at home.

His mother, also at the meeting, verified that her son had been able to turn an argument between her and the boy's father into a rational settlement.

Beyond its use in schools, the overall concept of community-based mediation has wide application to help solve disputes in government, business, and neighborhoods. Gene Stephens, writing in the *Futurist* magazine, cites a prediction for the future:

> Communities will resolve their own differences via the participatory justice model which is attuned to individual difference and recognizes that conflicts are normally among competing interests rather than between right and wrong.... This grassroots system of equitable resolution of differences seems to be the only method to create a harmonious environment for an increasingly pluralistic society [5].

Public Aid to Families

Welfare reform is an item high on the agenda nationally as well as locally in the state of Wisconsin. It is on the platform of every candidate for public office. In Racine County, the Human Services Department brought national recognition to Racine for its pilot Learnfare program, and its successful method of collecting child support. The British Broadcast Corporation (BBC) from London even paid a visit to the city to find out how the programs were working.

Learnfare in Racine County is a variation of Aid to Families with Dependent Children (AFDC). The actual amount of aid to AFDC families is lowered when school-aged children habitually skip school. Said Racine County Human Services Director Bill Adams:

> The program is not simply retaliation for truancy. We decided to use it as a tool that could encourage school attendance and use the state's Learnfare dollars to develop a case-management system to help families overcome the barriers to school attendance.

The Opportunity Industrialization Center is the county's contractor for Learnfare case-management services. When a student has piled up ten full days of unexcused absences in a semester, the family is offered a case manager who will work with student and family until an agreement is reached on a family services plan. Adams cites the following factors that have helped Learnfare do better in Racine County than in any other Wisconsin county:

- Dedication and competency of economic support specialists;
- Excellent cooperation from school districts; and
- The case-management system developed in Racine County.

Other counties look to Racine's Learnfare as a model. Racine 2000 participants are hopeful that local, state, and national welfare reform efforts will include jobs that can support a family and help provide adequate training, child care, and health insurance, until self-sufficiency is reached.

Empowerment Efforts and Payoffs

Several churches in Racine have joined forces with Racine 2000. People like Rev. Dennis Bade, pastor of Bethany United Methodist Church, have been involved in Racine 2000 from the very beginning. For instance, Bade has been a member of the Spirituality Taskforce that convenes quarterly prayer breakfasts at the YWCA to discuss and respond to local issues and needs, and has worked on an interfaith organizing effort to help local churches effectively address the needs of Racine. Also, Rev. Norma Carter, long-time Racine 2000 ally and an African-American pastor, has developed her own "Adopt-a-Neighborhood Program" to bring local resources to the communities where they are needed the most.

Pastor Jim Peters, president of the local Clergy Association, has acted on his belief that churches have a key role to play in social change. African-American and Hispanic communities and churches have drawn on the resources of Racine 2000 to develop their own agendas for action. Ken Lumpkin, editor of a local African-American newspaper, put the challenge to local churches and community this way, "Will the Racine community enter the 21st century with one group going in the front door and the other leaving by the back? Or will we enter the 21st century together?"

This point was pondered as the Racine community convened at the YMCA to address racism in Racine. Neighborhood groups formed to address crime and poverty. A resident of the central city, Moses Davis is an African-American disabled Vietnam veteran in his forties. His introduction to Racine 2000 began when he joined a group facilitated by Brenda Walsh and Barney Nelles in an alternative to incarceration class. He became interested in per-

Nine Principles for Change Agents

1. Established community institutions, such as the Dominican Sisters, can serve as building blocks for such important community development efforts. In many localities, churches as well as other established institutions, can play this role. The moral, financial, and evaluative support of the Racine Dominican Sisters was available from the start, and undergirded all efforts.

2. Key people concerned about a particular issue were contacted to ask for their support, to alleviate concerns about duplication of effort, and to show them the benefits of new developments.

3. A important goal is to focus on devising new solutions rather than repeating old ones.

4. Participation must be achieved across lines of age, race, gender, and economic status.

5. If projects are separately incorporated, use an umbrella organization to provide continuity through financial contribution, board membership, and support.

6. Make regular reports to funders and the general public help to retain interest and loyalty.

7. Identify underlying issues to link economic, political, social, and spiritual concerns for a holistic response.

8. Give solutions time. Changing structures and attitudes cannot happen overnight. Despite difficulties and slow progress at times, one must persist over the long haul for lasting results.

9. Involve public officials, both elected and appointed. Ask for ongoing support such as participation in events, funding for specific projects, and readiness to discuss community concerns.

forming services for the homebound people in his neighborhood through the Senior Companion Program. Now he is a very active outreach person. Says Davis:

> Working through Sister Brenda and Mr. Nelles, I've learned about the agencies in Racine and I can take the burden off of them by dealing with [the people] directly. Others I call them about, like an elderly person needing blankets or a single mother who is asking for baby clothes. Even though I don't drive, I get to visit outside my neighborhood by bicycle and do things like storm window changing. Seniors I visit have my unlisted number and know they can call me anytime, day or night.

Racine 2000 has been a catalyst for change, self-sufficiency, and accountability to the local community. Leaders of Racine 2000 list nine principles that have proved helpful in fulfilling their change agent role in Racine. These may also be of assistance in other communities which are seeking broad-based citizen involvement.

Problems in the Racine area, such as crime, poverty, and unemployment have not gone away. But systems to deal with them have helped move local residents toward the new century:

- Community problems no longer overwhelm and paralyze the residents into inaction, thanks to the attitudes engendered by groups like Racine 2000.
- Linkages and partnerships have been developed over the years, which can readily be called into action in response to local needs.
- Perhaps most of all, partnerships of courage and trust have been established, leaving the assurance that hope can take root and flourish even in dark times, and will bear fruit for generations to come.

Where Does Racine Go from Here?

Since its inception, Racine 2000 has generated inquiries from communities across the land. Word of the effort has been circulated through articles in national and international periodicals such as *Changing Work, Christianity and Crisis, Dominican Ashram* (India), *Development Forum* (United Nations). Workshops have been given for national groups at the

Center of Concern in Washington, D.C., and for two of the annual convocations of the World Future Society. Locally, Racine clubs and civic groups have frequently asked for input at their gatherings. But while sharing the story is important, the greatest joy comes from seeing people change and develop as a result of their involvement in the various Racine 2000 projects.

People see themselves continuing the work begun in housing, health care, strengthening families, and other areas. Above all, they are working toward a truly human community. They will work to defend it, celebrate it, and establish it in every area of life where that sense of community is diminished. The true test of our justice is how it is applied to every area of life — to race, to gender, to economics, to politics. Then they can truly look to a future rooted in hope.

References

[1] Holland, Dr. J. Speech given at Racine 2000 Conference held in Racine, WI, January, 1982.

[2] Parade Magazine, April 11, 1993, p. 1.

[3] Perkins, Dr. John. Speech given in Racine, WI, December, 1993.

[4] Gunn, Erik, "Wedding the Spirit to the Economy," *Christianity and Crisis*, June 22, 1992, p. 233.

[5] *Futurist*, Jan.-Feb. 1987, p. 23.

THE CALIFORNIA GNATCATCHER

Reprinted with permission from the *North County Blade-Citizen.*

Chapter 6
The Gnatcatcher Solution:
Breaking New Ground in Southern California

DOUGLAS A. WILSON, Ph.D.

*This is the story of a landmark case when groups
traditionally opposed to each other worked in an
unprecented collaboration to save the habitat
of the threatened species of songbird, the California
gnatcatcher. It is a tale of how diverse groups with
competing interests came to a table and worked out an
agreement that preserved coastal sage brush for the
gnatcatcher, and still created a project that made
economic sense for a large real estate developer,
Fieldstone La Costa Associates. In observing this
unusual success story, Jeff Opdycke, a U.S. Fish and
Wildlife Field Supervisor said in the San Diego
Union Tribune of May 7, 1992, "We want to use
this as an illustration of how to work through this
process (of habitat protection) or how to understand
what the community needs, the industry needs, and
the (various imperiled) species need."*

The California gnatcatcher is a small blue-gray songbird known for its plaintive, mewing call. Experts estimate there are about 2,500 nesting pairs of the four-inch-long bird remaining in the United States. Presently listed under the Endangered Species Act of 1973 as a threatened species, the bird and its habitat are both protected under federal law. Almost all of the gnatcatchers live in San Diego, Orange, and Riverside counties in California, and much of the bird's estimated 350,000-400,000 acres of coastal sage scrub habitat lies in San Diego County.

Introducing the Dilemma

This whole gnatcatcher story begins in 1988, when Fieldstone La Costa Associates, a Southern California residential homebuilder, purchased in partnership with BCED, the development arm of Bell Canada and the largest publicly held company in Canada, 2,800 acres of land in North San Diego County at a cost of $180 million. Their intent was to build approximately 3,000 homes in three major phases extending over a period of 12-15 years. The project was to be one of the largest real estate ventures in community development in the country.

Shortly after the purchase, Fieldstone discovered gnatcatchers on the property. Some of the rare songbirds' best coastal sage scrub habitat fell within the boundaries of the project's site—open, untouched habitat surrounded by urban sprawl. While the gnatcatcher was not yet listed, the U.S. Fish and Wildlife Service, the California Department of Fish and Game, the city of Carlsbad, the Endangered Habitats League, and a long list of conservation and no-growth groups were all offering ideas in the discussion regarding the protection of the gnatcatcher and its habitat. To avoid chaos in dealing separately with all of those expressing interest, Fieldstone knew that they would have to devise an overall plan for approaching eventual development of their land.

The Endangered Species Act, signed into law by President Richard M. Nixon in 1973, was written to protect animals, plants, and insects from extinction and to conserve their habitats. Species listed in it generally cannot be harmed nor can their natural surroundings be destroyed. In general the law has not resulted in increased available natural habitats, particularly on private property. "Too often listings have occurred and species have become extinct regardless," said Andy McLeod, spokesperson for the Resources Agency of California, which oversees all resource departments (such as the California Department of Fish and Game) in the state. "The law essentially is an 11th-hour warning system. A listing is comparable to bells and whistles going off at the point when a species is seriously endangered."

The Old Adversarial Model

Most developers take the traditional view when confronted with the possibility of an endangered species listing. They secure permits as quickly as possible, grade the land, and bypass any potential problems. The logic behind this approach is that if developers do not act quickly, they can be trapped in a hopeless bureaucratic morass for years, causing a significant financial impact and, in the worst case, resulting in the loss of the project. Fieldstone already had millions of dollars invested in the project and could not afford a multidimensional, protracted legal battle.

As members of the Fieldstone team, led by Senior Project Manager John Barone, sat down to discuss their options, they looked at the way developers had always dealt with such environmental conflicts in the past. If they decided to follow the old corporate tactic, Fieldstone would have to:

- Undermine the Endangered Species Act and, if possible, limit re-authorization of the act in 1992. They would have to lobby hard with their U.S. congressional representatives to help repeal the Endangered Species Act or water it down sufficiently to allow them to proceed so that the listing of a species would not be a problem.

- Defeat the listing of the gnatcatcher specifically. This effort would entail gathering as much scientific information as possible and dumping it on the agencies at the last minute in a continual series of stalling tactics until they could prove their case—that the gnatcatcher does not belong on the endangered species list.

- Develop a public relations strategy, particularly focused on California, to heighten people's awareness and fear of a doomsday scenario if the gnatcatcher were listed. This strategy would develop the bleakest picture possible, showing losses of jobs, development, infrastructure, and improvements.

- Keep the environmentalists out of the picture as much as possible and work with state and federal agencies independently.

The traditional view of environmentalists and conservationists was that they would go to any means to stop development. If discussion between developers and conservationists occurred at all, it was only through attorneys and hard-nosed negotiators, giving up as little as possible and bending only when necessary. The environmentalists were definitely prepared to do battle along the lines of the spotted owl conflict in the states of Oregon and Washington, where a listing resulted in the setting aside of millions of acres of forest, with the result of severely limiting timber foresting. This dramatically increased unemployment, and broke down some small communities.

Fieldstone's experience told them that the traditional perspective of the resource agencies and conservation organizations was that:

- Business is only interested in money. Environmental organizations and state, local, and federal agencies must prevent corporations from pillaging the environment.
- A good strategy for dealing with developers might be what people in manufacturing would call "over the wall." Developers would do the work and redesign what they considered to be a reasonable alternative to their original plan. They would then throw it over the wall to the agencies, who would critique and then throw the idea back over the wall to the developer. One example occurred when the resource agencies and conservation groups decided that establishing a "habitat corridor" (basically, a street for wildlife to travel from one area to another) was the best solution. They threw their idea over the wall to Fieldstone and said, "Make it happen." This kind of process resulted in many misunderstandings and angry reactions.
- An effective tactic of some environmentalists has been to slow down the development process to a snail's pace, give no data, and reveal no plans to business people.

Historically, the legal system has been the venue for resolving disputes of environmental versus economic interests. This adversarial approach is still predominant, in which each party tries to optimize its gain while minimizing any gains of the other side. As land disputes become more complex and involve more players, larger deals, and larger issues (i.e., environmental ones), the legal system is no longer the right venue for resolving problems.

A Developer's Dilemma

With this adversarial mindset at work at the city, state, and federal levels, a developer like Fieldstone was in a real bind unless there was a way to create a new model for problem solving. The task of working out a win-win solution seemed hopeless. As a builder the company saw no way to take the moral high ground and present itself as the "good guy." A builder is generally perceived by the public as the "bad guy." There was a great need to take a proactive position and challenge people to work with them in developing a creative solution.

From previous experiences, however, Fieldstone personnel knew they were up for a difficult battle. When they tried to negotiate with the government, sometimes they were rebuffed outright. Other times their programs were so heavily criticized they realized it would take years to make minimal if any progress. As a result of these realities, many private landowners are quietly killing off endangered species or destroying their native habitats to avoid the costly government restrictions. According to Firestone's team leader John Barone:

> The biggest risk was that by getting involved in an effort to negotiate a solution, we could have been red-taped to death. If the negotiations took ten years it would have cost us between $100-150 million in interest payments. We had to get going to dampen the interest meter running every day. It was potentially possible to be delayed right out of business.

Also, if the bird got listed, and Fieldstone had begun development, the company and any employee could face up to one year in jail or a $100,000 fine if any damage occurred to the sagebrush habitat. The listing would have completely stopped the project.

Developing a New Model of Planning and Collaboration

The Fieldstone team knew that the option to the adversarial approach was to challenge people to work with them to develop a creative solution. Mindsets and old paradigms would require significant shifting. Fortunately, Fieldstone already had a set of corporate values in place that supported collaboration. For instance, the company takes an annual reading to measure how effectively it is applying such values in its daily actions. Barone looked to Fieldstone's legacy of values, which reflect the company's dedication to:

- Excellence in everything we do,
- An environment of teamwork and trust,
- The value of each employee,
- A commitment to our homebuyers,
- The importance of profitable operations,
- Integrity in the conduct of our business.

Because these values were built into the ethos of the organization, Fieldstone's natural inclination was to avoid approaching the gnatcatcher problem confrontationally. Instead the company wanted to operate from a position that would inspire cooperation, trust, and a solution that was in everyone's best interest.

The Fieldstone management talked over the two points of view on conflict resolution. Historically, they knew that any developers who had tried to work with state, local, and federal government agencies in resolving environmental issues cooperatively had either failed or been involved in interminable negotiations. Their company could not afford that. However, they were also aware that grading the property quickly would still leave them with significant problems because they could only grade about one-third of the property and even that would not completely solve the problem. And, of course, if they went ahead they would anger the community. Fieldstone ultimately went with an approach that was more collaborative because, as Barone said,

> We had people in the company, including myself, who felt we needed to find a fresh way of working with the environmentalists and governmental agencies where it would be a win-win situation. The old approach was, "We'll get you before you get us." We felt we had to find something new.

The federal government had not yet actually listed the gnatcatcher, and so Fieldstone officials weren't sure whether they could even get the government's attention, because of higher priorities with already listed species. Still, Fieldstone wanted to go to them and say, "Let's talk about the gnatcatcher" and assume the bird was already listed. Barone outlined the predicament:

> We knew if we began working with the federal government, we would be taking the lead for the building industry in Southern California, particularly San Diego, because many of the builders around us all have gnatcatchers on their property as well. Concurrently, in an attempt to head off a federal designation of the gnatcatcher as endangered, [California] Governor Pete Wilson had been trying to persuade developers to voluntarily begin the planning to set

aside large tracts of coastal sage scrub. Unfortunately, if we went into a cooperative effort with the government, we would be perceived by other builders as caving in.

A Diverse Group Gathers

As Fieldstone worked to develop the operating principles for this new model of planning and cooperation, the company reached beyond their corporate boundaries to develop a team. Fieldstone asked a neutral facilitator hired by the city of Carlsbad to work with the group on some difficult issues. This choice of a facilitator was critical. They found someone with extensive experience in the San Diego Association of Governments and experience in the private sector as well. They also brought in Lindell Marsh, a creative attorney who had specialized in using collaborative processes for resolving difficult and complex land issues.

Fieldstone agreed to involve people with various orientations. The company approached the state and federal agencies, the city of Carlsbad, as well as the environmentalists; it also agreed to be a partner in a joint effort to create prelisting agreements to set aside land for the gnatcatcher as well as provide a permit for Fieldstone when and if the gnatcatcher was listed.

The next addition to the group was Dan Silver from the Endangered Habitat League, which represented over 30 different environmental groups. "From an industry point of view, inviting Dan Silver to the table was like inviting the devil himself," said John Barone. Silver then suggested they invite Dr. Jonathan Atwood, the nationally renowned gnatcatcher expert and the one who provided all the scientific documentation for the listing petition. Dr. Atwood and his people were thought by the building industry to be the source of all their problems. The building industry generally did not consider the environmental concerns of these people to be legitimate.

John Barone had taken the lead in developing Fieldstone's philosophy of planning and cooperation. But getting to a positive outcome was not easy. When Fieldstone went into the process of dialogue with the environmentalists, the company representatives discovered that they were naive about what the issues really were on the environmentalists' side of the table. Barone continued:

I had seen environmentalists in the papers and on TV and most of them were arm waving, irrational people screaming and trying to stop the whole world from growing. This was what I anticipated at the table.

At first, he went into the meetings with great trepidation, but his fears were eased as the group moved along. He began to see that he did not understand many of the environmentalists' points until he listened with a view of really wanting to understand, instead of trying to fight and find the holes in their thinking. The old model was to listen, find the holes, and poke. The new approach was to listen, find what was reasonable, legitimize it, and look for a way to build that legitimacy into a joint project.

John discovered that just as there are gradations of developers from bad to good in their willingness to be reasonable and ethical, there are gradations of environmentalists from bad to good in their willingness to be reasonable and ethical as well. Fortunately, the environmentalists Fieldstone was working with were not trying to stop the world from progressing. They knew they had to protect their own interests, but listen to the developer's interests as well. They were assertive in telling Fieldstone when something was unacceptable, but at the same time they worked to understand what Fieldstone needed.

On the other side, Barone observed:

The conservationists went into these negotiations with a naive view of developers. They too began to learn—about how developers must struggle with economics and how difficult it is to satisfy the needs of customers in a community, and at the same time preserve the environment in the best way possible.

Building Ground Rules

Once this diverse group got together, the company worked to develop an environment of teamwork and trust, based on one of the Fieldstone values. To succeed in establishing this kind of atmosphere, a group needs high levels of empathy. As John Barone asserted:

The golden rule says, "Do to your neighbor as you would want your neighbor to do unto you." Trust comes from a sincere desire to understand. It also comes from a willingness to shoot straight with people—not pull punches, try to hide information, or carry out a hidden agenda. We at Fieldstone decided the only way to make this project work was to put our cards on the table and let people see what we needed to make the project work. We were going to take a position of openness and candor. We were not going to roll over in order to get the job done, but at the same time we were not going to bully in any way.

The Fieldstone team knew that it needed to balance respect for the others' interests with the goal of producing tangible results. Throughout the process they not only valued teamwork and trust, but also each individual participant — not just because of their ideas, but because of who they were as people. As one Fieldstone team member commented:

We allowed each person to contribute fully and we genuinely wanted to understand. There was no manipulative approach to get people in the room and start maneuvering around a hidden agenda. We approached the problem with open minds and I believe everyone came with that sense of commitment. I'm sure people were suspicious to start with, but as I observed the process unfolding, people began softening into a willingness to cooperate.

Indeed, they had to spend a good deal of time establishing ground rules and agreeing not to discredit each other in the process. As the group built the ground rules, though, and felt the commitment to a secure, cooperative work environment, everyone got on board.

Fieldstone also knew the only way to make the negotiations work was to legitimize each group's interest in the project. The environmentalists had a legitimate stake in the survival of the gnatcatcher and the preservation of its habitat; the city of Carlsbad had a legitimate stake in the preservation of sagebrush and the need to construct public facilities that might have an impact on the gnatcatcher; and Fieldstone had a legitimate stake in the development of housing to serve the growth needs of the

City of Carlsbad
Community Development
Key Participants and Contacts

U.S. Fish and Wildlife Service: This is the principal agency through which the federal government carries out its responsibilities to conserve, protect and enhance the nation's fish and wildlife and their habitats for the continuing benefit of people. The Service's major responsibilities are for migratory birds, endangered species, certain marine mammals, and freshwater and anadromous fish.

California Department of Fish and Game: This is the state wildlife agency which is responsible for managing and conserving the state's natural resources. This also is the agency which has primary responsibility for administering the Natural Community Conservation Plan (NCCP), under the guidance of the California Resources Agency. The cooperative plan is a means of working with land owners, regulatory agencies and conservation groups to ensure protection of sensitive natural habitats while allowing for appropriate community development.

City of Carlsbad: City planners have established a Habitat Management Plan (HMP), a blueprint for citywide conservation of wildlife and habitat to offset impacts from new development and construction of public facilities.

Endangered Habitats League: A coalition of 33 Southern California conservation groups and many individual members. The coalitions' two main goals are to obtain endangered species listings for the California gnatcatcher and to help craft constructive solutions to conflicts between the environment and development.

The Fieldstone Co.: Developer of a group of master-planned residential communities in southern Carlsbad known as Fieldstone La Costa. The home-building firm is the largest single-family detached home builder in San Diego County.

county. It agreed that the solution should be scientifically based. At the same time, everyone also agreed that economic profitability would have to be the other consideration.

Fieldstone decided not to argue about the validity of the gnatcatcher listing. Their position was, "Let's assume the gnatcatcher will be listed, and let's act as if it is already even though it's not." This tactic took everyone off the defensive. No longer did anyone need to argue about how many birds were in the natural habitat or how many were on their land. Instead they worked with the environmentalists' assumption that, indeed, the gnatcatcher was endangered.

Another strategy in this process was to build consensus and to solve problems jointly by using strategic planning. The participants knew that any solution was going to be expensive and difficult, but that it would be definitely more expensive and more difficult to protract the situation.

As the group worked through the issues, there were some very difficult times, but Fieldstone agreed to give everyone a say in the success or failure of where they were moving. And they really meant it. John Barone felt strongly about the process and said, "Values without a willingness to risk, without being tempered by courage, go nowhere. They remain inscribed in notebooks but are never translated into action." Fieldstone was not going to back away if things got tough. Everyone had that attitude, and that determination went a long way. Another helpful factor was that the timing was right for this process. The environmentalists knew they needed a model to demonstrate that other developers were wrong when they painted pictures of economic disaster should the gnatcatcher be listed. They wanted to prove it was possible to have economic development and at the same time be environmentally sensitive. The risk Fieldstone took by bringing everyone to the table was that the whole project could blow up, and they could be perceived as one more greedy developer. If that happened, it could sever relationships that might never be patched up. But the team felt the risk was worth it.

Near Impasse

A potential impasse occurred when Fieldstone wanted to buy land elsewhere to mitigate the effect of the loss of gnatcatcher habitat on its project in Carlsbad. The resource agencies said, "No, a portion of your solution must include land being set aside on your project in Carlsbad." Fieldstone wasn't sure they could work this one out. By now the community and the media were watching their progress. Because these meetings had a high degree of visibility, none of the participants wanted to be perceived as caving in: they all had people to whom they were accountable. The banks as well as the financial partners were watching on Fieldstone's side, and the conservationists and the community were watching on the other side. In addition, many people in Washington wanted to see if the Endangered Species Act could work in its present form. This exposure made the situation even more tense.

At times the Fieldstone problem-solving team members felt that they were on the wrong track. There were meetings when they left the table, looked at each other, and said, "We're never going to reach agreement." They would start to think, "We've got to go to Washington...or to our congressman." Sometimes they felt they could not get through this process with the people who were in the room. It just seemed too difficult. At other times they felt that maybe a solution did not exist at all. Maybe they were trying to do something impossible. Maybe there was a good reason why every other developer had been mired in endless battles like this one was shaping up to be.

The Breakthrough

Newspaper articles came out talking about this process. They were very pessimistic. Many of the other developers wanted to see Fieldstone fail. They wanted to say, "I told you so. You can't sit down with these guys and work out a deal by consensus. It just won't happen." There were also people at The Fieldstone Company who thought that the Fieldstone team was never going to get this resolved and felt the company would be better off joining with other developers.

Despite the negative atmosphere, the Fieldstone team reached a breakthrough. They asked the environmentalists and agencies to draft a vision of the bigger picture regarding mitigation. Fieldstone challenged them to develop a plan for North San Diego. As they drafted their vision and Fieldstone listened, they were able to innovate together and create a solution that fit that vision. This clear joint vision allowed all the other details to be worked out. John Barone remembers, "By taking off our gloves and working with the environmentalists and agencies to think through what their vision was, we were able to build creatively." Here, the process moved out of a negotiation model and into a planning model. The planning mode made the Fieldstone project one part of a larger picture. The group was able to scope different alternatives for the future and forge a consensus on how to proceed. When the negotiations seemed to be at risk, John Barone remembers:

> Fortunately, there was a senior member of the team on their
> side of the table who said, "Wait a minute, we can make
> your idea work." The willingness of that senior member to
> see our point of view and how it fit into the overall con-
> servation vision was the breakthrough point that moved
> the project through to the end zone.

As they discussed specific items, the agencies often said, "This doesn't work. This works better over here." Fieldstone kept asking why and would help force them back to their initial vision. Finally, the group came to a critical meeting. Everyone remembers it vividly. The environmentalists came to Fieldstone and said, "Here's what we need and here's how we see this thing working." Once Fieldstone clearly understood what the vision was for San Diego county, they were able to find specific solutions on the property that fit within the framework of that vision. By looking at the vision, they saw what things they could and could not do. They understood where they could not cross lines.

A key here is that they had to think outside the concept of the property itself to arrive at a solution for the property. None of the participants could have done this individually in his or her own office. They had to do it together in an environment of teamwork and trust. Neither side had envisioned the specific solution they finally were able to develop. It came about together — cooperatively. The word cooperation was a key driving dynamic in the planning process.

The actual plan was outlined in a simple document called, The Initial Points of Consensus Document. It was initialed by the major parties to the agreement. The initials had no legal standing, but rather were an indication of each person's commitment to work together from then on. It is important to note that the parties did not have a legal document and the gnatcatcher could have been listed at any moment. But the agencies became

Milestones in Habitat Conservation Planning

1989 • State and federal wildlife agencies, Fieldstone and local environmental leaders begin laying the groundwork for habitat conservation planning on a large scale.

1/90 • Tours and briefings of Secretary of Interior staff.
• City of Carlsbad sponsors public discussions on environmental issues involving coastal sage scrub and sensitive species.
• The Alliance for Habitat Conservation is formed. This group comprises land development companies which collectively control 80 percent of the developable coastal sage scrub habitat in San Diego County.

2/91 • U.S. Fish and Wildlife Service agrees to use the Habitat Conservation Plan (HCP) process in San Diego, even though the gnatcatcher is not listed.

7/91 • Memorandum of Agreements (MOA) signed by both state and federal agencies agreeing to use the HCP process on a pre-listing basis with the city of Carlsbad.
• Resources Agency Secretary Douglas Wheeler announces a new HCP process, the Natural Community Conservation Plan (NCCP). It is authorized through legislation (AB 2172, Kelley) in August.

8/91 • California Fish and Game Commission votes not to list the California gnatcatcher as a state candidate for listing.
• Fieldstone halts development on its approved project, The Fairways, to assess mitigation of the post-approval discovery of gnatcatchers on the property.
• Fieldstone provides replacement habitat as mitigation for Fairways, a very degraded and heretofore unoccupied gnatcatcher habitat.

9/91 • Fish and Wildlife Service announces it will propose the California gnatcatcher for endangered status. This marks the beginning of a year long process of study.
• In an effort to produce the most resource-protective plan possible for construction of a vital, publicly mandated transportation link, Rancho Santa Fe Road, the city of Carlsbad formed a Habitat Conservation Plan committee comprised of City officials, U.S. Fish and Wildlife Service, Department of Fish and Game, Fieldstone representatives, and representatives of various local and regional conservation groups.

2/92 • Fieldstone becomes the first and only builder to sign a management and mitigation pre-listing agreement with the California Department of Fish and Game. The plan replaces a small parcel of disturbed and isolated gnatcatcher habitat slated for grading with quality habitat located nearby which also provides connectivity with adjacent habitat.

4/92 • After months of negotiations between participants of the Rancho Santa Fe Road and grading project HCP committee, an agreement was reached on the most appropriate mitigation for construction of the road and surrounding development. The conceptual agreement included providing wildlife corridors through and adjacent to the project with both on-site and off-site mitigation at a cost to The Fieldstone Company of over $12.5 million.

• The U.S. Fish and Wildlife Service and the California Department of Fish and Game begin work on pre-listing agreements for the Rancho Santa Fe Road and grading project.

5/92 • The city of Carlsbad held a press conference to publicly acknowledge the mitigation agreement on the Rancho Santa Fe Road and grading project. Participants include the city, The Fieldstone Company, U.S. Fish and Wildlife Service, California Department of Fish and Game, the Resources Agency, and several local and regional conservation groups.

3/93 • California Gnatcatcher listed as a Threatened Species by U.S. Fish and Wildlife Service (FWS). In a companion action, FWS proposed a "special rule" as provided under section 4(d) of the endangered species act. The rule states that take of gnatcatchers is not a violation of endangered species act if part of an approved NCCP plan.

12/93• FWS finalizes and adopts special rule which provides for take of gnatcatchers pursuant to approved NCCP plans. Short-term effect of the rule is to allow interim take of up to 5% of the existing coastal sage scrub habitat, subject to NCCP guidelines, prior to completion and approval of regional NCCP plans.

6/94 • The Fieldstone Company completes final draft of Habitat Conservation Plan for approximately 2,000 acres in southwestern Carlsbad. Carlsbad City Council authorizes submission of HCP to FWS and Calif. Dept. of Fish and Game as a joint application of city and Fieldstone.

7/94 • City of Carlsbad completes public review draft of Habitat Management Plan and releases plan for 60 day comment period.

12/94• Fieldstone HCP is in review by FWS. Carlsbad Habitat Management Plan is pending outcome of Fieldstone plan and progress on regional plan.

comfortable saying, "Look, guys, if the gnatcatcher gets listed, don't worry. We will deal with you in a fair way." This sort of commitment at a high level was unprecedented. By this time, they all knew they were breaking new ground in making a joint agreement to move together if and when the gnatcatcher was listed.

As this process was coming close to reaching a conclusion, the media talked to the parties involved. Reporters wanted to write about what was actually allowing this unlikely collaboration to succeed. The conservationists asked Fieldstone to set aside habitat and make design changes such as transferring densities, changing roadways, and changing the areas they would grade. Dan Silver said that Fieldstone showed a notable willingness "to design the hell out of their project to satisfy us, and the U.S. Fish and Wildlife Service," and also, that "Fieldstone essentially said we'll do anything you want us to do as long as we can still make a buck on this project."

When asked if there were better ways they could have sped up the problem solving, John Barone reflected:

> I think there were some ways we could have, but on the other hand, I don't think the mechanics of how we went about it were as important as the attitude and the ethic with which we approached the situation. I believe we had to flail, and find out where each person's bottom line was before we could really start to make progress. In a sense, we each came up against the wall and then knew what we had to do. My gut feeling tells me we just had to go through what we went through. We started out optimistically, things would fall apart, we patched them back together, and eventually we found we were making it work.

Everyone Wins

The mayor of Carlsbad, California, Bud Lewis, in speaking of this experience commented, "The proactive approach taken by the developer, the city, and environmental groups, stands as a model for future development proposals. It took courage for Fieldstone to do this and entailed a great sacrifice on their part." (San Diego *Daily Transcript*, May 7, 1992.)

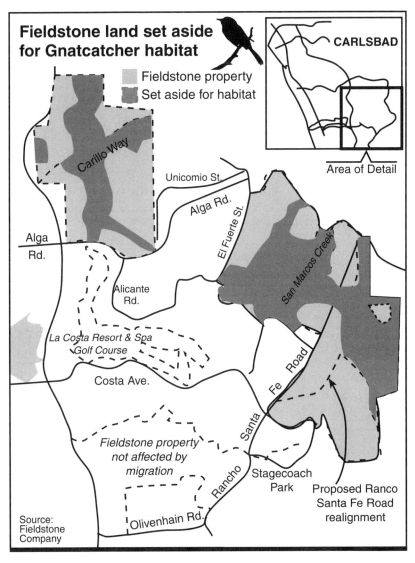

Fieldstone land set aside for Gnatcatcher habitat

Fieldstone property
Set aside for habitat

CARLSBAD

Area of Detail

Carillo Way

Unicomio St.

Alga Rd.

El Fuerte St.

Alga Rd.

San Marcos Creek

Alicante Rd.

La Costa Resort & Spa Golf Course

Costa Ave.

Santa Fe Road

Fieldstone property not affected by migration

Rancho

Stagecoach Park

Proposed Ranco Santa Fe Road realignment

Source: Fieldstone Company

Olivenhain Rd.

Fieldstone provided this early map as the group came to the first levels of agreement. As the process continued, details continued to change.

The hoped for outcome as of July, 1992 was a significant benefit to both the developer and the community. For the community, 645 acres of prime gnatcatcher habitat plus 240 acres of other habitat, which together addresses over 60 species, were to be preserved. Including land costs and additional conservation measures, the cost to The Fieldstone Company was to be at least $25 million. However, Fieldstone would have earned the right to develop land for as many as 3,700 homes worth a total of close to $1 billion in revenue over the next 12-15 years.

After July of 1992, several drafts of the document were produced and carefully reviewed by all participants. The process was far more time-consuming and expensive than anyone had anticipated. Then, on March 25, 1993, the U.S. Fish and Wildlife Service listed the California gnatcatcher as a "threatened species." A special "rule" was also enacted tying the bird's habitat to an innovative program proposed by Governor Wilson and enacted by the Legislature. This program was called the Natural Communities Conservation Planning Program (NCCP). The city and Fieldstone hailed the new program because it extended cooperative, proactive planning to the entire range of the gnatcatcher five county area. However, during this time the economy was taking its toll. Fortunately, both the city of Carlsbad and Fieldstone have weathered the storm so far, but the results are not yet in.

The final draft of the Habitat Conservation Plan (HCP) was produced in March, 1994 and has been submitted to the U.S. Fish and Wildlife Service, and the California Department of Fish and Game as a joint application of the city and The Fieldstone Company. While the HCP has been in preparation, a number of complementary habitat planning efforts have been initiated.

For instance, Carlsbad has initiated a citywide Habitat Management Plan of which the HCP will be the cornerstone. A subregional plan called the Multiple Habitat Conservation Plan is underway for North San Diego County. The city and the Multiple Habitat Conservation Plan are enrolled and actively participating in NCCP. This means that all the planning programs are interlocking at the local, regional, state, and federal levels. Final approval has not yet been given, so the story is a work in progress. However, participants agree it is a unique model that has tremendous potential for the rest of the country.

As John Barone says:

> Hopefully the outcome will demonstrate that the future for large scale development in Southern California lies not in developers fighting environmentalists and wildlife officials over sensitive habitats. It lies in creating an ideal future that integrates the interests of all parties into the best possible solution. Even the Endangered Species Act need not be an impediment to economic growth if developers, environmentalists, and government officials join in sensible planning efforts such as Carlsbad's conservation plan.

In the fall of 1994, the Institute for Local Self Government awarded the City of Carlsbad with the California Cities Helen Putnam Award for Excellence as a result of the city's joint effort in working with the Fieldstone Habitat Conservation Plan. The citation noted that people recognize that this is a new model that needs support to solve complex problems that will no longer work from the old adversarial negotiation point of view.

> *The author expresses special thanks to Julie Luckey for her important work on the development of this chapter.*

SECTION II
Entrepreneurship in Government

Putting the Citizen Customer First

A s I watch the evening news, I have a strange of *deja vu* sensation; once again I am witnessing the annual debate over whether there should be additional runways at Chicago's O'Hare Airport. The mayor of Chicago wants them; the mayors of the suburban jurisdictions surrounding O'Hare don't. It's that simple, so the news broadcast portrays. The news media desire to make things simple for us, because if the complexity were really known, they feel we wouldn't listen, watch, or read their news. So we allow ourselves to fall into the simple paradigms of "the-good-guys-versus-the-bad-guys" approach. This adversarial mind-set is an easy perspective from which to view the world, but we cannot allow the media to tell us, the American public, what and how we must think. We need to stand back, see the issues in their larger complex context, and genuinely assume responsibility for what is needed in today's world.

Pitting the urban against the suburban is a convenient way to avoid seeing the bigger picture. What would it mean to take a different look at the need for those runways at O'Hare? What if we eliminated the political jurisdictions all around O'Hare field for a moment and viewed this area from a satellite ten miles up? From up there, we can see all of the municipality boundaries. To begin to make responsible decisions, we need to look at wholes, rather than pieces.

The O'Hare runway issues set the stage for the stories that follow. These cases remind us that the efforts to transform government are for the common public good, as Carolyn Lukensmeyer asserts in Chapter 2. Until we can really focus on the big picture of just what the public good is, then perhaps all we are really doing is engaging in fruitless rhetoric. As Vincent Lane, Chairman of the Chicago Housing Authority said:

> Sometimes we need to start out with a blank slate and say, 'Hey, we've been doing this for the last forty, fifty years. It doesn't work.' Let's throw out everything, clear our minds…Let's have as a goal doing the right thing for the right reasons, even if it entails taking risks[1].

In this section a series of case studies describes how people from within their own administrative system have created pockets of success. Maybe one day a "critical mass" of such efforts will unleash an avalanche of change.

Many experts and organizations, as well as formal studies and reports, recount instances of reorganizing government from within. They demonstrate, along with the stories in this section, the many reasons to be enthusiastic about the future of government as agencies guide their own attempts to redesign themselves. Certainly, there appears to be a growing awareness of the need for change in our political institutions. Elizabeth Hollander in Chapter 1 reports on the work of the National Commission on the State and Local Public Service, referred to most frequently by the name of its chair, William F. Winter, former Governor of the State of Mississippi. Another example is the work of the Council for Excellence in Government, a network of private sector leaders who have previously served as public officials; this group has initiated a program to foster what it calls "mission-driven accountability."

The Federal Quality Institute (FQI) monitors the implementation of total quality management (TQM) inside the federal government and each year presents awards to select federal agencies who have woven TQM into their operations. In addition, the National Academy of Public Administration (NAPA) sponsors frequent roundtable discussion on the topic of government reform. One of its affiliate groups, the Alliance for Redesigning Government, is a clearinghouse of public innovations from all across the country.

Revolutionizing Bureaucratic Complexity

One place that cries out for reform lies in relation between the various levels of government itself. Too frequently state and local government bureaucrats become what could be described as "sub-federal level functionaries." An extreme example of this blurring of responsibility happened in Indiana when the head of the Department of Environment reported, "We have all these environmental mandates coming down, and we have all these cities and counties asking, 'Why are you doing this to us?'" Not surprisingly, the federal mandates have outstripped the state's ability to comply, and so Indiana is considering turning environmental programs back to the U.S. Environmental Protection Agency[2].

During the 1980s, urban areas especially experienced decreasing federal support of social programs. Many times the rules that accompanied the reductions in funding increased the complexity of administering those fewer assistance dollars, and the number of program administrators at the state and local levels increased in inverse proportion to the number of program beneficiaries. Something was wrong with the way government was doing its business. Jefferson said we needed an American revolution every ten years or so to think through what kind of government we wanted. Stories in this section reflect the hope of just such a revolution and show that an American Perestroika is underway.

Perhaps the greatest single effort underway in our country to reinvent government is being undertaken by the federal government. The National Performance Review (NPR) report, published in September, 1993, after a six-month study, identified myriad of success stories happening inside government[4]. Twelve months after the study's publication, the Vice-President announced that 90% of the 255 agency-specific recommendations were being implemented, proposed in pending legislation, or were to be included in the fiscal year 1995 federal budget. These results were accomplished not by politicians, but by loyal public servants fighting the war on bureaucracy.

Listening to Citizen Needs

One common denominator running through all the reinventing efforts is the need for government to listen more closely to what the citizens want. A simple truth in democracy, one might say. But somehow, over the years, layers of government have increasingly obscured this basic tenet. Attempts to resurrect it, however, have been underway for several years.

For instance ,the state of Virginia is taking citizen input seriously. Its Department of Housing and Community Development (DHCD) is charged with assembling the federally mandated CHAS — Comprehensive Housing Affordability Strategy. Most states and municipalities merely go through the motions, only masquerading citizen input; Virginia's DHCD saw this mandate as an opportunity to do something different and arranged for a series of regional forums — usually called public hearings — sprinkled across the state to ensure equitable citizen access to deliberations about the state's CHAS.

The first DHCD statewide public hearing took place in Williamsburg, a mere 15 miles from Jamestown, where English colonists first set foot in the New World. That April 27, 1991 morning, the people streaming into the nondescript meeting room searched unsuccessfully for a speaker sign-up sheet. Instead of the usual theater-style seating with a head table for state officials and a podium from which experts and dignitaries could expound on the needs of the citizens, there were many tables scattered around the room, each with a stack of yellow index cards and a pile of colored felt tip markers. Clearly someone had something else in mind besides a traditional public hearing. Four hours later, the 70 citizens had participated in a new form of government policy making. Each one was a part of an interactive process rather than a victim of a mind-numbing procession of those three-minute presentations that traditionally drag on to 15. On this day a public sector culture of participation had been born in the birthplace of America. Bob Adam, DHCD's Housing Division Director comments on his state's success:

> Aside from simply being the right thing to do to respect
> the views of citizens, the public participation process
> which Virginia used to develop its CHAS yielded a variety
> of benefits. The result is a much richer diversity of ideas

including some which are created on the spot through interaction. Unlike other states where citizens may not even recognize the plan that emerges at the end of the process, in Virginia there are no surprises.

Fashioning Community Forums

Not every area of the country is as successful at involving its citizens. While being pressured by federal and state agencies to take more and more responsibility for solving community problems, local governments are frequently losing the trust of their constituents. The siting of new facilities, landfills, waste management treatment sites, half-way houses, prisons, and other developments, even when widely recognized as beneficial to the community, are being blocked by the "not-in-my-backyard syndrome." A "Proposition 13" tax revolt has led to the repeated failure of governmental initiatives and bond measures vital to the health and welfare of the community.

In Suburban Chicago, though, local municipalities and park districts have been working with the Institute of Cultural Affairs (ICA) to fashion a type of community forum to allow citizen input that would provide village leaders with some sense of direction. Local community leaders in towns such as Aurora, Tinley Park, Buffalo Grove, Mt. Prospect, Deerfield, Bensenville, Woodbridge, and Norridge Park convened workshops where they asked residents what programs, services, facilities, and capital improvements they want to see in place in three to five years.

ICA consultant and facilitator Dennis Jennings, who leads most of these workshops, reports that this kind of town meeting becomes an opportunity for village leaders to clarify misperceptions citizens have about the constraints, the complexity, and the high cost of ready-made solutions that many bring to the meetings. "Participants learn that it's not so easy to adjust an expressway access and exit ramp to accommodate their own narrow purposes."

In all, as many as 40 Chicago suburban municipalities have employed this kind of "listen to the citizen-customer" town meetings. The village of Downer's Grove has undertaken a year-long effort to seek citizen input and participation in their "Village Vision for the 21st century." In turn, over 100 citizens served on committees and volunteered over 5,500 hours of time. Village Manager Kurt Bressner comments:

> It takes a tremendous amount of energy to sustain the momentum of citizen involvement, but once you start, there is no turning back. People learned to expect to be informed and involved and when they weren't, they became very upset. We learned that the rewards for taking the time to keep the citizens involved and informed were quite handsome....We do everything now in collaboration and partnership rather than in any kind of antagonism. We like to say we play softball, not hardball, in Downer's Grove. One of the things it takes—and fortunately we have it—is a group of elected officials not afraid of sharing their power with the people....We call our five elected officials the "community stewards."

Recovering Civic Responsibility

While applauding the efforts to make government more customer-oriented, citizens can never be complacent with being mere customers. Citizens are not just customers; they are owners as well. Admittedly, government reform has been supported by the carryover from the consumer movement in the private sector in the last few years. Nonetheless, citizen participation is more than focus groups and surveys. It is a hands-on partnership with the elected officials and professional staff.

References

[1] The National Performance Review, From Red Tape to Results:
     Creating a Government That Works Better and Costs Less,
     Washington: U.S. Government Printing Office, 1993, p. 37.

[2] National Commission on the State and Local Public Service, Hard
     Truths/Tough Choices. A report published by the Nelson A.
     Rockefeller Institute of Government, State University of New York,
     Albany, NY, 1993.

[3] Congressional Quarterly, Inc., *Governing*, Vol. 7, Number 4, January
     1994, p. 53.

[4] From Red Tape to Results, op.cit.

SERVICE MINNESOTA:

Taking Steps to Satisfy Your Public

Chapter 7
Building the Habit of Transformation

MIRJA HANSON AND SUE LAXDAL

*Achieving excellence in any sector is no small feat; in
the public sector, it's a miracle. The life of an agency
entrepreneur is mostly frustrating and hazardous to
one's health. One longtime state executive summarized
it well: "Public administration is like herding squirrels."
Carefully cultivated management reforms are
vulnerable to a quick death through politics or to a slow
withering due to administrative rules and competing
stakeholder conflict. However, in the state of Minnesota,
the continuing quest for excellence has become a habit.
The miracle behind the miracle of public reform
there is the invisible dedication of caring managers
and employees who weather the storms, continue to put
one foot in front of the other, and maintain the crazy
belief that government can change for the better.*

Long before total quality management (TQM) popularized quality
improvement efforts, Minnesota state government launched its
own efforts to improve the quality and cost-effectiveness of state
service — a testimony to the adage, "It takes twenty years to create an overnight success." Minnesota has been an incubator for
hundreds of productivity initiatives since the early 1970s. The
state has developed a homegrown approach that adapts TQM principles of
the private manufacturing sector to the realities and rigors of large public-
service organizations.

One method in the madness of Minnesota's reform is use of an in-house consulting group, the Management Analysis Division (MAD), one of the first competitive operations in state government and the only one of its kind in the United States. In 1995, it celebrates ten years of success. It has lasted through three administrations and continues to compete for state and local government business with all the big and small private accounting and consulting firms. It enjoys a reputation for objective, apolitical management consulting on agency downsizing, rightsizing, strategic planning, and service redesign.

Mixing Mission and Business

"In just five years, we went from $55,000 in billable hours to nearly $850,000," beamed Fred Grimm, current director of MAD. "We have tried to be a model enterprise in terms of how to run government like a business, using the talent that is within the organization." MAD's track record is impressive — hundreds of consultations dealing with small and large system transitions and transformations. In 1991, when the executive branch management shifted from a Democratic to a Republican governor, MAD was not only maintained but, due to its reputation, became trusted as a primary management consultant to the new administration. The division has facilitated planning and decision-making sessions for the cabinet and the governor's staff. Inquiries from other states indicate that MAD is a one-of-a-kind venture in the United States. A Minnesota *Star Tribune* article referred to MAD as "a group with an unusual status and sterling reputation" [1].

The mission of the group sounds deceptively simple: to help state agencies meet their bottom lines while improving the quality and cost-effectiveness of government services through better management. The impetus for this division to be a self-supporting group that could meet the needs of government "customers" was a 1985 legislative challenge to the division to charge for its services during recession-caused budget cutting. Today's MAD team of 20 consultants is not funded by general tax revenues, but supports itself by contracting with state managers who seek management consulting services. The division is housed with other management support services in the Department of Administration. In fewer than 20 years, MAD has emerged from a small unit conducting legislatively- mandated studies of troubled agencies and system trouble spots. Administration Assistant Commissioner Bock, a former director of MAD, recalled the early days:

We used to do a lot of analytical studies. During the late '70s into the early '80s we started to do change management because directive studies did not create agency ownership in improvement. We knew we needed to enlist top and middle management in those efforts. We realized over time that we needed to change the basic approach. We realized the business we were in was helping people to plan and manage change.

It began as a "mom and pop" operation. Grimm, Bock, and a core of ten consultants bid for every opportunity to sell their wares. No job was too small or insignificant. Grimm says of those days:

We found out the hard way that government is not built to run like a business — personnel systems and financial management systems tested our ingenuity. Without cash in hand, we juggled staff salaries with promised future dollars. Our propensity to underestimate our work hours challenged our ability to deliver quality and meet the bottom line. We learned the hard way that clients often do not know what they really want, resulting in many short-term engagements becoming careers for some staff.

The early struggles paid off. Initial work with units and divisions has led to widespread credibility and invitations to work with whole-agency change as well as with multiple-department efforts. The governor regularly calls on Management Analysis to help agency executives with inter-agency decisions and problem solving. MAD has served as process consultants on recent statewide policy efforts — long-term health care and sustainable development — initiatives involving two to five major agencies and over twenty private-sector groups.

The Competitive Edge

What leads a large number of first-time and repeat clients to choose Management Analysis? According to Grimm, price is one key to competitiveness. From the beginning of our consulting business, MAD has focused on bringing the best of private business to government operations. Our primary competitors charge fees that can preclude a government agency from hiring outside technical assistance for development. This has

Mission Statement

Management Analysis Division
Minnesota Department of Administration

The mission of the Management Analysis Division is to increase the capacity of government to manage resources and to create and implement strategies that improve the quality and cost effectiveness of public services.

We provide consultant services to state agencies, the governor, the legislature, and local governments.

We provide a continuum of management services ranging from analytical studies to design and implementation of change strategies. Our services include diagnosis, analysis, project management, operational and strategic planning, and organization development. Services are provided to individual agencies as well as on a state-government-wide basis.

We offer distinctive competencies that ensure professional, objective, thorough and innovative services specific to the client's needs:

- Comprehensive knowledge of and broad experience in state government operations;

- A disciplined team approach combining staff expertise;

- A track record of sensitive, yet tough-minded, work and a bipartisan reputation for integrity.

We operate with a specific set of values:

- Responsiveness: We design each consultation to focus on areas that have the most potential for significant impact on the organizational challenges of our clients.

- Involvement: We include in the diagnostic and decision processes the people who will implement decisions.

- Regard for employees: We consider an organization's employees to be its most important resource, and we treat them with fairness and respect.

- Objective viewpoint: We strive to maintain a fair, neutral, comprehensive perspective that is apolitical and sensitive to both management and employee needs.

- Inherent respect for public service: We support the mission of state and local government, believe in the dedication and competence of public-sector managers and employees, and support continuous improvement of government services.

—July 1991

meant an opportunity for Management Analysis and its clients. With lower rates, quality services are available to more clients and they receive more value for their dollar.

But Management Analysis is not just a "low-cost vendor." Many clients choose an in-house consultant over private-sector help because Management Analysis has firsthand knowledge of the intricacies and nuances of the public sector. The client saves hours of time not having to orient outside advisers to state systems. Furthermore, processes and recommendations are already tailored to fit the unique needs of public bureaucracies.

Skills Close at Hand

MAD uses multiple methods, skills and tools to customize help to every agency. Judy Plante, assistant director, describes MAD's approach as a "hybrid":

> What we have in place now is a wide variety of skills and abilities to apply to particular situations. We provide consultation that combines third-party analytical reports, organization development processes, and management advice based on wisdom acquired through many years of collective work and learning in agency management. It has been a challenge to customize approaches to meet client needs. It is exciting to actually see changes start to take place.

The success of MAD reflects state managers' willingness to seek and invest in neutral process experts. Such an investment will help to maximize participation and ensure that decisions are holistic, workable, and justifiable for everyone concerned. At the heart of MAD's consulting practice is the belief that effective solutions are derived from participation of all parties with a stake in a given issue or initiative. The role of a consultant is to provide a process that acts like a laser to focus the commitment and expertise of constituents, managers, and employees.

A driving business value is a strong belief in people. Grimm explains the philosophical foundations:

> In the early '70s, I was part of a community development project in the northern Minnesota town of Kinney, sponsored by the Institute of Cultural Affairs (ICA), an

international organization and community development group. I was interested in the planning and development process in Kinney, which was based on the premise that people, if given an opportunity, can chart their own future. I saw the potential for the same human development processes within the government service bureaucracies.

Close cooperation with clients is essential. Judy Plante describes them:

The clients we work with are a real joy. There is a sense of partnership in that these are all people interested in making their part of state government work as well as it can. We are in the truly enviable position of almost always working with people who want success. We provide the tools, but they do it. The goal is to enable agencies to direct their own continuous development.

Two satisfied clients describe their partnership experiences. Dan Collins, supervisor of the Trails and Waterways Unit of the Department of Natural Resources, said they turned to Management Analysis for their fresh ways. As he comments:

It was going to give employee groups an opportunity to not be hierarchical but relational in the way they come up with solutions and implementation. I did one of those plans that stayed on the shelf. We were looking for alternatives and rumor had it Management Analysis was successfully employing ICA methods of stakeholder participation. It sounded good. We have been able to create agreement in longstanding stalemates between constituency groups, such as fishing groups and trail users.

Jayne Khalifa of the Secretary of State's office attributes her repeated use of Management Analysis to the divison's credibility with the legislature for its analysis and, as outsiders, its capacity to allow those with an investment in current systems and decisions to discover the need for change and make new decisions:

With systems change, you must be aware that someone within the organization created [each system] and it's like a mother who has created a child. You don't come into a situation and announce that they have an ugly child and expect to stay. Management Analysis allows groups to admit the need for change, grieve and begin to break down the barriers that prevent change.

From Reactive to Proactive Service

Doing More With Less

"People are the most critical element as we look to the future," Public Safety Commissioner Michael Jordan declared:

> Everything else follows. Vince Lombardi, the late legendary football coach, described the elements of success for his football team like this: first, you have a common goal, second, you are the best at what you do, and third, while you are doing your job, you know others will do theirs. We emphasize quality service delivery that allows autonomy but with a parallel and equal emphasis on teamwork.

The growing concern regarding crime and crime prevention has given the Department of Public Safety a particularly prominent role in the public eye. In the last year it has been challenged to better meet public safety demands while resources decrease or at best remain constant. Stakeholder involvement of both internal staff and managers and external customers has been a primary requirement for streamlining, leveraging economies of scale, and focusing on outcomes. Management Analysis Division consultants were brought in to assist with the transition effort. As Jordan recalls:

> The Minnesota State Patrol was my first priority when I became commissioner last year. The patrol was a highly visible and political issue. Troopers had been working without a contract for more than 18 months and were very frustrated. Dwindling resources with related decreased staffing, subjective disciplinary practices, lawsuits, and leadership turnover added to the problems. It was key to the whole department to resolve issues here. Being the largest division in the department and perceived to be the most problematic, a success here would be a role model for other divisions.

Management Analysis Division
Popular Products and Services

Comprehensive Studies — An in-depth agency assessment to identify areas where change will increase effectiveness, reduce costs, or both.

Diagnostic Overview — A brief review of an agency. An objective look will quickly identify trouble spots and outline what needs fixing and how the repairs might be made.

Organization Development — Guidance to help an agency move onto a proactive course for the future. Working directly with affected employees, consultants assist in long-range planning and decision making. One-to-one managerial coaching and team-building are added tools.

Service Quality Improvement — Coaching, facilitation, and instruction in the use of total quality tools to improve client service.

Legislative Studies — Comprehensive research and analysis to aid policy decision making.

Organizational Structure — Design Analysis and recommendations for effective structure, authorities, and responsibilities.

Work Flow Simplification — Analysis and recommendations for eliminating duplication, unnecessary steps, and confusion in agency work processes.

Benchmarking — Comparing key components of service delivery with similar operations in government or industry to find a cheaper, better, or faster way to do a job.

Fundamental to MAD's approach was creating a basic, simple set of values:
- Treat people the way you want to be treated.
- Do the very best you can at all times.
- Have a fundamental dedication to the truth.
- Client Partnership

A critical element of the change effort was the development of a cross-functional Strategic Directions Team of 30 respected employees, selected from the one hundred fifteen that volunteered for the project. This group attended and helped guide focus group discussions with patrol customers, and analyzed feedback from more than 150 employees regarding patrol strengths and weaknesses. They also talked to quite a few states about new law enforcement trends and practices. The team identified issues that needed to be addressed and developed a plan to make the changes they identified. Once the plan was complete, they sold it to their co-workers. Jordan continues:

> Clearly the morale, behavior, and output of the organization have positively changed. There is a tremendously improved relationship with the troopers' association. For example, this year contract negotiations took just six meetings. Additional staff have been funded, the unfair discipline issue is being addressed. External customers were used in the selection of the new patrol chief. And the implementation of the plan continues with active participation from both the planning team and the overall organization.

> Overall in the Department of Public Safety, and in government departments in general, we are facing dwindling resources, and I'm not sure we can change that. In order to compensate for the resource reduction, we are looking for ways to improve the operating efficiency and effectiveness of the department. To that point we are clustering services and setting priorities at the department level to take advantage of economies of scale, even if we have to stop doing some things. This will reduce fragmentation and unnecessary duplication of effort.

> At a senior managers' retreat, we went back to the basics, establishing a broad vision for the whole department and developing a values statement. We are now coalescing around the vision and values. It is beginning to eliminate some of the competitiveness for resources and senior managers are beginning to see that they are a part of accomplishing each other's missions.

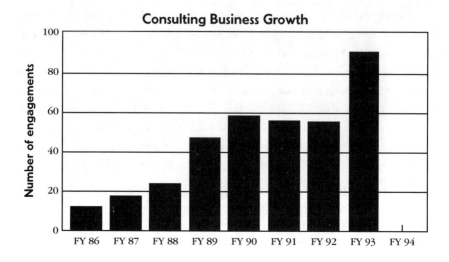

Consulting Business Growth

Policy Positioning

Government is often accused of being "too little too late" in important policy issues. That's changing. With public participation, government can draw attention to significant policy topics such as sustainable development. The Minnesota Environmental Quality Board (EQB) took the lead in designing a unique approach to building public policy that both drew major attention to the topic and formed early consensus. In the late '80s, the term "sustainable development" became more and more popular as a result of a report from the World Commission on Environment and Development. (The report, released in 1987, is known as the Brundtland Report, after Chairperson Gro Harlem Brundtland, Norway's prime minister at the time.) It defined sustainable development simply as a form of development or progress that "meets the needs of the present without compromising the ability of future generations to meet their own needs."

The Minnesota effort was a concrete response to the urgency of environmental protection. Composed of the fourteen state agencies with environmental mandates, the EQB named its year-long effort the Minnesota Sustainable Development Initiative. Its purpose was to educate people about the sustainable development concept and recommend strategies that support both a healthy economy and a healthy environment. Katherine

Barton, Department of Natural Resources Office of Planning, reports:

> The heart of the initiative was [the creation of] seven teams
> in the areas of agriculture, energy, forestry, manufacturing,
> minerals, recreation, and settlement. The EQB insisted
> that long-term consequences of each sector must be a
> central consideration of both environmental and eco-
> nomic decisions. Therefore, bridges must be built between
> and among people who have historically been polarized.
> To actively encourage dialogue, the 105 citizen team mem-
> bers included a wide range of interests and backgrounds,
> such as farmers, resort owners, corporate executives, pro-
> fessors, representatives from environmental non-profits,
> local government officials, and many others.

Each team successfully completed a strategic plan without, remarkably,
minority reports. A final congress drew together other interested participants to review team plans, expand awareness, and identify critical steps for
Minnesota. One major unanticipated outcome of the project was the positive relationships that were built between individuals and constituencies
that had previously suffered from misunderstanding and mistrust. One team
member said what she would remember most about the effort was the "willingness of individual participants from diverse backgrounds and with dif-
fering views to move with aligned agendas toward a common vision rather
than focusing on areas of disagreement."

Putting Mandates to Work

Participative planning has become a cornerstone in moving from reactive to proactive government as well as fostering employee commitment to
and involvement in new directions. Virginia Reiner, assistant section chief
of the Water Supply and Well Management Section of the Environmental
Health Division, Minnesota Department of Health, describes how her section
responded to a new mandate:

> Suddenly we were in charge of checking all holes in the
> ground. Our section is responsible for regulating public
> water supplies. In 1989, the legislature expanded our
> responsibilities to include a very high visibility program
> dealing with regulating past, present, and future wells in

Minnesota. We grew from thirty to close to one hundred within a period of two years. Not only did the numbers change, but the diversity of the staff as well. The newcomers were not all white male engineers, but included people with advanced education, many a lot younger than the veteran staff, and coming from a variety of backgrounds, including other state agencies. We needed a whole new way of doing business. We decided to go through a participative strategic planning process to help think through a whole new organizational structure in order to handle our new situation — we had outgrown our clothes. We pulled in the help of Management Analysis.

"I have worked for the state for 20 years and no one has ever asked me for my opinion on anything. This is the first time I have had the chance to say something," is one comment that sticks in my mind. We interviewed most of the people in our section, state decision makers and customers that we interact with. The portrait of what came out of the surveys was quite touching. A cross-section of the division formed the planning group, to transform the data into a plan with input from new and veteran staff and supervisors.

The basic plan was developed in two days! We brainstormed, we thought, we got lost and tangled in mazes, but at the end of two days, magically, I'd say, we came off with a basic tenet for a plan on where we wanted to be...more user-friendly, more external partnerships, and better internal systems. Even good group decisions aren't a guarantee to action. You can't put the plan on the shelf and think,: that's it. You have to keep perspective on your ultimate goal, keep track of how far you've gotten, and find ways to celebrate milestones to remind everyone we're on our way.

From Conflict to Public Consent

Customer participation in agency agenda setting can be a powerful tool for mobilizing public action. The term "customer" may not be the best term for describing the users and citizens who interact with government, because they are often in conflict with each other and exert more force on the deliverer than do the customers of private organizations. However, Minnesota government managers are realizing that implementable improvement requires that employees, citizens, and other stakeholders be partners in decision making, from generating ideas, to analysis, to recommendations and work planning.

Mediating Trail User Conflict

According to Department of Natural Resources Trail Plan Coordinator Paul Nordell, "There's been a tradition among some trail users — we don't talk to the other users because they are up to no good." He describes the department's action:

> We brought all the different users and their problems to the table and before it was over they saw that they had some common ground. Basically, we have enabled alignment of eight different groups, an attempt to get the agencies together on the same wave lengths and a discussion to get our own house in order on the issue of a public trail agenda.

Paul Swenson, then director, adds:

> State government can only do so much. The DNR has been viewed as the sole provider of trails. This isn't true. The Trails and Waterways Unit manages three thousand miles of state trails and holds administrative control over another twelve thousand miles through a grants-in-aid system. In total, Minnesota sports a roughly eighteen-thousand-mile trail system. We needed to get the trail users beyond 'what the department can do for them' if we were to improve our service. And within the bureaucracy, we needed to accept that we were only a 'player' in providing for the needs of trail users.

A state trail planning project provided a perfect forum to implement that perspective. Charged by the legislature with sorting out the opportunity that abandoned railroad corridors offered for trails, the group used a three-pronged strategy that was heavy on process and somewhat lighter on documentation. The first prong was to provide the legislature with an immediate "hit list" of rail-trail opportunities by tapping the instincts and knowledge of internal stakeholders. The second prong was to bring together agencies with an interest in the disposition of Minnesota's abandoned railroads: transportation, recreation, light rail, rural economic development, metropolitan government, and the University of Minnesota. We established with these agencies a dialogue that is being taken into the future and have established a plan for coordinated acquisition that moves in that direction.

Dan Collins, supervisor of trails and waterways unit, finished the story:

> The crowning jewel of the process was the third prong, how we dealt with our trail users. Minnesota has eight trail-user groups: bicyclists, hikers, skiers, equestrians, snow-mobilers, four-wheel-truck drivers, offroad motorcyclists, and all-terrain vehicle users. Trail plan coordinator Nordell was responsible for bringing each stakeholder group together and described what happened: In June, we brought each group to the table for two days of planning. Then in September we invited delegates from each of those eight groups to a congress and had another session, comparing visions and strategies. That was a real eyeopener.

The new agreement translated into dollars. In November, 1990, the trail congress organized as the Minnesota Recreational Trail Users Association. In November 1991, President Bush signed the InterModal Surface Transportation Act of 1990. In it was funding for trails. "That gave the association economic teeth, because it was in the position to become the congressionally mandated statewide trail advisory board with power to influence up to a couple of million dollars annually!," Nordell said.

Peace Between Fishing Adversaries

Constituents have had a big impact on policy and funding of the Fisheries Section of the Department of Natural Resources. Fishing is big business in Minnesota. There are two million anglers annually spending more than one billion dollars on their sport. In addition to many different anglers there are resorters, bait sellers, boat sellers and sports writers and environmentalists who have interests in Minnesota's recreational fishery. Jack Skrypek, Fisheries chief, said:

Minnesota Recreational Trail Users Association, Inc.

The Fishing Roundtable representing fifty stakeholder groups agreed to three main statewide goals — habitat improvement and protection, enlightened fisheries (individual waters) management, and new values education. "Participants, recognizing the common commitment to improving fishing regardless of conflicting strategies, agreed to respect all views and focus on quality fishing for Minnesota.

With four annual roundtable meetings complete, Fisheries management reported that these meetings have caused budget allocation changes, identified several necessary research projects, and refocused priorities on the three work areas identified. The Fishing Roundtable has drawn national recognition and is also well received by the legislators who appropriate funds and pass statutes needed to meet objectives.

Government Agencies
Learning to Buy Customer Service

There are two major benefits tax-paying Minnesotans are reaping from MAD's work. This section tells, in brief, direct results experienced in six state agencies.

Easy Service Access

A key to service improvement is to create a radical increase in user access to government resources. Currently, many useful goods and services are locked into thousands of bureaus and programs. Citizens seeking services are forced into a labor-intensive shopping trip to multiple government "specialty shops." For example, a Minnesota parent dealt with more than forty different government personnel in order to meet the social, physical, and educational needs of her handicapped child.

Minnesota state agencies are accepting the challenge to integrate state resources and are modernizing their access to the end users. The process begins by identifying customers and making changes to redesign service processes to be truly useful to the customers. Often this requires drastic measures that are difficult and painful to implement within civil service rules, union constraints, and years of tradition and past patterns. Specific efforts include education, natural resources, and internal management services.

Education

One agency that has attempted to redesign service delivery using staff involvement heavily is the Department of Education. After a twenty percent staff cut in 1991 and loud citizen calls to "fix" the education system, the department took a major leap to build a quality agency that meets the real needs of school districts and communities without administrative excess.

First, the department identified its ultimate customer and mission as "ensuring the success of every learner" and found the primary barriers to be fragmented delivery of state resources and support that was often not customized to school districts' specific needs. Furthermore, the state department was seen as the source of frustrating and restrictive rules, requirements, and mandates. Currently this all adds up to some six thousand or so rules with which school districts must comply while attempting to ensure learner success.

The Department of Education's staff and managers became actively involved in designing new systems. The department made a commitment to minimize controls and maximize support for outcome-based education at the local level. It launched a team-based organization with the hierarchy reduced from 55 managers to 25 team leaders. Frontline service teams were charged to customize the delivery of state resources to clusters of districts and communities with very similar requirements. For example, one team would serve the needs of the large cities while others serve the needs of diverse geosocial learner systems and segments. Specialized expertise areas such as school financing, special education, and curriculum support would be made available as needed to districts and communities.

But results were too slow for the governor. Midway through the implementation of the new approach, a new commissioner was appointed, resulting in a transition within the transition. As testimony to the value of involving staff, Mary Lillesve, assistant transition manager, said:

> Even though the change process has slowed, as an organization we are never going to be the same again. While the organization design plan has changed and looks more 'traditional,' a new pattern of teamwork and interchange has been established. I believe this new pattern is governed by a shared set of beliefs and goals across the department developed during the planning process.

Natural Resources

The Department of Natural Resources is also moving away from fragmented service. Although the various disciplines have consulted with one another informally for years, the goal is to create a healthy ecosystem through interdisciplinary coordination of information and personnel. In order to accomplish the ultimate goal of sustainable development, "Integrated Resource Management" is a priority approach to the stewardship of natural resources. The effort calls for maximizing the interrelationships and synergies among the department's resource-based disciplines, such as forestry, waters, minerals, fish, and wildlife. Currently, cross-disciplinary teams within the department focus on several demonstration "landscape projects" where management of resources and the interests of many stakeholders meet. Municipal and county governments are involved in planning for these areas. Other state agencies such as Agriculture, Pollution Control, and Transportation are actively involved.

Facilities Management

The Department of Administration's Plant Management Division became aware of the need for seamless services when customer interviews revealed frustration with the lack of coordination across divisions. A popular complaint involved newly laid carpeting being torn up for wiring projects; another was about custodial staff not being informed of projects affecting their work schedules. Why was cooperation between divisions so difficult? The Facilities Management Bureau, which is responsible for managing state government property, from delivering janitorial, landscape, and transfer services on the capitol grounds to monitoring state building codes, decided to do something to change the service. One major insight was that traditional vertical structuring within the bureau was a major barrier to communication and cooperation.

During planning, a staff-management team identified a systems approach as the key to their future. Moving to a "coordinated service management approach," the new system calls for cross-division responsibility for service to buildings and their tenants. It includes building managers who are responsible overall for their buildings and budgets. In a sense, they own them. To ensure implementation, the leaders have committed to involving all staff throughout the change process from the redesigning of the basic way to deliver services to the refining of almost every position. "It's a very simple axiom," said Dennis Spalla, assistant commissioner of the bureau, "but also very appropriate for the process we are experiencing: Teamwork works. It all started with a commitment to a set of goals, a change in the culture, a revival of basic values." With long-term goals established and mission and value statements as guides, the systems and structure changes are moving forward with surprising speed.

Streamlined Administration

Kudos are due to the often invisible administrative agencies that have begun to make real moves to shift traditional administrative monopolies into organizations that serve the needs of agency employees so they may, in turn, better meet the requirements of external constituencies.

They emphasize that in a service organization "there are two kinds of people, those on the front line and the rest of us" — a concept popularized by Zemke and Albrecht in their 1985 book, *Service America* [2]. In many agencies, the idea that "the rest of us" — the administrative and support services — are there not to control but to support line agencies, managers, and employees is slowly becoming a focus of active experimentation.

Personnel Systems

The Department of Employee Relations is taking steps to reform the 55-year-old civil service system, the single greatest barrier to agencies' flexibility to meet service demands. Many states share similar conclusions. One human resource system study in the State of Illinois, Cook County, and the City of Chicago represented a universal discovery that rules originally designed to minimize patronage and promote fairness were unable to do either. Even worse, observers found that these systems do not advance talented people, reward creativity, or permit flexibility in work assignments that could increase efficiency, allow creativity, and produce optimal results.

Civil service reform is one of many priorities mobilized in the Department of Employee Relations strategic planning process. As government change continues, it is clear to the department that it must play a central role in helping agencies work smarter because personnel affairs cannot be an afterthought. With more than seventy percent of agency budgets consisting of salary expenses, good human resource management is pivotal to service excellence. According to a recent agency newsletter, the Department of Employee Relations sees itself charting a new course much as Columbus did five hundred years ago:

> "We're not searching for a new world; we're searching for
> a better human resource system for the State of Minnesota,"
> said Commissioner Linda Barton. "We're talking about a

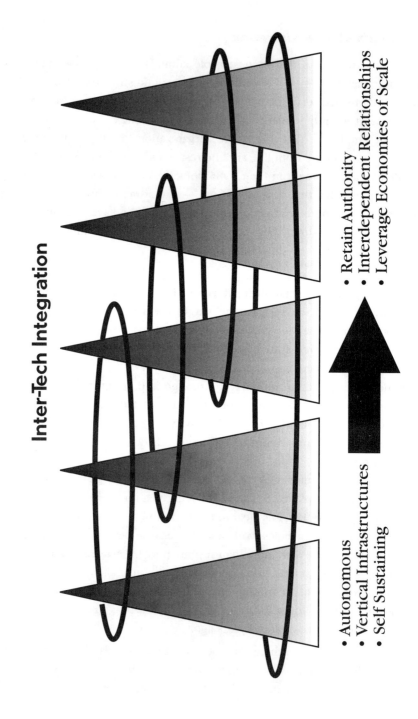

Inter-Tech Integration

- Retain Authority
- Interdependent Relationships
- Leverage Economies of Scale

- Autonomous
- Vertical Infrastructures
- Self Sustaining

major cultural change for our department and all of our customers and stakeholders. It may take us a while to complete the transition to our new approach, but it will be well worth it once we get there." The new system will be shaped with input from all stakeholders, with the objective of maintaining a necessary level of statewide consistency while allowing flexibility and delegated decision-making authority to agency managers. One immediate decision and commitment is to serve agency managers as priority customers. In providing technical assistance for hiring, promotions, classifications, and other performance management needs, Employee Relations managers and employees work hard responding to issues with advice, alternatives, and problemsolving approaches rather than the traditional dose of rules, restrictions, and regulations.

Jan Wiessner, Employee Relations deputy commissioner, noted:

One of the real lessons learned from the reform process is that stakeholder involvement is more than just getting input. Although we had involved people in focus groups, they really wanted much more, they wanted to be partners. So we formed a labor-management committee and what a difference in participation! There is a real level of commitment to outcomes, and although some of the things we are talking about now were things we had discussed during the process of the Commission on Reform and Efficiency, there is a real difference in participation. It is such a powerful message to send — that there needs to be a real investment in the change process, not just input.

Information Systems

Assistant Commissioner Bernard Conlin of the InterTechnologies Group (InterTech) of the Department of Administration called his reform effort "a fundamental reorientation." InterTech manages and operates information technology for state government and took more than a year and a half to refocus its services to customer needs in the '90s. Driven by strained relationships with agencies that were threatening to contract with outside services and staff who had seen several change efforts do little to improve the situation, InterTech's new leadership decided to try again with a different approach in 1991. This time the efforts paid off.

Conlin continued:

> Our refocusing has caused us to rethink every product, service, and position description in the organization and to realign business systems, structure, and internal communications to support lower cost and higher quality service. The amount of work it has taken to date has meant that involvement of many staff at many levels was necessary and the culture has changed as a result.

> A strategic planning effort with bureauwide and stakeholder involvement was the beginning of this reorientation. Using the mission statement and organization values as focal points, the refocusing team identified two new directions: to attain a position of state leadership in technology and to operate with a proven business capability. The main task of every participant was to focus on the future, and forget past answers to the problems. In the '50s and '60s, as technologies for managing information were emerging, single solution (mainframe) computing was the answer to agency information processing and storage needs. There were many signs that this old method was frustrating agencies. During preplanning discussions, this was verified, as agency customers indicated that this mainframe approach was out of touch with current needs. One element of our new direction is distributive processing, a different information architecture that better meets the growing information needs of agencies and their broader capacity to manage it. As we move ahead, there are no guarantees of success in implementing these fundamental changes in this complex environment, but we have to go ahead, and I am very optimistic at this point.

Management Analysis Division
Popular Products and Services

Comprehensive Studies

An in-depth agency assessment to identify areas where change will increase effectiveness, reduce costs, or both.

Diagnostic Overview

A brief review of an agency. An objective look will quickly identify trouble spots and outline what needs fixing and how the repairs might be made.

Organization Development

Guidance to help an agency move onto a proactive course for the future. Working directly with affected employees, consultants assist in long-range planning and decision making. One-to-one managerial coaching and team-building are added tools.

Service Quality Improvement

Coaching, facilitation, and instruction in the use of total quality tools to improve client service.

Legislative Studies

Comprehensive research and analysis to aid policy decision making.

Organizational Structure Design

Analysis and recommendations for effective structure, authorities, and responsibilities.

Work Flow Simplification

Analysis and recommendations for eliminating duplication, unnecessary steps, and confusion in agency work processes.

Benchmarking

Comparing key components of service delivery with similiar operations in government or industry to find a cheaper, better, or faster way to do a job.

Purchasing Systems

Of the many operations in government, the purchasing function is one system that affects virtually every state operation. The Department of Administration's Materials Management Division is responsible for the acquisition, inventory management, and disposal of state assets. Traditionally viewed by line agencies as a significant bureaucratic wall with sizable controls on purchasing and contracting, it has often been compared to the red-tape laden civil service system. Bob Schroeder, assistant commissioner of the department's Operations Management Bureau, which includes Materials Management, explained the changes:

> In order to become more user-friendly, Materials Management recently decided to shift to a commodity-based service delivery structure that enables its customers — the line agency managers and employees — to quickly access advice and technical assistance in acquiring the best valued product or service in any commodity area and gives more local autonomy for acquisition decisions. In the past, the division required the customer to interact through two units, purchasing or contracting. An important support for the new structure will be the comprehensive training arm of the division, which will not only aid acquisition, but also educate customers about their statutory responsibilities for society-valued purchases dealing with environmental, human rights, and small or targeted-group business considerations and purchasing.

Management Systems

One of many large agencies that acknowledges the importance of effective management systems is the Department of Natural Resources. Commissioner Rod Sando is a firm believer in the need for good internal processes to support agency leaders:

> Improvement processes take a long time to implement and get comfortable with, but the investment is worthwhile. The payoffs are there. We have seen gains in our external service capacity through real improvements in internal practices — conflict resolution, skills integration, internal

efficiency, implementing change, moving beyond the limits of traditional approaches, greater participation, higher morale, and quality decisions. I cannot underscore enough the importance of using professional, action-oriented processes to assist leaders in designing, enhancing, and coordinating management processes that produce results for users and taxpayers.

Making the right plans and decisions about Minnesota's natural resource use is a task we don't take lightly. The state of Minnesota is a top ten landowner in the United States and the DNR manages many acres of parks, forests, prairies, and wildlife areas. We employ between 2500 and 3000 people and our many divisions deal with all aspects of resource use and protection. We regularly interact with hundreds of customer and constituency groups that are critical partners in resource use and management.

We have a big push for productive internal systems, or 'ORGWARE,' that enable good ideas to really happen on the land. Top management must take and has taken a proactive role in directing continuous improvement in internal management and organization. Good management means (1) knowing when systems and practices need to change and (2) knowing how to change them. To assist the top managers, we have a department-wide management improvement team and professional staff who provide expertise in planning, organization development, information systems, constituent feedback mechanisms, stakeholder roundtables, employee participation vehicles, and teamwork systems. To stay current, we refine our directions every two years.

Continuous Improvement

The State of Minnesota is on a never-ending journey of invention. Current initiatives will continue, but fundamental change will require a stronger commitment to collaboration and performance accountability.

Seamless government will continue to be the challenge to improve service delivery. As a quick glance at the latest front page assures, much change happens within the state executive branch. But it only accounts for a mere 9.6 percent of state expenditures. The rest is allocated to local governments and school districts for the important business of delivery of direct services in education, health care, human services, transportation, and local government.

Close collaboration between federal, state, and local governments is no longer an option (if it ever were) if people's needs are to be met. For example, there are currently some 14 agencies dealing in some area of environmental protection and a similar number dealing with early-childhood education. Quantum leaps are needed to make government services simple, accessible, and useful to citizens, perhaps through neighborhood and community government service centers that handle everything from fishing licenses to welfare payments. Until all branches and levels of government join forces to eliminate duplications and integrate services to meet citizen needs, reform may amount to reinventing bureaucracy rather than to a fundamental change in delivering public service.

Linking Resources to Results

In an editorial on why government efficiency studies fail, Robert Walker, a retired program evaluator, said, "Committees studying government efficiency should realize that no one really knows if the government is effective or efficient because government does not measure what it does" [3]. A critical starting point to outcome-based government is to develop the common measures and common information sources that drive decision making, first about budget, tax dollars and, second, about targeting policy and programs. Easier said than done.

Small efforts are under way to install common goals and measures between the executive and legislative branches, but traditional gaps in trust, information, and communication continue to be fundamental barriers to decisions with a long-term view. A December, 1992 *Star Tribune* opinion piece described the governor's preparation of the state's budget and reported on the progress being made with respect to outcome-based management in government:

...Little noticed is a major change in state budget processes. It puts Minnesota in the forefront of government reform. More than states elsewhere, Minnesota broadly has begun linking budgets to measurable results. The change will take years to blossom fully. But if it succeeds, Minnesota policy makers, including the governor, agency officials, and legislators, will have better decision-making tools for achieving government effectiveness and efficiency. The public would get more for its tax dollars.

In June, 1994 [Gov.] Carlson told agency heads that the state's recurring financial crises require dramatic change in setting priorities and budgets. Spending must be linked to results. That would force agencies to set priorities, make choices, and defend their actions in understandable ways. The work of Minnesota Milestones, State Planning's effort to develop citizen goals, created a context for changing the budget process... A bigger impact will come in later years, when tomorrow's results can be compared with today's objectives — and when measurements and processes can be refined and improved. Evidence about program successes and failures can help sharpen management practices, determine priorities, and match limited resources and critical needs. All Minnesotans should welcome that [4].

The task ahead is immense. The primary challenge is to maintain hope — in the human capacity to envision desired futures and invent ways to bring them about. The Minnesota experience is a testimony to the age-old formula that where there is a will there is a way. The seminal learnings of the Minnesota case studies might be summarized as follows:

- All stakeholders in the system are needed to engineer transformation. Investment in participation processes that access wisdom and commitment of all people takes patience and time, but yields results that quick fixes cannot deliver.
- One size does not fit all—or even most. Every organization has unique system challenges and complexities that provide the raw material for producing customized innovations in service redesign and delivery.

- Unlocking the latent potential and motivation of all people is the fundamental task of management. Building the future requires risk-taking at all levels of the organization team. Committed leadership, good processes, and redeploying resources to truly support service people are the ingredients of real empowerment.

The American democratic experiment is only two centuries old. It is time to give it a major physical and spiritual exam. Corrections must—and can—be made to adjust the social innovation of another age to align with the realities of twenty-first century society.

References

[1] McGrath, Dennis J. "State seeking change in bureaucracy's core, plus big cost savings," *Star Tribune*, Minneapolis, Sept. 15, 1991.

[2] Zemke, Ron, and Karl Albrecht, *Service America*, Dow Jones-Irwin, Homewood, Ill., 1985.

[3] Walker, Robert A., "Why government efficiency studies fail," *Star Tribune*, Minneapolis, June 9, 1990. (Walker of St. Paul is a retired operator of a program evaluation service.)

[4] Inskip, Leonard, "Results-based budget will help Minnesota," *Star Tribune*, Minneapolis, Dec. 6, 1992.

Models of
Excellence

Chapter 8
Models of Excellence

CATHERINE A. RATEGAN AND KENNETH O'HARE

What if government officials were to tap the wisdom of their employees, the ones who know how things really work? What kind of creative governmental drama might empowered employees stage? What would it look like to reform local government from within, bit by bit? In Chicago, long known for its "machine" politics and patronage-heavy workforce, a nonprofit community foundation, the Chicago Community Trust, initiated a program called Models of Excellence (MOE). Since 1992, it has been posing a novel paradigm for reform.

The Models of Excellence (MOE) program is a tough-minded, Chicago-style attempt to bring the local public sector into the modern world of customer-driven, responsive, and efficient government. Working through problem-solving teams of government workers, MOE's mission is to instill quality management processes in Chicago's municipal and county governments. As part of its vision to improve public services through employee participation, MOE treats government workers as partners. According to MOE's creator, Joyce Hollingsworth, "Models of Excellence offers government workers a set of tools that lets them examine their own work and change it for the better."

MOE is sponsored by Hollingsworth's employer, the Government Assistance Project or GAP, a program of the Chicago Community Trust, a 78-year-old community foundation that uses the income from its endowment to fund charitable and civic initiatives in the Chicago area. In addition to backing MOE, GAP sponsors planning and networking among government agencies.

Facing Realities of Big City Government

Across the nation taxpayers want government to be cost-effective, businesslike, and even creative. Already, "privatization"—contracting out governmental functions—is an on-rushing reality for many government workers. But, the challenge to stem this trend is daunting. After all, the stereotype of the big city government worker is tinged with truth. Though not the rule, in big city government, patronage workers with low standards and retirement-oriented drones are a reality.

It is MOE's core belief that centralized, authoritarian environments encrusted with bureaucratic procedures sap the initiative of good workers. In their efforts to uncover the root causes of problems, the MOE teams are encouraged to ask, "Why do we do it this way?" They find that the most typical answer is, "That's how they showed me to do it when I started here." In such a setting, the bottom line too often becomes one of, "Make no mistakes and take no risks."

While some ask if participation can work for government, the real question is whether it can work in the big cities where patronage has been the rule for so long. Can government's own workers themselves improve governmental services? What new kinds of leaders and innovative approaches are needed? Recognizing that one obstacle to improvement in Chicago and other big cities is the high rate of turnover in appointed positions, MOE decided early to focus on what it calls the "B Team." "These are the people who will be there when top management comes and will be there when it goes," says Hollingsworth.

Within 18 months of its beginning in 1992, MOE's multirank teams of management and line workers in six agencies had begun solving real problems in ten city and county agencies, ranging from the park district, to the city human services department, to the county's purchasing office. By the end of that period, MOE was actually garnering rave reviews. The

Chicago Tribune, in a May, 1993 editorial headed "Extra! Government Made to Work!" said of the Models of Excellence:

> The results show this public-private partnership can, indeed, make government function better. There is also a less tangible benefit. It gives good people working in seemingly deaf and dumb government bureaucracies a chance to have their voices heard.

The accomplishments were noticed by officials, too. Said Hollingsworth, "When agency leaders saw the impact this new approach could have on their workforces, it really captured their attention. Many of them wanted to go deeper and apply the improvement process systemwide to more agency problems." The co-leader of an MOE project team in the city's Department of Human Services, Denise Kennedy, said that officials "were surprised that in-house people could put together something that was really consultant quality."

Delivering a New Public Library System

The experience of one agency, the Chicago Public Library, illustrates the dramatic results achieved by MOE's participatory approach. Versie Barnes is a determined person. But by the time she'd worked at the Chicago Public Library for 16 years, she no longer believed that the system for internal delivery of books and mail between the main library and any one of its 83 branch sites could ever be anything other than unreasonably slow. Then, early in 1992, Barnes was chosen to lead a team of library employees in a MOE program to develop a new delivery system.

In the past, outside consultants had been asked to improve the system, to no avail. This time, the actual workers who know the system set out to find a solution. The scope of the problem uncovered by team members surprised even those familiar with the Byzantine ways of a bureaucracy. A sampling proved that it took an average of six days for a book to be delivered from one library to a library in another district. Interlibrary mail required as long as three and one-half days to reach its destination. Library team member Dave Natelson describes the prevailing system, "We were dealing with 50 or 60 years of a built-up bureaucracy, with more rules being added all the time. We were in cement with all the rules." Adds Versie

Barnes, "Everybody knew for years that the system was bad. But we felt we just had to accept it."

One of the first steps in overhauling the delivery system was to analyze the routes of the book and mail delivery vehicles. In an effort to determine customer priorities, a one-page survey was sent to all library branch heads and regional library directors. Of the 93 survey forms sent, 90% were returned with telling comments. Team members found that most of the library's fleet of delivery trucks had been in service for well over four years. They also discovered that, on any day, at least one-half the trucks in the fleet were out for repair, at costs that could total as much as $900 for each repair job. A study revealed that the expense of running one particularly troubled vehicle actually averaged $186 a mile. When team members presented this data to management, library executives decided that it made better sense to lease trucks rather than own a fleet. "We didn't recommend leasing as a solution," emphasizes team member Roberta Webb. "What we did was focus on the problem. Then management came up with the solution."

Chicago Public Library

Control Chart

Cycle Time for Inter-branch Book Delivery

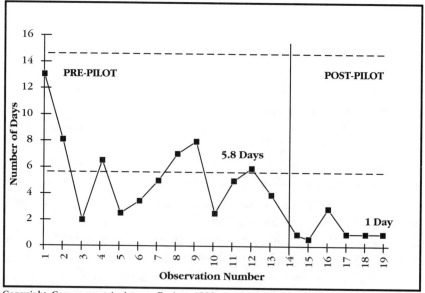

Chicago Public Library

Percent of Respondents Ranking
Delivery Characteristic as Top Priority

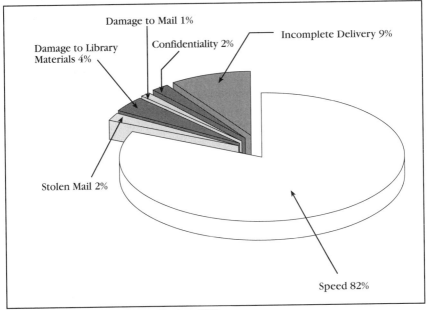

For a time, at the height of the problem-solving process, Versie Barnes' life was given over to it. "I lived it and breathed it," she recalls. "I took stuff home and worked nights and weekends. It was like a mystery and a challenge, and we couldn't fail." Why was she so compelled? "I'd been living with this problem for years, and finally we had a chance to make a difference—to come up with a solution." She smiles. "I felt so good doing it. I said, this is so sharp."

The team studied municipal library systems in other cities where they found that libraries with fewer branches often devoted more drivers, staff, and vehicles to the delivery process than were assigned in Chicago. Barnes personally studied the interagency delivery system in New York City, the largest library system in the country. New York has eight more branches than the Chicago library system and regularly meets its goal of 24-hour interagency delivery. "I got so energized by the system in New York," she recalls. "I kept raving about how they were so streamlined and efficient without a lot of layers."

Identify Potential Causes
Cause and Effect Diagram

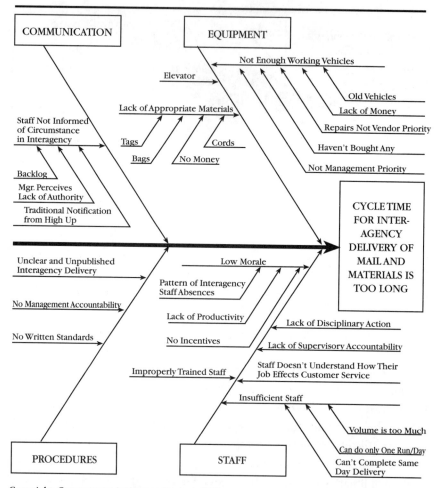

Copyright, Government Assistance Project, 1993

Moving Beyond Blame

Like many of the other GAP sponsored teams, library team members in trying to peel off extra layers of bureaucracy, faced opposition from their co-workers, many of whom saw the team as a threat. "People had a misconception about what we were doing," says Barnes. "They thought it was about finger-pointing." She sighs, "It wasn't easy to convince people that it's not about blame. You can say it a hundred times, but people who are responsible for a certain department or a certain operation think they're to blame for it."

Barnes continues, "They'd see us coming to a meeting carrying our easels, and they'd say, 'Who are they to think they can do this?' They felt we were part of the problem because we were uncovering inadequacies in the system. "It was a very difficult year for me," Barnes remembers, "very stressful and time-consuming. But it was also the most exhilarating assignment I've ever had. All the stress and pressure stiffened my resolve to make it work."

Another challenge was a series of personnel changes at the library, which had four different agency directors in the two years spanned by the project. However, team members received strong support from First Deputy Commissioner and Chief Librarian, Carla Hayden, who played a pivotal role in championing the team's work. "Support from top leadership is critical to any team," says Joyce Hollingsworth, GAP's program director, "and the team had to face the stress and tension associated with a transition at the commissioner level. However, they stayed focused on their primary objective, and they persevered." Team members combined the data they gathered with their first-hand knowledge of the library to design a new process for moving books and mail. Because the new system allows each site to sort its own materials, with no need to go to a central point for resorting, the new system cuts days out of the delivery process.

The next step was to test the process. Team members chose the system's northeast district with its 19 neighborhood libraries and one regional library as a test site — in part because District Chief Tamiye Trejo had asked that her district be the pilot site. While new to total quality management (TQM), Tamiye Trejo had seen what empowered workers could accomplish. Says Trejo, "The employees in this district were willing to do the extra work involved in trying out the new process because we wanted to see if we could change the whole system."

The GAP team members spent a week teaching staff members at the pilot sites how to use the new process. "We showed them the basics," says Versie Barnes, "and then they came up with some improvements of their own, including a lot of things we hadn't even thought of." What was the reaction of workers at the test site to the new system? "At first they were a little cynical," says district chief Trejo, "but once they saw how it worked, they were really enthusiastic. They felt it set our district apart from others in the system."

To demonstrate just how well the new process worked, team members measured the new delivery times and found they had reduced the time required for book and mail delivery up to 92 percent. In the process, they reduced the number of steps in delivering mail from 23 to 5, and from 34 to 10 steps for intradistrict book delivery. Best of all, the time required for intradistrict- to-district materials delivery was cut to a maximum of 24 hours— even to as little as half an hour. In one case, workers using the new system were able to deliver a book from another branch to a library patron while she was still in the library. All this without adding extra people, and without placing blame on anybody for what was really a faulty system.

Workers Designing New Systems

By July, 1993, library management had approved the new process for installation systemwide. Then, they phased it in, one district at a time, with each district helping to train the next one in line. It is expected that the new process will be in place throughout the library less than three years after TQM team members began their work. When that happens, all branches of the Chicago Public Library will realize for the first time the benefits of a delivery system designed by its workers. And, since continuous improvement is one of the cornerstones of quality management, two representatives of the original pilot district will continue to monitor the process, searching for ways to fine tune it.

Although she came to the library after the system for book and mail delivery began its phase-in, Library Commissioner Mary Dempsey is an enthusiastic supporter of the problem-solving process. "Rather than relying on reactive quick fixes, [TQM] uses hard data to uncover root causes," says Dempsey. "Recommendations that come out of TQM teams are realistic, practical and custom-made for our organization." Commissioner Dempsey is also a believer in worker input as she attests:

[This process demonstrates] that, given the opportunity, front-line staff are quite capable of solving complex problems. Using the TQM tools we've learned, we can solve a myriad of difficult issues, and the experience of one successful project [serves as] a catalyst for other improvements.

To work on those improvements, library management appointed two additional problem-solving teams, which began their work during 1993. One was assigned to simplify and standardize the process of preparing books for use by the public. The other was asked to establish standard purchasing guidelines throughout the library system. Commissioner Dempsey expresses delight at team members who found the TQM project the most rewarding experience of their professional career. "Many of these comments come from staff who've been with the library for over twenty years," says Dempsey. "As a commissioner, that gets my attention."

Serving as the team's facilitator throughout the TQM process was D. J. Smith, an independent training specialist. She comments,

The team has proven what employees can accomplish with the support of management. One reason for their success was that the team was made up of people who represented different parts of the library system. Each of them brought a different approach to the problem and a different viewpoint. People have the potential to use their imagination to solve their own problems. These team members knew what to do, and they got the go-ahead from management to do it. It shows how much talent and ability organizations lose when employees don't feel their input matters.

Smith contends that worker empowerment simply means giving employees a climate in which they can function.

For team leader Versie Barnes, her reward is being able to make a difference. "To see our work pay off like this, and to see it come not from a consultant but from a team within the library — that's the best story the library can tell."

FUNDAMENTAL ELEMENTS OF TQM

Shift Management

↓

Leadership

Reward & Recognize Team Achievements

Focus on Customers

Involve Line Staff on Project Teams

Educate the Workforce

Make Decisions Based on Data

Children Services Division

The experience of MOE in another agency, the Chicago Department of Human Services, Children Services Division, illustrates the critical role that executive leadership plays in effective worker participation. A profile of the activities of Maria Whelan, director of the division, shows the impact of a leader in action. One day she blew through the office like a tornado, her customary style, and loudly proclaimed, "I've found it!" as she unrolled a big poster with the word "WHINING" stamped out like a No-U-Turn sign. As the newly appointed director at the Children Services Division of Chicago's Department of Human Services she was about the business of developing the division's new corporate culture — one that would allow people to laugh with each other and move ahead with their shared mission of service to children.

The division, responsible for the quality of care given to 21,000 children enrolled in day care centers and Head Start programs throughout the city of Chicago, funds and monitors 110 contractors called *"delegate agencies"*—

non-profit groups that provide direct services to children and families at 300 centers. Yet, despite its key assignment, red tape and an old-fashioned bureaucratic structure stifled the division. Even worse, the adversarial rules-and-regulations stance by the division blocked a working partnership with the delegate agencies. Acting from the central office and isolated from the realities in the field, divisional employees were often arbitrary or erratic in interpreting rules. What could an appointed director, working through such a structure, do to improve the quality of child care in Chicago?

With the backing of her new boss, Dan Alvarez, the Commissioner of Human Services, Whelan challenged people to discard their hierarchical habits. When managers came to her, timidly, to ask what to do next, Whelan would reply, "I don't know. What do you think we should do?" Slowly, Whelan's message took hold. In a series of GAP-sponsored focus groups, the Children Services employees began to talk about the division's shortcomings — haphazard systems, painfully slow communications, and too much red tape in coordinating child care facility inspections with other government agencies, such as the health and fire departments.

Considering Agencies as Customers

Whelan knew she had to produce a sense of hope and teamwork. "The level of skepticism and cynicism was certainly very high," she said. To break through the division's malaise, she called an all-staff retreat to produce the division's first strategic plan. The result? — considering the division's delegate agencies as "customers" of the division, rather than as contractual subordinates to be ordered about. With this shift in perspective, and the boss's permission to be frank in naming problems and participatory in solving them, the most important part of Whelan's work was done. What remained was implementation.

Today, an MOE-sponsored monitoring systems team in the Children Service Division is gathering data about whether specialists at several select-ed pilot sites can use a new form created by the team to deliver better tech-nical assistance to its customers—the delegate agencies. Though their analysis is not yet complete, the team is convinced that this simple change will make a measurable difference in relationships with their customers.

"The agencies we monitor felt that we were talking down to them," said Lois Jackson, co-facilitator for MOE's projects in the division. To counter this perception, the team asked its newly found customers what was important to them and in the process made a surprising discovery. The delegate agencies most wanted two reforms at the bottom of the division's own list: more access to training and a more knowledgeable divisional staff, specifically one that could give more useful technical assistance. In response, a new reporting form, developed by the monitoring systems team and now being tested, should allow the division's specialists— nutritionists, facilities' inspectors, staff qualifications experts—to identify needed assistance accurately and deliver it quickly.

Despite the customer-responsive work of the monitoring systems team, skepticism about participatory problem solving remains. According to Jackson, "Folks have the notion we [the team] are trying to catch them, but we are not", according to Jackson. "We are just trying to improve the process." But resistance only stiffened the team's resolve according to team co-facilitator, Doris Fields. "The more they tried to downplay our work, the more determined we became to make it work."

Forming Communication Teams

Emboldened, some Children Service Division employees have identified other challenges and formed two more teams with MOE's help. Communications Team A decided to face the crisis of painfully slow written communications. It was a challenge at best to direct letters, announcements, policy guidance, and meeting notices initiated by divisional staff to the delegate agencies in a timely manner. Documents first had to run a bureaucratic gauntlet involving as many as 45 different types of delays.

Team A found that it took over seven days on average for a document to move from initiation to its final destination. Important, time-sensitive material would arrive well past the date it could be used. Using its insider knowledge of the division, Team A encouraged notice writers and typists to form production teams to streamline this unwieldy process. They triumphed when their redesigned process lobbed two days off the delivery lag time.

Communications Team B focused on the problem of how telephones are answered in the division. Callers with questions about meetings and training sessions frequently encountered staff members who knew nothing about upcoming events. Phones sometimes went unanswered, calls were bounced around, and messages did not reach their destinations, breaking the critical flow of information between the division and the delegate agencies who care for children. Team B asked its customers — people who call in and divisional staff who field incoming calls — for input. From customer responses, the team discovered a need to brief the staff who answer phones about upcoming events and to find a way to relay messages to divisional staff who work most of the time in the field with delegate agencies. To get a first hand experience of contemporary phone practices, the team went to private industry and visited the switchboard at the Motorola Corporation in suburban Chicago.

After analyzing their findings, Team B briefed top city executives on the division's jumbled approach to answering telephones. The executives were so impressed that they immediately approved the team's recommendations for updated equipment and methods at four pilot sites. The team applied for state and federal funds to underwrite the effort, and two of the sites soon installed new telephone equipment and voice mail systems. To cement its achievements, the team drafted new phone procedures and put them into a central information handbook, along with a calendar of events. They also set up a system of mailboxes and bulletin boards to convey needed information. The result: more promptly answered calls and a better informed staff.

Reflecting on the stresses of employee participation, the team co-leader, Ann Young, said that team cohesion grew only gradually. "We did a lot of storming, but after the storming we got on with the job. We worked by consensus, learning to bring everything to the team meeting and not to go off independently, unless something was assigned as an independent project." According to team co-leader, Denise Kennedy, getting buy-in from some team members was difficult. "At the start, some people didn't understand the whole idea of worker empowerment, and they caved in when their supervisors gave them a hard time about attending team meetings."

More Models of Excellence Projects

Additional MOE projects are now underway in nine agencies of city and county government in Chicago, where 12 MOE teams are working to streamline agency operations and improve the quality of service to the

The Problem-Solving Process

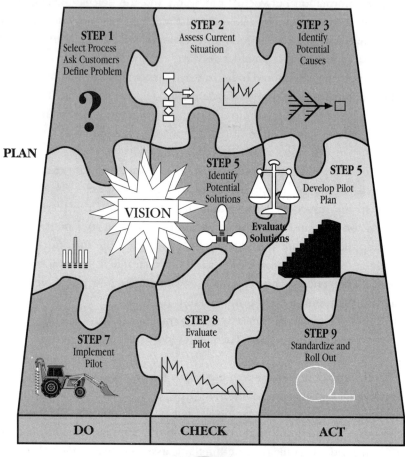

STEP 1
Select Process
Ask Customers
Define Problem

STEP 2
Assess Current
Situation

STEP 3
Identify
Potential
Causes

PLAN

?

VISION

STEP 5
Identify
Potential
Solutions

Evaluate
Solutions

STEP 5
Develop Pilot
Plan

STEP 7
Implement
Pilot

STEP 8
Evaluate
Pilot

STEP 9
Standardize and
Roll Out

DO

CHECK

ACT

CELEBRATE

public. Working in multirank teams that reflect the diversity of the governmental workforce and the need to decentralize decisions and accountability, team members are re-envisioning their agency as a kind of business, which must cut costs and red tape while increasing efficiency and productivity if team members' jobs are to survive in the long term. The work is hard, the changes are often painful, but the dividend for team members in several Chicago agencies is a sense of personal accomplishment and a welcome new quality of worklife in the public sector.

Chicago Department of Health

In 1991 the Chicago Department of Health's sexually transmitted disease (STD) clinics turned away 12,000 patients due, in part, to procedural inefficiencies. Staff members felt helpless. "We knew we were turning patients away," said the Department's Susan Albovias, M.D., "but we couldn't figure out what to do about it or where to begin." An MOE team of eight health workers set out to tackle the problem. "We found that a lot of employees weren't doing the work they were hired for," said Chris Kosmos, a co-leader of the team. Doctors were doing lab work and lab technicians were doing paperwork. Less than 2% of the time of licensed practical nurses was spent on direct patient care.

By acting on the underlying procedural causes of the problem, the team increased direct patient care time almost fourfold, from 10% to 37%. Health Commissioner Sheila Lyne observes, "It proves to me that we need not be restrained by barriers, real or imaginary, when we can tap into this kind of creativity."

Cook County Central Services

The Cook County Central Services Department, which handles installation and repair of over 35,000 government phone lines, was swamped with requests for help. When an MOE team was formed, they found that many work orders were incomplete, lacking authorization, or simply lost. No system tracked orders and their status. "Work orders came to us on memos, scratch paper, napkins, and paper plates," recalls MOE team member Sue Boyd.

To correct this mess, the team created a standard telecommunications request form, banned oral requests for service, and set up a system to log in and track work orders. At first, the task of changing the system met with resistance from team members. "They didn't believe that anything positive would come out of this," recalls team co-leader Deputy Director Dudley Donelson. Eventually, according to team facilitator, Don Bushman, "The team saw that no one involved in the old system was a 'bad' person." By the time the team reported on its accomplishments, a test of the new system in the offices of the county's chief judges had cut the time to process a telecommunications work order from six days to one day.

Cook County Hospital

Another organization to cut through the bureaucratic tangle was Cook County Hospital, one of the largest public hospitals in the country, admitting over 30,000 patients every year. From bandages to bedpans, the efficient distribution of supplies to the hospital's wards affects the well-being of patients. Yet critical care units were running out of supplies 44 times a day on the average. And deliveries were not scheduled on weekends, a real problem in the 24-hour, 7-day-a-week world of critical care. "It was frightening to come in on Monday and find that stock levels were down to zero," recalls MOE team member James Bluemberg.

To improve the availability of supplies, the hospital's MOE team set up a pilot program in eight critical care units. The team cut the delivery process from 26 to 14 steps, added Saturday delivery, printed a supplies catalog, and reassigned certain elevators for stock deliveries. The system is now being extended hospital-wide. "We took a chance on improving the system, and it worked," said Mariellen Mason-Gamble, the team co-leader.

Cook County Purchasing Agent

Part of the streamlining procedures involved county agencies in tapping into the miracles of modern technology. Before the MOE project took root, the Cook County Purchasing Agent's office issued about 8,000 requisitions every year to purchase everything from pencils to surgical equipment to buildings. Unbelievably, it was all done manually. "Emergency" purchases caused by expired contracts were costing the county big money. To expedite matters, an informal "sneaker" network walked contracts through a contract renewal process involving hundreds of pieces of paper.

Within a year, the MOE team saw the installation of a new, networked computer system, along with policies and procedures for timely notification of contractors. How could so much be accomplished by an employee team in so short a time? Team leader Dennis Coatar said, "It's a testimony to the team process. It's very intense. We all supported each other, and even when the process seemed to go on forever, we just put our heads down and kept plodding along." Woods Bowman, the county's chief financial officer said, "What they were doing was so engaging they took it on themselves to come in to work at 7:30 in the morning. They did it because they knew it would make everybody's life easier later on."

Chicago Department of Housing

The MOE's approach also succeeded in reducing utility costs for low-income households to safeguard residents against Chicago's merciless winters. Each year the Chicago Department of Housing weatherizes more than 3,000 homes in a process that includes weather-stripping, caulking, insulating, installing storm windows, and repairing furnaces. Delays in completing final inspection and approval were snarling completion of these important projects.

To speed up the inspections, the MOE team sparked Housing Department automation of the system for tracking inspections. By 1995, all weatherization jobs will go through the computer system. The team also set up a prototype weatherization training house to showcase everyday problems with weatherization and inspections. For team members, the work has offered professional advantages. Said Linda Shanks, team co-leader, "I learned how to work as part of a team, and how to analyze a situation instead of just reacting to it or assuming what someone else is thinking."

The Chicago Park District

During the summer of 1993, MOE team members at the Chicago Park District pretended to be citizens who wanted to register for Park District classes. They charted how much time elapsed between first contacting a park employee and actual enrollment. The results ranged from 30 minutes to 120 hours, with an average of 29 hours. The pace was glacial, with over 100 contributing causes of delay, ranging from misprinted course announcements to the entrenched practice of having the actual class instructor enroll each participant. If an instructor were not in, would-be registrants would be told to come back some other time to register. Not only was the registration process haphazard, there was little effort to inform citizens about Park District offerings.

Working from the point of view of the customer — the park patron — the MOE team revamped the entire process. They designed an informative and inviting program flyer, along with a new bilingual registration form to replace one used since the 1950s. In three local parks operating as registration test sites over a three-month period, registrations were completed in less than six minutes on average. "That's as much time as it takes to come into the park to get a drink of water," said team member Anita Hanserd. "Our success as a team proves that it's not just management that has the answers," says team leader Janice Geden, "and that you'll find the same caring and commitment at all levels."

Cook County Contract Compliance Office

Further focus on the citizen as customer occurred when the Cook County's Contract Compliance office set out to ensure that minorities and women gain access to county-generated business opportunities. According to law, at least one-quarter of county purchases must go to minority business enterprises (MBEs) , with another ten percent going to women-owned business enterprises (WBEs). Yet, the MOE team, which includes some of the office's "customers" as well as staff, found that notices to the two types of enterprises about contracting opportunities were infrequent, and often were mailed too late to be of use in preparing a bid.

To reach out to its customers, instead of merely reacting to inquiries, the office's MOE team created a mass-mailed newsletter and list of prime contracts. Says Gene Dibble, a team member and minority business owner himself, "Minority and women business owners must know who the prime bidders are so we can target our marketing efforts at non-MBE/WBE companies who might be interested in having us participate with them in the bidding process." Now, minority and women entrepreneurs have the information they need to prepare bids and identify potential subcontracting opportunities with prime contractors — a step toward improved business competitiveness for minorities and women.

Forest Preserve District of Cook County

An MOE survey of county residents revealed that customers of the Forest Preserve District (FPD) had one chance in ten of getting a busy signal, no answer, or being disconnected when they called for information. FPD manages 67,000 acres of land and 350 facilities throughout Cook County. Even when callers were successful in getting through to the staff, they often received incorrect or outdated information about FPD programs and facilities.

To better respond to their customers, the MOE team created a resource manual with answers to the most often asked questions, trained FPD telephone operators, and put in an 800 number. They recommended the creation of a separate department dedicated solely to customer inquiries. To accomplish all this, the team had to overcome significant resistance from co-workers. "Our co-workers were our first customers," said team co-leader Sue Holt, "and we had to convince them before we could improve our service to the public." Terry Lavenhagen, the team's other co-leader, said, "There's an overall awareness now that there's a new game in town, and it's called customer satisfaction."

Cook County Department of Facilities Management

In another example of Cook County inefficiency, governmental customers of one county maintenance agency were frustrated by slow service on everything from changing light bulbs to cleaning floors. Cook County's Department of Facilities Management maintains 39 county buildings. The system for managing this massive amount of space was mind-boggling in complexity. It took an average of 14.7 days for a work order to go through. As an additional snag, high priority projects for influential customers meant that lesser jobs had to be put on hold.

In the search for customer-oriented solutions, the department's MOE team surveyed users of the work order system and studied a similar private-sector operation at the John Hancock Center in Chicago. Using the 14-story Cook County Courts Administration Building as a test case, the MOE team cut the average time for a work order to move through the system to 3.9 days.

Lessons Learned

The string of successes outlined in this chapter may seem to be only small triumphs in a mammoth bureaucracy. But small gains are meaningful in an environment as large as the city of Chicago and Cook County, spurring quality government services through employee participation is a formidable challenge. It requires committed leaders who can encourage often entrenched employees to break old molds. Even with committed leadership, it takes time and persistence for stakeholder participation to take hold and grow. As MOE Director, Joyce Hollingsworth observes:

> Now that we are into our third year, it's clear the process is having a strong impact at our client agencies....City and county agencies are learning that they can streamline government services to be more responsive, and they can do it without adding staff or increasing costs.

In Chicago, the MOE teams' energy, accomplishments, and sheer desire to achieve change offer hope and a growing number of concrete accomplishments. "The teams," says the director, "are the wave of the future."

3 CORNERSTONES FOR BUILDING CHANGE

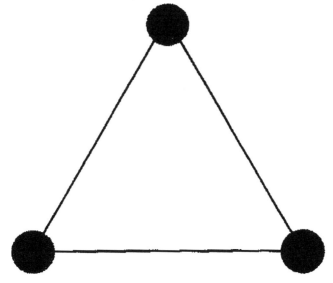

GUIDING IDEAS
- ▲ Mission and Vision
- ▲ Strategic Directions
- ▲ Values
- ▲ Goals and Measures

PEOPLE SYSTEMS
- ▲ Culture of Participation
- ▲ Cross-Functional Structure
- ▲ Team Recognition
- ▲ Communication & Feedback

COMMON TOOLS
- ▲ Management Theory
- ▲ Training Curriculum & Methods
- ▲ Planning & Analysis Strategies
- ▲ Reporting Formats

Chapter 9
Reshaping a Judicial System

HEIDI KOLBE

"We decided things could change. We decided we could work together to create new solutions to overwhelming problems such as increasing criminal case load, increasing incarceration rates, jail overcrowding and escalating costs. We had a new spirit and enthusiasm. Rather than jealously guarding our independence, we realized that all the justice agencies needed to coordinate our activities to solve the problems."
— Judge Roger Warren

t wasn't really a job he wanted. It didn't fit him. He had not counted on becoming a black-robed judge. Unfortunately it was too late. He had attempted unsuccessfully on February 27, 1976, the day of his appointment, to get "unappointed" from the Sacramento, California Municipal Court bench. But the Governor's office had released the news of his appointment to the press. So reluctantly, Judge Roger Warren reported for work to his new boss, the presiding judge. "He wasn't too impressed with my long hair and Birkenstocks," recalls Judge Roger Warren, "He just rubbed his forehead."

The Challenge Grows

Judge Roger Warren found that he had agreed to serve a system that seemed to be getting worse, not better. The problems escalated during the 1980s when Sacramento County experienced a 32 percent population growth. This growth brought an increase in crime and a greater demand for justice services. The government's response toward crime was to take a tougher stance. Police cracked down on substance abuse crimes and teenage gangs, and criminal sentences and penalties were increased by the legislature. As the criminal caseload grew, more police officers were hired, more judgeships created, and more offenders were arrested and incarcerated. The county constructed a new main jail at a great cost to house those incarcerated offenders. Despite all these efforts, and a tenfold increase in spending on the system, crime increased. During 1990, 61,342 adults and 7,792 juveniles were arrested in Sacramento County, representing 6.6 percent of the entire population. Analysis showed that the number of arrests was increasing at a significantly faster rate than the population growth. Felony adult arrests soared, with serious violent crimes and drug law violations accounting for nearly one-fourth of the total. Similar patterns were evident among juveniles. The increased arrests were overwhelming police, corrections, and courts, and seriously crowding the jails and juvenile facilities. Public confidence in the criminal justice system was at an all-time low. As Judge Warren recalls:

> Everyone realized that the local government did not have
> the money to handle the increasing criminal caseload, espe-
> cially if we just stuck to the standard response of arresting,
> prosecuting, and incarcerating criminals.

Agency administrators and elected officials also expressed their own concerns about the inadequacies of the criminal justice system. In 1990, they looked back at the changes made to the system and concluded that the increased staffing, the facility and technology modernization, and the additional funding had only barely allowed the system to keep pace with the rise in arrests without addressing the root causes of the increases.

As of 1994, the Sacramento Court system is viewed as a model both within the state and nationally. As Yolanda Williams, assistant court administrator observes:

> The experiences that the court has been involved with have
> resulted in a more focused court with a clear direction that
> is more flexible and adaptable to change. The court is more
> involved in looking at strategic plans where before strategic
> planning was not done. The relationship between the

county executive and board of supervisors has improved and the courts have been more able to adapt changing conditions. For example, the county has just had a fiscal crisis and required across the board budget reduction from each department. The courts were able to review and reduce budget costs without affecting the service levels to the public, while at the same time avoiding lay-offs. It has been easier to be more responsive because of streamlined budget preparation procedures. Sacramento courts have embraced the need to change. So much of the courts has been based on precedent (prior cases, rulings, etc.). Sacramento has taken the bureaucracy out and made the courts more responsive to the public.

What's Wrong Anyway?

The problem back in the 1980s was that the justice agencies themselves had different goals. Individual agency priorities were not clearly defined, well communicated, or coordinated with other agencies. For example, judges were sentencing criminals to jail, but because all the beds in the jail were occupied, the sheriff had no alternative but to release the criminal into the community. Often the court would order the Probation Department to monitor offenders even though there were not enough probation officers to do the monitoring.

There was no centralized planning for the delivery of justice. Budget and program proposals were submitted individually by each agency without regard to overall impact. Positive change in one agency often resulted in a negative impact in another. Special program approvals to crack down on crime often resulted in too many cases to process through the courts. Policy changes seemed to be reactive, rather than proactive, in responding to needs. The courts would hire additional staff to process additional work only after backlogs were out of control.

These public policy problems cried out for solutions. The human costs were very high. Children were taken into custody, prosecuted in the juvenile court, and then detained in the juvenile hall, boys' and girls' ranches, and finally the youth authority. (The youth authority is the maximum security detention facility for incarcerating the most violent juvenile offenders; it is the state prison or state facility for juveniles.) As the juveniles got older, many "progressed" through the adult system, beginning with work projects and then moving on to probation, county jail, and finally prison. It was clear from statistics that incarcerating adults had had little impact on their likelihood of reoffending. Because the average county jail inmate had been arrested eight times before, the courts were seeing the same criminals over and over.

The public policy issue of the use of scarce public funds was equally daunting. The more money that was spent to arrest, adjudicate, and incarcerate juveniles and adults, the less money was available for mental health programs and human services. Additionally, the amount of money available for these services was shrinking each year. "We didn't even realize how bogged down we were in our system of independent agencies until several of us attended the national symposium on Intermediate Sanctions in late 1991," said Judge Warren, who was then serving as presiding judge of the juvenile court:

> We decided things could change. We decided we could work together to create new solutions to overwhelming problems such as increasing criminal caseload, increasing incarceration rates, jail overcrowding, and escalating costs. We had a new spirit and enthusiasm. Rather than jealously guarding our independence, we realized that all the justice agencies needed to coordinate our activities to solve the problems.

Organizing for Change

To solve the problems, Judge Warren and 11 county officials created a high-level group named the Criminal Justice cabinet to study and offer solutions to system-wide problems. When the cabinet was formed in January, 1992, it was unique to Sacramento County. Since then other counties have adopted similar coordination mechanisms. The cabinet is composed of city, county, and state elected officials, as well as court, criminal justice, and human services department heads. The cabinet brought together top decision makers from the various agencies and institutions which could make the changes necessary to improve the system. The criminal Justice cabinet's official mission was "to study the juvenile and criminal justice system,

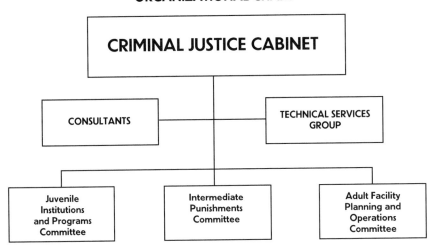

CRIMINAL JUSTICE CABINET
ORGANIZATIONAL CHART

CRIMINAL JUSTICE CABINET

CONSULTANTS

TECHNICAL SERVICES
GROUP

Juvenile
Institutions
and Programs
Committee

Intermediate
Punishments
Committee

Adult Facility
Planning and
Operations
Committee

identify deficiencies, formulate policies, plans, and programs for innovative change." To do this, the cabinet organized itself into three committees: (1) Juvenile Institutions and Programs, (2) Intermediate Punishments, and (3) Adult Facility Planning and Operations.

As a result of cabinet efforts since 1992, the average number of juveniles detained in juvenile hall has been reduced by 32 per day with an annual savings of $300,000. In January of 1993 the cabinet accepted a $75,000 planning grant. In addition, the cabinet received a $2.25 million grant in January, 1994 for the development of alternatives to incarceration, such as electronic monitoring of juvenile offenders.

The cabinet's first focus was on juvenile justice reform including reducing unnecessary reliance on detention of juveniles. This was a very nontraditional response. The traditional response especially when money is tight is to focus on the most serious offenders at the adult end of the system, adult felons. Instead this time, the cabinet wanted to focus on the other end of the system, juvenile offenders. The traditional response to rising crime is to lock up juvenile and adult offenders for longer and longer periods of time. Now the cabinet's response was to look for alternatives to locking up nonviolent juvenile offenders, such as alcohol and drug program referrals.

County Justice Cabinet Agencies

Board of Supervisors
(Elected)

County Executive
Chief Deputy County
Executive

Sheriff

District
Attorney

Sacramento
Supervisor
Municipal
Courts

South
Sacramento
Municipal
Court

Grand Jury

Procation

Other Justice Agency Members:
• Sacramento City Police Chief
• Sacramento City Council
• State Assembly Representative
• Board of Supervisors
• Sacramento Health Agency

The cabinet's second focus was to develop intermediate punishments that might have more success in preventing future criminal activity, such as day reporting. Under the day reporting system, offenders are allowed to spend the night at home but must report to a detention facility or work project each day by a certain time. This approach frees bed space and the use of the facility for those offenders requiring full-time supervision. As a result of cabinet action, the planned jail capacity has been reduced by 800 beds based on the expectation that successful alternatives to incarceration will reduce jail needs.

The cabinet's third focus was to prevent both juvenile and adult criminal behavior. The willingness of the sheriff, district attorney, public defender, mayor, board of supervisors, the probation officer, police chief, presiding judges, and director of human services to work together on a common goal of preventing crime is very unusual. Thus far, the cabinet has identified activities that could prevent future criminal behavior. The cabinet is pursuing multiagency improvements that have the potential of saving millions of dollars that could be redirected to prevention and other reform activities.

In 1994, the California administrative office of the Courts recognized the value and uniqueness of the cabinet's work by presenting it with an award for improvement in the administration of justice.

Now, when the cabinet reaches consensus on an issue, there are few impediments to implementation, because all of the primary players are involved in reaching the consensus. The cabinet's participative effort has required a commitment of cooperation from elected officials who are used to working independently. Sometimes, cabinet decisions that are for the good of the whole, limit funding and flexibility for individual agencies. Despite this loss of independence, bringing the heads of all the justice agencies together has proven to be an innovative approach to solving long-term justice system issues.

When Judge Warren was elected presiding judge of the Sacramento superior court in 1992, he began to realize the extent of the lack of coordination within the court system itself. Each county in California has one superior court and one or more municipal and justice courts. These courts provide many similar and redundant services. Judge Warren did not realize it then, but he was to lead one of the most transformational changes ever attempted by a court system. These changes had an impact on all of the

Sacramento Court's 58 judicial officers and 600 staff members located at eight different facilities within Sacramento County.

A Bigger Challenge

This transformation began with a participative process to eliminate redundancies, streamline and accelerate justice, and save money. The courts formed a team composed of staff from both the superior and municipal courts to identify opportunities for coordination and consolidation of the various court activities.

"We decided to go to the line staff, the people actually doing the work, to help us figure out what to do," said Judge Warren. The staff consistently suggested that the best opportunities for achieving the greatest long-term savings and increasing court access would come from consolidation rather than more coordination of activities. Each court had its own personnel, budget, and automation processes. Some of these processes were incompatible with each other. For example, different systems' platforms made it impossible to coordinate via computer, therefore much duplication of effort occurred. Everyone felt that consolidation of virtually every court function with control and accountability resting with a single administrator was the best way to go. This way, consistent methods of operating could be assured for all court functions.

Consolidation of two large complex organizations — the superior and municipal courts — would not be an easy undertaking. Both organizations had their own structures with managers and supervisors who were comfortable in their jobs and who might lose turf if the merger went through. At least one of the two court administrators would definitely lose his job.

There was also apprehension among the judges. Some municipal court judges feared that with consolidation they would no longer have their own administrator or staff. Some superior court judges were concerned about having to do municipal court work, which is volume-driven and not as exciting and glamorous as superior court work. Some judges had done municipal court work before and did not want to do it again. Others had been directly appointed to superior court and were not familiar with municipal court case processing.

Sitting in on early meetings of the judges was a very painful experience. The frustration and fear that come with anticipating change prompted anger.

The tension was palpable. No one attempted to hide any anger about resistance to the merger. Some judges even questioned the constitutionality of the consolidation in hopes of diverting it. There was an obvious perceived hierarchy at the meetings, with a handful of superior court judges openly sharing their opinions and a large majority of municipal court judges figuratively sitting on their hands and listening intently. As Judge Warren recalls:

> These early meetings in late 1991 were very challenging. I encouraged all participants to openly express their concerns. The fear and apprehension about change and how it would affect each judge surprised me, but it was important that it was expressed. Then the apprehension could be addressed. Ultimately, a better plan was created as a result.

Moving Forward

Another sign that progress towards transformation was actually occurring appeared when the courts used a team to develop the Trial Court Consolidation Plan, a blueprint to merge the policy making and staff functions of the superior and municipal courts. The goals of the merger were to:

A. **Increase access to the courts**. The word access here refers to eliminating all processing barriers such as language, handicapped access, and simplification of court procedures so cases can come in and out of the system in a reasonable time. To eliminate language barriers, the court provides interpretive services to customers, and customer service response cards are printed in different languages to get opinions from all groups. Many civil cases were taking months or years to get an available trial judge because of the clog of criminal cases taking priority for court time.

- Litigants should not have to wait for an available judge. For instance, prior to consolidation, law and motion items were heard intermittently in three or four courtrooms at various times. Now two courtrooms hear law and motion items full time. This improvement allows attorneys and the public much more access and flexibility in getting their motions heard and a decision rendered.
- Prior to consolidation there were separate local rules on which the fees were based. Now there is one fee schedule for the court, one set of local rules for the court, and a much streamlined process for the public and attorney in determining fees.

B. **Improve the use of judicial and staff resources by using the time of the judges and employees more efficiently.**
  - For example, assigning cases to available judges without delay.
  - Another streamlining tactic is the development of the tentative ruling system, which allows the case to be reviewed prior to court hearing. The judge reviews the file prior to scheduling and places a tentative ruling on the likely outcome of the case on a computer bulletin board. When attorneys check the bulletin boards, if they agree with the tentative ruling, an order is prepared for the judge's signature and the case is closed, thus saving court time and costs. Another similar process is the summary jury trial where attorneys argue their cases in an abbreviated form before a judge or jury.
  - The courts have also beefed up their involvement in Alternative Dispute Resolution (ADR) activities. As of July, 1994, attorneys are required to discuss ADR options with the client and file a statement with the court that they have done so. Mediation is now used in more areas (small claims, night court, civil harassment, and municipal cases) than before.
  - Since July, 1994, settlement conferences are mandatory for municipal cases where juries are requested. In these cases, attorneys sit as protem judges and negotiate settlements. In cases where settlements are successful, a judge will then review and create the order.
C. **Decrease overall court costs.** The consolidation reduced the expense necessary to process the escalating number of criminal and civil cases heard each year.

Ripple Effects

Before consolidation could take place, action by the California State Legislature was needed. The courts decided to initiate enabling legislation to allow for a single court system at the county level. This legislation was passed by the state legislature and signed into law by the governor; thus the Sacramento Superior and municipal courts were formally unified into one organizational structure, known as the Sacramento Courts.

This consolidation of the courts was very frightening to many employees. Many were asking, "Was the consolidation just another way to cut staff positions?" Most had good reasons to be concerned. At the same time the consolidation was occurring, Sacramento County was announcing the need to cut the budget and lay off employees. In addition, employees of the former superior court and county clerks offices had undergone an attempted merger 18 months earlier. This consolidation had not been completed and many employees were still upset by the experience. Five of the seven principal administrators from the former offices were gone. People were moved from one supervisor to another. Some had to learn new skills. Some had their hours changed. Many judges were still upset. Now, right in the midst of this turmoil, a larger, more complex consolidation had been approved.

As Judge Warren remembers:

> We knew this would be a tough change for everyone, not only because of the staff turmoil but because it is very difficult to integrate two separate organizations with individual ways of doing things. One thing we wanted to do was help people to let go of the past and realize that their fears, while real, were part of the past. We decided to have a ceremony. It was our way of honoring and ending the past while at the same time celebrating our birth as a single court.

The event, celebrated in January, 1993, was called "Yesterday, Today and Tomorrow" and served both as a wake and the celebration of a new birth. Television cameras were there to tape it. Many past and present employees and judges who had worked in the Sacramento courts were present to enjoy the court memorabilia, taped interviews, and live presentations that explained both the evolution and the future of the courts. The celebration helped the transition process, which involved all of the judges and staff of the court. They all had to cope with the impacts the changes made on them personally. A staff executive team created to lead the consolidation was made up of top administrators from both former courts.

Before the staffs from these organizations could come together, this executive team itself needed to coalesce. The team worked with an organization consultant who helped spotlight the first focus of getting to know one another and establishing effective working relationships. Personal and professional goals were shared. As understanding improved, hidden concerns, differences, and the experiences of working in different courts were expressed. Anger and fear began to surface. As the team looks back, however, they see now that this process actually reduced team conflict and helped team members foster behaviors which produced solutions and decisions that were truly beneficial. Early turf issues were neutralized. The executive team began to function as a team and was ready to lead the consolidation.

Positions of trust were reached by people working with each other. For example, Yolanda Williams and Debbie Fairweather represented each of their courts and were charged with developing an orderly process for consolidation. As Yolanda recalls:

> At first we didn't trust each other. I thought that Debbie had her own agenda and wanted to steamroll it through. She thought I lacked knowledge and should defer to her judgment. So we fought a lot. We did agree that it was important to present a united front and model the behaviors and values from the top down. So we spent time together talking about the outcomes we could work for, our motivations, and management styles. We spent time together collaborating on putting the task teams together to ensure there was no duplication of knowledge and that each individual would bring something unique to the team planning process. In time we began to trust each other.

There was steady improvement in the judges' meetings as well. The anger of some had tapered off to periodic expressions of discontent about the constitutionality of the merger by a handful of judges. There was equal participation among the judges and votes on issues did not follow court lines. The meetings were comfortable, with the only pressure being to make them briefer. The judges grew to trust the judicial leadership and the staff to do the right thing.

A Personal Champion

Successes began to build because the two courts were willing to work together to plan and develop the consolidation program. There was a commitment by judicial officers, especially Judge Warren and top court managers, to support each component of the plan. Judge Warren's personal contribution was his unique ability to be receptive and listen. He understood and respected all positions and issues thoroughly before advocating for a side.

He grasped concepts quickly and, asked "What if" questions for information on concerns about every aspect of the change. Judge Warren anticipated every question and every secondary effect of a decision. Once convinced, he became the strongest advocate. Specifically, sometimes when staff proposals were made by the executive team to the judges, these proposals were heavily questioned. In those instances, Judge Warren could sway the other judge's decisions by stating his analysis and support for the change. Also, in this way he helped the staff move forward on the consolidation.

Measuring Accomplishments

By March, 1992 a comprehensive consolidation plan emerged from the executive team's brainstorming. The heart of the plan was a list of functions to be consolidated and the order and priority in which they would be merged. The plan described the reasoning used. It contained an analysis of how cases were currently being processed and how they would be processed in the future. The plan described the level of involvement by staff, judges, and others in the process. Eleven task teams were established to coordinate all aspects of the consolidation. These teams consisted of judges, court personnel, and outside agencies representing a broad spectrum of ideas. The attorney from the legal community was represented on each team. Each former court was represented on each task team. This was to ensure that new ideas and fresh perspectives to the tasks were included. Employees who had an interest in gaining new skills joined on teams that reflected their interests. Wherever possible, champions, as well as detractors were included. "Devil's advocates" provided a good test for group consensus. Facilitators assisted task teams who reviewed current activities and developed recommendations and implementation plans for change.

The courts are very proud of the accomplishments which have resulted from the team process in the consolidation effort. Once duplicated in each court, activities such as personnel and budget/fiscal operations, master calendaring of court cases, and management information systems were consolidated under single directors. No one was laid off; overall though, there was a downsizing of management staff through early retirements and reassignments.

Accomplishments

1. The personnel task team identified positions for elimination that resulted in a first-year salary savings of $400,000.

2. The team established uniform court employee procedures which improved testing and recruitment.

3. In the first year, the management information staff was combined into a single systems unit under one director, resulting in a unified pool of technical experts who established standards for the combined court. Instead of each court developing separate systems, the unified court maintains one system for total court needs with lower maintenance costs. A single means of electronic mail has increased communication for all staff. Integrating technology also allows for sharing of programs, information, and documents. Prior to consolidation the two courts used many different software packages and two different systems' platforms.

4. Money was saved by combining units doing similar work in order to better distribute workload and eliminate duplication. For example, the criminal task team developed and implemented the Home Court Process, which expedites criminal case processing. The same judge hears felony proceedings in the municipal and superior courts where previously they were heard by at least three different judges. No longer does a second and third judge need to become familiar with the case.

- The public is getting better service. Creating single locations where the public can file documents, access records, and request information and direction increases efficiency and saves staff from having to maintain multiple locations.

- The centralization of the court's calendering function minimizes scheduling conflicts. Prior to consolidation, often attorneys scheduled court appearances in both courts at the same time. The new system monitors schedules and results in more communication about judicial availability. Having all judges in one court provides better coverage for vacations and absences.

- A single set of procedures provides consistent training among staff and eliminated policy conflicts between courts. For example, the facilities task team established uniform procedures for the purchase of supplies resulting in overall expenditure reductions in this area.
- Less complex judicial duties such as traffic violation hearings are now heard by subordinate judicial officers. This increases efficiency and availability of judge time for more complex matters such as felony hearings.
- Unifying the judicial system under a single leadership provides a clear line of direction for policy making and operations. For example, the county's total court priorities are established in a single budget request rather than two lists from each separate court.
- A new central accounting system provides consistency when dealing with other agencies and with distributing funds to the state. For example, portions of fees are easily transferred to the state to support the judges' retirement system. Also, the central accounting system has saved money by reducing overall duplicative contracts with outside vendors; now one contract, rather than two, for photocopy services is negotiated, prepared, and paid; better tracking of accounting transactions and better statistical record keeping. All this has improved public service and has sped up payments to court appointed attorneys, expert witnesses such as investigators and doctors, court reporters, and interpreters.
- Increasing the use of court attendants rather than sworn deputy sheriffs for court security services in some courtrooms has saved the court $300,000 annually. For instance, highly trained sheriffs do not attend in civil courts that process personal injury cases.
- Increasing the use of electronic recording equipment provides a cost-effective manner to produce verbatim court proceedings records. Prior to consolidation only court reporters were used. The cost savings for electronic recording will be approximately $9,300,000 over a 12-year implementation period.

Suggestions for Courts Contemplating Consolidation

- Develop a plan outlining goals and anticipated outcomes. Do your homework. The Sacramento team thoroughly evaluated its environment and determined it was prepared for the transition. Once a decision to consolidate was made, they were committed to "stay the course" regardless of the obstacles encountered.
- Involve all key organizational players. Sacramento used a task-team approach representing all levels of the organization as well as attorney/customers.
- Dedicate full-time senior level staff to manage the consolidation. If necessary, reassign projects to other employees. Transition managers need to be at a high level to gain support and credibility for the project. Much of Sacramento's success was attributable to its full-time focus on consolidation. A lesser obligation would have made it extremely difficult to get anything done.
- Allow adequate time to develop the consolidation plan and to achieve goals. Sacramento created a three-year plan to achieve results.
- Develop a sensitivity to the upheaval people experience during change. Sacramento's top managers attended a seminar on transition leadership. They planned not only for the consolidation but for people resistance and adjustment to the change. Had Sacramento not learned about transition leadership, they would have focused their energies on the processes for implementation rather than on the importance of employees. Change for many is an act of courage and an emotional experience. It requires a lot of patience and understanding to lead people through change.
- Increase communication processes because people do not hear as well during change. Sacramento established a reporting process and newsletter, designed primarily to communicate the progress of consolidation.
- Use project teams. Staff involvement fostered the acceptance and commitment needed for long-term success of the consolidation. Sacramento's cross-functional team approach generated positive outcomes throughout all levels of the organization. Some of these teams continue today.

Dealing with a Year of Change

The executive team discovered that the skills that had been sufficient to operate in a 300-person organization were not enough to run this larger, more complex organization of over 600. They discovered that they had to work together more closely and effectively if the team were to be successful. The biggest problem was that previously the managers had always had time and authority to do anything they had been asked to do. With the new organization, there was neither the time nor the resources to do everything. With the downsizing at the management level, each manager had more staff and could no longer be personally involved in every project.

The executive team members each had expertise in an individual area in an individual court. For example, operations managers had time to become completely knowledgeable in the operations of their sections. They had been able to spend time getting to know how things worked in detail. When judges asked them a question, they knew the answer. There was time to coach individual employees. In the consolidated court, managers had a larger number of staff reporting to them. Many were now managing functions that were merged, so often they did not know the operation and could no longer be personally involved. Being unable to do everything forced the managers to set priorities differently, and deal with their personal concerns as human beings facing major changes. People had to help one another.

Employees Continue Momentum

One transitional program that continues today is the Employee Organizational Support Team (EmOST), which began as the consolidation's "Organizational Wellness and Culture" task team and consisted of 16 court employees. Taking its new name — EmOST — after the consolidation, it continued the goal to be "the conscience of the organization and to explore the possible ways to find a balance between the basic business operation and the social health of the people involved." For example, this team finds ways for court employees to network and socialize in order to develop and strengthen relationships.

To do this, EmOST brainstormed 107 characteristics of a well organization and divided them into categories called employee morale, career development, creativity, personal development, training, performance, accepting supportive environment, and communication. These categories were then incorporated into the EmOST mission statement which reads:

> To assist the court in promoting high employee morale and a healthy organization through a supportive environment and to enhance employee performance in a continually improving organization.

When EmOST invited all of the courts' 600 employees to participate in one of four committees, 61 employees immediately volunteered. Over 110 court employees served in planning employee participation activities such as:

- Bringing supervisory training to employees who view supervision as a career goal.
- Expanding training available, such as that provided to courtroom clerks.
- Installing and improving 18 bulletin boards.
- Implementing a career development program, a suggestion award program, and a customer service improvement program.
- Planning the court employee recognition events honoring 92 employees in 1993 and 188 employees in 1994 nominated by their peers, supervisors, and managers.
- Improving court administration by involving line staff in court decision making, such as the decision for managers to provide one-on-one orientation to newly appointed supervisors.
- Sponsoring the first "Bring Your Kids to Work Day" attended by 155 children, and also holding a court picnic and holiday party.

The program success should not outshine the individual success expressed by the EmOST participants. One courtroom clerk writes:

> I believe EmOST is the main catalyst for making the Sacramento Courts such a rewarding place to work. The work of the committee is evident every time we have a training session, job enrichment opportunity or social event. Since the conception of EmOST, I have felt a sense of family at my workplace. I have felt more equality and respect for people.

Another employee writes:

> Being a part of EmOST has made me challenge myself to
> break out of a mold and grow to become all that I can be. I
> believe that being a part of the committees can give a person
> a respect for oneself beyond belief, and the insight that you
> can do anything you set your mind to do.

Employees who have served on the EmOST committees have expressed
their appreciation for the opportunity to participate in the development of
Court policies and programs, such as focus groups to develop and improve
training programs. EmOST gives employees a chance to improve their leadership and communication skills, and to feel that they are an active part of
an organization that cares about its employees, and invites their ideas and
active participation. The EmOST program represents the court's participative effort. As Judge Warren evaluates:

> We have used participation at all levels to increase justice
> system effectiveness. Everyone involved has had something
> valuable to contribute to our continued improvement. As
> the crisis in justice continues to mount, more courts will be
> forced to consider reinventing their organizations to meet
> the growing demands of the public. We hope that others
> can benefit from our experience. As for myself, I now real-
> ize that the change that I resisted so strongly in the begin-
> ning in accepting a judgeship, has proved to be one of the
> most rewarding experiences in my life.

References

Austin, Joyce A. Employee Organizational Support Team First Annual
Report, 1994.

Fairweather, Debbie. Sacramento Superior and Municipal Courts
Consolidation Plans and Processes, 1993.

Jones, Dennis B., Ralph N. Kleps Award Nomination Form, 1992, 1993.

Williams, Yolande E. Sacramento County's Transition Team Model for
Successful Court Consolidation: An Analysis of the Transition Team
Process That Reshaped the Local Court Structure and Service
Delivery Process.

Chapter 10
A Tribal Nation
Moving into the 21st Century

KIM ALIRE EPLEY AND JACKIE MILLER

It has not been an easy road for the Assiniboine
and Sioux people of Fort Peck, Montana. Their success is
a testament to their courage, perseverance, and instinct
for survival, all of which have their roots in hundreds
of years of existence along the banks of the Missouri
River. While there is no simple recipe for their success,
there are some key ingredients that have helped make
Tribal[1] government on the Fort Peck Reservation work.

Tribal Government: The Social and Political Context

Tribal government in the United States is one of the most complex and least understood forms of government in the world. Indian Tribes are sovereign, governmental entities with the right to self-determination, just like any other independent nation. There are 547 federally recognized Indian Tribes in the United States. In April, 1994, President Clinton held a historic summit with the heads of state of these Indian nations in an attempt to build a clearer understanding of Tribal issues and needs.

---

[1] The authors have asked that the words tribe, tribes, and tribal be capitalized in every use.
To comply with their request, we have departed from our standard style of capitalization.

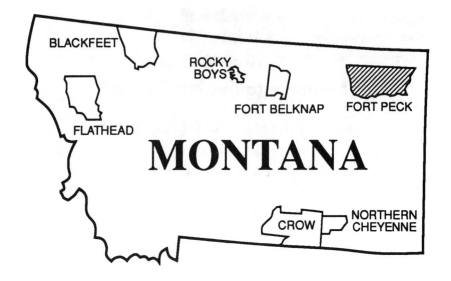

Billed as a "listening conference," the summit demonstrated the federal government's commitment to treat Tribes as "full partners" in a unique government-to-government relationship. At this conference, the President discovered that many Tribes were not waiting for federal initiatives; instead, they were proceeding with their own local development efforts. In some cases, those efforts were having a profound transformative effect on the Tribe's society and economy. This chapter takes a look at one of those Tribal communities, the Assiniboine and Sioux Tribes of the Fort Peck Reservation in Montana, and examines the roots of its success.

History of the Fort Peck Reservation

In the early 1800s, the Assiniboine people came to the Missouri River valley in northeastern Montana. They were joined there later in the century by the Sioux, who were evading the pursuing U. S. Cavalry. These two Tribes were jointly given this land as one reservation, the Fort Peck Reservation, which came into being by an Act of Congress in 1888. It is one of seven Indian reservations in Montana.

Today, the Fort Peck Reservation is about 110 miles long and 40 miles wide, encompassing just over two million acres (approximately 3,200 square miles). Of this, approximately 378,000 acres are Tribally owned and 548,000 acres are individually allotted Indian lands. The total of Indian-owned lands is about 936,000 acres. There are now about 5,800 people living on the reservation. Their median age is 22 years; it is a very young community.

Fort Peck: Transforming the Legacies of the Past

In forming the Fort Peck Reservation, the federal government not only "gave" the Assiniboine and Sioux Tribes a place to live, it also gave them a system of government, one that was alien to their tradition of consensus-based decision making. The bureaucracy created on the Fort Peck Reservation was built under the supervision of the federal agencies that had responsibility for overseeing the Tribes in that region. These agencies forced the Fort Peck Tribes to adopt a governmental system that mirrored the federal government; it was a system short on participation and long on paperwork, rules, and regulations.

The traditional and the new did not mix well. While their bureaucratic structure mimicked the federal government, the Fort Peck Tribes still retained their traditional styles of decision making as a means of ensuring broad community participation. As is common to many American Indian Tribes, tradition required the consensus of all members of a general council before they could approve a decision. The general council consisted of all enrolled Tribal members over the age of 18.

The combination of a lengthy decision-making process and an elaborate bureaucracy made this form of government extremely cumbersome. A growing population and increasingly complex governmental business exacerbated the situation. When decisions had to be made in a limited time-frame, the Fort Peck Tribes were vulnerable to those who would make decisions for them, such as the Bureau of Indian Affairs(BIA). Often those decisions were not in the best interests of the Tribes.

To add to the complexity of Tribal government, Tribal officials are frequently responsible for governing a people who are all closely related by blood or by marriage. It is difficult for leaders to be objective in their decision making when family members are involved. That Tribal governments persist and manage to serve their people in the midst of this tangle of regulations, funding sources, jurisdictional wars, political struggles, and familial conflicts is testimony to Indian strength and endurance.

Allotment Policy

In 1987, the U.S. Congress authorized through the passage of the General Allotment (Dawes) Act a general policy of parcelling Tribally held lands. The Act assigned set parcels to Tribal members and opened up for sale the remaining unalloted lands to non-Indian homesteaders. This policy resulted in the devastating loss of almost ninety million acres of Tribal land through the sale of this "surplus" land. This land was approximately two-thirds of the total acreage held by Tribes when the Act was passed.

To cope with these complex systems, the Fort Peck Tribes in 1960 began a political change process that would create a critical shift in the level of federal control at Fort Peck. The elected leaders at the time recognized that the Tribes needed a government that could respond more quickly to political issues. For example, the newly created business council was required to conduct the day-to-day running of operations on behalf of the larger Tribal community, such as approving Tribal agricultural and business leases.

The Tribal members created a new constitution that empowered elected Tribal government officials to negotiate with federal, state, and local officials. This framework allowed them a freer rein to sort out taxation issues and promote public health. The constitution also made it possible for Tribal members to take control of their own future, instead of being the victims of decisions imposed on them by outside agencies.

Role of the Tribal Council

Today, the official governing body of the Fort Peck Tribes is the Tribal Executive Board or Tribal Council, composed of 12 voting members plus a chairman, vice-chairman, secretary-accountant, and sergeant-at-arms. Council provisions emphasize the Tribes' traditional concern for dispersed power and direct participation. Council members come up for election every two years. These council members are the policy makers. Under the council are the program directors and staff, who organize and deliver the programs that care for the needs of the Tribal community—economic development, social services, health services, and infrastructure management.

Given the complexity of managing a multimillion dollar "family" corporation/sovereign government, the new Tribal government was not a panacea. But, for the first time since its recognition as a sovereign nation by the federal government in the 1800s, all Tribal decision makers were making all the critical decisions, instead of having the federal agencies making them by default. The new system of government was instituted in October, 1960.

Early struggles in the new government centered around identifying appropriate management systems for a Tribal governmental organization. There was little consensus on management; at one point each entity of the Tribe had its own checking account and separate bookkeeping system. There was no overall control over the various types of funds for which the Tribes were ultimately responsible.

The Fort Peck Tribes Today

After more than three decades of commitment to finding new solutions to their economic woes, the Assiniboine and Sioux Tribes of Fort Peck have proven that their leadership approach works. Fort Peck Tribes are successfully negotiating better working relationships with the federal government and the state of Montana, and they are taking a leadership role in Indian country, as well as in the surrounding counties. The Tribally owned Assiniboine and Sioux Tribal Industries (A&S) was at one time the third largest private employer in Montana. Fort Peck still leads Montana's seven reservations in economic growth. The Fort Peck Tribes were the first of the American Indian Tribes to develop jointly and wholly owned oil wells. To build a diverse economic base, they are expanding their involvement in agriculture, manufacturing, enterprise development, gaming, and tourism.

It has not been an easy road for the Assiniboine and Sioux people of Fort Peck. Their success is a testament to their courage, perseverance, and instinct for survival, all of which have their roots in hundreds of years of existence along the banks of the Missouri River. While there is no simple recipe for their success, there are some key ingredients that have helped make Tribal government on the Fort Peck Reservation work.

Keys to Success

Key 1: Forging Their Own Paths

First and foremost among the ingredients for success is the decision the Assiniboine and Sioux Tribes made to forge their own paths. There are hundreds of examples of failed development endeavors in Indian country. Some of these examples have even been on the Fort Peck Reservation itself. Historically, most of the businesses on the reservation have been owned and controlled by non-Indians. Typically, outside entrepreneurs have had little understanding of the special circumstances of business ventures in a Tribal context. Reservations in general have a relatively small, closed labor pool and a relatively small number of enterprises with employment opportunities. Fort Peck is no exception. The availability of specific skills can be more limited than in other areas, and, although entrepreneurial ventures are not necessarily more prone to failure on a reservation than elsewhere, the impact of such failure on the local community can be particularly severe.

From the standpoint of both workers and entrepreneurs, product and market diversification is a particularly critical element in guaranteeing the success of business ventures on a reservation. As Tribal members have a strong, vested interest in their economic success, it is important that they are directly involved in running the businesses on their reservations.

Recognizing their special circumstances, the Fort Peck Tribes resisted the temptation to use a cookie-cutter approach to economic development. Tribal leaders have relied instead on the creativity and resources of the Assiniboine and Sioux people to direct their activities. Tribal Chairman Caleb Shields says, "We have used participatory facilitation to harvest our most important energy resource—the creative energy of our people."

Key 2: Tapping the Tradition of Consensus Building

Participation of the Tribal community is the other major ingredient in the economic success of the Fort Peck Tribes. Consensus building has been woven into planning and implementing activities that range from economic development to the delivery of social, health, education, and housing services. In 1990, the Tribal Council began to seek the active participation of Tribal program managers and Tribal members in their planning efforts.

For many, including a participatory approach signaled a return to more traditional ways. Bringing everyone together to discuss, decide, and implement decisions was a common activity of the past. Vice-Chairman Ray K. Eder comments:

> In the past, we [the Tribal Council] let the planning department figure out what our priorities were, then we gave them a number [budget]. Now we develop our priorities ourselves with the community and staff in this process. It allows us to be in on the ground floor and understand better what it will take to reach our vision. The Tribes have been able to harvest the wisdom of their people to serve their aim "to move into the twenty-first century on our own terms."

Community Participation in Action

In August 1990, David Lester, executive director of the Council of Energy Resource Tribes (CERT), made a tour with other CERT staff to introduce participatory strategic planning to the remote reservations of northern Montana. CERT is a multi-Tribal organization founded in 1975 by 25 energy-owning North American Indian Tribes. CERT's membership currently stands at 53 U. S. Tribes and four Canadian Indian nations. CERT provides technical and professional services to Tribes to complement and enhance Tribal expertise. Fort Peck was one of CERT's founding members and has been active in shaping the direction of the organization.

Practical Visions, Tangible Strategies

The following wide range of issues motivated the desire for community-based planning at Fort Peck:
- Economic growth,
- Tribal management,
- Cultural survival,
- Financial control over Tribal programs,
- Natural resource development,
- The community environment, and,
- Health and welfare issues.

All of these concerns were being dealt with in a piecemeal fashion, instead of being addressed in a systematic way. For instance, before the strategic planning process began in 1990, communication between Tribal offices did not exist. There were over 30 Tribal programs with all their managers going their own separate ways. Although it did come through the Tribe, program management was usually tied to federal or state agencies. In practice, a program manager's first allegiance often was to funders rather than to the Tribe. By the end of the first planning session, all of the many issues, such as the managerial problems, had been addressed, one by one, and prioritized.

In the 1990 participatory planning session, Tribal staff and interested community members worked together with the governing Tribal Council to determine the key issues that needed further attention. Over 60 participants came to the session. Eugene Culbertson, a council member and chairman of the development committee, describes the event:

> We had never sat down together with such a variety of peo-
> ple to work on setting directions. The strategic planning is
> the first time we did this. In the past, the council couldn't
> always make a decision on what the priorities were....With
> the document at the end of the session, we had our prior-
> ities outlined.

Four diverse but major priorities emerged from this initial planning session:

1. Economic Development — A 47% unemployment rate underscored the need for new employment opportunities, but the reservation environment was not supportive of entrepreneurship and small business development. Those wanting to start a business on the reservation have a hard time getting financing, as banks are hesitant to invest; borrowers cannot use their land as collateral because of its trust status. In addition, while Tribal members may have a quality product or service to offer, they often have little knowledge of bookkeeping, marketing, or small business management systems. Grant availability, not Tribal priorities, was driving Tribal programs. At this time, the Tribe decided to reverse this direction. They would first design a comprehensive economic development plan and then seek funding for each element. This was a radical shift in approach.

2. Fetal Alcohol Syndrome — Alcohol destroys the brain cells of developing fetuses, a major problem on reservations such as Fort Peck where the rate of alcoholism is high. The destruction of the potential for greatness at a very early stage of development is considered by some to be the number one threat to Indian Tribes throughout the country.

3. Coordination of Social Programs — Tribal members evaluated the delivery of social programs on the reservation. They were surprised to see that, while a wide range of social services was available, there was considerable overlap in coverage; it was a powerful experience to see how ineffectively these services were coordinated.

4. Environmental Protection — Protecting the land and the human environment is a fundamental concern of the Fort Peck Tribes. Clean water, solid waste management, air quality control, pesticide regulation, and reforestation programs are all important elements of improving the Tribal quality of life.

Having the decisions on these four priorities written down was helpful, but the real gift of the planning was that this council had, for the first time, a sense of confidence in a broader Tribal consensus. These sessions provided an opportunity for a direct dialogue between the policy makers (council members), those who deliver services (program managers), and those who benefit from the services (Tribal members).

Priority One: Reestablishing Tribal Economic Foundations

Indian Tribes have a strong tradition of economic self-sufficiency, and have been able to support themselves for thousands of years without any outside help. For a brief moment in their history, and for many different reasons, that self-sufficiency was temporarily suspended. Nevertheless, the Tribe recognized those strong economic foundations could be reestablished. That is precisely what the Fort Peck Tribes set out to do.

Recognizing the need to engage the broader community, the Fort Peck Tribes invited city and county officials and local, non-Indian business people to join them in building a comprehensive economic development plan. While the non-Indian community is moving away from this rural region of northeastern Montana, the Tribal population is growing steadily; it is therefore no surprise to find the Tribes taking the lead in economic development.

One part of the Tribes' economic planning was a presentation made by the nationally recognized Indian historian, George Horse Capture. He introduced the concept that the cultural traditions of the Assiniboine and Sioux Tribes could serve as an area resource, drawing tourists to the region. Instead of viewing the reservation as an impoverished place to be avoided, Horse Capture suggested that it was a place that people might want to visit precisely because it is a reservation. Creating a tourist industry was just one element of the comprehensive, five-year economic development plan that emerged from these facilitated participatory sessions. The main areas the Tribes' economic development plan focus on are:

1. Agriculture — Develop a profitable irrigated farming/ranching operation using land specifically acquired for this purpose.
2. Small business development — Establish 50 new Indian businesses on the reservation.
3. Manufacturing — Improve the marketing of the Tribal manufacturing industries and expand employment.
4. Tourism/Recreation — Develop tourism and wildlife-management industries, such as issuing hunting and fishing licenses.
5. Public works — Improve the community infrastructure — paved roads, electricity, sewers, etc. — to improve the quality of life on the reservation and to make it easier to establish new businesses.

This five-year economic development plan was translated into a funding proposal that led to an award of $440,000 a year for five years from the BIA. The only Tribes to receive this special BIA grant were the Assiniboine and Sioux Tribes of Fort Peck, and the Navajo Nation. This award was quite a testimony to the Fort Peck Tribes' planning skills. Ironically, the BIA is finally beginning to recognize the need for participatory planning; their only recommendation to the Tribes was to add more in the budget for continued "strategic planning."

The BIA award created a real challenge for the Fort Peck Tribes. They were expected to meet certain targets and produce tangible results on a short timeline. The first step of the five-year plan was to create five taskforces to work on each of the economic sectors. These taskforces meet regularly. Every three months all the taskforces come together to ask, "How are we doing and what are the next steps?" This pattern of participation keeps the taskforces on target. Regular, large, and eventful plenary sessions help to keep the comprehensive plan connected and sustain long-term participation.

Agricultural Initiatives

To further their agricultural objective, the Tribes purchased 1,200 acres of irrigated farmland. Tribal land lies in the midst of some of the most fruitful land in northeastern Montana. After years of watching non-Indian farmers make a living from the land, the Tribes decided to try their hand at "large-scale" farming. Tribal staff are now working on several strategies to develop the farm. They are planting irrigated spring wheat and alfalfa, which have proved to be lucrative crops for other farmers in the region. They have also received a U. S. Direct Loan for cattle. The agriculture coordinator is working with Montana State Extension Services to make the farm an experimental station. The Soil Conservation Service inventoried the range unit and developed a plan to improve the resources by developing off-stream livestock watering facilities. Carry-over grant funds from the Clean Water Act are being used to implement that part of the plan.

Small Business Development

The most ambitious goal of the economic development plan was the creation of 50 new businesses in five years. The taskforce responsible for growth created a plan addressing the unique challenges a Tribal entrepreneur faces. At the local bank, the Tribes established a Tribal loan guarantee that helped provide credit, and also organized a Native American Chamber of Commerce as a supportive network. With the backing of the Tribal planning office, they initiated a system to assist in creating business plans to help with start-up efforts. The plan is right on schedule, with 20 new businesses in place in 1994 as the program began its third year.

Manufacturing Expansion

Manufacturing is the one area in which the economic development plan had a serious setback. As noted earlier, the Tribally owned Assiniboine and Sioux Industries (A&S) was, until recently, the third largest private employer in Montana. During its 20-year history, the company had its trials and errors. Tribal leaders worked diligently to convince the federal government that Indian people were reliable workers and could produce quality products. That effort paid off with contracts with the Department of Defense. For example, during Desert Storm, A&S built water tanks, nets, and other equipment and had a workforce of nearly 500. With the downsizing of the defense industry, A&S attempted to enter into a joint marketing effort with the other Tribal industries, West Electronics, and Great Divide Manufacturing. West Electronics, a manufacturer of sophisticated electronic products, currently produces security systems for the United States military. Great Divide specializes in processing paper and fiberboard as well as in silk-screening. The Brunswick Corporation, which managed A&S, attempted to diversify from defense to private industry contracts, but failed, bringing about the A&S closing in July, 1994. In an effort to compensate for the closure of this major employer, Tribal leaders are pursuing legislation that will make it easier to attract businesses to the Fort Peck reservation. Currently, the Tribes are aggressively pursuing new markets and are confident they can revive A&S Industries.

Tourism and Recreation

The fourth taskforce of the economic development program is tourism and recreation. Gaming is the current economic boom industry in Indian country. However, the Tribes have entered into gaming very cautiously. A sure attraction for tourism dollars, gaming has created a unique and unprecedented opportunity for over 100 Tribes, according to Tribal Chairman Caleb Shields. He notes that since 1980, American Indian Tribes have netted over $100 million from gaming, and in addition, some Tribes have nearly eliminated unemployment. There are several small gaming operations run by autonomous Indian communities on the reservation and the Fort Peck administration is planning to build a Tribally managed casino.

In another tourism venture, a traditional Assiniboine village has become one of the key tourism attractions on the Fort Peck Reservation. The village is living testimony to the early history, traditions, and customs of the Assiniboine people prior to 1880. Featuring camp activities such as hide scraping, the village was opened on Memorial Day in 1992. Over 1500 tourists visited the village in its first summer season.

Maintaining a Solid Infrastructure

This kind of ambitious economic development can flounder without the community infrastructure services that most of North America takes for granted. For this reason the infrastructure taskforce addresses the basic water, waste removal, and transportation needs of the Tribes. Working with the Tribal planning office, this team took the lead to ensure that the new U.S. Environmental Protection Agency (EPA) regulations for low-level waste management were met. The taskforce guided the installation of a solid waste disposal system that is a model for rural communities. Before the taskforce tackled the issues, solid waste was openly dumped, and the water/sewer system suffered from improper maintenance. The Indian Health Service and the BIA constructed the sewer system, but there was no government program to maintain the system; nor was there suitable funding to assist the Tribe with ongoing maintenance.

At the end of 1991, the public was invited to an open session at which the economic development planners described their accomplishments and outlined the priorities for the next phase. This sort of community accountability and open sharing of information is one of the keys to the success of the Fort Peck development strategy. Dick Scheetz, a federal Soil Conservation Service employee assigned to provide technical assistance to the Fort Peck Reservation, shared his perspective on the participatory process:

> I am a resource to the reservation. I am here to provide information. The planning process helped get my information into a different group. We were able to focus on coordinating ideas and resource information. I have worked with different planning processes, but this is the best method because it produces more ideas and gets more people involved.

Ironically, this "new" approach to economic development is based on the traditional Native American practices of consensus building and cooperative implementation.

Priority Two: Fighting Alcohol Abuse

Alcoholism is a daily reality for the residents of Fort Peck Reservation. Many organizations address the problems that stem from alcoholism, but none are more important to the future of the Tribes than the Fetal Alcohol Syndrome (FAS) taskforce. This syndrome, which threatens the next generation of Tribal members, is a consequence of the abuse of alcohol by pregnant women. The great urgency of stopping this abuse is felt throughout the Tribes.

A small group of medical professionals and community residents came together as the FAS taskforce to focus attention on this tragically destructive problem in the reservation community. It was the only taskforce originally staffed entirely by volunteers, a core group of dedicated people who wanted to find a way to keep FAS in the public eye.

The taskforce started out with high participation levels; 30 to 40 people attended the early meetings. However, the group's lack of leadership, structure, and definite goals resulted in very short-range targets and no long-range cohesive plan. There was no schedule for implementing goals. At one time the taskforce had 14 committees, but, although there was plenty to do, the work was not allocated in a way that sustained people's involvement. The lack of babysitters at meetings also meant that many women could not attend.

Having heard about the Tribes' success with participatory planning, the FAS taskforce members decided to develop their own strategic plan. This goal enabled them to outline effective strategies to give visibility to FAS. They organized educational events and opportunities for raising awareness and encouraging involvement. By developing clear strategies and systematically dividing up the responsibility for implementing these strategies, the taskforce emerged with a guideline to focus their energies: their overall goal is to curb FAS by discouraging pregnant women from drinking.

Since their initial planning session, the FAS team has organized a successful conference, co-sponsored by the Tribes, and has been recognized formally by the Tribes as an important entity in the community. After seeing how effective the FAS team was, the Tribe decided to fund its work directly. The taskforce now publishes a column in the weekly Tribal newspaper to educate the public on FAS and a related, but less devastating, problem known as fetal alcohol effect. An active speakers' bureau responds regularly to requests for presentations.

Indeed, the Fort Peck FAS taskforce has become a leader in its field and is actively participating in the nationwide network of individuals working on this critical issue. Their strategic plan is being hailed as a model in Indian country. Other Tribes recognize the value of addressing the FAS issue as the Fort Peck Tribes have done. A coalition of 19 Sioux Tribes has asked the Fort Peck FAS taskforce to help them prepare similar plans for their Tribes.

Using a taskforce to tackle a social issue can be a difficult struggle. The initial energy and excitement easily wane and leadership roles can change frequently; it can also be difficult to retain the consensus-based approach that makes the taskforce effective and keeps its members motivated. The FAS group learned that they needed to have a multifaceted plan in which different people take responsibility for implementing various parts of the plan that they all created.

Priority Three: Redefining Social Service Delivery

Another initiative that grew out of the original strategic plan was a comprehensive assessment of the reservation's social service programs. The social services taskforce decided to develop a comprehensive strategic plan to deliver social services, and invited delegates from the state, county, Tribes, local towns, churches, private agencies — anyone who had anything to do with delivering social services to Tribal members. The turnout was excellent. Representatives of 35 agencies that serve the reservation communities took part, covering a wide range of programs such as family advocacy, job opportunities, basic skills training, child care, community services, and sexual abuse.

While economic development planning activities focused on implementation, the key issues in the social program planning arena were coordination and collaboration. Lack of communication between agencies caused considerable duplication in services delivered by the different agencies. "Look at the services we're delivering. Look at the overlap," one participant exclaimed. The taskforce knew that program delivery had to be revised to be based on need, not just on the availability of program funding.

During the first planning meeting, it became clear that protectionism was a main barrier to communication between agencies. Because program managers were striving to maintain funding for their respective programs, many were reluctant to discuss their budgets and funding sources openly. This kind of "turf protection" cut off the option of developing joint responses to the daily social crises that these program managers faced.

The Tribal Council wanted the social service program managers to create a comprehensive model for effective service delivery. They could not accomplish this without teamwork — a major stumbling block at first. During the initial planning, interagency teams were created with a mandate to find ways to improve cooperation. The taskforce applied for and received a $300,000, two-year grant for this project from the Administration for Native Americans (a federal agency). Though the grant has greatly facilitated the in-depth investigation of social service delivery to Tribal members, this investigation is proving to be threatening to some program staff . They are concerned about retaining their jobs as managers in those cases where the plan might call for program integration. Streamlining the delivery of social services continues to be a challenge to implement. One way the taskforce addresses the managers' personal concerns is by ensuring that the Strategic Model for Social Service Delivery clearly includes opportunities for everyone's participation in carrying out activities, even after streamlining is implemented. The taskforce places a heavy emphasis on team accountability and ongoing collaboration.

Priority Four:
Tribal Sovereignty through Environmental Protection

Though the Tribes perform a wide array of traditional government functions, some aspects of environmental regulation are managed by external federal, or state agencies. This external regulation was troublesome to the Tribes, particularly because their lack of regulatory structure was not caused by inability or legal barriers, but due, in part, to inadequate funding. In 1989, the EPA introduced multimedia funding for its programs with Tribes. Prior to this, EPA funding for Tribal programs was linked to a specific environmental medium: water, land, or air. The Clean Water Act, Section 106 grant program, for example, deals only with the management and abatement of surface water and groundwater. Funding for pesticide control had to be applied for separately, yet pesticides sprayed on the soil can leach into the groundwater, thereby affecting the water supply.

The new multimedia funding was intended to help the Tribes develop environmental protection capabilities on their reservations, as well as infrastructure and regulatory mechanisms for comprehensive rather than piecemeal environmental protection. The general consensus among the Tribes is that the program has fallen far short of meeting Tribal needs. The multimedia concept has not proved to be as comprehensive as was perhaps intended. And, of course, there is a limited availability of multimedia grants.

The Fort Peck Tribes, who have been implementing EPA programs since 1979, decided they wanted to design a comprehensive environmental program that was both effective and practical in making the best use of multimedia grants. Debi Madison, director of the Fort Peck Office of Environmental Protection, decided to bring a group together to focus on the Tribes' multimedia grant.

Debi is a skilled Tribal program manager. In her ten years with the Tribes, she has learned how to be innovative within the federal constraints that have often stumped other managers. She wanted to build a sensible structure to organize all of the environmental programs, to weave together the regulatory and nonregulatory mechanisms that protect the environment of the Fort Peck Reservation, and to fill in the gaps in environmental program coverage. To do it right, she called together a taskforce consisting of Tribal program managers from environmental health, enterprise development, housing, minerals management, and environmental planning.

The taskforce decided to look at every possible regulation, code, policy, or environmental issue that concerned the Tribes or the EPA. Sifting through the data uncovered eight key programs that should form the basis of the emerging Comprehensive Tribal Environmental Plan (CTEP):

1. Water quantity and supply,
2. Water quality (surface and groundwater),
3. Land resource protection,
4. Solid waste management,
5. Air quality control and management,
6. Hazardous materials,
7. Environmental health, and
8. Pesticide regulation.

After identifying these eight key programs, the taskforce needed to address the remaining half of the issues raised in the data analysis. Then a real breakthrough occurred. The question was posed: "What is the rest of this about?" "Sovereignty," was the reply.

The topic of Tribal sovereignty is part of any discussion of the past, present, or future in Indian country. The fundamental right of Indian Tribes to exist has been under attack since the days when the first Europeans entered this land. Today, the discussion of sovereignty centers around the ability of a Tribe to govern and manage itself effectively, and to put its sovereignty into practice. In this case, Tribal sovereignty centered on the careful management and protection of Mother Earth — and on being taken seriously by federal, state, and county bureaucracies, as well as by Tribal members.

Carrying Tribal Self-Reliance into the 21st Century

This discussion of sovereignty led the taskforce to develop a core structure of four elements that had to be present in each of the environmental programs: management, community education, community involvement, and intergovernmental relations.

The word "management," often considered a dry, bureaucratic term by many people, took on a life of its own when defined by this group. Their management component focused on making environmental protection a consideration for all Tribal program managers. It pushed these same program managers to be proactive in considering the connection between environmental protection and their specific program development efforts.

The community involvement and community education components highlighted the need to assist Tribal members in understanding the right of the Tribes to make and enforce environmental codes. The community needed to know that this action represents the Tribe acting on its sovereign authority; defying a Tribal order to clean up an environmental hazard on one's property is denying Tribal sovereignty. This perspective puts enforcement into a different light, and helps to build respect for Tribal environmental codes and laws. Some Tribal members felt that the Tribal leadership should not regulate their decisions on housing construction, pesticide use, waste disposal, and other factors that affect the common environment. This meant that each Tribal member had to have the opportunity to participate in developing the regulatory codes.

The intergovernmental relations component was designed to support and enhance cooperative relationships and reduce the duplication of effort among Tribal, federal, state, and local governments. The component emphasized that the Tribes can and should continue to take the leadership role in the region's environmental protection efforts. This strategy further enhances the Tribes' sovereignty.

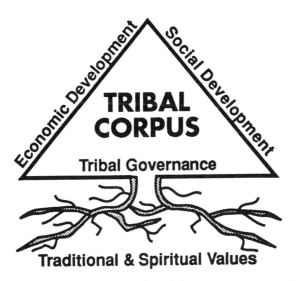

Tribal governance, economics, and social programs are rooted in, and nurtured by, the traditional spiritual values that have been the lifeblood of Tribal people through the centuries.

The Fort Peck Comprehensive Tribal Environmental Plan stresses the need for all Tribal members to see themselves as protectors of the environment and guardians of the future. The EPA recognized the importance of this element and decided to use the Fort Peck plan as the template for their requests for funding proposals from other Tribes. The Fort Peck Tribal staff is now fielding questions from other Tribes on how to replicate their work.

Although a competent program manager would have been tempted to develop such a plan herself, Debi Madison recognized that if the plan were to have any broad impact — if it were, in fact, to be embraced as a community environmental plan — it had to be developed by the people who would eventually carry it to success.

Assessing Tribal Accomplishments

This focus on individual responsibility was nothing new to the Assiniboine and Sioux people. For thousands of years before their contact with the Europeans, Tribal communities had been economically self-sufficient and socially self-reliant. That early visitors to this continent thought they had reached a virgin land is a testament to the Indian people's history of environmental management and low-impact lifestyles. One of the highest compliments to Indian forms of governance is the fact that the U. S. founding fathers modeled The Bill of Rights after that of the Iroquois Confederacy.

These and other Indian contributions point to a foundation of strength that serves Indian country today. The Fort Peck Tribes are using participation to reestablish these strengths in their own community, and create benchmarks for successful development in rural Montana and in Indian country elsewhere. They are involving the community in an authentic dialogue and moving into the 21st century on their own terms.

A number of key factors have contributed to making participation work in these efforts at Fort Peck:

1. Creating opportunities for individuals to take responsibility;
2. In planning sessions, recognizing that respect for the individual is paramount;
3. Inviting people to participate to the extent that they wish; it is an open system.

Like most reservations, Fort Peck is a most intimate community. The participatory methods introduced by the CERT staff have helped avoid the personalizing of issues and stances that could easily become very political. Instead, traditional shared responsibility and communication styles have been emphasized. However, participation has not been a free-for-all. Carefully structured participation has been at the root of their successes in development planning.

The planning and participation of the council, staff, and members of the Fort Peck Tribes are not new, but comprise the latest evolutionary stage in a long history of consensus-based decision making. It is important to note that while briefly summarized here, these planning and development activities have actually spanned three-and one-half years. The struggles have not ended and the need to come together in planning sessions will continue. What has been established, though, is that the people of the Fort Peck Tribes, as successful consensus builders, now realize they can carry on the legacy of their ancestors.

Ogden, Utah Service Center

Chapter 11
The Quality Flag Flies Proudly

ELIZABETH W. KATZ

*The theme for the 90s can be summed up in two words:
QUALITY and CHANGE! Automation is modernizing
our tax systems and challenging us to look at what
we do in a new way. In order to meet these challenges,
we must constantly strive to achieve our goal of
"Excellence in Everything We Do." Never before has there
been such an abundance of opportunities to excel in
the quality process. Here at the Ogden Service Center
each employee has the opportunity to take advantage
of these unique prospects. I challenge all of you to
become personally involved as we move toward
becoming a Total Quality Organization with ever
increasing momentum. Challenges still lie ahead. We
must all generate the energy to face these challenges as
we continue our pursuit of excellence. We do this by
always thinking of the needs of our customers, and
doing our job in the most efficient manner possible.
American taxpayers deserve the very best.*

—Director Michael Bigelow

Singing the praises of the U.S. Internal Revenue Service (IRS) has
never been a national pastime. In fact, most American taxpayers see
themselves as victims, certainly not fans, of the federal tax collection
agency. But miracles can happen, and one has definitely been in
progress at the Ogden, Utah, Internal Revenue Service Center for the
past decade.

According to a report in *The Public Innovator*, the newsletter of the Alliance for Redesigning Government, the IRS as a total agency is "already working to change its operational culture and management." As stated in the April 14, 1994 issue:

> ...the IRS has become the largest "pilot" designated under the 1993 Government Performance and Results Act (GPRA), covering IRS' entire $7.4 billion budget, and 116,000 full time equivalents[employees]....The IRS chose to offer its entire operational overhaul as a pilot because its organization is so interdependent, IRS officials say. "We've been organizing, reinventing, and reshaping everything," says Tyrone Ayres, IRS director of planning [1].

Racking up Savings and Awards

Taxpayers will be happy to know that this kind of innovative overhauling is not just a recent accomplishment of the redesigning government movement. The entire IRS began a system-wide program in the late 1980s. The Ogden Service Center (OSC) has been busily redesigning itself since 1985, and racking up enough tax-dollar savings and efficiency improvements to impress even the most jaded IRS watcher. On March 28, 1994, Vice-President Al Gore presented OSC with the Hammer Award "for outstanding initiatives in reinventing government through new dealings with customers and empowerment of employees"[2]. The Hammer Award is actually a carpenter's hammer mounted in a display case, with a note from the Vice-President saying, "Thanks for building a government that works better and costs less." The hammer is a reminder of the 1980s Defense Department's procurements when the government paid $600 for a hammer. In presenting the award to OSC, the Vice-President pointed out that the hammer in the display case costs $6.

As reported in the OSC newsletter, *Newscope*, of April 15, 1994, Ogden received this award because the OSC "forged a partnership between management, employees, and the National Treasury Employees Union (NTEU), which resulted in dramatic improvements in productivity and service to taxpayers through a commitment to quality"[3].

Nancy Fisher, NTEU Local Chapter 67 president, described the new employee/union/management partnership in which attempts are made, up front, to resolve issues, informally, rather than rushing to file an employee grievance. Grievances and labor-management disputes have been remarkably reduced as a result of the partnership effort to build trust through continued communication.

The news release also observed that the present OSC director, Mike Bigelow, and the preceding Ogden director, Robert Wenzel, have worked persistently to improve service to their customers—the taxpayers. For example, the OSC developed the Professional Letter System (PLS) that, for the first time, gives tax examiners the opportunity to feel ownership of a case. The PLS allows employees to personalize and sign letters to taxpayers. It also gives the customer the name of the employee who is handling his or her case. Under the "old" system, the employee prepared a response to the taxpayer by choosing text that "most closely fit" from a menu of several hundred standard paragraphs. As a result, customers often received what OSC describes as some very "interesting" correspondence.

Other examples of improved customer service cited in the release included:

- Increasing walk-in taxpayer service assistance programs at OSC, which offer taxpayers free electronic filing; and
- Making outreach to tax professionals a priority by developing the annual Tax Practitioners' Symposium and establishing a 24-hour electronic information bulletin board.

Further achievements of the OSC will come to light as the story of their quality efforts unfolds, but the one meaningful accomplishment to taxpaying onlookers is that as of 1994, OSC had achieved a projected cost savings of $27 million. In 1993, they received 26,047,360 returns, all processed by 3,400 permanent employees and 2,900 temporary hires who work as needed during the peak seasons. Service centers, like Ogden, form the data processing arm of the IRS and work under the guidance of the national office. The OSC is aligned with the Southwest Regional IRS office and has the largest service area of the 10 service centers in terms of geographical area; it serves taxpayers and tax practitioners from 14 states.

Tackling the Workload

The Center is organized along two lines: one that directly involves the processing of tax returns (pipeline) and one that accomplishes correspondence, legal, and other functions (non-pipeline). The Center receives and processes tax returns, reviews them to ensure that necessary schedules are included, codes them, and enters the data into the computer. All returns are assigned a unique serial number for easy location, and payments are deposited in the Federal Reserve Bank within 24 hours of receipt. Built-in computer checks verify math and identify other kinds of errors. Next, examiners correct returns rejected by the computer through the on-line error resolution system. If additional information is needed at any point in the process, an employee corresponds with the taxpayer. Ogden then transmits data containing correct return information to the Computing Centers in Martinsburg, West Virginia; Detroit, Michigan; and Memphis Tennessee, where permanent records are established. From here taxpayers receive refunds or notices of taxes due.

The non-pipeline functions at OSC include:
- Correspondence audits of individual tax returns;
- Processing taxpayer correspondence involving delinquent taxes;
- Checking returns for fraud potential and criminal intent;
- Matching information from employers and financial institutions against taxpayers' returns;
- Processing taxpayer inquiries;
- Answering taxpayer inquiries by telephone, mail, and in person at the Customer Service Counter, open daily from 7:00 a.m. to 4:00 p.m.; and
- Maintaining the general ledger accounts for all tax processing operations of the center.

With such a staggering and detailed workload, it's difficult at first to understand how Ogden employees remain so enthusiastic and cheerful. But after a few conversations with Nancy Sandall, an OSC quality improvement program analyst, one begins to feel the positive energy of the Ogden workplace. Reviewing employee descriptions of the work environment, its ethics and its commitment leads to only one conclusion: the Ogden Center is a great place to work—one dedicated to serving its internal and external customers while saving more and more tax dollars.

Take a look at the pictures in Ogden's colorful brochure, Quality Begins With Me, and it's obvious that Ogden's physical location surrounded by the Wasatch Front of the Rocky Mountains and big skies of Utah helps lift the load of serving taxpayers and professionals well. But it involves more than inspiring surroundings and a glossy brochure to win awards and nationwide respect. It has taken ten years of commitment to quality to move the OSC to where it is today: an arm of the IRS nearly completing some goals and tackling even more. The OSC is definitely not resting comfortably on its laurels as winner of the 1992 Presidential Award for Quality, the highest prize for quality in the federal government.

The Federal Quality Institute (FQI) issues these awards to federal agencies that display what a difference a commitment to quality can make to an agency's responsiveness, productivity, and teamwork. Located in Washington, D.C., the FQI is a semi-independent federal organization set up to assist agencies in transforming themselves to customer-centered operations through quality management. Ogden's decision to apply for the Presidential Award reflects another facet of the Center's experience with quality management. When a team was formed to prepare the 30-page application, Nancy Sandall remembers asking then-director, Robert Wenzel what he would like to be included. He told her to go out and ask the OSC employees themselves because they would know best what they'd accomplished. He did not interfere in the process, but encouraged the teams to tell of their accomplishments. His trust in Ogden's workforce paid off when the Center's application was accepted for the award. Wenzel later accepted the

Quality—A Way of Life

Quality improvement at the Ogden Service Center is a way of life. It involves all employees, their efforts, and commitment. Employees and managers work together to provide the methods for early identification and resolution of problems. These methods provide better products and services to our customers. We are creating a climate that fosters respect and desire for total quality. Each employee is encouraged to contribute their energies and ideas to continually improve the work process and environment of the entire Center.

—*from the Center 1994 brochure*

1992 prize with these words, "All of the recognition we have received would not have been possible without everyone's personal commitment toward serving our customers and working together to ensure it took place in Ogden."

"Today," as the employee brochure states, "the quality flag flies proudly over the OSC, a reminder to all employees of their commitment to excellence...and of the workforce's united efforts to produce a quality product, one that reflects each individual's belief that 'Quality Begins With Me.'"

Moving Beyond Quantity to Quality

In 1985, however, the quality level in the IRS as a whole, and also at the OSC, was no model. An explanation in the Federal Quality Institute's Presidential Award for Quality booklet refreshes some memories about the tax situation in the 1980s. During the spring of 1985, newspapers around the country contained headlines such as "IRS' MISTAKE RATE HIGH," "IRS ADMITS REFUND ERROR," "TAX FILERS GET UNHAPPY SURPRISE" [4].

Clearly at this time the IRS, along with the American taxpayers, was caught in the middle of a crisis resulting from the nation's drive for production at any cost. As in the rest of the public and private sectors, IRS' problems in 1985 were symptoms of the nation's misplaced focus on production at the expense of quality. The emphasis on quantity led the IRS to adopt the quick-fix approach of addressing symptoms rather than root causes. Major delays in tax processing triggered problems across the IRS. With volumes of erroneous notices, unlocatable tax returns, and a tremendous increase in the volume of taxpayer correspondence, unfavorable public opinion of the competence of the IRS was painfully visible. The IRS was in the middle of a crisis that was beginning to erode the very foundation of its operations.

Caught in the same negative position, the OSC saw the need to refocus priorities and channel the energy of the workforce in new directions of quality management. As the Federal Quality Institute describes in its 1994 publication, Lessons Learned From High-Performing Organizations in the Federal Government:

> The initial stimulus to the Ogden quality effort came from
> a general awareness that communication had broken down
> between top management and others in the organization.

The director at the time was a self-described traditional command and control manager. He gradually became aware that the Center had a communication and morale problem, so he commissioned an outside consultant to assess the organizational culture. The consultant concluded that the leadership style was impeding communication within the Center and the effectiveness of operations. The director acknowledged the problem and investigated possible solutions. The top management team participated in selecting quality training courses, which led them to adopt a formal quality training effort at the Center [5].

As the FQI continues to relate, despite the obvious problems, when the OSC began its quality effort it was widely seen as one of the most effective and efficient IRS centers. However, the leadership at Ogden began a quality effort partly in response to a cultural survey the Center conducted that showed employees felt left out of decisions. At this time, morale was generally low. The workforce, which embodies the well-known Utah work ethic, was not comfortable when fast production was the strongest push. Though the Center director at the time, Dominic Pecorella, described himself as an autocratic, top-down, driven manager, he reacted in a constructive way to the survey, and saw the need for a new vision involving everyone in making quality and customer-service improvements. He introduced top-level managers to a leadership training course that had influenced his own thinking. This training helped trigger a communication breakthrough among participants, which encouraged managers to actively support a quality management effort with input from everyone. Leaders at the OSC credit this breakthrough with convincing most managers and employees of the need to change.

Six Driving Principles

Incorporating quality into an organization the size of the Ogden facility is a complex job. The OSC organized the huge task around six interlocking driving principles: structure, commitment, education, customer focus, involvement, and recognition. In documenting its quality efforts for the 1992 Presidential Award for Quality, the OSC explained how the six principles worked in helping the Center move down the road toward an effective, centerwide quality program. "We saw each as a gear, with each interrelated principle adding momentum to our efforts," one manager explained. The trip was not always smooth; there were several bumps and detours along the way. But having a well-defined roadmap of principles definitely helped.

Principle 1: Structure

The OSC structure, the mainspring of the driving principles, includes councils, quality improvement teams, task teams, a value system, and techniques for measuring progress. The OSC partnership with the NTEU strengthens the overall effect of the quality improvement process. In 1986 the OSC senior executives established a Service Center Quality Council to lay the foundation for the quality movement. The local president of the NTEU served on the coordinating committee of the Council from the beginning. In 1987, union officers became voting members of the Council, which was then renamed the Joint Quality Council (JQC). Once the Council was expanded beyond senior executives only, OSC was on a clearer path toward becoming a total quality organization. Because it takes managers, union, and employees working together to achieve quality, IRS changed the reference from Total Quality Management to Total Quality Organization, forming the acronym TQO. The mission statement developed by the JQC reflects the expansion:

Despite these significant achievements, midlevel managers throughout the Center initially felt left out of the quality effort, and voiced their concerns to the JQC in 1986. One complained, "All this talk about quality improvement. I'm a manager, but they haven't asked for my input." Responding to this feedback, the director recommended subcouncils be formed for each division with linkage back to the JQC. To enhance the quality initiatives on the night shifts, the OSC formed a Night Quality Council including firstline managers, a section chief, and NTEU representatives, bargaining OSC employees, who are NTEU members. This same format spilled over to the day shift, where some grass roots subcouncils were formed, composed of firstline managers, employees, and union representatives, which promoted the quality process across the working levels.

This type of quality partnership between managers, employees, and union was reinforced nationally in October, 1993 with President Clinton's Executive Order 12871, encouraging all federal agencies to form partnership councils. In line with this order and recognizing the need to expand

---

Mission Statement
A Total Quality Organization:

- Trusts and empowers employees to deliver a quality product.
- Has a common vision shared by everyone.
- Upholds the highest standards of ethics and integrity.
- Advocates, recognizes, and rewards risk taking and creative thinking.
- Focuses on long-term improvement.
- Improves work processes to prevent mistakes from occurring.
- Bases decisions on customer-focused quality standards.
- Inspires all employees to take ownership of the quality process.
- Openly discusses problems and sees defects as opportunities for improvements.

---

partnering more into day-to-day operations, OSC changed in October, 1994 from a JQC to a Partnership Council with equal representation from management and the union.

Cascading Through the Ranks

Once the structure reached out to all the OSC employees, the mechanisms were in place to deal with the chronic problems at the Center. The FQI refers to this deployment of the quality process throughout the entire organization as "cascading." In its assessment of high-performing federal agencies, FQI notes that many organizations when they first begin a quality program confront the dilemma of whether to spread the effort across the board or to confine it to areas that welcome innovation. Organizations also have to decide if they should deploy quality management efforts at the

Payment Tracers
1987-1993
Ogden IRS Center

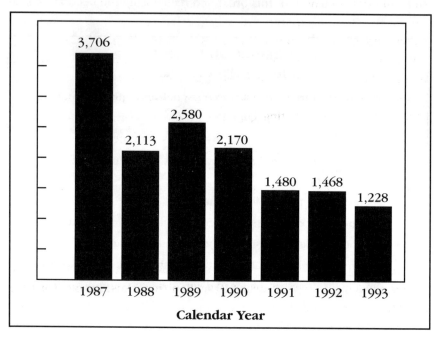

Payment Tracers 1987-1993 — Ogden IRS Center

Calendar Year	Value
1987	3,706
1988	2,113
1989	2,580
1990	2,170
1991	1,480
1992	1,468
1993	1,228

operational levels or with mid-level managers first. The FQI analysts report that some of the effective organizations spread their quality improvement efforts to selected operating areas very early in the quality movement to achieve early, measurable results. In the process they bypassed several layers of management. But in each case, top leaders of these organizations report the bypassed managers were confused about the quality effort, suspicious about what was going on, resentful that their subordinates were working on something of which they had little knowledge, and ultimately opposed the effort. In addition to including mid-level managers on subcouncils at OSC, these managers also participated on teams that gave them first-hand experience in using problem-solving tools.

The deployment of the quality program filtered throughout the workforce when a series of quality improvement teams (QITs) were formed to work on specific problems. The charter of one QIT, the Taxpayer Caused

Notices Team, states that the "IRS wants to mail quality, correct notices of errors to taxpayers, even when the taxpayer has caused the problem. The team's purpose is to identify the primary causes for taxpayer errors that result in erroneous notices"[6]. To support the team efforts, program analysts of the Quality Improvement Staff combine the roles of teacher, promoter, and facilitator, and train teams in decision making and group dynamics. When teams form, the members sign contracts that set boundaries and expectations to define roles. Employees from all levels of the organization nominate and submit team projects to the division staffs, which set specific criteria for selecting QIT team projects. They ask the following questions about team problem-solving suggestions:

- Is it a chronic or systemic problem?
- Is it doable?
- What is our return on the investment?
- What impact does it have on the customer?

Special Team Results

The OSC currently has formed 58 QIT teams involving over 500 people with a projected savings of over $19 million from those teams that have completed their analysis and recommended solutions. The Improper Payment and Deposits QIT team addressed the problem of payment documents being put into the system incorrectly, causing erroneous refunds and notices to taxpayers. The team discovered that unclear instructions in the mailout package of the 1040-ES Estimated Tax Payment Vouchers caused confusion and inconsistency when taxpayers completed their vouchers. The unorganized information of the vouchers led to incorrect posting of taxpayer accounts.

To remedy this situation, the team submitted form change requests, approved nationwide, to standardize the estimated tax voucher package and clarify the instructions. The overall team actions contributed to a reduction of over three million unidentified remittances and over one million fewer payment tracers. Of course the intangible benefits to such a quality effort include improved customer service, but the tangible result to applaud is the cost benefit of $297,720.

Correspondence
Processing Areas
Ogden IRS Center

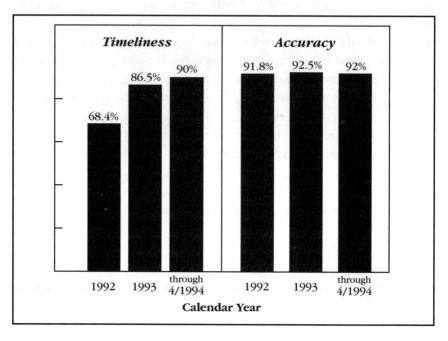

Timeliness
68.4% 86.5% 90%
1992 1993 through 4/1994

Accuracy
91.8% 92.5% 92%
1992 1993 through 4/1994

Calendar Year

Principle 2: Commitment
Among Managers

The OSC recognizes that commitment from all levels of the organization—top management, union representatives, and employees— keeps the quality program moving. One of the most concrete signs of management's commitment to quality is that managers have opened up meetings to all employees and have listened to employee suggestions. In interacting with OSC staff on a daily basis, managers move around the workplace and hear actual staff concerns up front. For example, an employee asked one senior executive, "Why do we transport 50,000 documents through the warehouse, then up a ramp to gain access to an area that is 15 feet away on the other side of the wall?" The executive listened to the question and made the necessary contacts. An opening now offers easy transport of the documents directly.

Another example of such involvement is the story of the OSC night shift employee who wanted to sit in the Ogden director's chair one time before leaving the center to attend dental school. When the director heard this, he made arrangements for the employee to come to his office where he invited the young man to sit in the director's chair. While sitting there, the employee turned to the director and said, "I have worked in a lot of places, but I have never worked where quality has been emphasized as it is here. I know it has to come from your level or it just wouldn't happen."

Among Union Officials and Representatives

At OSC, the president of the local chapter of the NTEU and two other union representatives are members of the Partnership Council. The chapter president and one other NTEU representative also attend the director's staff meetings, as well as budget and staff meetings. The NTEU President Nancy Fisher, and OSC Director Bigelow work together on almost all matters connected with the quality effort. When other agencies visit OSC to learn about the quality program, the union president joins the Ogden management officials to explain their quality efforts and accomplishments. As one union official notes," I've been involved in the quality process since the beginning and I can see it working through an improved working atmosphere, overall communication, and better rapport among management, union, and employees."

Among Employees

From the minute new employees walk through the Center's door, they understand the OSC position on quality. First off, they receive copies of the brochure, Quality Begins With Me. So from the start they are plugged into the program. As one employee comments, "Start with quality as a part of our new hire orientation and it becomes a daily part of processing our work." Such workplace commitment and energy are necessary to cope with the never-ending workload. The OSC receives or sends out over 49 million pieces of mail each year. Cynical taxpayers, ever ready to take a few verbal shots at the inefficiency of the IRS, would be silenced by the statistics of how the employees of the OSC deal with this avalanche of mail, and of how they have reduced the number of errors.

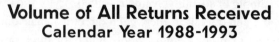

Volume of All Returns Received
Calendar Year 1988-1993
Ogden IRS Center

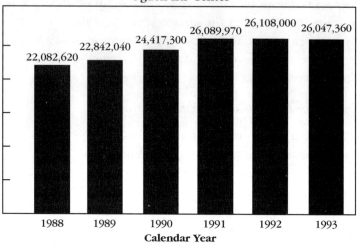

26,108,000

26,089,970

26,047,360

24,417,300

22,842,040

22,082,620

| 1988 | 1989 | 1990 | 1991 | 1992 | 1993 |

Calendar Year

Money received with returns is deposited within 24 hours 100 percent of the time, (except peak), well ahead of national requirements.

Such employee diligence is gaining OSC nationwide recognition as a proving ground for new technology. The OSC is currently a development site for several new IRS automation projects, such as the Totally Integrated Examination System (TIES), which has had a positive effect on improving taxpayer compliance and relieving taxpayer burden. With TIES, information from tax returns undergoing examination is available immediately to tax examiners. The computer is programmed to make various mathematical computations and generated reports. Detailed planning of this system includes everything from computer hardware and software to systems furniture designed to meet employee needs. The total estimated annual savings and benefits for TIES are over $3 million, resulting in:

- Increased revenues
- Improved quality
- Faster response
- Reduced overhead and clerical costs

Principle 3: Education

One OSC employee has observed that "employees will give quality service and job performance when given adequate instructions, support, materials, and motivation." At OSC, management believes that when employee training includes information on the Ogden approach to quality, the employees become involved in the Center's quality vision. For example, technical skills training classes reinforce the commitment to quality and customer service. The following goals are introduced to all new hires and reemphasized in all training classes:

- Establish a quality climate where quality is first among equals with schedule and cost.
- Emphasize product and service quality by eliminating systemic flaws upfront.
- Improve responsiveness to the customer inside and outside the OSC.
- Focus on improving work systems and processes through the use of project teams.
- Integrate quality standards and measurements.

Innovative training concepts at OSC help keep the workforce willing to accept new ideas, a characteristic not usually associated with overworked federal employees. Holding brainstorming sessions is one training tool that stimulates employee enthusiasm because workers realize someone is taking time to listen to their ideas. A significant training program at OSC is a one-day course called Close Encounters of the Customer Kind. The course was developed at the Southwest Regional Office. In Close Encounters, participants:

Identify their customers, particularly internal customers (co-workers at OSC, other IRS centers and offices, as well as at the national agency);
Zero in on their customers' requirements; and,
Map the processes used to meet those requirements.

Once they have completed the course, participants are encouraged to design a plan for improving customer service when they return to their jobs. The FQI notes that much of the day-to day-quality effort at Ogden stems from this initial training. This kind of employee education explains why and how the OSC focuses so successfully on customers.

Principle 4: Customer Focus

The FQI Management Handbook, Lessons Learned From High-Performing Organizations in the Federal Government, mentions that the National Performance Review report advises leaders of federal organizations to pose a series of critical questions about how an organization operates, before they begin to decide how best to transform their own organizations. In the area of customer focus and satisfaction, they advise leaders to ask:

Do you know what your customers need?

Do you relate well to your customers?

Do you have a method to determine customer satisfaction?[7]

The OSC has been asking these questions for almost a decade. At OSC, workers and managers recognize that every tax return represents a taxpayer. To improve customer service they first identified their internal and external customers and their needs. As mentioned earlier, the internal customers include anyone within the IRS — at Ogden, other IRS centers and offices, and at the national agency. External customers are taxpayers, tax practitioners (such as professional tax preparers and CPAs), congressional staffs, other government agencies, vendors, and suppliers. A top-level OSC manager comments, "Before this definition, we didn't recognize in-house people as customers. We did not consider that some actions taken in one area may be detrimental to another area down the line."

Internal Customer Service

The OSC actually has outreach programs to solicit feedback from customers inside the Center. For example, the Communications and Customer Service operation in the computer room sends an annual questionnaire to all branches within the OSC asking them to rate the computer room services they receive. After compiling the questionnaire responses, Communications and Customer Service workers meet with all IRS service center branches, one-on-one, to discuss corrective actions. As OSC Quality Improvement Program Analyst, Nancy Sandall, observes, "At the IRS we are…our own customers." Another example of outreach to internal customers is the Problem Resolution effort in which OSC representatives visit the 14 district offices served by the Ogden Center to find out what problems the OSC might be causing for the district offices. Managers at OSC then receive feedback for problem resolution.

External Customer Service

In its efforts to improve services for external customers, the OSC established in 1988 a walk-in customer service desk to provide easy access for drop-in taxpayers. Many Americans would love to have access in their neighborhoods to such an instant problem-solving service that welcomes taxpayers off the street to discuss problems or even to file electronically. Ogden reports that 96% of the problems brought to the desk are solved on the spot. The most popular issues discussed are questions regarding collection and retirement issues. The OSC is planning to expand this service and is building an entire wing of the center for drop-by customer service.

Another service to external customers, this time for tax practitioners, is the Tax Practitioner Forum consisting of five representatives of the tax practitioner community served by OSC. A link between the center and the practitioners, this group also assists in organizing the annual Tax Symposium sponsored by the OSC and co-hosted by Weber State University. In 1994, more than 280 tax professionals from 17 states attended.

Practitioners can also benefit from an OSC service called the Tax Practitioner Priority Case Program, allowing tax professionals another avenue for case resolution. Now practitioners with problem cases can contact the Center's Taxpayer Relations Branch directly by phone or mail. These cases receive priority handling, and, in most cases, are resolved in 14 days or less. A FAX machine is also on-line 24 hours a day to allow practitioners to correspond directly with the Center.

Principle 5: Involvement

In ticking off the driving principles that keep the OSC on the quality road, it's no surprise that employees themselves as well as managers are spurring the quality mission along. After reviewing how the OSC serves its internal and external customers, even the most critical onlooker can see that everyone at the Ogden Center is involved in making excellence a priority. Management seems to grasp the OSC quality vision, then models it. Director Bigelow is said to show his commitment by example. He doesn't force the employees. He doesn't need to. Teams keep the momentum going. In fact the director would like to have every significant process of the OSC operation handled by employee teams, who would take ownership for initiating specific improvements.

At first the Quality Council assigned team slots to employees. But it soon realized that handing out team assignments did not ensure employee buy-in. A worker's knowledge and interest did not always match the team designation. Now management and the union jointly develop criteria for team members on a project-by-project basis depending on the knowledge required to address the particular problem assigned the team. The union also ensures that teams are composed of at least one-third bargaining employees, a configuration which allows for valuable input from the working level when solving problems. One method used to obtain names of employees who would like to participate on teams was interest letters. The divisions sent out the interest letters so employees could explain in a letter why they should be on a particular team. At the bottom of this letter, the manager stated that he or she would support this employee, who would be released from regular duties without hassle to attend team meetings. As Nancy Sandall, who has been very involved in this process, notes:

> Sometimes employees decide they need to be working and cannot spare the time for a team meeting. Sometimes a worker will plead, "My work has to get done." When that happens, we ask if someone else in your unit can help you with your work. That's how seriously team involvement is taken at the OSC.

Often the ideas for streamlining the bureaucracy come from the OSC individual employees themselves. Out of concern for the diversity of the IRS' external customers, workers at Ogden formed a group to meet one hour each week for a Spanish self-study course. Of course they realize that this is not nearly enough time to develop Spanish language proficiency. Their goal is to be able to understand key words and phrases, so they can better serve their Spanish-speaking customers.

Examples like this one show how public service employees can tap their own energy resources to redesign government, not because the Washington agency hands down an official program, but because of personal initiative that is as entrepreneurial as any seen in the corporate sector. Accomplishments at OSC are hard evidence that the team commitments outlined in the Ogden quality brochure go beyond mere words to measurable constructive action.

Principle 6: Recognition
From Within

One top OSC executive observes, "Our real momentum comes from all persons making hundreds and thousands of small changes that continually raise the overall quality of the entire organization." The Ogden Center has designed several in-house means of rewarding these quality actions. Bimonthly awards ceremonies recognize Quality Champions, OSC workers whom managers, union representatives, and fellow employees can nominate as individuals whose work performance and attitude reflect true quality characteristics. At the ceremony, the director, division chiefs, and NTEU officials personally recognize each champion. The following definition of champions, designed by an OSC employee is reflected in each Service Center champion:

> Customer oriented
> Hard working
> Ambitious
> Make sure the job's done right
> Proud of their work
> Innovative
> Open to new ideas
> Never shirk assignments
> Sold on quality

Descriptions of some of the Ogden champions are, "She has saved the service center thousands of dollars by stopping fraudulent refunds from going out." "He has developed such an effective work method...he has been requested by other managers to present his work method to their employees." "To her credit she has processed 248,188 federal tax deposits with a 100 per cent accuracy rate." As a permanent tribute, the names of these outstanding employees are engraved on the OSC Service Center Quality Champion Board, highly visible to all who enter the main door of the OSC.

Each October the Center celebrates Quality Week as part of National Quality Month. During one celebration, peer-selected employees who exemplify quality received a badge, rotated daily, which read, "I was recognized for quality." During the October celebration in 1994, a new peer recognition was instigated whereby employees can recognize quality efforts of co-workers with balloon bouquets highlighting the theme "Without 'U' there is no quality." Top management at Ogden is also very involved in personally recognizing valuable, quality-minded workers. Each year the director writes hundreds of thank you notes to those who go the extra mile to perform quality service. His comments in these letters include, "It is individuals like you, showing commitment to quality and concern for the customer in your efforts everyday, who ensure, 'Excellence in Everything We Do.'" These notes are hand delivered to the recipients. Since 1988, over 5,000 employees have received another form of recognition, the on-the-spot quality award given by a manager or union official who observes a worker going that extra mile.

A very recent addition to the in-house recognition list is the "Tim Bucks" program whereby exemplary employees earn an hour of administrative leave, instead of a more typical award trinket. These "bucks" can be accumulated over time to equal days off.

From Outside

The Ogden Center has received a large measure of recognition from outside its walls as well. Prizes such as the Hammer Award in 1994, the 1992 Presidential Award for Quality, the National IRS/NTEU Joint Quality Improvement Process Award presented to OSC's JQC in 1990, and the 1989 Office of Management and Budget's Prototype Award for Quality and Productivity Improvement, all prove the Center's competitiveness in the national leagues. Nearer to home, Ogden in 1990 received the Innovative Corporate Excellence Award from the governor of Utah. The Center's outstanding accomplishments in equal employment opportunity practices, community commitment, and child care services merited the governor's prize.

In fact, the OSC Child Care Center received accreditation status by the National Association for the Education of Young Children. Kindergarten classes are also available at the Center, a feature that has helped OSC parents who faced the dilemma of dealing with the problem of the local public school system's half-day-only kindergarten. Having this kind of facility at the Center is further proof that the OSC not only includes productivity and customer service in its goals, but also recognizes how the quality of worklife is another parameter of excellence affecting worker motivation and outlook.

Moving the Principles Forward

The interlocking principles of structure, commitment, education, customer focus, involvement, and recognition obviously serve Ogden very well. Yet, no hint of complacency is detectable at the OSC by even the most sensitive evaluator. In fact, interviews with Ogden personnel always result in new material, hot off the press accomplishments and initiatives. Ogden watchers also have very positive reactions to the OSC continuous improvement program.

In its 1994 analysis of eight relatively recent winners of the Presidential Award for Quality or the Quality Improvement Prototype Awards, the FQI shows how Ogden went beyond formal structures and integrated quality into day-to-day operations. The FQI uncovered ten broad approaches used by these organizations to ensure that quality practices become a part of the way the organizations are managed and operate routinely[8].

Ten Effective Strategies

- Focus on a Few Major Elements
- Establishing the Need to Change
- Approaches to Planning for Quality
- Process Analysis and Reorganization
- Comprehensive vs. Targeted Implementation
- Strategies for Involving Mid-level Managers
- Employee Involvement and Communication
- Union Involvement
- Measurement
- Leadership

In weighing the importance of each of these ten strategies, the FQI decided that the exercise of effective leadership appears to be the most important factor in transforming an organization through quality. In their analysis, the FQI concludes that the most effective top leaders display personal ownership of the quality effort and consistency in the overall direction of the quality effort in the event of turnover at the top[9]. It was exactly this kind of leadership transfer that actually took place twice at the OSC in the midst of the quality initiatives. As noted earlier, Director Dominic Pecorella began the quality process in the 1980s when he introduced top-level managers to a leadership training course that helped shatter communication barriers and encouraged managers to glean everyone's input in quality activities. Leaders at Ogden point to this breakthrough as one reason for being able to raise the low employee morale that had previously permeated the OSC atmosphere and push on toward a full-fledged quality movement.

In June, 1986, Robert Wenzel became OSC director and set into action his management and leadership style of communicating fully with everyone at the Center and delegating as much authority as possible to lower levels in the organization. Under Director Wenzel's leadership, OSC developed the framework to harness the quality initiatives that had previously been somewhat random and unstructured. His philosophy of "doing it right the first time" appealed to employees frustrated by a system that didn't always function as they wanted. Recognition such as the 1989 Director, Office of Management and Budget Prototype Award for Quality and Productivity Improvement and the 1992 Presidential Quality Award attest to Wenzel's effectiveness. So does the 10-minute standing ovation he received from OSC employees at the Presidential Awards ceremony held at Ogden. As the FQI notes:

> One observer [at the Ogden ceremony] commented that it was the most emotional and inspiring display of federal employees he had seen and much of it was because of the employees' personal identification with Wenzel's leadership[10].

Current OSC Director Michael Bigelow continues the OSC tradition of close communication between the director and employees at all levels. He has instituted the "If I Were Director" program that encourages employees to fill out a form detailing their suggestions for quality improvements at Ogden. Though a coordinator helps Director Bigelow collect the data, he reviews every form himself. Workers who make the best suggestions receive a recognition award plaque and have their picture taken while sitting at the director's desk. Town meetings conducted by both the director and NTEU chapter president are held monthly on both shifts and have become an effective tool for two-way communication. Ideas such as this help Michael Bigelow achieve his goal of making employee involvement more systematic and routine at OSC. They also reflect his systematic and organized approach to management. As Director Bigelow commented to the FQI, "I couldn't have stopped the quality effort here at Ogden even if I had wanted to. I would have had a revolution on my hands"[11]. He went on further to say:

> It is an honor to be singled out as a leader in the arena of reinventing government. The challenging aspect of quality improvement or reinvention is that "the more you learn about quality, the more you realize how much you still need to accomplish." Through partnering and tax-systems modernization efforts, we are striving to provide the kind of quality service the American taxpayer expects and deserves.

References

[1] Alliance for Redesigning Government, "Performance Pilot at IRS," *The Public Innovator,* Issue No. 2, April 14, 1994, Washington, D.C., p. 2.

[2] IRS Center, Ogden, Utah, "Hammer Award drives home partnerships," Newscope, Vol 26, No.4, April 15, 1994, p. 1.

[3] Ibid.

[4] Federal Quality Institute, Presidential Award for Quality Booklet, Ogden Internal Revenue Service Center, Washington, D.C., 1992, p.1.

[5] Federal Quality Institute, "Lessons Learned from High-Performing Organizations in the Federal Government," The Federal Quality Management Handbook Series, February, 1994, Washington, D.C., February, 1994, p. 54.

[6] Presidential Award for Quality Booklet, p. 7.

[7] Lessons Learned from High-Performing Organizations, p. 16.

[8] Ibid., p. 16.

[9] Ibid., p. 44.

[10] Ibid., p. 45.

[11] Ibid., p. 47.

SECTION III
Empowering Employees

Recovering the Role of Public Servant

The mayor of a city was being driven to work one morning when he noticed something odd. Along the edge of the boulevard, a municipal workman was digging a row of holes. But as soon as he finished digging one hole, another workman would step up and fill it in again! The mayor had his driver pull over and sent his aide to investigate. The aide returned to the car looking relieved: "Nothing out of the ordinary, sir. They're usually a three-man crew, but the fellow who plants the trees is out sick today!"

One hopes that this story is apocryphal. Especially since these days it is possible to find public servants who model the best in public sector behavior. They don't deserve the cynical government-bashing that many find fashionable today.

Initiatives from Within

Joan Hyatt Wickersheim, an inspector for the Department of Labor's Occupational Safety and Health Administration (OSHA) in Denver, Colorado, is a prime example of one such model[1]. She is part of a team of people whose job it is to ensure the safety of our country's workplaces.

OSHA's mission is to investigate reports of unsafe working conditions, instruct workplace managers to correct bad conditions, and propose fines for workplace violations. Previously, inspectors had to consult with their supervisors during every step of the review process, ultimately passing off their cases to administrative personnel and other specialists.

However in 1993, OSHA held what the National Performance Review calls a "reinvention lab" or conference in which Joan and 50 other front-line workers and supervisors participated. They were asked to determine ways that they could make their jobs better, reduce their excess paperwork, and focus instead on their main assignment of inspecting the workplaces. At the end of that reinvention conference, the 50 participants had come up with 22 initiatives and called in top OSHA management officials to approve or disapprove of those initiatives on the spot. Nineteen of the initiatives were approved.

One of 19 called for a revision of what OSHA inspectors call their "field operations manual," a tome of 400 pages. This manual dictates to workers like Joan the large amounts of paperwork they must fill out and the kinds of documentation they need to provide. And, as Joan says, "It also tells how to put one foot in front on the other and walk down the aisle of a workplace to do our inspections." As a result of their management-approved initiatives, Joan and her colleagues whittled the manual down to 100 pages. The end result is that OSHA inspectors now will have fewer paper barriers to jump before they can get into the field. In the new system, which Joan and her colleagues created, the OSHA field investigator "owns" the case from start to finish. Now, inspectors ask for advice when they need it, and are responsible for making decisions on site. Freed from their desks, they are able to fix unsafe conditions faster. And when they visit a worksite, they are now taken more seriously.

Empowering Public Servants

In this illustration of one federal agency initiative, one sees in microcosm what is meant about worker empowerment. Joan, like most of us, simply wants to do her job and do it well. Reinventing government does not require millions of dollars paid to high-priced consultants. Rather, it can be done by asking people like Joan to be what they were called to be—public servants.

Many people—both inside and outside of the public sector—believe government is simply a big jobs program, another entitlement to be taken advantage of. If success stories like Joan's are to increase, everyone must reject this cynical view while inspiring those inside government to remember what initially lured them to government careers. Nineteen million Americans are public servants who work for either the federal, state, or local levels of government. If this powerful human potential can be fully tapped what a wonder one would behold. Cynics may ask, "Isn't the empowerment of public servants an oxymoron?" As these case studies show, the answer is "no."

Many public servants have become institutionalized by the very institutions that were meant to care for others. They've become hardened in their efforts to carry the weight of society's problems while at the same time being constrained by a framework of paperwork geared to the needs of the 19th century. They've become mere functionaries. Yet, at one time, public service was the most noble of professions, second only to the priesthood. Plato said that these ones who accepted the responsibility for running government were the philosopher-kings.

Encouraging Entrepreneurs Within Government

Happily, the concept of public service as a noble profession may be resurfacing as we witness the emergence of public heroes. Exceptional government performances are recognized by The Public Employees' Roundtable, which has a Public Service Awards program identifying federal, state, and local governmental agencies that have recognized the achievement of empowered public servants.

One agency winning the Roundtable Award in 1993 was the Office of the State's Attorney, 18th District of Florida, Titusville. Workers in that agency concentrate on crime victims and witnesses who for decades have been ignored, inconvenienced, and revictimized by the very system designed to protect them. Their Victim/Witness Services program ensures that victims and witnesses receive the attention, assistance, and support they need and deserve throughout every step of the court process. Individual needs assessments are made of the emotional, psychological, and physical state of victims. Intervention is then often provided to help them deal with employer relations, financial hardships, creditor problems, landlord difficulties, and questions about the return of property. Both staff and volunteers work closely with other public agencies—the police, the courts, hospitals, and community services. The result has been an increase in the number of successful prosecutions and convictions.

Governing magazine conducted a poll of readers in regards to the recommendations of the National Commission on the State and Local Public Service in its report, "Hard Truths/Tough Choices: An Agenda for State and Local Reform." A high-performance workforce was the number one area of concern for readers who enthusiastically endorsed the report's recommendations for improvement, including new styles of labor-management communication and skill-based pay systems. More than 66 percent of the respondents gave that recommendation top priority [2].

Governing and the Council for Excellence brought together 120 top state and local officials gathered to discuss the recommendations of the Winter Commission Report. The officials identified two road-blocks to empower front-line workers and shake up the old bureaucratic governance model: the historical mistrust between labor and management, and the resistance of many managers who are not interested in a closer working relationship with the front-line people. The participants identified a variety of ways to deal with the issues, but ultimately confirmed there is no secret to success. It remains the task of leadership to guide the transformation process.

Consulting from Within

One of the ironies of the desire to reinvent government is the notion that high-priced reengineering consultants will be needed. As the stories in this section indicate, just the opposite may be true. Once competent facilitators, who engage stakeholders in agency change, are injected into an organization, management frequently discovers that the only consultants they need are the ones already working for them—their dedicated employees. This became evident at Chicago's Department on Aging (CDoA). Midway into the first year of implementing the CDoA staff-designed strategic plan, Nora Jones, the department's union steward, found a smaller number of employee grievances being brought to her attention. As she studied the phenomena, she saw that it wasn't so much a matter of there being fewer concerns. Instead labor and management were dealing with the issues more openly and frankly at the source long before the concerns festered into actual labor complaints. This, most agreed, could be attributed to the newfound candor that resulted from the strategic plan being designed by all 200 department employees. In these facilitated planning sessions, everyone had a chance to articulate their visions for the department and vent their dreams and frustrations. This openness led to real implementation of their strategy, because, as everyone knows, no one implements someone else's plan.

When the employees are engaged in the planning process on the topics that affect their jobs and when they are genuinely asked to participate on an equal basis, something akin to a "mind-shift" occurs. This does not happen without top management's support. The people in charge must give their blessing to authentic employee involvement, not just tacit consent. This will require a new type of leader—one who will seize today's new way of doing the business of government. For public sector leaders to reinvent their units of government, they must reinvent themselves. Dedicated public servants are not merely a "cost." They represent an investment, and if leaders want to make long-term improvements in their organizations, they will wisely make long-term investments in their people.

As our case studies demonstrate, managers create boundaries, walk them, and create a "safe space" to allow employee participation to take root. Providing time for training and planning is not a luxury but an integral way of life in an organization. Wise leaders know the important role of training as an investment in the human factor: people come first.

References

[1] The story of Joan and OSHA is retold from the transcript of a White House ceremony on the occasion of the six-month report of the National Performance Review.

[2] *Governing,* February, 1994, p. 60.

Chapter 12
Change Agents in Purdue University Libraries

NANCY S. HEWISON AND DONALD O. BUSHMAN

Purdue University, located in northwestern Indiana, is a state school with over 35,000 students and a total of 15 libraries scattered across the campus. As recently as 1985, the Purdue University Libraries[1] had been described as "a loose confederation—15 libraries connected by a budget." That situation began to change when Emily Mobley joined the library administration in 1986 and set in motion the Purdue Libraries' transformation — a success story of people shaping and owning the future.

The Problems

The difficulty in getting consensus on any issue on a college campus is well known. Peter Drucker, for example, reportedly has described a university faculty as "a group of anarchists united by a parking lot"[1]. However, at Purdue University, there has long been a guaranteed way to set heads nodding in vigorous agreement: mention "the library problem."

When Emily Mobley became dean of the Purdue Libraries in 1989, she inherited "the "library problem," which was really many problems. People described the situation in different ways. Too few books and journals. Not enough library computerization. Too much attention to computers. Too many libraries, too far apart. The lack of special-subject libraries. Almost everyone, though, pointed to inadequate funding of the Libraries by university administration.

---

[1]It is Purdue University's style to capitalize the word Libraries when referring to the campus-wide library system. We depart from our standard style to comply with Purdue's usage.

The whole campus was aware of these problems. For instance, when Pennsylvania State University became a member of the "Big Ten" in 1990, this letter appeared in Purdue's student newspaper:

> The addition of Penn State to the Big Ten means that despite the efforts of Dean Mobley and all of the other library professionals, Purdue's library system is sinking into what was once a comic metaphor: eleventh place in the Big Ten [2].

Today, in 1994, people speak differently about the Libraries. "Try that agricultural database on the Libraries' system," a student advises a friend. "It's easy to use and all the journals in its index are here on campus. It'll really help you with your term paper." A faculty member remarks, "Every time I go into one of the libraries, there's something new. It's exciting!"

How did the change occur?

Planting the Seeds of Change

The change began in 1987. A small group of library faculty and staff studied the library system, comparing it to other university libraries, interviewing the campus community, and then sharing its findings with the whole campus. That was the first step.

Next, the Libraries held a retreat and focus groups that included the entire library faculty and staff. At these gatherings the entire group developed a vision of what the the Libraries' future could be, and defined its role— to be a partner in the university's mission of teaching, research, and service to the campus community.

Finally, the group invited the Libraries' users to join 19 "action teams"; at this point campus interest in the Libraries grew. All told, nearly 100 individuals participated directly in action-planning teams. These teams spent three to nine months addressing issues such as the following:

Resource Materials	Physical Facilities
Accessibility	Archives
Teaching Partnerships	Preservation of Library Materials
Research Partnerships	Staff Morale and Common Purpose
Collaborative/Interdisciplinary Efforts	Staff Workspace and Tools

Productive Information Users Staff Development
Technology Training Internal Communication
Lifelong Learning Public Relations
Service Partnerships Organizational Structure
Information Transfer

Early results of the planning, such as the addition of new databases to the Libraries' computerized catalog, made a positive impact. Yet even within the Libraries, some doubts hovered, and some in the group were unsure whether any real changes could take place. These nagging doubts surfaced when the group coordinating the Libraries planning asked Dean Mobley, "What if we do all this planning and come up with a lot of great ideas, but there's still no money?" Undaunted, Dean Mobley issued a challenge: "What if we never have any more money in our budget than we have right now? Will we just sit back and do what we've always done?" Then to acknowledge that money is important, she continued, "I can just about guarantee that if we don't have a plan, we won't get additional funds. But if we have a plan, we may just get the money we need to carry it out."

By the end of 1992, when the 19 teams completed their plans, the number of proposed actions totaled more than 350. It was time to pull all this together into one strategic plan, a flexible blueprint that would enable the Purdue Libraries to respond to the changing needs of users. And so, on a cold January morning in 1993, while Purdue students were home for winter break, 37 leaders and members of action-planning teams put their heads together. The group defined 11 critical directions for the Libraries. They then ranked the actions within each direction. Next, as a team exercise, they designed an elephant wearing a rocket pack to symbolize what the critical directions say about the Libraries.

This "gang of 37" came away from the winter meeting in an optimistic mood. When asked, "What did you people do all that time?", they focused on the group's achievements. "We decided on the future of the Libraries!" said one, and, "We took the important parts of all the action plans and made them into one," boasted another. One delighted person said, "We did something I never thought we could do, and we did it by consensus." And one woman, in a voice full of wonder, answered, "A co-worker asked me that, and I said to her, 'There may be a place for me here, after all. We used the word "risk." And then we actually had a discussion about building risk taking into the Libraries."

Planning Pays Off

The Libraries confronted the reality of the risks head on. When Purdue administrators prepared the 1993-94 budget, the university faced continuing economic uncertainties. "I think it is fair to say that we must anticipate another lean year, and perhaps another three lean years, as we look at the economy of the nation and the state," Purdue University President Steven C. Beering told the faculty senate in November, 1993 [3]. Would all the planning pay off for the Libraries, even in the middle of a recession? To some it seemed unlikely, partly because his assessment reflected the nationwide experience of tough economic times for publicly supported universities. As *The Chronicle of Higher Education* reported in January, 1994, "Even where economies are recovering, higher education often falls into the budget queue behind prisons, Medicaid, and the public schools"[4].

In the on-campus budget queue, the library may be far back in line. Faculty members and campus administrators often describe the library as "the heart of the university," seeming to recognize that it provides major support for all academic programs. However, when university budgets are tight and all departments are asked to take cuts, the library's budget may also be reduced, further undermining the teaching and research programs of the university.

Yet, in the Purdue 1993-94 budget, the Libraries received the highest percentage increase on campus. The administration increased the amount allocated for books and other library materials by over 18 percent. In addition, the library system was one of only two units on campus that was not required to reduce its staff. "The university administration was more supportive this year than in any of the seven years I've been around," Dean Mobley said. The planning was working at the university level as well as within the Libraries.

Don Bushman, a strategic planning consultant for the Institute of Cultural Affairs (ICA), paid a visit to Purdue part way through the Libraries' planning effort. He had taught a leadership course at a library association conference several years earlier. One of the attendees at that meeting was Nancy Hewison, who had applied what she learned at the conference to her work as coordinator of the Purdue Libraries' planning effort.

Two Profiles

Purdue University

Location: West Lafayette, Indiana.

Established: 1869, as a land-grant university under the Morrill Act of 1862, by which the federal government offered to turn over public lands to any state which would use the proceeds from their sale to maintain a college to teach agriculture and the "mechanic arts." Named for John Purdue, an early benefactor.

Students: 35,161

Faculty and staff: 12,250.

Degrees awarded annually: Approx. 8,000.

Schools: Instruction organized through the schools of Agriculture; Consumer and Family Sciences; Education; Engineering; Liberal Arts; Management; Pharmacy, Nursing, and Health Sciences; Science; Technology; and Veterinary Medicine; and through the Graduate School.

Annual operating expense budget: $671 million.

Physical plant: 145 principal buildings; 647 acres.

(Information from *Facts at Your Fingertips 1993-94: A Resource Book for Those Who Speak and Write About Purdue and Facts About Purdue 1993-94,* West Lafayette, IN: Purdue University.)

Purdue University Libraries

Faculty and staff: 200.

Annual budget: $12.25 million.

Computerized access: Online catalog plus databases covering periodicals in agriculture, biology, business, engineering, humanities, and social sciences. Over 100 CD-ROM and diskette databases. "Gopher" server which provides connections to databases, library catalogs, news, etc., available on the Internet worldwide network.

Collections: 2 million volumes; 1,800,000 items in microform; over 16,400 periodicals; plus government publications, company annual reports, technical reports, maps, slides, motion pictures, videotapes, and theses.

15 libraries: aviation technology; biochemistry; chemistry; consumer and family sciences; earth and atmospheric sciences; engineering; humanities, social science, and education; life sciences; management and economics; mathematical sciences; pharmacy, nursing, and health sciences; physics; psychological sciences; undergraduate; veterinary medicine.

Planning Timeline

1986 • Emily Mobley comes to Purdue as associate director of libraries.

1987 • Libraries director names Mobley head of Library Futures Steering Committee, made up of ten library faculty and professional staff.

• "Futures Committee" studies Libraries' history, develops comparisons to other university libraries, interviews and surveys faculty and students, and begins sharing data with campus.

1988 • Entire library faculty, professional staff, and clerical staff (totalling 220 people) meet in 22 focus groups to develop Libraries' mission statement.

1989 • Mobley named acting director upon death of Libraries director.

• Futures Committee issues "Information Report," analyzing data collected to date.

• Library faculty and professional staff meet in groups over six weeks to develop Libraries' vision.

• Mobley named dean of libraries (position upgraded from director).

• Library faculty and professional staff go on retreat to further refine vision, develop a sense of unity, examine opportunities and threats to success.

• Retreat Recap Committee reports to entire library faculty and staff on retreat activities, learnings, and outcomes. This committee also proposes that planning process continue via action-planning teams and coordinating council.

1990 • Futures Committee determines make-up of its successor, a Futures Planning Council. Mobley agrees to finalize draft planning document, developed from work to date, as basis for next steps in planning process.

1991 • Mobley, finding herself unable to continue work on planning document, creates planning librarian position for Nancy Hewison, to head Futures Planning Council and coordinate planning process.

	• Planning Council completes planning document, including strategies for achieving Libraries' vision, and refines it in meetings with entire library faculty and staff.
1992	• Convened by Planning Council, 19 action-planning teams composed of library faculty and staff, plus others from university community, work to turn strategies from planning document into recommendations for action.
12/92-1/93	• Thirty-seven team leaders and members review 350+ actions proposed by teams, prioritize them, and develop eleven "critical directions" in which Libraries will move. Group also works on possible new organizational structures.
1993	• Planning Council prepares near-final draft of strategic plan, reworking eleven critical directions into five "key strategic directions," each expressed as set of strategies with specific programs and actions. Council refines draft in discussions with entire library faculty and staff, and completes final version of plan. Proposed new organizational structure also presented and discussed.
	• Libraries' strategic plan printed, presented at faculty and student senates, and distributed to all campus faculty.
	• Dean presents new organizational structure, including clusters of related-subject libraries and new policy-making council which will include clerical and professional staff representatives.
	• Planning Council's "implementation audit" in August shows all but a few of 1992-93 actions and programs have been implemented. As its final duty, this council reviews implementation milestones for remaining four years of plan, adjusts them among years, and prioritizes those for 1993-94.
1994	• Planning continues as new policy-making council works on Libraries-wide issues, project teams implement actions, and various units determine specific plans under umbrella of Libraries' strategic plan.

Critical Directions for the Libraries

Toward improving user access

Toward taking creative risks

Toward improving and enhancing collection quality

Toward redefining and growing library instruction

Toward building library esprit de corps

Toward developing human resources

Toward enhancing information delivery

Toward improving physical work environment

Toward extending outreach to state and under-served

Toward building public relations and support

Toward facilitating cooperative research with faculty

(Determined in December 1992 by "the gang of 37,"
made up of leaders and members from nineteen action-planning teams,
working with 350+ actions and programs recommended by the teams.)

Don Bushman had heard about the emerging transformation of the Purdue University Libraries and had come to campus to see the situation for himself, and to meet Dean Mobley, whom he understood to be the "prime mover" of this transformation.

When Emily welcomed him into her office, Don began to hear the Libraries' story in her own words. Looking back to the days of the late 1980s, she told Don:

> I saw planning as a vehicle to create change in an environment, rather than to solve short-term problems. When I came to Purdue, I found an excellent library staff. And we know this because surveys and reports from the faculty and students tell us this over and over.

The users, she explained, continually found fault with collections, equipment, and facilities, but never failed to praise the staff. This support for their work, however, did not prevent the Libraries' faculty and staff from agreeing painfully with the generally held, negative appraisal of the Libraries. Emily continued, "The Libraries had a major image problem. Part of changing the culture was for our own preservation. We needed to do something that allowed us to feel good about ourselves."

One challenge that Emily identified was helping the faculty and staff of the Libraries "choose to differentiate beyond the fiefdoms." In using the word "fiefdoms," she emphasized that many of the directors of individual libraries operated as if they were autonomous units, competing for resources with the other libraries. Emily recognized this attitude as a reflection of the university culture, in which money, staff, and space were largely under the control of the deans of the ten schools, with competition among the schools for these resources. Recalling her assessment of the situation, Emily told Don, "We needed to see that our self-worth is not based on working with a certain school or department, but on being librarians."

Eliminating a Top-Down Culture

Additionally, Emily had seen the need "to change from a top-down culture to a sharing of power." She wanted faculty and staff of the Libraries to become comfortable in making decisions at their own levels in the organization. "Planning rests on actions that carry responsibility," she observed, and continued, "There were problems at the systemic level, that is, at the level of the libraries as a system. People needed to feel successful about creating their own destiny. I saw the need for empowerment of the staff and looked for what it would take."

It was obvious to Don that Emily had recognized that a staff revitalized by planning would respond better to significant developments in the university, such as the creation of a new school. This energy would help them respond creatively to trends in the larger environment of higher education, such as the decline in state and federal funding. The staff would also need to increase their ability to develop and adopt new strategies, such as implementing new information technologies. Such flexibility would be critical if the Libraries' were to continue to meet the needs of their users.

Shifting Mindsets

In the process of empowering the staff, Emily wanted to set in motion several cultural shifts. She described one as a shift from a mindset of "all we need is more money" to creating, instead, practical suggestions for doing what could be done immediately, with the Libraries' present resources. She felt the need to "force an environment that understands there are things we can do right now."

As Emily explained to Don, "We needed to shift from an emphasis on our local collection of books and materials, to an emphasis on access to information, no matter where it's stored." Part of such a shift involved moving from hard copy to electronic storage and retrieval of information. It also meant beginning to look at the entire collection as one large, campuswide resource, instead of building the Libraries' individual collections in relative isolation from one another. Emily told Don:

> We needed to move away from the feeling that we can't give up any of our journal subscriptions, toward making a campuswide decision to go from three subscriptions to a particular journal down to one.

As she talked with Don that day, Emily shared some of her thoughts on the transformation to date:

> People in the Libraries are willing to look out farther into the future than we were two or three years ago. Action planning has been a way to get people to articulate their visions. People are more involved in the Libraries' role in the university.

Outside the Libraries, she observed:

> The faculty are giving us praise among the complaints. And as the university administration talks about library services that are "cutting edge" and "state of the art," librarians are coming to be seen as allies.

New Ways of Working Together

Don felt great anticipation as he finished his visit with Emily. He was about to find out whether the changes she had hoped to catalyze were really taking place. He planned to talk with ten members of the library faculty and staff, each of whom had been involved in the planning process in one way or another. Using the appreciative inquiry method, which invites people to reflect on their own experiences, Don and each individual would explore the planning effort [5].

The Libraries Vision

In the twenty-first century, the Libraries will utilize sophisticated technologies to provide optimum access to and delivery of information, regardless of its location, rather than serving as a major local repository. An expert staff will assist the members of the Purdue community in becoming proficient and productive users of information.

(From A Shared Commitment to Excellence:
A Plan for the Future, 1992-1997,
the strategic plan of the Purdue University Libraries)

Don talked first with Jean Poland, a library faculty member. She didn't hesitate over her answer to Don's first question, "What was your peak experience in the planning process?" "The action team on morale and common purpose was the most important element for me. This gave the staff a voice." As a faculty member, Jean reflected on the sharp contrast between the past and the present. Before the planning process started, those in the lower levels of the Libraries' faculty, professional, and clerical staff hierarchy were only rarely consulted on issues affecting the Libraries:

> We had Emily's support of the process and a team made up primarily of clerical staff members who were given a chance to say what they liked, and to feel that what they said was important. This team was harnessing the abilities of the staff. And our conclusion was, "We've been heard."

As the ten interviews with the Libraries' faculty, professional, and clerical staff unfolded, Don heard over and over about the value of working together in a group that included people from all job levels. "At these meetings I could disagree with professional librarians," Jill Smith, a clerical staff member, told Don. "I felt a real part of the process." From Jill, Don learned that the faculty and staff hierarchy in the Libraries was a direct reflection of that in the university itself, a sort of caste system that he had wrongly assumed no longer existed in universities.

Don found that Jean and Jill were not alone in sensing a change. Everyone spoke of it, including Pat Carmony, a clerical staff member who had not been on a planning team because there just was not room on the

The Libraries Mission

The Libraries are partners with the schools and departments
of the university in meeting the teaching, research,
and service commitments of Purdue University.

The five components of the mission are:
- A partner in teaching and research
- Information literacy and lifelong learning
- A partner in the university's off-campus service programs
- Information transfer
- A repository of the intellectual record

(From A Shared Commitment to Excellence: A Plan for the Future, 1992-1997,
the strategic plan of the Purdue University Libraries)

teams for all who had expressed interest. Don spoke with Pat to gain the perspective of someone who had not been deeply involved in the planning. "The most engaging part of the planning process," she said, "was having all the different teams with faculty, professional, and clerical staff."

Faculty and professional staff members agreed with their clerical colleagues on including people from all staff levels. "The planning process empowered the clerical employees," one staff member told Don, reflecting on the large number of clerical staff involved. She also talked about the respect their ideas received within the teams and in the planning effort in general. "It's the end of the clerical staff as a forgotten voice."

The issues and problems that the clerical staff needed to discuss included inadequate wages, unclear job descriptions, supervisors who did not understand the jobs of those they supervised, and the desire for more on-the-job training. In addition, clerical employees were as passionate as the Libraries faculty about improving services for the user. Clerical staff who perform many of the front-line jobs in the Libraries brought to the action-planning teams a strong advocacy for simplifying procedures and standardizing policies, to make library use easier. They also spoke clearly about the need to improve public relations with the university community, and to broaden communication within the Libraries.

The Role of Technology

A common thread unifying the components of the mission is the use of technology for the identification and delivery of information, in both local and remote collections, and information services. Today's libraries are technology-rich learning centers for information literacy and lifelong learning skills. The Libraries will research new technologies for the creation, storage and retrieval, analysis and transmission of information, resulting in the design of innovative systems for students and scholars.

(From A Shared Commitment to Excellence: A Plan for the Future, 1992-1997, the strategic plan of the Purdue University Libraries)

Don interviewed Dot Fultz, a clerical staff member for whom the changes in the Libraries as a result of the planning process had special significance. Prior to her planning team experience, she had worked on a universitywide committee to improve communication between clerical staff and campus administrators. When asked what personal rewards she had received from the planning, Dot answered very directly: "Sharing what I feel: knowing we can break down ranks. I had the satisfaction of working along with faculty and professionals." She was equally clear on her requirements for the future of the Libraries' planning process. "From now on we'll have involvement of everybody at all levels," she said, referring to the need for continued participation of clerical staff as well as the professional staff and faculty. "This is the way it's going to be."

One Interactive Community

Throughout the interviews, Don found the theme of "one library" recurring. This was a new concept for the Purdue Libraries' employees, who had long defined themselves mainly in relation to 15 different client groups. Library faculty member Jean Poland had suggested that a basic value enlivening the planning process was "the sense of community building, the sense that this is all one community that interacts in different ways." Don's talk with Judy Nixon further underlined this shift. Serving on the planning council that advised the action teams, she saw "a strong undercurrent of need to work as a single system," and a willingness to "change a procedure if it's for the good of all."

Shirley Coleman, a team leader, found that the planning process "clarified direction." She also observed, "There seems to be more support than in the past for a unified approach." For example, all libraries reached an agreement on how long a user could borrow a book. Then, staff across campus who were in charge of loaning library materials, reviewed the multiplicity of user-notification forms. They created one standardized form for each type of notification, such as an overdue book reminder. The 15 libraries were taking practical steps toward becoming the "one unit" Shirley described.

Don saw another example of this changing perception. Mark Tucker, a team leader and a member of yet another team, reflected on what he saw on the horizon:

> We need to recruit differently. We used to just get specialists. Now we need to recruit so that people think more like an entire library, rather than a group of specialists. We are different; we need to think differently and, therefore, we have to recruit differently.

Search committees for the Libraries' faculty positions were beginning to reflect this change. Starting to reflect this change,they began to look for signs that a candidate could work well in a group, and would also have expertise in a subject area, such as history or chemistry.

Mark went on to say:

> We'll need different kinds of people because we'll interact with the university differently. We'll be telling the deans and faculty, "This is how we fit into the university." We'll be educating people about the Libraries and this "educating about" will result in creating more support.

A New Sense of a Larger Role

Many of those involved in the planning realized the growing importance of information technology in the university setting, and in the world at large. They also recognized the increasing role librarians would play in teaching users new information skills. This concept of a "teacher-librarian" was already in practice among the science librarians and those in the undergraduate library. Now, this idea was beginning to challenge another model also in use in the Libraries, that of the "scholar-librarian," whose expertise lay mainly in building and managing library collections in particular subject areas.

Staff Levels in the Libraries

Faculty

Dean and directors of divisions

Heads of school and department libraries

Assistant heads of libraries

Reference librarians, subject bibliographers

Planning librarian, technology training librarian

Professional staff

Heads of access services and technical services

Managers of circulation, interlibrary loan, information broker service

Catalogers, information technology managers and coordinators, some assistant librarians

Business manager, development officer, personnel director

Clerical staff

Front-line and behind-the-scenes positions in all fifteen libraries, all support departments (such as cataloging), and Libraries administration

---

Don knew that the "educating about" mentioned by Mark had begun early in the planning process, when the Libraries had shared the results of a campuswide survey of faculty and students. More recently, people from outside the Libraries had been involved in one-half of the action-planning teams. For example, Pat Greer spoke about the preservation team:

> My action team included a non-library faculty member. It was great to have him there. He gave a new perspective on our suggestions from his experience in setting up a small laboratory for preserving printed materials. This matched up with the team member from the library mending unit.

Incorporating user group representatives into the Libraries' planning may have helped staff extend individual ownership of the Libraries mission into a sense of alignment with the Libraries' role in the university. In early 1992, for example, with the impetus to "internationalize" the university becoming a growing concern on the Purdue campus, the Libraries faculty enlisted the help of foreign language faculty and graduate students to produce a brochure giving a brief introduction to the Libraries in eight languages. The brochure was made available to international students and visiting scholars. Copies were also sent to all the deans and university administrators, for use with international visitors.

Don observed that the library staff was already experiencing a change in the university's perception of the Libraries. "We're getting a lot more press," one staff member told him. "The president has talked about the Libraries more, and the students have seen that we are more responsive." Members of the student government, for example, approached the dean of Libraries with a plan to demonstrate the usefulness of linking computerized databases to the Libraries' online catalog. At a reception to celebrate the installation of such databases, both the university president and a student body officer praised the Libraries for bringing these important information services to Purdue students and faculty.

Jeff Garrett, a library faculty member, told Don that one of the personal rewards of the planning was "having contributed to something that will be implemented at the highest level." For instance, several teams proposed installing an "electronic gateway" to computerized information at Purdue and worldwide. Within months, the project received funding. The team on morale also experienced immediate results from their planning. Their report strongly stated that every search committee for a faculty or professional position should include a clerical staff member with a stake in the outcome. Just such an individual was subsequently appointed to the search committee for a new associate dean.

Becoming Active Change Agents

Don found that, from the first interview to the last, library staff cited the Libraries' accomplishments. They appreciated that Emily used every window of opportunity to implement recommendations as the teams' plans emerged. Several teams, for example, had suggested ways to improve internal communication, including a new in-house newsletter. Emily found a way to create a half-time position for a staff newsletter editor. "She has convinced people she will push for things," Judy told Don. "For example, she got funding from the university administration for a new document delivery service. And money to provide a better collection of journals for undergraduates."

However, the library staff members, Don learned, did not simply sit back and watch the dean work. Nor did they wait for her assistance or blessing before taking certain actions with Libraries-wide consequences. A group of clerical staff from across the Libraries organized tours so that staff members could visit libraries and units other than their own workplaces. The faculty and professional staffs of two of the libraries began meeting regularly to explore ways to share service responsibilities. And librarians from the subject-related libraries volunteered to join the undergraduate librarians in their program of on-request term paper clinics.

"We are changing other people's vision of the Libraries," Dot had told Don, who now realized that an even more fundamental shift had also occurred. The Libraries staff had changed its self-image. While one person suggested that the Libraries "are in a position to make changes," another took this a step further, declaring, "We are change agents."

Factors for Success

As Don reviewed his notes from the interviews, he realized that the planning process itself was a key factor in the transformation of the Purdue Libraries. Participation in the planning had allowed the library staff to experience new behaviors first, before they had to decide about the implications. For many clerical staff members, working with teammates from across the Libraries to explore common issues was a new experience. Accustomed to spending their entire work day in one library unit, they previously had only that unit's concerns as a point of reference. Even for many members of the Libraries' faculty and professional staff, the "whole-Libraries approach" required new behaviors and attitudes.

In addition, new patterns of interaction for the entire staff had been built into the planning process by including everyone at critical points. From the first meetings of the early focus groups, reports of the planning were repeatedly brought back to the entire library staff. One person told Don that a strong underpinning of the process was how communication increased as the plan proceeded — with everyone gathering as a group to discuss each important step of the plan.

Don learned that informal interactions changed as well. As the planning process unfolded, people talked about it throughout the Libraries. At undergraduate library staff meetings, people discussed ideas emerging from the technology-training team. In one library workroom, intense conversations focused on ways to improve the Libraries' public relations. People sent each other articles and news items related to their action team topics, and also networked with people outside the Libraries. One faculty member from the Foods and Nutrition Department attached this note to information he sent to his former action teammates: "I keep thinking of all of you when I run across stuff like the enclosed."

The growing involvement of the staff was not limited to those who had worked in the Libraries throughout the planning process. They drew others in as well. A new staff member commented that several of his co-workers returned from a planning meeting to start "quite a discussion among the rest of us." He suggested, "Maybe the most important thing about these meetings is the discussions that happen afterwards."

As Don came to see how individuals had experienced the planning effort, he also began to understand how they viewed Dean Mobley's part in the changes occurring in the Libraries' corporate culture. "Emily provides the will," one person told Don. He could see that Dean Mobley's confidence in the planning process was visible and widely felt, and that she valued the contributions of each individual. "She communicates it every time you encounter her," faculty member Jeff Garrett told Don:

> When you take a problem to her and ask what we should
> do, she says, "I don't know. What do you think?" She has
> the courage to let other people's innovations go forward.

When she helped turn such proposals as the electronic gateway and the staff newsletter into visible outcomes, Scott Mandernack observed that the effect was a growing "confidence that there'll be results."

Emily had been a leader in creating and modeling a new role for librarians on the Purdue campus. She had created the example and sustained the environment for the staff to participate in the Libraries' future. Don found it almost a paradox that the staff gave such credit to Emily's leadership, because the heart of that leadership had been to empower staff members. They themselves had become leaders by expressing their willingness to take responsibility for change.

Changes and Accomplishments, Challenges, and Threats

By the spring of 1993, when the Libraries released the strategic plan, the staff had accomplished all but a few of the implementation milestones that they had set for 1992-93. "It seems there's something new every month," a user observed. A number of other projects were years ahead of schedule, including work on a course in information skills and the equipping of a new electronic classroom.

Internal changes were also taking place. By fall of 1993, the 15 libraries were organized into "clusters," groups of libraries related by subject matter. The biomedical and natural sciences cluster explored ways to share the time and expertise of reference librarians. In the libraries of the physical sciences and engineering cluster, several clerical staff members began to trade jobs one afternoon a week, creating more flexibility in staffing. At its first meeting, the new Libraries Council defined itself as operating from a "philosophy of one library," representing its constituencies but "thinking bigger picture." Led by Dean Mobley, this group included several other administrators, the cluster coordinators, and staff representatives. This was the first time that clerical and professional staff joined faculty in making decisions and setting policy for the Libraries as a whole.

As 1994 began, Emily saw that the Libraries' planning had "helped communicate a direction that the university feels it can support." Most exciting for her was that "the university now sees the Libraries as knowledgeable about the electronic future, the information future of the 21st century."

Key Strategic Directions

In achieving its mission, the Libraries will pursue five key strategic directions, each of which is expressed in the plan as a set of strategies with specific programs and actions.

- User Access Increased
- Collection Quality Enhanced
- Library Instruction Redefined
- Information Delivery Expanded
- Internal Resources Optimized

(From A Shared Commitment to Excellence: A Plan for the Future, 1992-1997, the strategic plan of the Purdue University Libraries)

Within the Libraries, the thrill came from changes in people:

> We're doing it! We're doing something! We're breaking
> people out of the mold. It's exciting to see librarians try
> things without first getting the money to do them.

The rough spots have not all been made smooth, of course. "The more things change, the more they stay the same," Emily remarked, explaining that, at the university level, "We're still not at the table when the deals are cut," regarding some issues of policy or funding. Even here, however, she saw progress, observing, "We are now asked before the crumbs are slung on the floor — this is a step forward." She described, however, what remains as her greatest frustration within the Libraries:

> There are people who aren't coming along into this future.
> I find myself asking, "How do we get them to come along,
> and what will I do if they don't?" One of the inherent
> threats is that when our own people decide "their" schools
> are more important than the Libraries, we don't get their
> help in influencing key players in the university to change
> their embedded image of the role of the Libraries.

A significant issue that the Libraries face today, Emily declared, is that "our personnel model of the past doesn't fit our personnel needs of the future." The need for teacher-librarians, rather than scholar-librarians, is foreshadowed in the future directions outlined in the Libraries' plan. But not all of the Libraries' faculty members are comfortable with this shift. As the global access to information defines new skills and attitudes needed to work in libraries, the Purdue Libraries will also face challenges in filling other staff positions.

Emily concluded, "As a university, we now have no choice but to take steps to get ready to access information." The Libraries are using increasingly sophisticated computers and establishing electronic connections to information all over the globe. To keep this information technology going, money will be diverted from all schools and departments, and the Libraries, to create a new infrastructure. For example, all campus buildings must be wired for connection to the information superhighway. Emily predicted:

> We'll be required to pay for things we've never paid for
> before, and to figure out what to cut to pay for it. Priorities
> will have to be set. People will have to plan, and do major

goal setting throughout the university. This is all part of the "threats" for the Libraries of moving into our vision for the 21st century.

Will the Transformation Continue?

In their book, *Corporate Cultures*, Terrence Deal and Allan Kennedy have written that organizational or cultural change means "real changes in the behavior of people throughout the organization." And they warn the reader that "this kind of deep-seated cultural change...takes a long time to achieve"[6]. Recent events in the Libraries suggest that the transformation in this organization, begun in 1987, will continue.

At its December, 1993 meeting, the Libraries' faculty debated whether to respond as a group to the report released by the Purdue administration, entitled, Discussion Drafts of the Committee Reports on Challenges [for Purdue] of the 21st Century. Someone suggested leaving it to interested individuals to write letters to the university administration. Then came the heartfelt statement, "We have something of a reputation on this campus for leadership in planning." Those words clarified the issue, and the faculty decided to prepare a corporate response to the report. The result: a concise document that set forth the library faculty's view of a reconceptualized university, and the critical role that the Libraries will play in that university as the information future unfolds.

In a concrete example of undertaking new roles and responsibilities, the six-person staff of the management library set out in the first few months of 1994 to plan a way to better use the main floor of their library. They developed a practical vision of this space, with walls removed to create an open atmosphere, computer workstations arranged for user-staff interaction, with service points and collections reorganized. Next, they identified obstacles to their vision, which included everything from constraints inherent in the building's structure to attitudes resistant to change. After determining the requirements for a new floor plan, the group proposed its own floor plan. They have now formed taskforces that will weed out and consolidate library collections, work with university staff regarding structural changes, get a detailed plan down on paper, and stage the actual movement of library materials and equipment. The group's own words best describe their resolve to move from planning to action:

> We, the staff of the Krannert Library, are committed to a reorganization of the library, which would improve the efficiency of service and provide an attractive, pleasant, scholarly environment for the Purdue community and the citizens of the state of Indiana.

In spring of 1994, a team of library staff and faculty, with a student's help, developed new statements of the purpose, mission, and philosophy of the undergraduate library. When it was time to request feedback from their co-workers and Libraries administrators, the team unhesitatingly selected its clerical staff members to lead the discussions. The new statements generated much excitement with their messages of the need for partnership in information literacy, active learning, student-oriented services and attitudes, the leadership role of the undergraduate library, and a cohesive staff that works together toward goals.

The team found its colleagues ready to move on to the next step, planning strategic actions to fulfill the undergaduate library's purpose and mission. The Dean highlighted the more far-reaching implications of the team's accomplishment when she suggested that they had, in essence, written "next generation" statements for the entire Purdue Libraries system.

The head of the undergraduate library recently called for volunteers from the Libraries' faculty and professional staff to present orientation programs for students attending freshman summer camp. One-half of the librarians who were contacted signed up. When asked why they volunteered, they said that getting freshmen off to a good start is critical for the Libraries, and that the undergraduate library faculty shouldn't have to do it all.

There are many hopeful signs as people of the Libraries are express new personal and corporate images of leadership. The new models, created for the Libraries, also work for the university as a whole. In an organization which historically has divided up its clientele by schools and departments, the orientation of freshmen is beginning to be considered a responsibility across all the Purdue Libraries. Finally, the Libraries' faculty and staff are learning such participatory methods for group work as the idea-generating and decision-making methods introduced during the strategic planning. They are using these techniques in the work of committees, project teams, and library units. Had someone in the mid-1980s predicted that the Purdue University Libraries would move into the new century with a vision, and with practical plans for achieving it, those who worked in the Libraries would have been as skeptical as anyone. Today, these same people speak with excitement and pride of their accomplishments, then add in the next breath, "...but we've learned that planning never stops."

Their stories prove that participative planning is most effective when it incorporates a strong link with action and includes a leader who creates an environment that supports new behaviors. When this combination is present, the individual and the group can adapt entirely new roles in creating the future of an organization. "We are different," Mark told Don. And from Dot, Don heard, "This is the way it is going to be."

As 1994 began, an engineering professor and long-time Libraries watcher observed, "This is the year of the Purdue Libraries' empowerment in the university." His use of the word "empowerment" was unusual. The word is generally applied to individuals, not to an organization. Here, however, the word is appropriate on both levels, because the transformation of the Purdue Libraries really is a story of people—people engaged in an ongoing process of both shaping and owning the future.

References

[1] Heany, Donald F. *Cutthroat Teammates: Achieving Effective Teamwork Among Professionals.* Homewood, IL: Dow-Jones-Irwin, 1989, p.8.

[2] Trauner, Eric. "Library staff needs support from P[urdue] U[niversity]." [Letter to the editor] *The Purdue Exponent,* Jan. 22, 1990, p. 6.

[3] Beering, Steven C. Remarks to the University Senate, Purdue University, West Lafayette, IN, Nov. 29, 1993.

[4] Mercer, Joye and Kit Lively. "Higher education and the states." *The Chronicle of Higher Education,* Jan. 5, 1994, p. A25.

[5] The application of this method was based on the work of David L. Cooperrider and his colleagues from the Department of Organizational Behavior, Case Western Reserve University, Cleveland, Ohio.

[6] Deal, Terrence E. and Allan A. Kennedy. *Corporate Cultures: The Rites and Rituals of Corporate Life.* Reading, MA: Addison-Wesley, 1982, p.158.

Building Austin's Standard in Customer Service

Chapter 13
Back to BASICS:
A City Investing in Its Workforce

BERET E. GRIFFITH

*A city with customers? That is how the city of Austin,
Texas, treats the citizens of Austin as it delivers city
services. The city's vision is ambitious: "We want to be
the best managed and most livable city in the country.
We will accomplish this through people who genuinely
care and who provide responsive, quality service."*

In 1990 Austin made a commitment to providing consistent quality in customer service, delivered by a trained and responsive workforce. Since that time, by investing in its workforce, Austin has changed the way it does business with its customers, the citizens of Austin. Wanting each customer encounter to be better than the last, Austin strives toward exceeding customer expectations, not just meeting them. To achieve this goal, the city manager's office in 1990 designed a process called BASICS — the acronym for building Austin's standards in customer service. The BASICS initiative is a commitment to bring total quality management (TQM) into all city operations, "to redefine the way we work, linking leadership, teamwork, and a focus on continuous improvement of our services to achieve customer satisfaction"[1].

How Basics Began

Austin, Texas, a city of nearly 500,000 people with approximately 10,000 city employees, is one of the largest and steadiest employers in the area. City employees operate all of the public services, as well as enterprise functions including the airport, electric and wastewater utilities, and the convention center. Austin's council management form of government mandates the mayor and council set policy and hire a city manager to carry out policy and manage daily city operations.

In 1989, a new city council and a new city manager received data suggesting that the people of Austin were not happy with the services they were receiving from city employees. This feedback gave city government an opening to change the way it served the community. As a first step toward responding to their citizen customers, Austin's leaders began to look to success stories in the private sector, where organizations were using a TQM philosophy. Austin's Quality Officer Kim Peterson recalls, "Dr. Camille Cates Barnett, at that time the new city manager, began talking about the importance of customer service. She said that the bottom line for public service was customer satisfaction, which meant more than just providing services at the lowest possible cost."

Today, the city of Austin continues to be concerned with how the city services and enterprises are run and with the education and development of its employees. The quality revolution has been a factor in doing business in the private sector for a long time. Austin adopted this approach because people running the city felt it made good sense. Once Austin made its own commitment to TQM, city leaders accepted clear lines of responsibility for putting it into effect.

The city manager is responsible for the change effort with top managers required to become educated about quality and to use BASICS approaches in their operations. Department directors set the tone and requirements for their individual departments where participation is voluntary.

First Steps: Performance Assessment and Goal Setting

As Monica Ahring of the Institute for Education and Employment notes in her case study, *The City as a Teaching Firm: The BASICS in Austin*:

When former City Manager Dr. Camille Cates Barnett began her tenure [in 1988], she set out to discover just how well this huge "organization," as he called it, was performing—both internally as employer, and externally as service provider. She surveyed employees, meeting with as many as she could in each department. She asked individual citizens as well as corporate leaders how well the city met their needs. "Essentially," she recalls, "I thought this was an organization that was very demoralized, was not well thought of, didn't think well of themselves, and most importantly, had lost its bearings"[2].

An internal evaluation of Austin's municipal government indicated that training had virtually ceased within the organization as a result of an economic downturn in the early 1980s. Training, organizational development, and human resources services had been targeted as "extras" or luxuries not to be wasted on the public sector.

Since then Austin has been challenged with difficult times. Shrinking revenues and repeated departmental reorganizations have strained operational systems, while budget cutbacks and staff reductions have dampened employee motivation. Management instability, including turnover of the city manager, assistant city managers, and department executives, has contributed to the cynicism that can be found within the organization [3].

Nevertheless, despite recent difficulties, Austin carries a long tradition of quality customer service. In 1991, a team of city employees developed a seven-year plan. In the report of this plan, *Blueprint for the Way We Work*, the design team of the city of Austin describes this renewed commitment to quality, "We have drawn on emerging management trends, but more importantly we have built on the examples of quality customer service found throughout the city organization"[4].

The following specific common sense goals emerged from the blueprint's assessment of problems facing the city in its role as an employer and service provider. The following three goals were focused through the lens of the city manager's commitment to leadership as development, not as top-down command:

1. *Focus on customer service,* since "everybody said the city government...isn't providing good service."

2. *Invest in the workforce,* instituting training as a legitimate, even cost-effective tool for enabling staff to do good work.

3. *Live within our means,* so that all these efforts can be sustained [5].

Improvement From Within:
Following a Personal Commitment

The Ahring case study highlights many specifics of the new approach and observes that uncovering weaknesses and failings did not deter Barnett. She held on to her conviction that this was "an organization with a lot of strengths, a lot of good people working here"[6].

Ahring's research notes the ongoing, substantial efforts to revitalize the city into a "teaching firm," an environment that builds teaching and learning into every part of the work at all levels. A workplace where teaching and learning become an integral part of an organization results in fully engaged, challenged, and satisfied employees. Such an environment improves quality and delivery of services and products resulting from the work of motivated employees. In studying Austin, Ahring observed that the reinvention of government in Austin did not start out as an attempt to live out any particular organizational development theory or ready-to-use framework for change.

Instead, the study notes that City Manager Barnett cautioned that the idea of implementing TQM or fundamental change as objectives in and of themselves would be senseless. She worked, instead, from the basic and clear conviction that improvement in worklife and in performance would come to the city of Austin, if she could "invest in the workforce." As the co-author of the book *The Creative Manager,* Barnett underscored her conviction that experimentation and learning are essential elements in the workplace[7]. This belief naturally led her to focus Austin's improvement efforts on city employees—all employees. As she explained:

> ...in the beginning, I didn't know how we were going to do it. I just knew that it all had to be done. And I don't think that you can have a learning organization or a teaching firm or any variation of it if the people in charge don't feel like they're learning too. So, if I had come in thinking that I knew how to do all this, I might have been teaching,

but I sure wouldn't have been learning. I don't think you can sustain an effort like this unless the people who are leading it are also changing....So the first thing that we did was to say, we don't know how to do all this, but we know it needs to be done [8].

Marketing New Ideas Internally

What the city manager knew was that everybody really wanted service to be improved. This meant that Austin's first goal, to focus on customer service, was already something people accepted. What they couldn't accept was the possibility that the three goals would work together. Talking about the relationship between the city's goals of working on customer service and investing in the workforce at the same time became a critical part of Barnett's job. In public speeches and in private discussions with city council members, the *Teaching Firms* notes that Barnett made clear her commitment to improve customer service.

This determination did not mean that it was all smooth sailing for Barnett. As *Texas Monthly* magazine of March, 1994 reported, there were people who felt "that she cared more about her public image than about running the city" and that "her energy went not into governing but into networking outside of city government"[9]. According to Austin Quality Officer Kim Peterson, there were some highly successful individuals in Austin who felt there really was no need for change. However, despite these problems in getting everyone on board, Barnett then wove the city's other goals, to invest in the workforce and live within our means, into her conversations, saying over and over, "If you want service to be improved, pay attention to the people who are providing the service." Next, together with a small taskforce, her office produced a Customer Service Issue Paper in January, 1990. Here, in more formal language, the concept of investing in the workforce was articulated and the process called BASICS outlined. Members of Barnett's taskforce began to hear their ideas affirmed by others as a result of the internal marketing effort. Investing in human resources was the recurring theme, Barnett recalls, "...in everything we read and everything we said. When we talked to other people, they all said, 'That's key; you've got to treat your employees differently'" [10].

City of Austin
Management Plan
1992-94

Vision

We want Austin to be the best-managed and most livable city in the country. We will accomplish this through people who genuinely care and who provide responsive, quality service.

Values

We will honor the public trust through:

- Respect and dignity for our customers.
- Respect and care for the environment.
- Equal Opportunity.
- A workforce selected with care, treated with respect, rewarded for performance.

- Open, honest communication.
- Positive action and innovation.
- Teamwork.
- Responsible use of public resources.

Goals

We will focus on customer service by:

- Supporting the city council's priorities.
- Cutting red tape.
- Improving effectiveness of internal support services.
- Following the BASICS implementation plan.

- Listening and responding to our customers.
- Improving public awareness of city services.
- Increasing employment and business opportunities for minorities.

We will invest in the workforce by:

- Treating employees as customers.
- Involving employees in decision making.

- Maintaining competitiveness in wages and benefits.

We will live within our means by:

- Operating within budgetary limits and adhering to financial policies
- Emphasizing preventative maintenance.

- Seeking new sources of funding.
- Focusing on continuous improvement of quality, productivity, efficiency.

From the beginning, BASICS was promoted as and continues today to be a visible, living opportunity for change within city government. Training, celebration, and communication from the city manager have been important elements of the plan. Twenty-two separate city departments are involved in the process of change. Top managers are trained in quality techniques and philosophy, and training is cascaded down to employees. Additional factors identified as crucial to the success of BASICS included the following approaches usually associated with the private rather than the public sector:

- Supportive corporate culture
- Stable workplace environment
- Top management leadership and involvement
- Employee involvement
- Customer communications
- Training and evaluation
- Patience and discipline

As Austin's new ways of managing the key goals became more widely understood and adopted, the city manager's office developed more formal and sophisticated ways of talking about what was happening. The BASICS program organized a wide range of initiatives in creativity, literacy, and quality assessment into a connected concept of government. Colorful, upbeat pamphlets, one, a step-by-step guide on BASICS, helped the city to market the idea to all levels of Austin's government.

Learning from the Private Sector

Part of the reason Austin's style of running the city sounds so much like a business approach is that Barnett asked business leaders from Motorola, Xerox, and IBM to provide her with collegial advice and feedback. She started talking with executives and managers from these firms when she was trying to figure out what kinds of improvement efforts were working in the corporate world. Stories from corporate leaders were of more immediate and practical value than academic research, so she went to business leaders to see what they were doing. As it turned out, *The Teaching Firm* notes, the TQM ideas the corporate leaders were implementing were very similar to what the city manager envisioned for Austin.

Barnett recalls first drawing on the corporate leaders to help move her agenda within the city when she faced city council members doubtful about some of her ideas on the importance of training. She invited a group of Austin executives to join city council members in a meeting, and as Monica Ahring remembered, Barnett let the CEOs do the talking. At first, some council members felt that the TQM approach was too "touchy-feely" and resisted going to meetings[11].

However, the private sector provided tremendous support for the BASICS initiative. The Xerox Corporation and Motorola openly shared their quality initiatives. City government then was able to borrow from what was working in the private sector and adapt it to municipal government.

After the initial success with the budget process and citizen involvement, the Greater Austin Quality Council was formed as a joint public/private partnership of the city of Austin, the University of Texas at Austin, and the Greater Austin Chamber of Commerce. The council's goal was to "create an Austin in which quality and value of its people, goods, public and private services, education, and overall quality of life are renowned"[12]. The Greater Austin Quality Council provides the city council with consultation on how to invest in the workforce to improve services. Education on quality is the primary goal of the quality council. It holds two annual conferences and supports the University of Texas Quality Center. The annual Austin Quality Awards program, modeled after the federal government's Malcolm Baldrige National Quality Award, is also sponsored by the Austin Quality Council.

The language of quality service and investment in human resources set the stage for new actions. It also took a healthy dose of what City Manager Barnett called "management 101" to inspire the city council to pass a radically new budget during her first year on the job. She commented further that giving the council "a budget that was balanced at a tax rate they could stomach politically," was critical to establishing the credibility and merit of new goals and processes[13].

Austin's 1992 budget received the Distinguished Budget Presentation Award of the Government Finance Officers Association (GFOA). As a GFOA award winner, the budget document was recognized as a piece of work that serves as a policy document, an operations guide, a financial plan, and a communications device. The new language of quality and participation showed up in "everything we read and everything we said."

Citizens who embodied public needs and demands for service were called "customers." The words "investment," "sensitivity," and "vulnerability" replaced traditional language of costs and benefits[14].

What was perhaps most encouraging about the budget was that it went beyond being organized by particular departments or budget categories. To reflect the new way of doing business, the budget was organized around those priorities the city council identified as critical to the health of the city. What was perhaps most daring about the budget was that it paired priorities with specific descriptions of expected outcomes. As noted in the Executive Summary and Transmittal Letter of July, 1993, the city was prepared to measure its success or failure in meeting customer expectations. The city involved citizens more in finances and the budget process by setting up Budget Information Booths in local shopping malls and conducting call-in shows on Cable Channel 6 to answer citizens' questions.

Blueprint for Action

Once the budget process was in place, Austin tapped into its long tradition of quality customer service and sought to renew this core value and have it to become a part of the entire city organization. The Blueprint for Action document set strategic goals for each year of the BASICS planand showed that the model for implementing goals at the department level depends on a learn-use-teach-mode of action[15]. The BASICS approach does not change traditional management authority and accountability. What does change is the way responsibilities of managers and employees are viewed and shared, and the way the roles of managers and employees are communicated to reflect a shift from old to new patterns. The blueprint set a list of ten essentials of customer service, illustrated by a series of different shoe styles,which employees were encouraged to try on for size.

A Look at Investing in the Workforce

Austin wanted improvements in customer service as well as improvements in employee morale, personal productivity, and job security. Austin employees were advised, "Just put your best foot forward. And take it one step at a time." This quote from the BASICS guide illustrates how the initiative worked in three city departments—the Austin Public Library, the Electric Utilities Department, and the Department of Finance

Ten Essentials for Success

"Quality is what the customer perceives it to be, not what we think it ought to be"

Austin wanted improvements in customer service as well as improvements in employee morale, personal productivity and job security. All city employees were asked to try on ten essential elements for size.

What To Do

Step into a "moment of truth." Every contact with a customer is a contribution to customer satisfaction.

Put yourself in the customer's shoes. Understand what the customer wants.

Keep everything "customer friendly." Systems and procedures need to be easy for customers to use and understand.

If the shoe fits, wear it. We are all customers and our time at work can be satisfying and rewarding.

PUT YOUR BEST
FOOT FORWARD

How To Do It

Pave the way. Top managers and key individuals, chosen for their commitment to TQM, will nurture quality improvement within each department.

Walk the talk. Senior management will make sure that management at all levels practice the principles of BASICS day in and day out.

Teach the steps. Employees will be given a working knowledge of the tools and techniques of quality service. Training will be delivered in "natural work groups."

Stay on your toes. Improving customer service is an ongoing job.

Remember you're walking a two-way street. Communication is crucial. We will share our observations and ideas about customer service.

Say thanks. Recognition and reward are important.

Illustrations by Edd Patton of Austin, Texas

and Administrative Services. The various departments and their leaders have different stories to tell about how all the words of advice, the policy budget goals, and business approval add up in the day-to-day functioning of the Austin government.

The Austin Public Library

Brenda Branch, director of the Austin Public Library, says that opening people up to their own creativity is "a real obsession" for her. When she learned about the city's goals to support learning in the workplace, her obsession shaped the initial investment in the library's workforce. She proposed that workplace education at the library focuses on unleashing staff creativity, which she believes leads to more daring and better problem solving at all staff levels. The city manager gave Branch free rein to develop what became a far-reaching program of "funshops" with the slogan, "Quality Begins with Creativity." As Kim Peterson explains:

> The funshops were the city's first efforts to encourage employee participation in problem solving. The funshops are one-day training sessions that use a series of group activities to support the value of thinking outside the box to come up with creative solutions to city problems.

Middle and upper managers interested in quality and creativity were among the first group of participants in the funshops. Some who took part decided they would like to run creativity sessions themselves and signed on for additional training to become leaders for other groups. Even now, volunteer facilitators responsible for the success of the funshops come from all over the city and include professional trainers, librarians, telephone operators, utility meter readers, an architect, engineers, emergency response planners, a police fingerprint specialist, and a traffic planner.

Library Director Branch says she has faced surprisingly little negative feedback on the funshops. "You're spending money on 'fun shops?' Give me a break!" was a comment from only a few constituents. While she has no hard data on the effects of these workshops, Branch knows how popular they are with the city staff. She also observes that requests from libraries across the country and from Austin's residents to open the program to the public provide evidence enough of the program's value.

The Austin Public Library also developed a Workplace Literacy Program offering educational opportunities for its own staff, for other city employees, and for community members. Because the literacy initiative promises concrete outcomes—specifically, to make city employees more productive and promotable—Branch is concerned about being able to actually measure results. But good accomplishments are already surfacing. Some staff have been promoted as a result of their participation in the program.

First steps have been taken to find meaningful ways to document the achievements of those who participated in the literacy program. In 1993 the Austin Public Library won the Library of the Year Award sponsored by Gale Research and the *Library Journal*. The June 15, 1993 issue of the journal states, "A unique quality of this outstanding public library is the [number of] very close bonds it has created with the government and the people of the city of Austin, Texas." The article further noted:

> According to Branch, and to Lynn Wolff, the library's coordinator of the program, it really works. "This program is really transforming lives," Branch told *Library Journal*. "People who went through it have been promoted at work. Whole families go through it and are changed." The literacy program now operates in a brand new facility that includes a classroom for Graduate Equivalency Diploma programs and separate tutoring areas for one-on-one sessions. It is open long hours to allow workers on all schedules to drop in anytime. Currently, some 220 students are enrolled, and 237 city employees have been trained as tutors. Austin may be the first U.S. city to try to bring full literacy to its workforce.... Branch feels that the emphasis on TQM brought to the city by Barnett has had a positive effect on the library system. "We're very lucky," Branch said. She encourages risk taking, innovation. "We'd been trying to improve the quality of service all along, but the TQM program made it systematic. It gave us tools and processes to make it more effective." Branch coordinated the city TQM program. Its tools and processes are part of the library routine now[16].

The list of library success stories is long. The Job Information Center, aimed at adults with less than a 12th grade education, serves over 7000 customers a year. The library partnership with the Austin Independent School District serves 2,113 youths in a low-income neighborhood, with 72 different programs. The project was the winner of the Texas Library Association Project of the Year Award in 1992. The people of Austin are satisfied library customers. There are over 200 active volunteers a month, contributing an annual 24,000 hours of work that would have cost the library at least $260,000. In reporting these positive statistics, *Library Journal* exclaims:

> ...and that's not all. In 1992 the citizens of Austin approved a bond issue to raise $16,395,000 to improve the Austin History Center and to build or renovate six branches. It was clearly a vote of love for and confidence in the Austin Public Library. "The city has done the best it can by us," Branch is quick to say. "Quite a contingent in Austin is opposed to all taxes. Yet a progressive city council has actually raised taxes here to support our library. We owe them our gratitude"[17].

The Electric Utility Department

Another Austin city department to refocus on worker participation in customer satisfaction is the Electric Utility Company. Director John Moore said that before BASICS got moving, the most basic training, even in essential areas like safety, had been neglected for years. Since BASICS got underway, he sees that the "old mentalities, attitudes [of] trying to keep costs down and short-term thinking" are beginning to give way to new ways of thinking about learning in his department. While the basic understanding that learning and quality are linked was growing in this part of the organization, the utility company was still struggling to get beyond talk to actually work in new and different ways[18].

At the utility Moore has taken a more structured approach to shaping investment in the workforce than Director Branch is using at the library. He set up an organization development (OD) staff to serve as a training resource for the department and to draw on the utility's own workforce as educators. Moore has found that the training needs are huge because the department is trying to develop two strands of learning at once—training people in customer-service orientation as a new way of thinking and working and addressing essential work skills, ignored for years. According to Ahring, he sees the agenda for this group as "almost overwhelming" [19].

Moore and the OD group are still concerned about how to integrate training into the ongoing life of the workplace. Moore's group is facing two questions:

> How should they balance the two major training needs? How much does learning need to focus on specific and technical skills, and how much on overarching concepts and attitudes? Moore told Ahring that the utility has gone back to a focus on "the basic stuff about total quality management." So far it seems that very basic changes in thinking are needed before willingness to do specific tasks differently can be opened up.

The utility's OD group wanted to create more opportunities for staff to practice what they learn in training sessions. According to Moore, the usual format in which "you send a person downtown for three days, they sit in a seminar, some of them are real interested...they get out, go back to the workplace, business as usual" has got to change.

Kim Peterson observes that Moore's department now sees opportunities for practice as critical to integrating new learning into work behaviors. The division offers a full range of training to utility employees in areas including safety, supervisor skills, TQM, and diversity. Employees can use their new skills in teams and work units, and some cross-functional teams have been active at both the department and city levels.

Like the library, the utility is beginning to determine the kinds of tools needed to measure how education is really affecting the organization's work. One problem is not having established baseline data or measuring performance on new dimensions. Moore notes:

> "Bottom line here is what does it cost to produce a kilowatt hour,"...but statistics relating that bottom line allow the organization to see performance only "from a very high level." The problem with these kinds of measurements, Moore says, is that they have typically been used to

manage short-term change. "I can go out and finagle numbers and it'll improve, but I ain't fixing processes. I can go out and liquidate assets, and it'll improve." His struggle is finding numbers that tell the larger story of quality of life within the Public Utility Department and the quality of service it provides[20].

Moore has found it difficult to balance two key messages of TQM. On the one hand, he says, TQM "puts a big focus on measuring and having goals that you can measure," but, on the other hand, "there's a real tricky balance between doing that and driving out fear, as quotas and fear tend to go together." Moore's group backed off on trying to assess specifics on performance or service, and tried to follow through with a "focus on attitude change and how you measure some of that"[21].

The Department of Finance and Administrative Services

The third Austin municipal department highlighted in this study is the Department of Finance and Administrative Services. Director Betty Dunkerley describes how meter readers used to be managed at the utility:

> The front-line employee reported to a field supervisor, then three or four of those field supervisors reported to another supervisor. That supervisor reported to the officer who is over the division of utility customer service. And that officer reported to me"[22].

The situation has changed quite a bit in the past few years.

According to the 1993 Proposed Budget Transmittal Letter, the Utility Customer Service Office now trains all service representatives to deal with all of its customers. As a result, employee productivity is up—and customer waiting is down. Over the past five years, the number of utility customers served per employee has increased 3%. Kilowatt-hour sales per employee have increased 7%. Service to new electric customers has improved dramatically:

- 1-day wait for service—down from a 3-7 days
- 20 steps in the installation process—down from 35 steps
- 400 extra trips a month were eliminated
- $12,000 saving for ratepayers

Successful Team Results

City of Austin

Founded by Congress,
Republic of Texas, 1839

EMPLOYMENT IMPROVEMENT TEAM has reduced the error rate in application process from 11% to 2%.

PUBLIC WORKS OVERLAY TEAM has improved their quality scores in identifying problems and solutions, implementing improvements and measuring results in the division's street overlay project from 73.8% to 95.4%.

PUBLIC WORKS PROJECT QUALITY IMPROVEMENT TEAM includes eight division functional teams responsible for improving the quality of street resurfacing and rehabilitation projects. They have raised their project quality score from 70.8% to 96% since October, 1992.

STREET AND BRIDGE DIVISION SEAL COAT TEAM reports that quality of work increased by 50%. Productivity increased by over 250% from 29 tons of hot mix placed per hour to 100 tons per hour. Customer surveys indicate an 80% to 90% favorable response on the helpfulness of employees, receipt of adequate notice, and timely completion of work.

EMERGENCY SERVICE RUN FORM RETURN TEAM has developed a process for getting patient report forms back to the central office within 24 hours, down from a previous two- to three-day process.

ROSEWOOD-ZARAGOZA HEALTH CLINIC PHOENIX TEAM manages to have the adult health clinic staff see 82% of their patients in 1 hour, up from 8%; patients report 78% to 94% "good" or "excellent" satisfaction with their care.

As the February, 1994 issue of *Financial World* notes:

> According to Dunkerley, "Employees came up with a proposal to manage themselves. We were able to cut out two layers of management." Surprisingly, the meter readers set higher standards for themselves, not lower. Recounts Dunkerley: "The meter readers proposed daily, weekly, and monthly measures to monitor work and progress. We now measure error rates on individuals, teams, and the whole function. The employees themselves decided that an error rate of 0.25% was the target. The first month it came in at 0.22%. This last month was 0.11%"[23].

These stories of three different Austin departments show a glimpse into the results of ongoing employee involvement in the continuous improvement process. They also point out how Austin's venture into quality municipal management is paying off.

Measuring Change for the City

To help quantify the actual results of Austin's TQM efforts, the city created an Organization Research Division to get city employee and citizen feedback on services provided and the quality of municipal government worklife. The Austin Quality Award application is used as a self-assessment tool. In 1993 each department of the city went through the process of examining where it stood in seven key areas:

- Leadership
- Information and analysis
- Strategic quality planning
- Human resource development and management
- Management of process quality
- Quality and operational results, and
- Customer focus and satisfaction.

This assessment is one data source for the city's long-range strategic planning. It will continue to be used to look for trends as the city manages the ongoing continuous improvement process and all city departments are involved in solving problems.

Austin's Mayor, Bruce Todd, asserts that it is important to understand the difference between cost and investment when an organization undertakes long-term improvement efforts in human resources. He indicates that BASICS has now moved beyond its infancy, and the city of Austin is beginning to get some results. However, assessing outcomes is especially difficult in the public sector where some of the "warm and fuzzy...quality of life" issues that determine citizen satisfaction with the organization's responsiveness are hard to measure. Todd knows that new instruments for measuring return on investment in the public sector are "imperative" and many city departments are now reporting results[24].

One area of quantifiable success is in the individual work units, which continue to improve work processes and to develop specific measures of change. Austin's present City Manager, Jesus Garza, recently recognized city teams for their achievements. While many teams have been acknowledged for their work, what follows are reports from Garza's files on a few of those teams.

Belief and Ownership

What has motivated these kinds of measured achievements of Austin employees? When she began Austin's quality push in 1989, City Manager Barnett saw changes in her staff's ability to "believe" as important. When she set out the three basic goals for Austin, she said people believed that focusing on good service, investing in the workforce, and living within the city's means were, "mutually exclusive, that you couldn't do all of those." Over time that perception changed, she said, "When people talk about those three goals, they rattle them off without thinking that they're mutually exclusive—and they sure do pay a lot of attention to investing in the workforce." She believed that over time, departments would find ways to describe new behaviors and the results they bring about in narrower, concrete terms.

According to the Ahring case study, in the early days of the BASICS Initiative, neither Mayor Todd or Barnett pressed department heads to produce quantitative results right away. In fact they both expressed a great deal of faith in the city's ability to live by relatively new goals, and stressed the importance of waiting for opportunities to reflect on change over the long term. Ahring points out the willingness of Todd and Barnett to "believe" and to emphasize subtle shifts in thinking as indicators of progress seemed clearly supportive of efforts to change. They felt they needed to consider a range of ways to pass on their belief and truly empower other managers across the organization to create teaching and learning opportunities, as well as define and make appropriate measurement of effects. According to the May, 1994 City of Austin Report, in 1993, 83% of the executive management team and a total of 29% of all employees had participated in teams during that year.

A January, 1994 assessment was taken right after Jesus Garza became acting city manager. Now as the official city manager, Garza states that BASICS has had a positive impact on the city of Austin; consequently, he is continuing the BASICS initiative. In his words:

> I am committed to continuing the city's efforts to improve customer service through employee involvement. It is through this commitment that we are able to achieve positive results—the kind we've been experiencing now for some time with BASICS. To further enhance BASICS, the city will expand on its performance-based budgeting and strategic planning efforts. In addition, I believe that we need to fully empower *all* of our employees to adopt the customer service and quality approaches so that they may use them in their daily work.

Both City Manager Garza and Quality Officer Peterson provided much of the data and measurements that helped bring BASICS up to date. Peterson states:

> I hear from employees who welcome the opportunity to be heard and to have a part in addressing issues in a meaningful way. Worklife is less stressful because city employees have a common understanding of the importance of customer service to the organization and are getting the tools they need to provide that service. This means fewer negative interactions with customers and more success on the job.

Nationwide Recognition

The rest of the country is also taking note of Austin's accomplishments. The 1994 edition of *Quick Facts,* a publication of the Greater Austin Chamber of Commerce states:

> In 1993, Austin ranked 8th in *Financial World*'s third annual "State of the Cities" list of America's 30 largest cities. Cities were judged in four areas of municipal management: accounting, program evaluation and measurement, budgeting, and infrastructure controls. Contributing Editor Katherine Barnett said, "Of all the cities we've looked at, Austin has made the most progress at applying the principles of total quality management to government. The city has a planned, priority-driven, team-oriented approach that's a model for others"[25].

The September, 1993 issue of *Money Magazine* ranked Austin number 10 in the article titled "Best Places to Live Now." Even U-Haul International, Inc. noticed Austin, claiming the city as the 8th most popular destination for families who moved during the summer of 1993.

As the change effort continues, Peterson expects that employees will become even more active in problem solving and more focused and skilled at providing customer service, because of their better understanding of where they fit into the organization. As Austin continues its initiative, the spotlight should focus even more on the city's model program. All along, those involved have understood that the change process is a long one. Now, five years old, the BASICS Initiative has primarily focused on training and building the foundational systems for change. The next phase for the city of Austin will be to look at outcomes and determine future trends. As Peterson noted in her June, 1994 interview:

> No change effort can be effective...if there is not a good business reason for it. After five years, we are seeing improvements that justify continued attention to a systems approach that includes customer satisfaction, leadership, employee participation, and continuous improvement.

After all, the city of Austin did set out to become the best managed, most livable city in the country.

References

[1] Ahring, Monica. *The City as a Teaching Firm: The BASICS in Austin, Texas*, The Institute for Education and Employment, Education Development Center, Inc., Newton, Massachusetts, 1993.

[2] City of Austin, Texas Design Team, Blueprint for the Way We Work, Austin, Texas, August, 1991.

[3] Blueprint for the Way We Work, op. cit.

[4] Ahring, op. cit.

[5] Ibid.

[6] Barnett, Camille. The Creative Manager.

[7] Ahring, op. cit.

[8] Barnstone, Robert. "City Mis-Manager: Camille Barnett," *Texas Monthly*, March, 1994, p. 66.

[9] Ahring, op. cit.

[10] Barnstone, op. cit.

[11] City of Austin, A Status Assessment of the City of Austin's Total Quality Management Initiative Through December 31, 1993. Austin, Texas, 1994.

[12] Ahring, op. cit.

[13] Ibid.

[14] Blueprint for the Way We Work, op. cit.

[15] Berry, John. "Library of the Year 1993, Austin Public Library." *Library Journal*, June 15, 1993, pp. 30-33.

[16] Ibid.

[17] Ahring, op. cit.

[18] Ibid.

[19] Ibid.

[20] Ibid.

[21] "The Restructuring of Austin." *Financial World*, February 1, 1994, p. 48.

[22] Ahring, op. cit.

[23] Ibid.

[24] Ibid.

[25] The Greater Austin Chamber of Commerce. "Austin in the News—1993," *Quick Facts for Newcomers & Prospective Citizens*, November, 1993.

Chapter 14
The FDA as Maze and Model

DAVID DUNN

In early 1994, when U.S. Food and Drug Administration Commissioner Dr. David Kessler announced his interest in a national dialogue about the regulation of nicotine in cigarettes, the tobacco industry and millions of smokers hit the ceiling. It isn't often that remarks by a federal bureaucrat cause a significant percentage of the American population to go ballistic. But the FDA and its work now touch the lives of every citizen and the quality of every food and drug product manufactured here. While FDA employees from the top down work to provide these basic services, they must also balance competing interests and manage a productive workplace.

From Every Consumer Dollar—25 Cents

Throughout the U.S Food and Drug Administration (FDA) hierarchy, scientists, investigators, and compliance officers take their mission to protect the public's health and safety seriously. Here is a federal agency that often makes front page news. The debate over regulation of cigarettes is just one example of the FDA's daily impact on our lives. Over 9,000 employees and an annual budget in excess of $746 million are required to keep tabs on nearly 100,000 establishments that process, manufacture, label, repack, store, distribute, or test products under the FDA's jurisdiction. These products include foods, human and veterinary drugs, human biological products, medical devices, cosmetics, and consumer products, such as TVs and computers that give off radiation. FDA staffers work with thousands of strong-minded individuals aggressively pursuing highly secretive, competitive ventures involving millions of investment dollars. The FDA alone regulates over $960 billion worth of commercial products—25 cents out of every dollar spent annually by consumers in America[1].

The FDA is not an impersonal monolith however. Commissioner Kessler oversees a network of some 20 national offices and centers, six regional offices, 20 district offices, and 130 resident inspection posts. When you call the Denver district, for instance, it isn't long before you connect with a real person like District Director John Scharmann, his secretary Sue Sherlin, Public Affairs Specialist Virlie Walker, or Compliance Branch Director Gary Dean—just four of the 110 real people in the Denver district, all of whom have families, hobbies, and a full plate at work each week, just like the rest of us.

A district's experience can be instructive at many levels. The FDA's history and corporate culture illustrate the clash of attitudes and approaches that occur when federal workers take on the challenge of figuring out what reinventing government really means. District-level managers acknowledge that change requires significant employee participation. It's not surprising that exploring a more open, participatory style of management leads to both enthusiasm and frustration. The mixed results of experimentation illustrate the complexity of decentralized management without autocratic control. To get a feel for the challenge of reinventing, a look at the Denver district is a must.

The FDA as Maze and Model

The FDA Denver district offices are located on the sprawling Federal Center campus, 15 minutes west of downtown Denver. The route to the Denver district director's office is a complex maze with surprising left and right turns. It's easy to get lost. The FDA's route to a leaner, less complex organization has also been circuitous. In May, 1991, following a series of committee reports, FDA Commissioner Kessler issued a directive to expedite case processing by doing away with all the layers of review.

As Compliance Branch Director Gary Dean put it:

It prompted us to look at how we do cases. We no longer had to have all layers sign off. [The signature of] only one person was needed. A lot of folks [in the districts] had been practicing participatory management; now we were hearing about it from the highest levels.

In short, what the troops were trying out—local initiative and decentralized authority—the generals had decided to bless. Now, nearly four years later, the projection that the Denver Laboratory, a major component of the Denver FDA campus, will be closed by the year 2010 hangs over everyone's head. The mandate to do more with less is an undercurrent in most discussions about the future of government at all levels. In the Denver district, the possibility that self-directed work teams represent a positive management innovation has led to a significant investment in staff training and management soul searching. But the long-term outcomes are yet unclear, and the 110 workers at FDA Denver are a bit uneasy.

Why is it so difficult to reinvent the FDA? Size and complexity are a part of the challenge. The FDA is a "classic bureaucracy," a hierarchical agency whose monolithic form and function served the public need for universal service and reliability well. Some 88 years after President Teddy Roosevelt signed the original Food and Drug Act of 1906, and 67 years after the U.S. Food and Drug Administration left the Department of Agriculture, the FDA is nested within the Public Health Service within the Department of Health and Human Services. And yet the FDA is not the only Federal agency empowered to use the tools of science, technology, and the law to protect Americans' health and safety. At least ten other Federal agencies have FDA-related duties. To ensure the political viability, management liaison, and scientific integrity of such a complex regulatory effort, the FDA maintains a working relationship with four Senate committees; seven House of Representatives' committees; each of the ten related federal agencies; and some forty-four expert panels, boards, and advisory committees.

In spite of the complexity of the organization, FDAers are proud to be such a science-based enforcement agency. And herein lies an important dilemma: increased public expectations for health and safety are confronted with diminishing public resources. It's one thing to keep up with rapidly advancing scientific knowledge and quite another to keep up with the state of the art in management systems design and human resource development. Furthermore, when Washington, D.C., orders, "Flatten the hierarchy, extend the span of supervision, inaugurate self-directing teams, do more with less," the mandate is bound to sound like the old saw, "Build me an ark!" — to which a district is likely to reply, "What's an ark?" In the midst of the day-to-day pressures of district business, it is hard to see a clear blueprint of the future.

In the preface to *Reinventing Government*, authors David Osborne and Ted Gaebler quote the French novelist Marcel Proust: "The real voyage of discovery consists not in seeking new lands, but in seeing with new eyes" [2]. Reinventing is not just a matter of demanding that employees behave differently, take a new direction, or organize themselves in some innovative way. It is a matter of inviting them to be more explicitly what human beings are essentially—self-transcending creatures with the capacity to continually see new possibilities and to redefine themselves in new and surprising ways. At bottom, entrepreneurial governance means government that can continually reinvent itself, i.e., government that is continually self-transcending. If the three districts in the Southwest region are any indication, reinventing government is a major preoccupation of FDA district and regional directors. District Director John Scharmann, Doug Payne, Mike Rogers, and Regional Director LeRoy Gomez catalyzed significant changes toward entrepreneurial management of the FDA in the southwestern states. These efforts have led to a learning process that could permanently change the way the FDA does business.

The Southwest Region: Arena of Experimentation

Before his retirement in 1994, LeRoy Gomez managed FDA activities in 11 states from his Southwest region office in Dallas. Gomez talks about a major staff development effort, initiated during 1992, which came to be called the Southwest Regional Training Academy:

> The germ of an idea started with me, my three district directors, and our executive director. We saw several things come into focus at the same time. Retirement was going to create a significant loss of talent, especially among managers and supervisors; a regionwide survey revealed a widespread negative attitude about the supervisor's role; and,

funds for training were to be cut by 50% in the near future. If we were going to [address these concerns], we were going to have to act during 1993.

For the FDA, the resulting regional training strategy was decidedly innovative. Gomez created a cadre of three employees, all experienced in training and staff development, whom he empowered to invent a new training program. They were given a budget and permission to operate in any way needed, anywhere in the region. This first self-directed project team in the Southwest region created the Regional Training Academy, now a permanent program for staff development throughout the region.

Regional Training Academy participants took a two-day course on the administrative aspects of supervision, and a one-day course, "Is Supervision for You?" Graduates were involved in follow-up projects and were encouraged to choose additional course offerings for self-development or supervisory development. Participants who entered the pre-supervisory track attended a five-day seminar on the skills needed for effective teamwork: good communication, effective meetings, conflict resolution, problem solving, and constructive coaching. This course was followed by a month-long "detail" as an acting supervisor, with the guidance of a volunteer mentor.

At about the same time, in the fall of 1992, John Scharmann and his management team in Denver spent two days away from the office in a strategic planning event remembered as "The Go-Away." Action projects identified at this workshop paralleled projects identified by participants in the Training Academy. As one of the participants in both reflected, "People gravitated to projects they felt strongly about." During late 1992 and throughout 1993, the initiatives catalyzed by the Southwest Training Academy and the Denver district strategic planning Go-Away tended to merge and support each other. The list of accomplishments is impressive.

Go-Away Training Academy Grads' Accomplishments

- Director Scharmann created a "Guidance Group" to ensure implementation of projects after the Go-Away. Each follow-up taskforce has a member on this group, which is empowered to make all implementation decisions, except those involving major commitments of time or money.

- A monthly information-sharing luncheon was launched to increase communication among the district director, branch managers, and supervisors.

- This district management team decided to gather opinions about the district from all 110 employees. Workshops were facilitated by Go-Away participants.

- Investigations Branch and Compliance Branch supervisors participated in job exchange details. As a result of this cross-training experience, Director Scharmann observes, "They now 'understand' each other better. People are not so quick to jump."

- One taskforce created a flextime scheme. Scharmann and Regional Director Gomez signed off on it, and the proposal went to headquarters where it was approved.

- Another taskforce launched a new inventory method using bar-code labels and computers, which achieves major time savings in conducting the annual equipment inventory. With input from everyone concerned, implementation is faster and reliability higher.

- The *Effective Meeting Guide* was researched and published by a team of Training Academy grads and Go-Away participants, many of whom worked on the guide in their off-duty time. There has been tremendous satisfaction in its publication and distribution.

- The *Effective Meeting Guide* group and others have become an informal network of facilitators in the Denver district, recognized for their skill in conducting productive meetings. They are asked to facilitate meetings throughout the Southwest region, and even for national FDA staff in Washington, D.C., action-oriented planning to catalyze innovation.

But there were other, indirect results, some of which were quite unexpected.

- Regional Director Gomez received feedback that Training Academy grads were more supportive of their supervisors, had a higher stake in successful completion of work, and were visibly better at teamwork.

- The mood in the Denver district remains noticeably upbeat. People say: "People are more relaxed and comfortable;" "The psychological climate is more open; we are relaxing the rules;" "There is a ton of stuff happening; the momentum is enough to make me giggle;" "We're learning, the climate is changing."

But of course there has been short fall.

- A Computer User Group was commissioned to make recommendations for the use of computers in the Denver office. But uncertain leadership and technical expertise, unclear authority and focus bogged the group down in too many meetings with too few accomplishments. Nevertheless, some of the most valuable lessons about participatory management have come from this experience. Success requires that people have technical expertise, a sufficiently focused task to permit results, and the authority to act. Compliance Officer Shelly Maifarth comments, "Management wanted us to make management decisions, but we weren't managers and didn't have authority over time, assignments, or spending. It's wrong to use an internal, volunteer group to make management decisions."

- When a new computer group was formed, its technically knowledgeable members didn't solicit input from less computer-literate users. The results were less than user friendly.

LeRoy Gomez noted that some projects have fallen by the wayside and observes, "We've learned that support is key. Enthusiasm and interest generally prevail, but alongside mixed reviews, many in the Denver district are on tenterhooks about implementing participatory management and self-directed work teams. Teams are treated like a strategy for special assignments, rather than as a way to manage the daily routine. Their members' comments reveal the difficulty of making personal changes. Commenting on hesitation among some older employees and impatience among the new ones, some observe that "the Denver district has a lot of 20-year people and a lot of 2-year people." Some doubt their own ability: "Can we do it?" Others are concerned about getting their regular work done. Karen Kreuzer, manager of the Denver Lab's Microbiology Assay Section, says, "We are trying, but our old ways are a block. The new isn't necessarily fostered quickly. Stuff has to be batted around."

Familiar issues like difficulties in interbranch communication and an expanding workload are joined by new challenges. Denver employees voice some of their concerns:

- District Director Scharmann now has to pay attention to new questions of balance: "How much time should I make available to [new] projects? Too little time and people say, 'I don't have enough support.' Too much time and I'm 'giving away the farm.' Regular work suffers. We've had to 'sunset' one or two groups because they didn't contribute to the FDA's mission."

- The prospect of serious experimentation with self-directed work teams has generated both a high level of interest and a high level of anxiety. Will a team have enough expertise? Will people be good at time management? Who will handle the complexities of budgeting? Kreuzer comments, "The idea of quality circles or self-directed teams is great. But they still need coordination and facilitation, and some people don't like that role."

- Will people be able to work together in new ways? Shelly Maifarth recalls, "We did a project on diversity and how people and organizations are tackling diversity. Because we lacked team-building training, my group was really dysfunctional. We each believed that we could come up with a good project alone—but not as a group."

- Another staffer observes, "First-line supervisors are under pressure to produce numbers and paperwork—it's the channel by which feedback goes back up a hierarchy. To do self-directed work teams we're clearly going to have to change the FDA culture."

Despite some discomfort with the new order of FDA business, authoritarian management, punitive supervision, or mindless routine, if not completely gone, are clearly discredited and seldom missed. The easy assurance of things running smoothly, comfortable routines that get the job done, and an occasional twinge of boredom are also gone. The end of the present course—flattening the hierarchy, launching pilot self-directed work teams, changing to a more open management style—is not yet in sight. The path toward "entrepreneurial government" is neither clear, nor is there any promise that it will become clear soon. The Denver district is betwixt and between, caught more or less self-consciously in an uncomfortable, if exhilarating, space between the FDA culture of the past and an emerging, as yet undefined, FDA culture of the future.

Tylenol, Terror, and Teamwork

The year is 1986. About 1 A.M. on February 8th, a healthy young woman dies suddenly in her bed in Peekskill, New York. An autopsy reveals traces of cyanide in her stomach and blood; the police find three Extra-Strength Tylenol capsules containing cyanide in her home.

Three years after the passage of the 1983 Federal Anti-Tampering Act, the U.S. Food and Drug Administration is called in to conduct an intensive search for other adulterated capsules. Scores of field staff and 60 laboratory technicians are put on 24-hour emergency duty. Within hours they implement a systematic seizure of Extra-Strength Tylenol capsules in a one-mile radius of the A & P supermarket where police know the dead woman purchased the adulterated capsules. Hundreds of stores are inspected and thousands of capsules are tested. The stakes are high. Human lives, a trusted pharmaceutical company's reputation, and the public's trust are at risk. Nothing unusual turns up on Monday. Or Tuesday. Or Wednesday.

Five days into the investigation, the FDA Sample Custodian for the New York Regional Lab in Brooklyn reports the arrival of three new samples to Sample Room Supervisor Jim Yager. They are the latest of some 67,000 which have arrived for analysis. Yager assigns each sample to a staff microbiologist. Within minutes he receives a report: five of the capsules found on a local Woolworth's shelves are visibly darker than normal. Tylenol powder is pure white; analysis confirms the presence of cyanide. FDA field staff revisit area outlets to confirm that all Tylenol capsules have been removed. No one is ever caught, but no other lives are lost in Westchester County due to cyanide poisoning.

The Challenge of Reinventing Culture

Many FDAers wear their culture on their lapels like a badge. The FDA is an enforcement agency whose core values include rigorous attention to good science, careful detective work, demand for compliance, and high energy responsiveness in crisis situations. Following the FDA's investigation of the Chicago Tylenol deaths in 1982, the agency was instrumental in helping to design the Federal Anti-Tampering Act of 1983. For the first time it became a federal crime to tamper with consumer products. The FDA can work with lightning speed to investigate health hazards, especially when criminal activity is suspected in a highly emotional and visible national scare. Ironically, however, the very values of which the FDA is justifiably proud, e.g., rigorous investigation and enforcement, prevent some managers from seeing more effective ways to ensure the health and safety needs of the nation. For example, after 30-some years, a demonstrably superior process for ensuring food safety, the Hazard Analysis Critical Control Point technique (HACCP), is just beginning to gain limited national acceptance. Pioneered by Pillsbury under contract with NASA in the early 1960s to guarantee the health of astronauts, training in the use of HACCP techniques has only recently become a part of the FDA plan of work nationally.

The Clash of Cultures in the FDA	
The old culture that isn't quite gone	The new culture that isn't all here
• hierarchy, multiple layers	• fewer layers of review
• autocratic, top-down	• cooperative, networking
• law enforcement; know it all	• empowerment; mutual learning
• inspectors can't help	• trainers can coach
• improvement through criticism	• improvement through learning
• reactive	• preventive
• customer vulnerable to inspector	• customer creates own destiny
• "scalp" system: bringing in seizures, prosecutions, etc.	• "star" system: bringing in results e.g., no poisionings.

Understanding the FDA culture and the clash of mindsets that both influence it and are influenced by it is a major factor in understanding what it takes to help a national agency change the way it does business. Tampering and prevention of adulterated drugs are regulatory matters and the FDA is skilled in effectively regulating the manufacture and packaging of over-the-counter drugs. But though the food industry requires regulation, implementation of HACCP techniques is more a challenge of meeting an industry need, catalyzing new practices, and empowering ownership of new food safety training programs. Also, the FDA must build public awareness to support its intention to expand its use of the HACCP system.

Because challenges like nationwide implementation of the HACCP system would require a 180 degree about-face in the mindset of FDA staff, federal officers who carry the club of regulation have a hard time shifting gears to the flip charts and overhead projectors of education. In the not too distant past, an FDA investigator who tried to help a restaurant owner solve a food-related problem was liable to receive a reprimand from a supervisor. This clash of cultures makes it difficult to implement new ways of working.

So what is to be done? The principles of reinventing government, exciting and full of promise on paper, fly in the face of the very ways of doing business that have allowed the FDA to create public trust. As Jim Yager, director of the FDA Laboratory in Denver points out, "Congressional committees may criticize us, but people feel safe; Americans have improved health because of what we do." Regulation of over-the-counter drugs and promotion of food safety are just two of the scores of concerns that occupy the FDA. Under pressure to change when such a complex mission must proceed with limited funding, nothing short of miraculous transformation seems adequate to support the practical, personal transcendence needed to reinvent the FDA. The question comes to this: How do managers and employees help each other continually to let go of old, self-limiting images in the necessary process of transcending the very structures that have given meaning to their labors?

Seeing with New Eyes

As Peter Senge suggested in his 1990 work, *The Fifth Discipline*, there are five characteristics of learning organizations: systems thinking, shared vision, team learning, mental models, and personal mastery [3]. It's instructive to look at the FDA through the "set of eyeglasses" these characteristics create. If the real challenge of redesigning government has to do with seeing with new eyes, how does a whole system create new eyes? In the face of change, some employees tighten up, shut down, and watch out for the next assault of ambiguity. Others take an expansive relationship to change and many staff members in the Denver district are living examples of this refreshing response. They speak about the excitement of learning, taking courses, and trying out new approaches, i.e., in various ways having their eyes opened. In the face of change, they have been able to open up in an attempt to see and understand more.

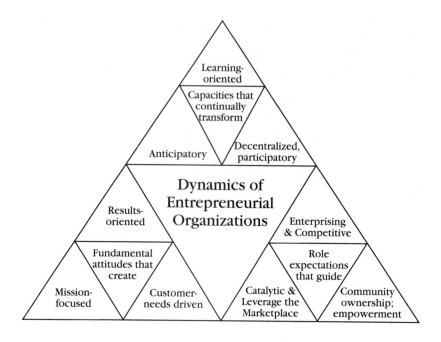

Their positive mental attitude and openness allow them to see adventure where others see ruin.

The Denver district, for instance, has a somewhat outdated and not universally shared vision; employees struggle to function as an effectively connected, united system; many employees have been deeply appreciative of their team learning, but have little opportunity to share their learnings with other teams or the whole district. District managers have few mental models for management innovation or organizational change; and yet many people are proud of increased personal mastery in various fields of endeavor, though they have limited opportunity for recognition of their prowess. Each of these observations has a fairly concrete, constructive implication for a manager's consideration and illustrates the power of Senge's image of the learning organization to create a new set of eyes.

The entire Southwest Region began to develop a new set of eyes during 1993 and 1994. At the same time that the national Office of Regulatory Affairs (ORA) was distributing its strategic plan, "ORA 21"—a call for decentralization, streamlining, cultural change, and exploration of self-directed teams—managers and employees throughout the region were noticing the interest generated and energy released by involvement in the

Denver district management Go-Away and the Regional Training Academy. These three influences, a mandate for change from Washington, a demonstration of effective employee involvement in district management, and a visible commitment to training catalyzed discussion about a regionwide change effort.

Working Through Change

Just before the end of FY 1994, the decision was made to influence all 440 employees across the region with new images of increased involvement in managing their own work. A series of 13 orientation workshops was held to support the launch of pilot self-directed teams in each district.

Participants' reactions ranged from fierce anger to enthusiastic appreciation that someone would honestly acknowledge their capacities for self-management and that someone would recognize the difficulties involved in trying to shift in this direction. Surprisingly this kind of positive reaction was the most common experience across the region. Everyone understands that energy and creativity are released by participation in teams. They also know that the FDA creates teams when something needs to be done. Various cross-functional teams are frequently used to make the system work in spite of itself, though the general mythology of the FDA does not yet acknowledge this fact of significant employee involvement. Most employees' operating images lag behind the reality of participation and teamwork.

The most striking finding to emerge from this face-to-face encounter with an entire region was the degree of alignment. People want to be able to work better; they also wish for more involvement and better morale. At the same time, they doubt their own capacity for managing change or the FDA's commitment to supporting change. Whatever is said in Washington about reinventing, FDAers are doubtful that it means anything different in their lives. But even if change were expected, employees see two remaining obstacles: their own anxieties about working more closely together, and the system's limited ability to either reward change or change what it rewards.

By the end of a day spent candidly discussing the prospects for change, employees are ready to take constructive action. Though said in different ways in different places, the consensus was:

Let's commit to a positive attitude and give more employee involvement a chance. Let's open up communication so we can all think through where it would be sensible to try our self-directed teams. Let's see a real demonstration of commitment to change by removing barriers to our working more effectively together.

The greatest obstacle to change in the FDA may turn out to be the absence of any mechanism for revealing an actual consensus of change in the districts across the nation. In the Southwest region, managers and employees alike are ready for a more entrepreneurial approach, but do not yet have clear operating images of what that looks like.

The Dynamics of Entrepreneurial Governance

What does entrepreneurial governance look like? Osborne and Gaebler give examples of organizations experimenting with a more entrepreneurial approach, but do not describe and explore the role of their principles in a single organization. Entrepreneurial governance is needed in an organization like the FDA that hopes to create greater output and benefit. The new set of eyes provided by seeing Osborne's and Gaebler's principles as dynamics in entrepreneurial organizations makes it possible to visualize the activities needed for entrepreneurial leadership.

The Denver district's experience in implementing HACCP is a clear example. HACCP, a state-of-the-art system for food safety, is clearly mission-focused. The system meets a "customer" need — a reputation of safety translates directly to the industry's bottom line. HACCP implementation is results-oriented: the goal is to reduce the incidence of food poisoning or food-borne infection to zero. In the FDA's Denver district, HACCP training efforts have been organized to catalyze the entire food service industry. FDA trainers and inspectors cooperate with food processors, distributors, and retailers to identify hazardous practices. State and local government and private industry partners have teamed up with federal FDA officials to sponsor and conduct training seminars. Industry experts have been brought in to share their on-the-job experience, to empower the food industry itself to take on the challenge of putting HACCP into action. In Colorado, HACCP's implementation has been both anticipatory and participatory. At a statewide seminar to introduce HACCP principles, seminar participants themselves set HACCP action plans.

A dynamic model of entrepreneurial organization also helps reveal weaknesses and opportunities. While HACCP has touched all of the dynamics of entrepreneurial governance in Colorado, it has been weakest in catalyzing other players to broadly influence the marketplace. If the food service industry took ownership of HACCP, might it be possible to leverage total statewide implementation? Might a business or university partner be able to offer statewide trainings at no cost to the government? Or might the FDA itself create a training service that would be totally self-supporting? Nationally, HACCP principles and technology offer a perfect opportunity for the FDA to experiment with more entrepreneurial approaches.

FDA's latest efforts to seek public comments on expanding its HACCP program is one further step to involve the food industry more directly in food safety monitoring. The HACCP program is just one example of how looking more deeply at organizational dynamics might help the FDA become entrepreneurial.

Anticipatory Posture

If the essence of an entrepreneurial organization is a capacity for "self-transcendence," what are the elements that facilitate this? How do conscientious workers shed the old images that have guided their actions, so that they can at least see clearly new needs and responses? More pointedly, how can the FDA overcome the blinder effect of the scientific, regulatory culture which has been its solid foundation for many years? Social scientist David Cooperrider suggests a new frame of mind for a start. One way to transcend the past, he says, is to deglorify it, to notice where the structures have not been so successful. In *Appreciative Management and Leadership,* Cooperrider makes the point that our old images can be a serious obstacle to creating a more adequate vision of the future:

> To repeat, our positive images are no doubt the best we have, but the best is often not responsive to changing needs and opportunities. The real challenge, therefore, is to discover the processes through which a system's best affirmations can be left behind and better ones developed [4].

He suggests that we acknowledge that our old visions are, after all, only our own inventions, and can be replaced by new inventions.

Seen in this light, the FDA's scientific culture could become its greatest ally for change. Scientists, after all, experiment and learn by observation. If old ways are no longer adequate, experimentation could reveal more adequate replacements. Clearly, continuous visioning is needed to replace the perspectives from the past with even more powerful outlooks for the future. Osborne and Gaebler point in this direction when they write about "anticipatory government"—government that looks to the future. But anticipation means more than prevention. Anticipatory government implies leaders who transcend the past because the very feel of organizational culture has shifted. Culture is no longer an artifact of the past, but a quest for the empowering vision, values, and beliefs adequate to a future they desire. Cooperrider notes, "Fundamentally... it can be argued that every organization, product, or innovative service first started as a wild but not idle dream, and that anticipatory realities are what make collectives click." Culture, in this sense, is not so much what we remember and guard, as what we anticipate and invent. Anticipatory culture stimulates transcendence.

Participatory Access

A second way to transcend the past is to shift from autocratic decision making to reflection, critique, and shared responsibility. One of the negative impacts of autocratic leadership is anger. When people are left out, they feel stifled and get angry. Sometimes the anger bursts out in the violence of a postal worker gone berserk. But more often it is buried and then gets in the way of doing the job effectively. D. J. Inman, a regional food specialist who conducts food safety education in the Denver district commented, "We have endured bureaucracy. But the comforts are no longer enough to make up for the negative impact of an autocratic system and people who have worked outside the federal bureaucracy know it." Bottled-up anger makes any organization dysfunctional, from families and teams to national agencies. Transcending the past requires that we take the lid off, give people a chance to be heard and to have an impact on their work.

Lloyd Beaston, one of two compliance officers in the Denver district, ran into fierce anger when he was asked to help the clerical, administrative, and secretarial staff develop a mission statement:

> That was an awakening. They felt unappreciated and under-supported. I was unprepared for the hostility, all the negative feelings. It took two sessions to get to the issues. [We discussed several specific points but when] it came to the bottom line, you had to deal with all the feelings. Their anger may block them from taking a step. Taking the lid off was just the beginning. After the feelings get out, it takes careful, assertive leadership to ensure constructive follow-up.

Participation is more than a strategy or goal. Participation is the way an open system operates. One long-time FDAer notes, "Participation helps managers see real problems; it helps bureaucracies get new messages about reality." Continually soliciting ideas and responsibility, from employees and clients alike, is a way an organization can get uncomfortable information. Information which upsets the apple cart creates an opportunity for transcendence.

Learning-oriented Posture

A third way to transcend the past is to transcend the limits of one's own imagination. Time after time, the Denver district managers interviewed spoke about stretching, flexing, and growing. Literally dozens of employees, only a few of whom have been mentioned here, self-consciously decide day by day to explore the greater contribution they can make in their work as they enlarge themselves, connect with others, and try new ways of getting their jobs done better.

Sandy Cross is one such person. She was one of the creators of the Denver district's Effective Meeting Guide, and is now a member of the Denver district facilitation team. Sandy recalled the immense difficulty the guide team had getting to work, narrowing its focus, and producing results. But, she said, the seven were committed to their project and set strong guidelines for themselves early in their work, even requiring each other to raise hands for permission to speak. Sandy described this experience:

There was a lot of learning on our part, but we came to really enjoy one another. We've become strong advocates for good meetings. What made it possible to stick with a task under difficult circumstances? This is the first time I have been a part of a truly self-directed team, with real cooperation and sharing. It was exciting to be a part of a group that functioned well as a team. I wanted to see us grow and I wanted to be a part of the growth.

An organization whose employees continually seek their own enlargement, balance, and effectiveness is a system whose very foundation is in the hearts and minds of growing human beings . When people and their teams adopt a posture of learning, every moment is a lesson, every assignment releases entrepreneurial spirit, and every challenge is an opportunity to practice change.

References

[1] U.S. Federal Food and Drug Administration, Almanac, Fiscal Year 1993 (Rockville, MD: Department of Health and Human Services), 1993.

[2] Osborne, David and Ted Gaebler. *Reinventing Government* (Reading, MA: Addison-Wesley Publishing Company, 1992), p. xxii.

[3] Senge, Peter. *The Fifth Discipline: The Art and Practice of the Learning Organization* (New York: Doubleday), 1990.

[4] Cooperrider, David L., S. Srivastva, et al. *Appreciative Management and Leadership: The Power of Positive Thought* (San Francisco: Jossey Bass), 1990.

Chapter 15
Labor Management Partnerships

ELLIE HAYDOCK

*In 1992, City and State Magazine presented City Manager
Odio, along with six colleagues around the country, its
"Most Valuable Public Official" award, honoring
excellence in public service. Odio brought all four
union presidents, whom he referred to as partners in
the award, to Washington, D.C. for the ceremony. He
acknowledged them and other city employees saying,
I'm proud of this award because I'm only a small piece
of it. Every city employee has a piece of it...employees
now take part in the city's operations and management
policy-making process. Every city department has an
LMC and every employee has a word to say about how
we run the city. They have as much at stake as I do, so
why shouldn't they have a say in what we're doing.*

I t is well documented that the response time of paramedic rescue units
is the critical factor in determining the chances of survival in times of
medical emergency. Rescue units aim for four minutes or less; they
consider six minutes tolerable. In Miami's west side, however, the
average response time was seven minutes and more. Because of a low
number of emergency requests, the fire department could not justify
assigning an advanced life support (ALS) service unit to the neighborhood fire station; it housed only a single fire truck called a "pumper." The
department wanted to upgrade station resources but understood the city
had no funding for a new ALS rescue unit.

Despite these problems, this story doesn't end in a bureaucratic logjam so common in most large municipal governments attempting to resolve such issues. Several positive actions helped avoid such a blockade. First, Miami's network of labor-management committees (LMCs), charged with unblocking administrative nightmares, stepped in. The fire department LMC worked out a novel solution bringing benefits to all concerned. The single pumper unit staffed with one fire lieutenant and three fire fighters were upgraded to officer, and two fire fighter positions to the position of fire fighter paramedic. The paramedic fire fighters, after receiving special training, received pay increases equal to those of ALS unit paramedics. The pumper itself was outfitted with all the medical equipment necessary to make it an ALS unit.

Citizens on Miami's west side now receive ALS response time within four minutes. Building on this model, a plan is now in place that places a paramedic pumper in all twelve fire stations. These units back up regular rescue fleets and ensure that citizens receive the quickest, best service in the country with very little additional cost to the city of Miami.

Labor and City Management as Partners

This story is one tiny indicator of the way the city of Miami does business these days. Here, labor and management work together to benefit each other and their customers, the citizens of Miami. This result is the focus of this case study: how labor and management can work cooperatively together in government for the well being of all parties, citizens, workers, and management. This cooperative spirit was not always present.

A partnership emerged from management's invitation for labor to participate in a problem-solving and decision-making process. Motivated by hopes for mutual improvements, participation in the joint sessions anticipated specific rises in quality of work life, productivity, service, and communication. They had high expectations to change interpersonal relationships from adversarial to collaborative.

Typically, in the past, and to some extent still, decisions in Miami city government, as well as most government and private businesses, have been made at the top and communicated downward to rank-and-file employees, who rarely are asked for ideas or solutions. No one seemed to be listening; no one seemed to care. Service suffered. Morale was at an all-time low. Conflicts were resolved by arbitrations, civil service proceedings, or court action.

Initiating Change

Such was the case when City Manager Caesar Odio took over in 1985. Odio is recognized both locally and nationally as a progressive city manager in a highly complex, multiethnic and fast growing city. This came partly from his ability to work creatively with the City Commission (the locally elected city council) and to forge alliances and cooperation between his administration and four major unions of city employees: the International Association of Fire Fighters (IAFF), the Federation of Police (FOP), the Sanitation Employee Association (SEA), and the American Federation of State, County, and Municipal Employees (AFSCME) who represented the rest of the city workforce.

After representatives of the local AFSCME and the city's bargaining team attended a win-win negotiation training session sponsored by the U.S. Department of Labor, Odio executed a new contract with that union in record time. This prompted him to ask, "What if labor and management sat down together to deal with shared issues regularly, not just when it is time to negotiate contracts?" With that idea, he established LMCs in each department of city government. He wanted to inspire people to resolve issues themselves early on without having to create bureaucracy.

The process began in March, 1991 with a Labor Management "Shared Visions" Conference of 120 participants, including 4-6 union representatives from every department, each department head, assistant department head, and assistant city managers. Most had never heard about LMCs and did not know what this conference was about. Participative planning consultants, Cynthia Vance and Larry Ward of Strategics International, designed and conducted this two-day conference. At the beginning, Odio said,

> Labor Management Committees are here to stay. We are totally committed to a participatory form of management by which employees actively contribute to decisions affecting their jobs, their departments, their city, and consequently their future. Management and labor will work together, streamlining procedures, policies, and services.

At the end of his presentation, he held up a sign that said, "I BELIEVE," an action which shocked the group. He went on to say that if any members of his own management team refused to participate in the new approach, "they could work someplace else!" His challenge was met with skeptical enthusiasm.

Participants then worked in department teams, making every decision along the way. They forged mission and role statements for LMCs, identified their membership, key values, leadership, communication modes, meeting frequency and sub-committees necessary to work on a list of 5 - 8 issues they would tackle in the first year. The group created department mottoes for the first set of LMCs:

Budget Dept.	"Balance It!"
Computer Dept.	"Excellence Through Teamwork"
Finance Dept.	"Turning Sense into Dollars"
GSA/Solid Waste	"Employees for a Better Miami"
Planning/Building/Zoning	"Make It Happen"
Public Works	"Working for Progress"

Union leaders were enthusiastic about the LMC process. William "Shorty" Bryson, president of the IAFF Local #587, says:

> The intent of the labor management concept is to open up problem solving to all levels of the department, create a 'we' attitude, resolve issues without spending time and money on arbitrators or courts, give better service to the citizens, find new, creative ways to save dollars or generate revenues and much more.

Charles Cox, president of the AFSCME Local #1907, echoed Bryson's enthusiasm.

> The labor-management process will foster employee involvement in the big scheme of our city government. This will help the City operate more cost effectively and stop the 'us vs. them' attitude.

FOP Lodge #20 President Al Cotera added, "This is a new concept that can become a very successful way of improving the workplace for both labor and management." Enthusiastic support for the process convinced the Federal Mediation and Conciliation Service (FMCS - the U.S. government's full-service conflict resolution agency), to grant the city $62,000 in 1991 to give their LMC program a boost over an 18-month period, plus $12,500 in continuation funding for an additional six months. Out of 101 applicants, Miami was one of only 13 which received grants. Throughout the initial phase of the program, the money was used for staff support, training, supplies, and a quarterly newsletter. "There was something about the application that said success," noted Peter Regner, FMCS Grants Program Director. "I said to myself: 'People in Miami really want this. It takes guts to embark on this process.'" "It is time to recognize we have things in common," said Robert P. Baker, national representative of the FMCS director. "The time has come for the public sector to show the private sector a more enlightened approach to management."

Once the process started some teams worked harder and faster than others. Although there was not 100% effectiveness across the board with the LMCs, there have been significant breakthroughs. A number of departments have instituted an "employee of the month" recognition. One department has monthly "employee town meetings" to gain increased input into their LMC work.

Ordinary people doing what many consider extraordinary things can produce amazing results. In reality, it is simply a case of people doing their jobs smarter. Take, for example, Charles "Chuck" Postis and Oscar Valido, who are both members of a departmental worksite LMC and who each received the mayor's commendation for excellence in public service. Postis is an air-conditioning mechanic and has been with the city since 1989. He submitted an idea that the city install sub-meters for cooling towers at the police and administration buildings. He realized that the city was billed for sewer charges on readings of a single meter that registered total water usage. Since the city implemented his idea, sewer charges have dropped approximately $6,000 per year, providing a cost savings to the city. Valido is an electrician and employed by the city since 1982. One day at the city garage, he saw that the overhead high energy lights were on all day. He decided to run a test and turned all the lights off. Surprisingly, no one there noticed any difference. He then told the garage supervisors what had happened. Afterwards, he installed a timer so that lights go on only at certain times, providing a high cost savings to the city.

The Process at Work

The LMCs are authorized and established by the city manager and various union leaders. Essentially they try to improve the quality of work life, productivity, procedures, service, communication, and interpersonal

Results of the Labor Management
Committee Approach in Miami

- Decreased employee grievances by 12%, civil service appeals by 75% and legal actions by 38%.

- Lowered absenteeism in the AFSCME bargaining group in 1992 by 72% through implementing a sick leave policy resulting in 30,000 hours of sick time saved, or approximately $750,000.

- Updated 50% of the administrative policies and renamed them labor-management policies by an administrative policy review committee.

- Established an education committee to seek other avenues and sources for employee education tuition reimbursement.

- Eliminated an employee classification called "managerial confidential" describing an employee group that does not fall under the bargaining group and is still civil service. All but 49 of these positions then became eligible for union membership.

- Developed a perfect attendance award program for which 300 employees became eligible for a $100 drawing which 25 won.

- Amended the donation of time policy to allow employees the option to donate vacation and earned time to another employee for reasons other than illness.

relationships. The committees develop a variety of means for communicating to all employees. These include routing of meeting minutes, posting information on bulletin boards, memos, department and divisions meetings and newsletter.

Committee members can be contacted in writing or directly by other employees with an idea, suggestion or problem. Also, in many departments suggestion boxes keep communication lines open. Most LMC's meet at least once a month, and if there is a long agenda, they meet more often. The length of the agenda determines when and how long the LMCs meet. Some members serve on the LMCs as volunteers, but in most departments,

- Agreed to promote 39 stand-by (temporary) workers in the solid waste department to full-time status to reduce overtime, absenteeism, and injuries.
- Permitted alternative work schedules, such as flex time and a 4-day/10-hour work week.
- Provided for annual physicals for the hazard materials team within the fire department.
- Extended a physical fitness program to include all fire department employees assigned to a 40-hour workweek, allowing a few hours a week for each employee to maintain physical fitness.
- Arranged for police management and union to meet with vendors to negotiate equipment purchases.
- Created a fairer employment interview and promotion process.
- Initiated a "swap program," which allows paramedics from other less busy departments to "swap" with the fire departments of other municipalities to gain additional experience.
- Standardized the fire fighter's previous "just cause" disciplinary code to reduce the wide variance in its application. This change has resulted in decreased employee union grievances filed against management.
- Developed and instituted a fire fighter sick time incentive program funded by unused overtime monies.
- Implemented a new form of employee self-management in the motor pool and property maintenance division of the General Services Administration/Solid Waste Department.

members are appointed by labor and management, or are selected by their peers. It takes 4 to 6 months to develop the skills and abilities to participate effectively as a member, and to feel comfortable with the process. Once members reach that level, they are expected to serve and contribute for another 6 to 12 months.

Effective committee members must be committed to the process because this responsibility can be very difficult and frustrating, especially at first. Members must be flexible, patient, open-minded, enthusiastic, and assertive. They also need to be willing to learn new things and listen effectively. In total, they must be willing to learn how to participate and how to allow others to participate. In other words, the LMC process is a self-development process. Effective communication, planning, decision-making and leadership skills are developed by all the participants. The sum total of all their work has been increased satisfaction on the part of employees who are watching improvements in their own department. Employees are now being heard, a very positive development for them.

Training and development support is necessary for the success of the LMC program. In fact, members reported that the more they knew about all the surrounding concerns they were examining, the better they were able to address each problem. In addition, members have requested and received training in productivity techniques, problem solving, running effective meetings, and developing good listening skills. To be successful, members reported needing the skills for reaching consensus and for equal participation in decision-making processes.

Experimentation to Learn

The labor management process allows for experimentation: it does not have to guarantee immediate success. An experience of the Sanitation LMC is a case in point. One of its first suggestions concerned a new system of streamlining the process of backyard garbage pickup to reduce the potential for injuries. Barrels with wheels were abandoned after a pilot test because the physical impediments for rolling the barrels from the curb to the backyard took too much time. Later, however, the union representatives to the LMC agreed to a management suggestion to achieve a worker injury reduction goal by employing curbside pickup. The SEA union was reluctant at first, expressing concern about possible job layoffs, even though the backyard method of pickup tended to be inefficient and prone to create injuries. Together, labor and management, through the committee process, eliminated this concern by agreeing that extra workers not needed in the new system would be assigned to neighborhoods to perform litter and special cleanups. Results: the city saved money and labor lost no jobs. Now, the work is more efficient and safe. Workers are happy and more productive because their ideas and concerns on how to do their job were listened to and implemented. And citizens are pleased with the new service because it results in a cleaner environment.

With this new burst of collaborative success under its belt, the SEA's next idea was far more dramatic. The Sanitation Employees Association (SEA) and Miami negotiated an amendment to their contract for residential curbside recycling pickup services to all single and duplex residences. This action provided extra jobs to residents of the city and a profit for all members of the SEA union through the sale of the materials. This program lasted until mid-1994 when, due to failure to meet some of the stipulations of the contract, the city rescinded the agreement and returned the program to its previous arrangement.

So, the LMC is not always an instant success. It has ups and downs, just like every other successful change process. But the leadership is undaunted. As Lionel Nelson, the past-president of the SEA said, "It [the LMC process] will work if the city manager sticks to his word. And it can only work if we all participate and are patient. It is time to make a change. We are the people; we can do it."

Continuing the Process

Thirty LMCs have functioned well for some time now. In addition, subcommittees or worksite committees are often formed to create more employee involvement and additional resources. These committees address and solve specific issues and make recommendations to the departmental LMC.

In addition, each bargaining unit established its own summit committee with the city manager, labor relations officer, and others appointed by either the unions or management. This summit committee meets once a month to review and resolve departmental concerns such as issues within departments that cannot reach a decision by consensus, issues that affect the departmental budget, and procedures and policies that affect the employees citywide. This committee also offers an appeal process for the LMCs within each bargaining unit. An additional part of this process is the executive summit held to address citywide matters that involve more than one bargaining unit. Members of the executive summit include the city manager, AFSCME President, FOP President, IAFF President, SEA President, the fire chief, the police chief and the labor relations officer.

Since the LMC process began, both sides have come to realize that it is not easy to reach agreement when each side has to give a little. But, unions have participated in finding more efficient methods for providing service, redesigning systems to save money, and improving working conditions for city employees. The city also benefits by saving money and raising the level of employee morale.

Says IAFF President Bryson,

> The labor-management process has worked for both union and management. Prior to the process we went to arbitration about twelve times per year. Now we arbitrate about once or twice a year. Service is better and benefits have improved, but it is not a simple process. Both sides have to be willing to make it work.

Success of the process varies between employee groups and departments. Some groups are highly successful while others have not used the process to their advantage. Much of this variance can be attributed to personalities on both sides. As FOP President Cotera said, "In the police department, with its regimented para-military focus, the labor-management process can be frustrating at times." However, as time passes, if the process successfully continues in Miami, department directors and others will be evaluated and appointed partially by their ability to work within the LMC system.

The city of Miami has found that to achieve success, the labor management process must start at the top with the city manager and the union presidents, and permeate the entire municipal government organization. If employees feel they are not getting a fair shake, whether from the manager, the city commission or their department director, they really can not be expected to work on issues such as managed health care, decreasing pension funding requirements, or improved disciplinary systems, which are topics the city wants to take on next.

The Miami labor management process is an experiment in participative management and consensus decision making. Each committee makes its own procedures, goals, and objectives. Organizational decisions are reached in such a way that input and responsibility extend to the lowest level appropriate to the decision being made. Miami has learned that participative management cannot be delegated; it must be led. Some departments welcome this opportunity more easily than others. Some directors want to include employees, while others feel they don't have the time or have not yet recognized the value of employee involvement.

AFSCME President Cox has said:

I am confident this program will spread throughout the city workforce; employees have the unique opportunity to become the masters of their own destinies and eliminate what has always been the biggest complaint about work. We rarely hear complaints about money; rather, we hear complaints about working conditions. By becoming a partner with the city in establishing exactly what those working conditions will be, we can improve productivity, which results in continued guarantees of secure employment and economic advancement.

Ground Rules Matter

Two important elements in the labor-management process are: first, the freedom to express one's feelings and ideas without the fear of retribution, and second, the ability to listen to each other. While there is resistance to the LMC concept in Miami, the most difficult obstacle is changing people's attitudes. Some people have complained for so long that it is difficult to direct their energies to solution thinking. And there are those conditions that can never change, which are part of working in the public sector. It takes commitment, common sense, and perseverance to pursue those concerns, problems and ideas that can be changed.

Miami has also learned that this whole process does need a coordinator who can champion its cause on a day-to-day basis. Guarding and nurturing this process requires a lot of pushing and prodding. A project director is the resident "on call" facilitator and guide for each committee. Other responsibilities for this position include helping LMCs document their work, leading department retreats, assisting participants to distinguish between LMC issues and personnel/staff/budget issues, coordinating and conducting training, publishing LMC accomplishments, and motivating directors and participants to stick with the process. The coordinator can be coach, counselor, or whatever else is needed to keep the process moving. The Coordinator is directly accountable to the city manager and works out of that office. It is driven, supported and monitored out of the city manager's office, which is another major key to the success of the LMC process.

Dollars Saved

One of the most dramatic success stories of the LMC process was the 1994 settlement of an 18-year controversy over the city's pension fund for its employees, known as the "Gates case."

In 1976, city employees determined that funding problems existed in the City's pension plan. After many years of discussion, a joint settlement was reached in 1985 which created an amortized schedule of payments that the city was responsible to fund for a period of twenty years. The city also started a cost of living account (COLA) for all retirees, which was funded by both city and employee contributions. The fire and police pension board, structured in favor of the employees, had managed its funds well but problems still existed. The 5% increasing annual liability payments were creating an adverse impact on the city's financial position, and retirees were receiving a cost of living adjustment at less than the rate of inflation.

Through the labor management process, this case was resettled in a way favorable to all parties. While scheduled payments were removed for the city, the city also agreed to make much larger contributions to the COLA fund, providing better benefits to retirees; also active members were no longer required to make contributions to the COLA fund. A $128,000 liability was removed as a result of the application of an alternative funding formula and city contributions were reduced by several million dollars per year. This settlement agreement took almost three years to complete because the fire and police bargaining units had to approve it, along with the city and the courts who oversaw the process. Such a settlement would not have been possible in an adversarial era that had dominated labor-management relationships for some time.

Miami is proof that the old models are giving way to a new one of cooperation for the benefit of citizens. The bottom line is that the labor-management process in Miami operates like a marriage; both sides have to work together, give a little, take a little, keep from burning bridges, and once in a while tell each other how they could not survive without one another.

Labor-Management Partnership in the City of Miami

*The cover of the June, 1994 conference handbook shows
one artist's interpretation of how differences were
managed by both labor and management before
the partnership became so effective.*

SECTION IV
Facilitating Collaboration

The New Business of Government

Networks, coalitions, alliances, partnerships, collaboration. Buzzwords to be sure, but their increased use in our vocabulary of government—and in all walks of life—point to a new way of organizing the political landscape. This new approach vests our public institutions with confidence and the capacity to reform themselves, so that they can fulfill their missions. Part of the reason for this is the growing awareness that we live in an integrated world. Everything we do affects the whole. This new science of organizations is beginning to permeate how we think about getting things done.

Actually, government has used collaboration for many years, but has not necessarily called it by that name. In a commentary in the December, 1993, issue of *Governing,* Steven Ratgreb and Michael Lipsky, point out:

> Prior to the 1960s, social services consisted of private charities on the one hand and, on the other, a few government agencies that provided services, usually through large, impersonal institutions such as training schools for youth and mental hospitals. After 30 years of extensive contracting with nonprofit organizations to provide key

social services, American governments have made these organizations hidden partners. From prenatal clinics to home health care for the elderly, 65,000 nonprofit service organizations currently serve Americans from cradle to grave. As such they are subject to government demands regarding regulations, minimum requirements[1].

While the idea of using this network of nonprofits works well, a problem persists: the government unwittingly intervenes too much in determining how these "ear to the ground" groups deliver their services. Presumably, accountability is the reason. For example, instead of allowing competent lay leaders to serve in a shelter for battered women, the government contract requires the shelter to replace them with professional social workers. Of course, some argue that it is warranted to challenge the lay person to become certified, gain additional training, and learn valuable new career skills. Such advancement will produce more effective care. But when this argument gets carried too far, no one is served.

Therefore, establishing common ground where partnerships of service can flourish is the most important step in the collaborative process. There must be a shared vision that everyone "builds" together. No one can create a vision for someone else; each partner has to be part of the visioning process. That is why key partners gather together around a table and allow a facilitator to guide them toward a shared vision of their common future. This is also the reason the role of the facilitator with experience in guiding this kind of vision session has become important.

Because there is an increasing awareness for the need to deal with problems of government and society at large from a holistic perspective, many groups and organizations are stretching themselves to think beyond their boundaries. They are attempting to form alliances and partnerships with other groups who can help them fulfill their charge.

An important example of partnership is the worldwide Healthy Communities movement that developed out of a renewed understanding of the relationship between the health and well-being of a community and the decisions and responsibilities of local government. The World Health Organization (WHO) is sponsoring Healthy Community initiatives around the world. The Canadian Healthy Communities Project, established in 1987, has been the catalyst for the development of over 200 local

Healthy Community projects across that country. Healthy Community Projects are based on three strategies: 1) Fostering public participation; 2) Strengthening community health services; and, 3) Coordinating healthy public policy.

Each community assesses its own situation, proposes strategies for action, and implements its own solutions. In so doing, it creates a framework for community decision making that ensures public policies contribute to the quality of life in a community. An example of the Healthy Communities approach appears as one of our case studies, the story from Escondido, California, and its Youth Empowerment Project.

Community Policing

Another new form of collaboration is "community policing," the concept of getting police officers out of the cruisers and back on foot patrol so that they can become more familiar and "user-friendly" to the citizens they serve. This community policing strategy is emerging as the centerpiece in the national war on crime. Several large cities have pronounced it a winning, workable solution. One of those is Portland, Oregon. A city of 470,000, Portland has one of the lowest ratios of police to population: 1.9 police officers to every 1,000 citizens.

One key to Portland's success is its holistic approach of marshalling neighborhood residents in the battle against crime. During the program's first four years, Portland's crime rate dropped. Police respond more quickly to emergency calls, and residents say they are satisfied with the performance of the police and feel more secure. Portland's Community Policing program trains police officers to be enterprising problem solvers who prevent crime, not just report it, through such initiatives as carrying blue pocketbooks stuffed with information about the city's social service agencies[2].

When city officials assess what makes community policing work for Portland, they cite several factors, including the addition of nearly 200 officers. Another reason is that the program was implemented throughout the entire police department, not just in special police units or districts. While not pronouncing the program a complete success, city officials in Portland are very pleased with the results. .A critical place where collaboration in government is needed — and already exists in a few cases—lies between the different layers of government itself. The myriad number of federal programs and the labyrinth of local government rules and regulations is a serious detriment to delivering quality services to local citizens. To avoid these mazes, some state governments have come up with innovative approaches:

- The Texas Department of Human Services took the 14 separate federal programs for the 22 different children and family eligibility groups and designed a single enrollment form.
- West Virginia merged all of the state's federal funding for children and families into one pool focused on improving their health and well-being, thus avoiding the current mismatch between federal money and the real needs of low income residents.

Collaboration Experiments

In San Diego

Regional cooperation among municipalities is another arena where collaboration is being experimented. San Diego County, California, is working on forging new relationships between its various local government agencies and its network of nonprofit organizations. Faced with yet another year of a sizable state deficit and subsequent downsizing of budgets in the regional government, Chief Administrative Officer David Janssen, approached the executives of the not-for-profit corporations providing services to the population of over 2,800,000 citizens residing in the eighteen cities, neighborhoods, and unincorporated areas of the County. His questions to them were:

How can we streamline costs and maintain quality service without losing our committed staff?

What new ideas in cooperative initiatives, coalitions, and collaborations could we jointly employ?

What services and activities is the county currently providing that the community-based system could provide more effectively and efficiently?

Receiving a better reception than he anticipated, Janssen continued to provide a format that allowed the groups to meet. Soon, however, it became evident that groups of "partners" needed to build a common language, create guiding principles, and work out mutual agreements on the administrative requirements of a genuine, community partnership. So, in March of

1993, 30 public officials and 30 community leaders spent a two-day retreat to create a new way of doing business together. The object was to leave all preconceived ideas at the door and come up with a brand new approach.

In Idaho

Another place where collaboration seems to be working is in Island Park, Idaho, where irrigators and conservationists battled angrily from the early 1980s until 1993, disputing water quality in the Henry's Fork of the Snake River, one of the country's premier trout streams [3]. Through all the tumult, conservationists won a couple of limited victories, but failed to arrest the decline of the fishery. "We felt that there had to be a better way," said Jan Brown, a longtime resident and environmentalist. Brown heads the Henry's Fork Foundation which represents fly-fishermen. But it is now cooperating with its former adversary, the Fremont-Madison Irrigation District, which represents potato and grain farmers. As of October, 1993, the two organizations began to "co-facilitate" the state-chartered Henry's Fork Watershed Council .While the council accomplished no miracles in its early stages, Brown and her counterpart, Dale Swensen of the irrigation district, are optimistic. They feel the council can improve both the quality of Henry's Fork and the civility of eastern Idaho. "We've had dinners together," Brown said. "We're on parallel tracks. Our people have learned that they aren't Neanderthals, and they've seen that not all environmentalists wear ponytails." Swensen agreed: "As we talk to one another, we find that we have more common ground that what we thought we had."

In Ohio

This same spirit of collaboration is manifest in the Wraparound Services at Huckleberry House in Columbus, Ohio. Modeled after similar programs in Alaska and Vermont, Wraparound Services provides highly individualized services to troubled youth and family. Its approach requires a fundamental shift in the vision we have of serving the needs of families. It is a process that gives both the youth and family a voice, access to, and ownership of the interventions and outcomes. Wraparound Services wraps the resources of the community around the youth, based on what they need. It is a matter of "seeing" the world through the young person's eyes as best as possible.

Sheryl Nordin-Caruso, executive director of Alternatives for Children and Teens (ACT) in Columbus, Ohio, which oversees the "Wraparound" projects in several private agencies in Central Ohio, says:

> It's clear to me when programs are owned by the people they're serving, the success rate is much greater. Building on the strengths of a family and community, rather than looking for the limitations, allows creativity and hope to emerge. Participation by each member of the child's system is the key element to a positive outcome.

A Government By the People

Is collaboration the new business of government? We think it is. The stories in our anthology point to the kind of success that happens when local groups and government agencies come together to form a level playing field and solve social problems together. Some collaborative efforts involving community groups and public sector agencies represent a form of "counter government where programs and policies are being shaped outside the mainstream of the traditional government activities. Gradually, these activities create a change process within government itself, an "in but not of" tradition of public service, giving rise to a new of hope for the future.

In these collaborations, the citizen regains the role as the primary owner and user of government, while the role of the public servant changes from "solver of all problems" to "resource-provider," enabling citizens to be the change agents of their own destiny. The role of the public servant then becomes akin to a midwife—enabling and supporting, but not causing.

The public servant as resource broker can bring about a new sense of civic responsibility on the part of the local people themselves who come together in a new model of government that works.

References

[1] Smith, Steven Ratgreb and Michael Lipsky, "Commentary"
     Governing, Vol. 7, No. 3, December, 1993, pp. 10-11.
[2] Dellios, Hugh. "Residents Like New Approach," *Chicago Tribune,*
     Feb. 25, 1994, p. 1.
[3] "Virtues of mediation changing old politics," *Chicago Tribune,*
     May 14, 1994, p. 1.

Chapter 16
Rallying to Save Louisiana Wetlands

JEAN WATTS WITH KIRK CHERAMIE

*Resource management is fraught with special
interest politics. Each group of citizen stakeholders
has its own pet issues and answers. Each state
government agency competes for the same dollars
and their missions frequently overlap resulting in
"turf battles." This was certainly true for the coalition
meeting on the Bartaria-Terrebonne Estuary. Steve
Mathies took a chance. He bet that 80 people would be
able to reach a consensus on rules and regulations
for marsh management, pollution control, and
public access rights.*

One muggy south Louisiana day in 1992, a group of people gathered to resolve the almost insoluble problems in the nation's
largest coastal estuary. Many were historical antagonists, vet-
erans of bitter conflicts over use of this fragile ecosystem.
Several were government scientists committed to an already
prescribed approach to problem solving in the environment.
Some were passionate environmentalists fighting to save a way of life.

Around the table sat Phil Boydston, representing land owners, some of
whom still believed that "if you trespass on my property I have the right to
shoot you," Vince Cottone, an environment engineer from Texaco; Kay
Radlauer, an environmental activist representing local citizens; Karen
Gautreaux, from the Governor's office; Kirk Cheramie, a Houma Indian

The Barataria-Terrebonne Estuary: A Nationally Significant Ecosystem

Between the Mississippi and the Atchafalaya rivers in south-central Louisiana lies the Barataria-Terrebonne estuary. It's a unique land, bounded by great river levees, rich in natural resources that sustain the oldest French-speaking culture in the nation. These estuarine wetlands are one of the most biologically productive systems in the nation.

The Barataria-Terrebonne Estuary includes over 6,300 square miles of cypress swamps, timberlands, farms, residential and commercial communities. Here, freshwater drains from the land into the estuary's lakes, bays, and bayous and meets the salty tides of the Gulf of Mexico in miles of coastal marshes. It is in this transition zone from freshwater to saltwater that a national treasure of plants and animals thrives, fish and shellfish spawn, and approximately 630,000 humans live and work.

But the estuary is in trouble. Since 1932, over 656 square miles of valuable wetlands and barrier islands have been lost—nearly 11 square miles a year for the last 60 years. Land loss threatens the way of life and the ways of making a living.

What causes the loss? Forces of nature as well as the residential and commercial activities of the people who live and work in the estuary. As land is lost, saltwater from the Gulf moves deep into the estuary's freshwater areas, affecting water supplies and destroying productive freshwater marsh. Estuarine lakes, bays, and bayous are polluted from known and unknown sources and contaminated by human waste. Fish kills have been an annual event in recent years. Every year nearly half the Barataria Bay oyster beds are closed because they are affected by sewage contamination.

Although primarily known today as French-speaking Cajuns, the people who live in the estuary are a melting pot of French Creoles, Italians, Anglos, Spaniards, Germans, Acadians, Chinese, Filipinos, Native Americans, Dalmatian Croatians, Canary Islanders, African-Americans, and many multiethnic descendants of the raiders of Jean Lafitte, based in the area more than 200 years ago. The people here love the solitude and beauty of their wetlands where they can maintain their distinctive ethnic and cultural diversity.

Drawn to the estuary because of its teeming abundance, they built their homes and businesses on stilts because the fragile wetlands are flood prone due to tidal and storm waters; they are too soggy to walk on, let alone support a permanent structure. Most of the people still live in small communities along the ridges or natural levees of the major waterways, such as Bayou Lafourche, Bayou Terrebonne, Bayou Teche, and Bayou Black. Hurricane storm surges exceed 13 feet above sea level and can cause extensive flood damage. Some communities have had to move inland after particularly severe hurricanes, such as the 1893 hurricane that destroyed the bustling fishing community of Cheniere Caminada and killed 1500 of the 2000 residents.

The estuary is a sportsmen's paradise. The freshwater marshes of the middle and upper Barataria and Terrebonne basins are vast feeding and nesting grounds for migratory birds, and both indigenous and non-indigenous animals including a number of endangered and threatened species, such as the bald eagle and black bear. Fishing is a year-round leisure-time activity for the people in the estuary and for fisherman from larger urban areas within a one to two hours' drive from the estuary. At least 60 different fish species live here.

The traditional economic base of the estuary has shifted in recent years from oil and gas exploration to commercial seafood production and recreational fishing and hunting. These activities bring Louisiana over one billion in revenues a year. But today most of the land is still controlled by oil and gas interests, which in the past seldom connected business activities with environmental problems.

member of the Policy Committee; Kerry St. Pe, a Cajun representing the Louisiana Department of Environmental Quality (DEQ); Myron Knudson, Water Management Division Director of Region VI, Environmental Protection Agency (EPA); David Muth, a bird watcher; Don Lirette, representing shrimpers and oystermen; Windell Curole, whose family has lived and worked in the estuary since the 1800s; Greg Ducote, representing the Louisiana Department of Natural Resources (DNA); and Neal Bolton, a sugar cane farmer.

What brought these people to the same table? They had all been asked by the Governor of Louisiana to be members of a coalition to create a conservation and management plan to preserve and restore the Bartaria-Terrebonne Estuary. They came representing conflicting interests as well as diverse perspectives and wondering, "Who is really in charge here?" "Who would be making the decisions?" "Why am I really here?"

An Innovative Approach to Natural Resource Management

Dr. Steve Mathies, a soft-spoken southerner and a biologist from the U.S. Army Corps of Engineers and Director of the Barataria-Terrebonne National Estuary Program (BTNEP), wondered how these folk and 70 others would ever be able to reach a consensus on rules and regulations for marsh management, pollution control, or public access rights. They represented stakeholders or user groups from federal, state, and local governmental and regional planning agencies, the oil and gas, fishing, and sugar cane industries, the agricultural, cattlemen's, forestry, and tourist associations, local business and large landowners, the Houma Indian Nation, the Audubon and Sierra clubs, as well as scientists from Louisiana's universities. His challenge was to produce a plan for management of the wetlands in this most southern part of the state.

Recognizing the national significance of this unique area, EPA had selected the Barataria Terrebonne Estuary in 1990 as one of 21 National Estuary Programs, among them Corpus Christi Bay, Long Island Sound, Puget Sound, and San Francisco Bay. The EPA's selection acknowledged that natural and human forces are affecting the viability of this ecosystem in sustaining wildlife, human life, and commercial opportunities.

The BTNEP differed from most of the other National Estuary Programs because habitat loss instead of water quality was its primary focus. The EPA had provided over three million to BTNEP, matched with one million by the state of Louisiana. Each of the National Estuary Programs was to draft its own Comprehensive Conservation and Management Plan (CCMP).

All estuary programs were to begin with a set of critical problems determined by a local planning group and then approved by the EPA. The priority problems identified for this estuary were:

- hydrological (water flow) modification
- reduction of sediment flows
- habitat loss and modification
- changes in living resources
- pathogen contamination
- toxic substances
- eutrophication (oxygen depletion)

"Our planning efforts have been unique," says Dr. Mathies, "in that they did not address one problem with one solution, but demonstrated how a group of related problems can be addressed by developing comprehensive, multifaceted groups of solutions to be implemented simultaneously."

In the beginning, many of the stakeholders and user groups were hesitant to volunteer their time to a government-sponsored program. They perceived the traditional top-down hierarchical style of management by command and control as excluding them from participation. There had been few successful cooperative planning or implementation efforts between state agencies. Furthermore, until now Louisiana's elected politicians had not made preserving and restoring the wetlands a priority. Not surprisingly, the general public had come to view government programs with suspicion and lack of trust.

The lack of trust goes both ways. Many Louisiana bureaucrats had mistrusted the public, assuming them to be uninformed and emotionally motivated. Private-public partnerships, although recognized as important, had seldom been pursued. Neither the private nor public representatives were very optimistic about improvements. Kirk Cheramie, policy committee member, remembers sitting in on the first national estuary planning meetings, "There was much tension at the onset of the BTNEP among the state agencies over who would be the major decision maker in the program and who would provide the money to support it." However, 85 representatives decided the attempt to diffuse tension had merit. They optimistically volunteered to serve on one of five committees organized as shown in this diagram:

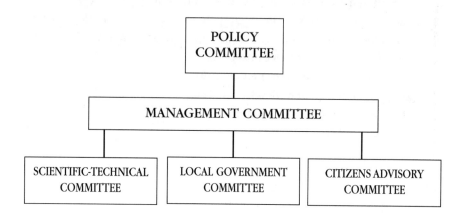

Selecting a Nontraditional Planning Approach

At first all participants brought their own agendas to the table, certain that they would have to fight for them to be considered. Committee members did not know each other and were suspicious of each other, as well as members of other committees. The scientists and engineers were committed to delivering their expertise in planning the water quality and capital construction projects to divert fresh water, nutrients, and sediment to wetlands in order to reverse long-term land loss trends. Although they were convinced that solutions to the estuary's problems could not be implemented without major changes in the political, economic, and educational structures of the estuary, they felt unqualified to build a plan that included socioeconomic and public involvement solutions. Yet at the same time, the nonscientific members felt overwhelmed by the highly technical issues.

Steve Mathies had just participated in a workshop of a similar environmental initiative when he became director of the Estuary Program. At this workshop he had participated in a traditional "buy-in" or agreement process to plans written by an "expert" or contractor. He had noted that when people affected by the problem are not part of determining solutions, they are not empowered to implement the plan. He realized that stakeholders and

Planning Phases of CCMP Development

ACTION	OUTCOMES	TIME LINE
ARTICULATING A COMMON VISION	**GROUP VISIONING PROCESS** SHARED VISION — STRATEGIC DIRECTIONS UNDER-LYING BLOCKS — STRATEGIC ACTIVITIES	**PHASE I 1991** Set context for group planning Establish 5 Standing Committees & Program Office Initiate CCMP characterization Initiate the CCMP Taskforce Hold Nov. '92 Conference Workshop
BUILDING THE ALLIANCES FOR IMPLEMENTATION	**IMPLEMENTATION FRAMEWORK** PROGRAMS PROJECTS CAMPAIGNS	**PHASE II 1993** Develop 12 Program Goals Establish CCMP Task Force Create Conceptual Planning Framework Hold July '93 Conference Workshop Hold Nov. '93 Conference Workshop
DEVELOPING THE CCMP OUTLINE	**PLANNING FRAMEWORK**	**PHASE III 1994** Build Implementation Plan Complete Characterization Conduct Public Review Workshops Establish Informal Alliances Hold '94 Conference Workshop
WRITING THE DOCUMENT	**ORGANIZATIONAL FRAMEWORK** COMMITTEES STAFF TASK FORCE TEAMS ALLIANCES PARTNERSHIPS	**PHASE IV 1995** Establish Formal Alliances Develop Organizational & Monitoring Structures Conduct Public Review Workshops Write Final CCMP Doc Hold Celebration to Begin Implementation

user groups might not sign onto his plan if they had not been involved in the early design process or experienced it as a living, breathing entity. In light of this, BTNEP sent out Requests for Proposals to design and facilitate the planning conferences.

As the New Orleans Director of the Institute of Cultural Affairs (ICA)— a research, training, and consultant organization specializing in facilitating participatory events—I was glad for an opportunity to submit a proposal. I was excited at the possibility of demonstrating an innovative participatory methodology that would allow all stakeholders an equal voice in decisions. Our group had experience using a comprehensive systems planning approach that would be valuable in designing this type of long-term environmental planning. Our proposal recommended using a bottom-up approach to gather and assemble the collective wisdom of its stakeholders. The implementation of all the steps in our plan would take four years.

Since this approach would require more than just rubber stamping a contractor's plan, Steve Mathies wondered if the management committee would approve it. Could he trust the decisions and deliberations of the conflicting user groups? He asked himself if members' participation in a cross-committee taskforce would limit or interfere with their ongoing participation in their assigned committees. Furthermore, the scientists and engineers from governmental agencies were more familiar with buying into an expert's plan than with beginning from scratch.

The EPA mandates maximum stakeholder involvement and public participation in the decision-making process for all estuary programs. Most of the other estuary programs had accepted contractor-generated plans and recommendations. Stakeholder involvement usually begins at the point that plans have already been generated by outside experts. Several contractor-generated proposals were submitted to BTNEP by coastal ecology groups. Steve Mathies finally decided to combine the ICA proposal with another one that recommended a traditional linear problem-solving approach used widely in academic and governmental circles. He asked our group to facilitate the conference workshops using a highly participatory consensus-based approach; he asked an ecology expert to draft the CCMP outline using his expertise and knowledge on environmental sustainability. No one realized that the two planning approaches would clash with each other. Although they shared a common philosophy—an understanding of the estuary as an ecosystem and a common belief in environmental sustainability— the two proposals did not share a common approach to facilitating decision making or long-term strategic planning.

Airing the Concerns

The facilitators met with each committee to determine what they had accomplished to date and what they expected to accomplish at their first conference workshop. Committee members shared for the first time what had motivated them to become a part of the BTNEP coalition and what most concerned them. The fishermen, who regularly harvest the abundant shell-fish, fish, seafood, and wildlife of the estuary, were concerned about low oxygen levels in the wetlands. Thousands of miles of oil and gas pipeline canals bisect and cause atrophy of natural coastal Louisiana waterways that have historically been used by the public for access to fishing and hunting grounds. In recent years, private companies and landowners who dug these artificial waterways have been closing off public access to many fishing and hunting grounds by constructing levees, dikes, weirs, gates, fences, and other blocking structures. The landowners cited liability concerns, economic opportunities, and private ownership development rights as the reasons for closing off public access to fishing and hunting groups. Many private landowners had found themselves in legal liability conflicts with fishermen and hunters over damages to persons or watercraft created by accidents such as collisions with submerged objects.

Many stakeholders believed that wetlands in the estuary had been destroyed and water quality degraded as a result of altered water circulation patterns due to oil and gas development practices, such as dredging activities for exploration. Some stakeholders wanted federal government agencies to enforce environmental regulations that would protect wetlands. However, the oil and gas producers complained about the enforcement of inconsistent, inequitable, and technologically unachievable environmental rules and regulations. Environmentalists were concerned about the drainage canals inhibiting the natural cleansing ability of the wetlands. Boaters feared navigation hazards created by weirs and other shore protection restoration structures. Swimmers wanting to protect the recreational benefits of the coast worried about the high bacterial count in the waters and the health hazards it generates. People who live and work in the estuary were deeply concerned about the overall pollution of surface waters that endangers not only their livelihoods, but also destroys the aesthetic value of their environment. Landowners were concerned with the invasion of traditional property rights. The academicians saw a lack of scientific consensus on solutions to land loss, wetland restoration, or protection.

Almost everyone complained about the public review process used by government. Many had felt left out of past public policy and regulation processes. For instance, they felt that flood control projects were not coordinated among the parishes, with each parish primarily concerned for its own residents. Furthermore, everyone was concerned about the altered water circulation patterns that inhibited sediment and nutrient flows to vegetated wetlands, the effects on fishery resources of toxic agricultural runoff, and poor drainage systems around the basin. All users complained that conflicts addressed in expensive law suits frequently do not resolve the environmental problems. Local government representatives complained that estuary resources such as oil and gas had produced billions of dollars for corporations and nonresident landowners, with little of the wealth returning to the estuary for maintenance and sustainability of the resources.

The general mood of the whole group was almost surly. How could so many questions and concerns be addressed? How could a viable plan come out of this cross-current of ideas and feelings? The answers to those questions would reveal themselves only over time, after seemingly endless sessions. The huge plus was that people, while unveiling marked differences, nonetheless agreed to participate. Everyone knew and agreed that something positive had to be done. This mission statement provided a base of agreement for everyone who signed on.

Phase I: Working Toward a Shared Vision

Eighty stakeholders gathered at Nicholls State University in Thibodaux in November, 1992 for the first conference workshop to begin the CCMP visioning process. Everyone came to the workshop asking: What needs to be done? How long will it take to act before it is too late? Who will pay for the expansive and expensive preservation and restoration projects needed? Since no one really knows what will work, how soon can we begin to try some things out?

Mission Statement

The Barataria-Terrebonne National Estuary Program (BTNEP) will work to develop a coalition of government, private, and commercial interests to identify problems, assess trends, design pollution control and resource management strategies, recommend corrective actions, and seek commitments for implementation. This coalition will provide the necessary leadership, will facilitate effective input from affected parties, and will guide the development of coordinated management measures. The BTNEP will provide a forum for open discussion and cooperation by all parties that includes compromise in the best interest of natural resource protection.

The BTNEP's long-term objective was to develop consensus at the advanced level on policy and action, so that various members of the coalition could act independently but in concert with one another to implement measures designed for the long-term good of the estuary. Of course reaching consensus is cheaper and more effective than having to enforce regulations or pay people to implement measures the public does not own, understand, or necessarily agree with. People knew that consensus was going to be the answer, but reaching consensus never happens automatically. And they had no idea how we would do that.

Consensus exists and is built on successive levels of consciousness or shared understanding. At the most basic level, consensus involves discovering the collective wisdom of the group by listening to and hearing each other's perspectives until all have a common sense of what they are talking about. Most traditional decision-making processes stop here. At the second or intermediate level, consensus has to do with making a decision together, without individuals giving up part of their wisdom by compromising or polarizing the group by voting. At the third or advanced level, consensus has to do with committing to a common ground and taking action together by owning the inclusive wisdom of the group, rather than just clinging to one's personal opinion or perspective. The third level is built on the foundation of the first two levels.

Session 1

The first session was designed to get all members thinking together by first listening to the other's vision of the future. The ICA consultant facilitating this session began by asking ,"What do you want to see in place within the estuary in 25 years?" The conference participants met in small groups where they discussed and wrote down their dreams and hopes. Each shared these dreams and hopes with the whole group, forming clusters of ideas into ten major vision components. People then worked to reach consensus on a name that held all of the wisdom within that cluster.

The conference participants then broke into 10 small groups to discuss the long-range significance of each vision cluster and summarized their discussion by writing statements to be presented to the whole group for further discussion and clarification. The participants then wrote the following:

Vision Statement

We, the people of Lousiana and the Barataria-Terrebonne Estuarine Basin, believe that our ecosystem is a national treasure which represents a unique multicultural heritage and that our ongoing stewardship is critical to its preservation, restoration, and enhancement. This stewardship can only be maintained by public education, informed participation, and national recognition and support. People living and working in the basin believe that we should have an environmentally compatible infrastructure, sustain and/or restore our basin's land mass, integrate our watershed planning, and have harmonious resolution of user conflicts. Economic development should be done in an environmentally responsible fashion, which would include elimination of pollution to create a healthy, aesthetically pleasing environment and to enhance production of fish and wildlife, as well as other natural resources.

Those stakeholders who expected the conference workshops to conduct business as usual were surprised. "It is so refreshing to come to a meeting where my input is not just asked for but required," remarked a representative of Louisiana Land & Exploration Company, one of the largest land owners in the estuary. The workshop was highly participatory and everyone had an equal voice. By discovering common ground and reaching consensus, the members were more able to respect their differences.

Session 2

In the second session, the intermediate level, the participants broke into small groups to discuss and identify obstacles that could prevent the coalition from achieving their vision. The whole group organized these obstacles into clusters, naming the root cause of each cluster and specifying the particular malfunction that needed to be addressed. They determined that societal interests and values lead to conflicting agendas and that many estuarine resource users were inadequately informed; that ineffective governmental action has produced mistrust and resistance to regulations; that there was a distorted image and historic perception of the estuary; and that parochial attitudes caused resistance to management. Then the conference divided into small groups to discuss and write statements articulating the implicit challenge or goal that each cluster illuminated. These were presented to the whole group for discussion and clarification.

Vision Chart

Session 3

In the final session, the conference participants built an advanced level of consensus by proposing what actions would be required to meet the challenges and realize their vision. Within each workshop session, the conference participants went through each level of consensus. The first level began with an intuitive brainstorm. The second level grouped and named related insights. Finally, participants discerned the implications for the future. During all the sessions everyone had a place at the table and a voice in all the decisions. The willingness of the EPA representatives and BTNEP staff to roll up their sleeves and work alongside the stakeholders was a surprise and a delight to the conference participants. It gave many of them a renewed hope in government.

Barbara Keeler, the EPA project officer for BTNEP, thought the visioning process prepared the members to develop details of the CCMP action plans. She felt there would be less chance that the conflicts among agencies that usually bog down the planning process would occur:

> Now, they will more likely reach consensus in working out their specific action plans, rather than just compromising. When people compromise, they feel they have given up something. But when consensus is achieved, they feel the plan contains their ideas and wisdom and there will be greater willingness to implement the plan as their own. Compromise sparks debate. Consensus incites action. A consensus-built plan will be a higher quality management plan because it has meaning to those involved.

She thought the success of the visioning process was a result of allowing the broadest array of ideas to surface, but with no time for prioritizing, debating, or lobbying and, therefore, less opportunity for squelching anyone's thoughts. One participant noted, "Everyone felt validated. Confidence in the process was enhanced by the recordkeeping and data analysis process that places equal value on all ideas contributed." Another observed that when exchanging ideas, people from various agencies often seemed to realize the same underlying problems. Yet another observed that all stakeholders are really closer together in their ways and wishes than they normally believe. By discovering common ground and reaching consensus,

UNDERLYING CONTRADICTIONS (BLOCKS)
and CHALLENGES
Management Conference Workshop   November 12-13, 1992

CONFLICTING AGENDAS
23
Discover common ground within the management and user groups

INADEQUATELY INFORMED PUBLIC
23
Develop and implement a comprehensive program to involve and inform all users

INEFFECTIVE GOVERNMENT
18
Involve all levels & political jurisdictions in long-range planning & implementation

PAROCHIAL ATTITUDES
13
Create a pathway toward regional pride and long-term stewardship of Barataria-Terrebonne Estuary

NATURAL RESOURCE LIMITS
18
Identify the limits of our resources & seek a balanced usage of those resources

MISTRUST & RESISTANCE TO ENVIRONMENTAL REGULATIONS
16
Develop clear, fair, practical, and enforceable regulations with strict penalties

DISTORTED IMAGE
13
Assemble a promotion package which emphasizes unique elements of basin & provides in-depth factual background

ADJUSTMENT TO NATURAL PROCESSES
2
Understand how to be compatible with natural change & use existing infrastructures to enhance the ecosystem & minimize impact of natural disasters

DATA GAPS & INTERPRETATIONS
16
Organize & interpret data into information readily accessible to decision makers & public

the members were able to learn from each other's viewpoints and began to respect their differences.

Phase II: Creating a Conceptual Planning Framework

Following the November workshop, a cross-committee taskforce funneled all work done up to that point by contractors and the elements of the visioning process into a single, interrelated conceptual planning system.

This system is visually presented in a conceptual model as interlocking triangles to represent the highly interrelated ecology and management of the estuary. The 12 triangles of the conceptual framework represent 12 program arenas. They are grouped into four major "systems" or factors: Natural, Human, Management, and Linking. In each system there are three goals, each divided into three program areas.

The triangle framework "gave everyone a way of visualizing the complex set of systems that affect the estuary," Barbara Keeler reflected. "It allowed us to talk about the ecological relationships in more concrete terms. The active forces became more tangible, something we could get a grip on." One of the research scientists commented, "By using the comprehensive conceptual-planning framework we can make this plan more than just a proliferation of Band-Aids."

Snags in Planning

In planning for the second conference workshop, the two outside consultants disagreed on which planning approach would best meet BTNEP needs and on what facilitation style was appropriate. The ecology expert preferred the traditional goal-oriented approach, which moves linearly from problem to goal to objective to action, with each action relating directly to one objective. The facilitators preferred a more integrated-systems approach in which the actions that will accomplish all the goals are determined first. Then, grouping the actions by intent/purpose exposes the objectives and reveals that one objective can be related to more than one goal. Thus, the action plans would accomplish more than one objective and relate to more than one goal.

There was also disagreement on which facilitation style would be acceptable to the coalition. Most were accustomed to the traditional top-down, command-and-control model in which those at the top do all the planning.

Those at the bottom of the bureaucracy and the public were expected to accept or "buy into" whatever was planned on their behalf. Were the contractors responsible for the drafting of the plan in command? If so, should they not develop a plan for the coalition to modify or change? Or should they continue to expand an approach that would build the plan from the bottom up?

When consensus could not be reached between the contractors, Steve Mathies joined the planning team. Having three perspectives instead of two made a difference, and we were able to reach an agreement. But more importantly, we saw how valuable it was for partnerships to work together informally before establishing formal or binding relationships. The parties in the partnerships must not only share a common vision, they must decide on a common approach. Although each contractor group had agreed that its task was to facilitate development of a CCMP, they had not agreed earlier on the approach or steps necessary to accomplish the task. In planning the July conference workshop, the new three-party partnership reflected on the fact that most of the stakeholders had welcomed the initial nontraditional meetings, and decided to elicit suggestions to inspire in participants a sense of meaning and control, even ownership.

Working Toward Solutions

At the July, 1993 Conference Workshop, the participants identified the central problem within each goal arena, related it to the priority problems, and then brainstormed actions that would both deal with the central problems and accomplish the goals. The conference participants clustered these actions by similar intent and wrote a brief statement for each cluster of actions. Then they brainstormed a list of agencies or organizations that might be involved in implementing the actions and filled in as much detail (how, when, where, cost, etc.) as time would permit. Every individual had equal input into the discussion, and every perspective was considered by the whole group. Because the group as a whole did not know from which individual proposed solutions came, each suggestion got equal consideration. "There were many surprises," said an educator who had worked in a group on education and involvement problems. "Some of the best ideas came from the engineers. I never realized they cared about the importance of education."

Phil Boydston, who represents large land owners, recalled that the academicians usually felt more research or study was necessary before a solution to the land loss issues could be suggested. The citizens and environmentalists proposed practical solutions that could be implemented relatively quickly, including: creating a Barataria-Terrebonne Foundation, using volunteers for 'hands on' activities such as collecting Christmas trees to use as landfill, and holding public meetings and workshops. Agency representatives working on more than one regional environmental program suggested actions that would coordinate BTNEP plans with other plans to avoid duplication and to develop better communication among agencies. Business people and commercial fishermen suggested developing ecotourism, promoting current and new products, establishing value-added processing of basin raw materials, and developing new equipment technology transfer. Government representatives made sure that actions were included that would require treatment of sewage, stormwater, and pollutants, and modify legislation to limit commercial and recreational harvests. They also suggested providing sufficient funding and authority for regulations and statewide planning. Residents of the coastal areas favored solutions to restore barrier islands and long-term freshwater sediment diversion, while the residents of the upper, inland areas of the basins suggested solutions that dealt with water quality.

All user groups proposed giving tax incentives for land owners, establishing one-stop permitting, fostering public/private partnerships, encouraging conflict resolution using a nonconfrontational process, developing procedures for multilevel involvement in the regulatory process, and generating comprehensive public education programs. Participants accepted actions equally and made no attempt to eliminate or evaluate the action. Frequently, the solution to realizing a goal in one factor was accomplished by an action in another factor. For instance, improving interagency coordination and planning, which is part of the management system, was a primary objective of the Natural Factor goals. Likewise in the Management Factor, fostering public education concerning effective regulations (Human Factor) was an objective equal to consolidating and streamlining the permit process and improving the enforcement of regulations.

It was at this conference that stakeholders began to realize that the solutions were as interconnected as the problems of the estuary. The stakeholders also began to appreciate the diverse insights that each brought to the table. By sharing their suggestions on the solutions to the problems, members reached a clearer understanding of each stakeholder's perspective. The experience of cooperating and discussing in a nonconfrontational mode was new to many of the user groups. Reflecting on the effectiveness of the planning process, 70 percent said they had a better understanding of the views and concerns of members with different or opposing viewpoints. Some members began to realize how much more could be accomplished by using a structured participatory workshop process rather than traditional methods. "Many of our committee meetings lasted all day," said Jane Ledwin, a U.S. Fish and Wildlife Service representative, "but by all of the committee members coming together, we accomplished what it would have taken over a year to do in our regular committee meetings." Vince Cottone, of Texaco's Health & Safety Department, who represented the oil and gas interests remarked:

> Gathering the stakeholders who will be affected by the policy decisions in developing the management policies will save millions of dollars just in lawyers' fees from lawsuits. That money can now be used to replace equipment or improve processes to reduce the discharge of wastes. Had we been involved in the writing of the regulations from the beginning, they would have been written in a way that allows us to comply.

Winding Up the Year

During the conference workshops and in committee meetings there were few disagreements. However, again, in preparing for the third conference that would begin the implementation phase, there was no agreement among the contractors on how to proceed with the planning. To resolve this dilemma, Steve Mathies felt that the cross-committee taskforce should be given the opportunity to decide on approach. He was surprised when the taskforce chose the more systems-oriented approach. "Most of the stakeholders are accustomed to using a linear approach," he reflected. "Deciding to do programs that cut across more than one goal is different from what we are used to doing."

At the November, 1993 Conference Workshop the stakeholders enjoyed the challenge of selecting the "catalytic actions" from a list of over 400 possibilities. An action was considered to be catalytic if it:

1. Initiated and/or accelerated completion of other actions,
2. Were strongly linked to actions in other arenas,
3. Produced powerful results, or
4. Were a significant priority action, i.e. without it, the goal would not be accomplished.

The stakeholders placed these catalytic actions onto broad timeframes, clustered, and grouped them into five major programs containing related catalytic actions. They further decided that the action plans for each program would be developed by an "informal alliance" of stakeholders who would be affected by the plan or who would be implementing the plan. They then chose the initial core leadership team for the alliances, organizations, and individuals who would be involved in developing the action plan for each program. By the end of the third conference workshop, the stakeholders had grasped a broader vision of the complexity of the CCMP and the importance of having a comprehensive conceptual model for working through the complex estuarine issues.

Evaluation: the First Two Phases

Following the November, 1993 workshop, the planning committee met to evaluate the results and reflect on the year. It was exhilarating to realize how much progress had been made in just ten months. Steve Mathies began the discussion by remembering:

> Last year at this time the stakeholders didn't even know one another. There was a strong mistrust and an assumption that members from other agencies were adversaries, and were plotting to undermine the program. Now there is a genuine willingness to work together. People who traditionally have not been considered colleagues are actually enjoying dealing with one another as partners.

Kay Radlauer, designated reviewer for the contract to facilitate the CCMP workshops asserted:

> Yes, and the committees themselves have come such a long way. In the beginning, EPA told us what to do. They would come in with stacks of papers and even films. Now we are generating all our ideas instead of being handed a list of what other estuary programs are doing to emulate or adapt.

Kirk Chermanie added:

We are reinventing government by giving our members a way to engage in the business of government. The public and frontline state bureaucrats are working together to not only identify and prioritize problems, but also to determine mutually acceptable solutions. In the traditional top-down methodologies used by government, a major factor in making decisions is the level of support of constituencies. The CCMP will already have obtained the level of support necessary to guarantee sustainability of the estuary. The diversity of BTNEP will bring pressure on bureaucratic and political bottlenecks. If we can build a comprehensive plan that we accept, we can get it past any bottle-necks....The only reason we will not get funding or obtain political will is if we fail to rely on our diversity or revert to a top-down approach.

New Ways of Thinking

"Over the last year we have shifted our way of thinking," said Kerry St. Pe, chairman of the Scientific Technical Committee:

The major shift has been that of seeing the diversity of per-spectives, interests, and viewpoints as a gift of the program rather than a problem. Last year we brought to the table our own private interests and were prepared to defend them to the end. Now we see that the various perspectives and interests of each stakeholder contribute to creating a more comprehensive and inclusive plan.

Kirk Cheramie stated:

BTNEP has created a new model for public decision mak-ing for South Louisiana. And God knows, it is necessary to our long-term survival. With the more traditional method-ology of formal voting, those not in favor of the majority decisions can distance themselves from the results should they prove unbeneficial. With the bottom-up methodology of building teams that decide by consensus, everyone owns the decisions, whether good or bad.

Windell Curole, chairman of the Local Government Committee said:

> We move from the use of words like I, he, she, and they, to words like us and we in the evaluation of the results of the decisions made. Everyone is to blame or to take credit for the results. This methodology breaks gridlock and makes government move in a positive direction, even considering the few bad decisions that can be made.

Before the last workshop conference, members were waiting for a plan for their agency to react to; now they saw that their agency would be involved in creating the action plan that they will be implementing. Before the workshops, the stakeholders were primarily aware only of the biological and physical problems of the estuary. Now, they saw these problems in relation to the socioeconomic and human problems that exist. Vince Cottone concluded, "Before members from the large oil companies saw government regulations as the primary problem. Now they see the need for effective regulations and they want to have a voice in making those regulations."

During the first three years of the program, the overall task was to set in motion a series of scientific research tasks on the present state of the estuary, establish communication and partnerships among the members of the coalition, and produce a CCMP draft outline. The conference workshops and CCMP cross-committee meetings were designed to generate content or data for the CCMP draft outline and provide a mechanism for the coalition to experience consensus-based decision making. And what did the evaluation team report? It identified at least four benefits of the participatory approach:

1. BTNEP has accomplished a great deal in a shorter period of time. As a result of the structured participatory workshops and follow-up meetings, BTNEP was able to produce far more than an outline. It generated a several-hundred-page document.

2. Involvement in the three conference workshops promoted a greater sense of individual responsibility for writing the plan. Participants felt empowered to challenge previous assumptions and some of the suggested actions of the ecology expert and each other. Many volunteered to redraft parts of the document. This personal investment in the CCMP will ensure its promotion and in the long run its implementation.

The Barataria-Terrebonne National Estuary Goals

	NATURAL FACTOR	HUMAN FACTOR	MANAGEMENT FACTOR	LINKING FACTOR
SYSTEMS	Systems related to physics, biology, or chemistry and the movement of water or land within the estuarine ecosystem. Addresses the science and technical problems and are tightly linked to one another.	Socio-economic systems which presently have the greatest impact on the estuary. Involves informed public participation and the cultural patterns and attitudes related to economic development and natural resource value.	Systems of decision making and management which involve integrating comprehensive, holistic environmental considerations into the planning, coordinating, and regulating of the human and natural resources.	Systems which serve as criteria to achieving environmental sustainability.* Represents how the natural, human, and management systems are dynamically linked and were referred to by the stakeholders as the "heart or soul or conscience" of the ecosystem.
	LAND MASS Preserve and restore the wetlands and Barrier Islands by developing agressive and effective programs.	**ECONOMIC DEVELOPMENT** Promote environmentally responsible economic activities and estuarine-based jobs that sustain estuarine resources.	**COMPREHENSIVE DATA BASES** Create an accessible, comprehensive data base with interpreted information for the public.	**BALANCED USE** Formulate indicators of estuarine ecosystem and human health and measures of balanced use of natural resources.
BTNEP	**DIVERSE BIOLOGIC COMMUNITIES** Realistically support diverse, natural biological communities.	**NATIONAL RECOGNITION AND SUPPORT** Gain national recognition through informed advocacy to attract federal funding and strengthen federal policies to support the Barataria-Terrebonne Estuary.	**EFFECTIVE REGULATIONS** Create clear, fair, practical, and enforceable regulations with balanced participatory input and interagency coordination by increasing quantity and quality of public participation.	**COMMON GROUND SOLUTIONS** Discover common ground solutions within management and user groups to ensure implementation and obtain voluntary protection of resources.
GOALS	**WATER QUALITY** Develop and meet water quality standards that adequately protect estuarine resources and human health.	**EDUCATION & INVOLVEMENT** Implement comprehensive education and awareness programs that enhance active public participation and maintain the cultural heritage.	**COMPREHENSIVE WATERSHED PLANNING** Develop and maintain multi-level, long-term comprehensive, watershed planning by establishing a tradition of upfront, inclusive stakeholder involvement in all planning efforts.	**COMPATIBLE WITH NATURE** Be compatible with natural, physical, and biological change by using existing and future infrastructures, providing harmonious, socio-economic activities, and minimizing the impact of natural disasters.

* "Environmental sustainability" was defined as the relationship between dynamic human economic systems and the larger dynamic ecological systems in which (1) human life can continue indefinitely; (2) human individuals can flourish; (3) human cultures can develop, but in which (4) the effects of human activities remain within bounds so as not to destroy the diversity, complexity, and function of the ecological support system.

3. Team spirit, trust, and willingness to listen have increased. Communication among committee members has continued beyond the planning workshops and committee meetings, and trust is beginning to develop among stakeholders from different and often opposing viewpoints.

4. Familiarity leads to congeniality, which leads to cooperation and collaboration.

Consensus is not synonymous with ownership. Consensus does not mean that everyone has taken ownership of each idea or concept. Some may have bought into some aspects of the decisions and taken ownership of others. Thus, during implementation, when one meets a roadblock, only the parts that they owned will be implemented because ownership motivates the creativity and persistence required to move around the roadblock. Neither does reaching consensus guarantee implementation. As Barbara Keeler concluded, "We have had a series of three good conferences. But it would be presumptuous to imagine that consensus is now assured." Without continuing the consensus-based planning process to the next phase, implementation will be delayed and the past attitudes about government decision making will be reinforced. Many stakeholders are worried that implementation will not happen if top level agency management is not more directly involved in the planning process from now on. "When top level agency management is involved only in understanding what their personnel have proposed, they have little ownership in the process," notes Vince Cottone. "Thus, at the point of implementation, they do not hesitate to change what their personnel have spent considerable time and resources developing."

Unfortunately, in the year following the third workshop, Cottone's prediction came true when top-level management in the Department of Natural Resources decided to stall the BTNEP program. It has taken a year for the stakeholders to mediate a new agreement to continue the program.

"It is like trying to ride a razor blade. One wrong move, however unintended, and you're in serious trouble," remarks Steve Mathies. The stakeholders are approaching the second level of consensus, which will involve deciding specifically what actions to take to move towards their vision. He is optimistic because of the degree of ownership already developed; he sees that the members have banded together to independently solicit support and commitment from appropriate state legislative delegations and politically influential constituencies and to seek opportunities to tout the accomplishment of the program thus far.

Structured participatory workshops that include all the stakeholders and the general public can prevent conflicts from escalating when the conflicting parties' perceptions get transformed. Their views of their opponents change from one of adversary to one of colleague. Each begins to value the other's knowledge and experience. Miracles do occur.

Participating in the decision making is only the first step in responding to the trends that cause wetland loss. The second step is participating in the changes required. For government agencies, this means getting the budget flexibility and accountability necessary to make the changes. For the oil companies, it means getting consistent and compatible regulations and one-stop permitting into operation. For the land owners and fishermen, it means participating in the decisions affecting public access to the diverse natural resources. The people who live and work in the Barataria-Terrebonne Estuary, and who participate in the decisions of the National Estuary Program, have become empowered to chart their own destiny. In the process, their national treasure is preserved, protected, and sustained.

Chapter 17
Do It For The Kids:
Advocating For the Childrens' Agenda

SANDRA TRUE AND JANIS ELLIOT

*The United States is the only industrialized country in
the world without a comprehensive system for early
childhood care and education. How can a country with
such resources and creativity fall so far behind its
world partners? Why, with all the child care models
available, has the United States still not been successful
in creating its own? One factor stands out when child
care advocates are looking for an answer: the lack of
agreement on who will "lead" the early childhood cause.
Often called the debate over sponsorship, this conflict
boils down to skirmishes over who receives the money,
controls the budget, and makes the decisions.*

Teresa became pregnant when she was 15. Family life had been difficult ever since Mom and Dad split up when she was ten. School hadn't been any better. The counselor at the teen program really encouraged her to stay in school after the baby was born. She knew she'd need some training if she and the baby were to be o.k., but couldn't imagine ever going back to high school, let alone college. "It had been terrible before, so what will it be like with a baby?" she wondered. "People will really give me a hard time now." But the school had a young parent program. She gave it a try and was really surprised. The staff really understood what it was like to take care of a baby and try to keep up with both work and school. Teresa could take her daughter, Megan, to school with her and leave her in the day care center there. She also helped in the center, performing volunteer work, which improved her parenting skills. She's now in her first year at the community college, studying to be a paralegal. Maybe when the baby's older, Teresa can become a lawyer. Thinking back, she can hardly believe what's happened. She won't have to raise her Megan on welfare and is excited about having an interesting, well-paying job. Things are much different for her than they were for her mother and older sister.

Teresa's story is being repeated all over the state of Oregon, which has the highest rate of teen parent participation in school and work training programs of any state in the country. An estimated 1,000 children of teen parents per year now receive child care, more than twice the number formerly receiving benefits before new programs like the one Teresa attended were put into place in Oregon. Schools, community groups, and state agencies are all working together to develop programs that make this kind of increase possible. Education and child care funds are used together to create integrated, community-based services that make a difference in the lives of children.

Oregon's Children's Agenda

What brought about the change? Everyone involved knows it didn't happen overnight. Parents, child care advocates, providers, and community groups have worked for almost a decade to improve conditions for children and families in Oregon. Most people agree that Neil Goldschmidt is one agent of change. In 1986, Goldschmidt was running for governor of Oregon. At that time, a group of his advisors asked him, "What do you want to be remembered for as governor?" An earlier Oregon governor, who was much loved and respected by the people, Tom McCall, was known for cleaning up the state's beaches. What, his supporters wondered, would be Neil Goldschmidt's legacy? "For the children," replied Goldschmidt, "I want to be remembered because I made it better for children. Now it is time for this generation of Oregonians to meet our challenge: to become stewards of the child." So began the Oregon Children's Agenda.

Other governors of other states have made such declarations. What was different this time? The first and most important factor, said Goldschmidt, is that everyone must be invited to the table. So he began a demanding tour of the state, inviting, cajoling, coercing, and demanding that everyone—parents, social workers, businesses, youth, politicians, government agency staff—everyone sit down together in each Oregon county to develop strategies to improve children's lot in life. Goldschmidt had read the statistics. He knew that every grand idea he could conceive of as governor for the economic recovery of the state depended on the health and well-being of Oregon's citizens. Commitment to children was the foundation upon which every strategy must be built. The difficulties that Oregon parents have in caring for their children while they work or attend school are the same difficulties faced by families all over the United States. Oregon is unique, however, in its solution to the problem.

A New Way Of Doing Business

Today, Oregonians are working together for children. The fragmentation and divisiveness are gone and the many groups involved in children's issues have come together. Janis Elliot, administrator of the state's Child Care Division, says,

> Wherever we work, whether it's in a state agency, a school, a community-based program or a hospital; whether we care for children directly in our home, or work in a child care center; no matter who pays our salary, we all have a common purpose. We want families and children to thrive. That's what we're working for, and when we remember that, we make big strides towards our goal. We (the workers) aren't important; it's families and children that matter!

To help keep their "eyes on the prize," Oregon's key agencies responsible for childhood care and education have developed a Statement of Values and Purposes that expresses this common understanding. This statement has served them well over the past few years and will continue to do so as they take on new challenges.

How did Oregon get to this place? Everyone involved believes success came because of the strong commitment to participatory decision making and the involvement of every sector of the state and local community: parents, children, public and private agencies, businesses, and government.

Getting to this place of common purpose wasn't easy, however. Years of groups protecting their turf had resulted in fragmentation, discord, and competition in Oregon's communities. Divergent professional perspectives resulted in disagreement about who "had the right answers." To further complicate the situation, cultural and religious differences led to strong disagreement about the role government should play in this arena. One school board member from a rural community in eastern Oregon said, "If women would stay home and take care of their kids like they're supposed to, schools wouldn't have to worry about the child care problem."

Despite these stumbling blocks, the story of Oregon's success with parents and children's programs proves that by working together, people of diverse backgrounds and interests can create change.

Only In America

There is an African proverb, "It takes a whole village to raise a child." Children's advocates have quoted this truth widely because they believe it reflects a reality that the United States has avoided for too long. Changes in the economy have propelled ever-increasing numbers of parents into the workforce. In 1960, 10 percent of American children in the U.S. lived with one parent; by 1989 that number had increased to 25% [1]. Of the Oregon mothers with children under age six, 54% work outside the home. This means more children are in child care while the parent works[2]. A report on 1990 census data says that only 51% of America's children live in "traditional" nuclear families. The rest live in single-parent, blended, adoptive, or other extended-family households.

The United States is the only industrialized country in the world without a comprehensive system for early childhood care and education. How can a country with such resources and creativity fall so far behind its world partners? Why, with all the child care models available, has the United States still not been successful in creating its own? One factor stands out when child care advocates are looking for an answer: the lack of agreement on who will "lead" the early childhood cause. Often called the debate over sponsorship, this conflict boils down to skirmishes over who receives the money, controls the budget, and makes the decisions.

This sponsorship question has blocked an effective resolution to the child care debate in the United States for 20 years. As Abbie Klein notes in

The Debate Over Child Care, "The result is a patchwork system... composed of [different] sectors, each with a vested interest in maintaining or expanding its claim to controlling child care services" [3].

Childhood care and education programs in this country fit no single pattern. Administered by many different organizations, each has a slightly different focus. Thus it has been difficult to build a common identity. Day care center operators see themselves as different from people who care for a small number of children in their own homes. Those who operate preschools consider themselves early childhood educators, seeing little relationship to the day care providers whom they consider "baby-sitters." Private not-for-profit programs look with disdain on proprietary programs operated by national chains, as if the profit motive somehow sullies the true work of caring for children. Providers, whether they be public, private, or volunteer, day care or pre-school, struggle over sponsorship and dollars. But whatever their origins, all are working to deliver affordable, quality services under difficult circumstances. Unfortunately, competition, rather than cooperation, has been the norm for these groups.

Day Care Wars

In Oregon, as in the rest of the country, the struggle for control over this important area erupted in the 1970s, a period now referred to as the "day care wars." One "survivor" of this period tells of breaking out in tears at a public hearing as groups shouted at each other across the hearing room. There was no strategy to work together at the local or state levels. Many advocates were even afraid to come to the table lest hostility break out again.

Meanwhile, families were falling farther and farther behind. Ann Clark, an educator in Alsea, Oregon, remembers how it used to be. She'd heard the same story repeatedly. Parents in her community were desperate. They couldn't find the kind of care they wanted for their children. Even if they did find it, they couldn't afford it. Ann recalls a phone call from one worried parent, Margaret. The baby sitter who had cared for her baby since last October was moving and Margaret couldn't find anyone else she felt comfortable with. Quitting work wasn't an option; Margaret's husband used to work in the mill but now was able to find only part-time work. They couldn't support the family on his income alone. What could she do?

The CCDBG Framework

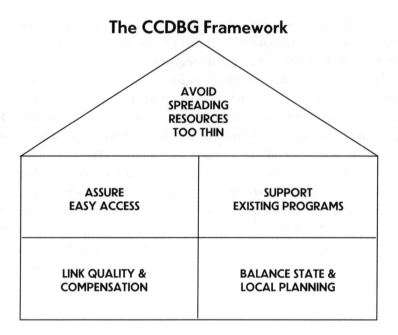

AVOID SPREADING RESOURCES TOO THIN

| ASSURE EASY ACCESS | SUPPORT EXISTING PROGRAMS |
| LINK QUALITY & COMPENSATION | BALANCE STATE & LOCAL PLANNING |

Ann knew that Margaret was not alone. More than 59% of Oregon's families with incomes under $25,000 pay more than 10% of their household income for child care, an expense second only to housing [4]. Yet Margaret, and many others like her, cannot afford to go without this expensive care; someone must watch two-year old Sarah and six-year old William while Margaret is at work. The problem is especially acute in rural communities such as Alsea, a small timber-dependent town nestled in the coastal mountain range of Oregon. Its population of 500 is spread out over 20 miles. The downtown has a public school, two churches, a library, and a community store. Badly hit by the declining timber industry, families now need two incomes to provide the same household support that one income could provide 20 years ago. Ann resolved to make a difference for families like Margaret's.

The Government Gets Involved

In 1973, President Richard Nixon vetoed a major piece of legislation designed to address the dilemma of working parents. Nothing further had happened on the federal level until 1990, when Congress got involved in a significant way and passed several pieces of important legislation. One, the Child Care and Development Block Grant (CDBG), addressed child care concerns like Margaret's in Alsea. As a result of the CDBG, states would decide how to spend the funds within federal guidelines. Each state was required to submit a comprehensive plan after soliciting public input. The legislation also addressed the issue of sponsorship by giving authority to the governor to appoint a "lead agency." All other agencies must work cooperatively with the lead agency. Everyone must be at the table.

Oregon's Commission for Child Care

Oregon had not been idly waiting for the federal government to act. In 1985, the Commission for Child Care was established to recommend child care policy to the governor and legislature. Commissioners worked closely with Governor Goldschmidt to create an Office of Child Care Coordination and bring forth an ambitious legislative agenda.

The following four major accomplishments of this commission laid the groundwork for successful use of the new federal CDBG funds in Oregon:

1. Increased business involvement;
2. Focus on early childhood;
3. Community involvement, especially on the
   part of citizens and parents; and
4. Enhanced cooperation among state agencies,
   private providers, and funders.

Business Involvement

Businesses in Oregon began to get involved in the child care arena. Large companies like US Bancorp, Nike, US West and Hewlett Packard lent executives' time to state and local child care initiatives. At the same time, growing numbers of small businesses became involved as well. This agenda was a key to the well-being of the whole state. US Bank President Kevin Kelly spoke out strongly for corporate involvement in child care. "It's not just a passing fad; it may be now, but certainly will be in the future, the most important issue for any size business." Nationally, most employer interest has come from very large businesses such as the one Kelly heads. However, small businesses across the country have been less responsive. Oregon has a higher proportion of small businesses than any other state in the country;

but fortunately for Oregon, small businesses there are highly involved in childhood care and education.

Jo Rymer is President of Pro Tem, a temporary service that provides a child care subsidy to employees. Rymer is an active promoter of quality childhood care and education, and speaks from her experience: "We found there's a propensity for employees to stay with Pro Tem. Some will stay here because they believe in what we're doing. They like that we're involved."

Focus On Early Childhood

Research has shown that Head Start, the early child education program started in 1965, has been effective. Despite its success, however, only about 16% of eligible children were enrolled. Early childhood educators launched a campaign to create an Oregon version of Head Start, the Oregon Pre-Kindergarten Program (OPP). In 1987, OPP found favor with the Goldschmidt administration and the legislature. The state set a goal of serving all eligible children by 1999 and made a major investment of state dollars to take the first steps toward this objective. The result was an increased awareness and understanding of the importance of early childhood, an emphasis that now underlies Oregon's nationally recognized efforts at education reform.

Community Involvement

The Children's Agenda created an unprecedented excitement and interest in children's issues. Goldschmidt created the Oregon Community Children and Youth Services Commission (OCCYSC) to keep the momentum going, as well as to provide state-level assistance to communities. Charged with planning and coordinating services for all children from birth to 18 years and their families, OCCYSC relied on Oregon's strength—the communities—for people support. State staff provided guidelines and technical help, but counties decided what best would meet local needs. The state and counties worked together, supported and guided each other, and created a climate where services for children could flourish.

County OCCYSC members in one rural county included business people, early childhood and elementary educators, as well as juvenile corrections officers. The county commissions called on citizens to join planning groups to do research and advise the commission on local child care issues. This small county involved more than 115 people in creating programs for children.

Interagency Coordination

In an area as complex and widespread as the child care system, enthusiasm and interest just aren't enough. The inability of all of the state agencies involved to work together caused confusion and frustration on the community level. One mother, thoroughly fed up with the array of Oregon agencies involved with her family said, "I have 3 children and 12 social workers trying to help my family. Last month, in one day, I had a visit from the school, the health department, the child services agency, and the church. All these helpers, and nothing is getting better!" To answer such objections, the Office of Child Care Coordination invited all involved state agencies to create an Interagency Child Care Group. This group got state government out of the way of communities and helped families to gain access the child care they needed to get on with their lives. The business voice was significant in moving this effort forward. Jo Rymer, of Pro Tem, put it best when she said, "We don't have much tolerance for the government making excuses. We want results, not another agency report!" Thirteen Oregon agencies signed on. The work began.

With the advent of additional federal money, the child care system stakes were higher. Interested parties started coming out of the woodwork. Child Care Coordinators, Mary Louise McClintock and Janis Elliot, realized the importance of getting all these people and agencies together in order to create trust. Working with the Commission for Child Care and others, they formed a strategy of broad-based participation to envision a childhood care and education system, while at the same time creating consensus.

State Child Care Summit

On February 16, 1991, a Child Care Issues Summit entitled, "Child Care: Creating the Vision," launched this community-planning process. People came from all points in the state to the central location of Linn-Benton Community College, in Albany. Oregon's 36 counties sent representatives from all interest areas. Little did participants know that this Child Care Summit of 1991 would be a major turning point for the early childhood care and education community. Two hundred plus people met at the same place, agreed on the major issues to be addressed in the plan, as well as how to address those issues. Governor Barbara Roberts, who succeeded Neil

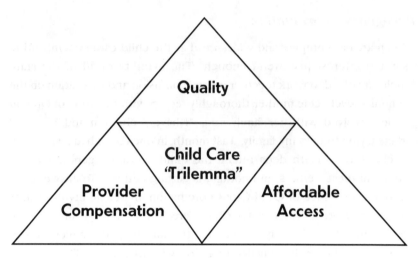

The "Trilemma" of Child Care

Goldschmidt as governor, designated Oregon's Department of Human Resources as the lead agency, with a charge to ensure "meaningful community involvement in creating the plan."

At the summit, small groups formed, each with good representation from the different kinds of providers. Tense energy charged the summit meeting atmosphere. Clusters of advocates huddled, discussing how to approach the day to best advantage. With everyone at the same table, the participation strategy brought the real issues to light. Quality of child care was a growing concern. Parents wanted healthy, safe environments, age-appropriate activities, and discipline practices that fit with family values. Parents needed help finding, choosing, and paying for the best care for their children. Providers needed training.

Compensation was another issue. Susan Giese, with the Worthy Wage Campaign in Oregon, produced results of a study presenting a bleak picture: child care workers, often with graduate degrees, barely earn more than minimum wage. Couriers delivering packages or persons who wash trucks get paid more than teachers in early childhood programs. For example, Kay, a single parent working full time in a child development center, had to rely on food stamps and state-assisted medical care to support herself and her young children. "I went to graduate school and I'm still below the poverty level," she exclaimed. Because of low wages and lack of benefits such as health insurance, the turnover rate in Oregon's child care industry had nearly tripled since 1977, from 15 percent to 41 percent, resulting in a shortage of qualified staff and disruption to children's care [5]. One provider tells of a two-year old in her program who put her hands on her hips and said,"I don't have to listen to you; you won't be here tomorrow!" Obviously, turnover creates a real dilemma. Parents, already strapped by financial burdens, cannot afford to pay more.

Accessibility was another major concern discussed at the summit. One county reported that 71% of the children needing care were left on their own or in a relative's care. The county had 7,600 child care slots when the estimated need was as high as 29,000. Despite the growth in Oregon pre-kindergarten and Head Start programs, only 30% of eligible children benefited from those programs. Employers found it difficult to recruit and retain a workforce. After the summit discussions, the issues were clear to everyone; now it was time for the solutions.

The intent of CDBG was to support working families. Yet, many feared that the Oregon Department of Human Resources, as the lead agency, would divert child care support from working parents. Those who had worked long and hard to pass the CDBG on the federal level feared that others who had not been involved in the advocacy effort would claim funding. Some expressed concern that larger center-based providers would receive preferential treatment over the smaller family-based providers. All were prepared to defend their causes.

Common Ground Discovered—A Major Turning Point

The different agendas soon surfaced, but the process chosen for the summit meeting brought unexpected results. Merrily Haas has more than a decade's experience with child care issues in Oregon. An earnest advocate of quality early childhood education, she was delighted: "The Ah-ha of the morning happened in sharing concerns. The participatory process helped us see how our concerns related. Our perspectives broadened."

Much to the pleasure of summit participants, the process included everyone. Each perspective had a voice. One participant remarked, "I've been fighting for day care for years. My enemies were in my group. It was amazing to see my issues actually fit with theirs. Before today, I had just never heard it."

At the end of the day, each small group reported to the entire group with spirit and fanfare. Consensus on a plan for Oregon was clear. Together, they developed five concepts to be used as a guide for the rest of the decision-making process and as the backbone of the plan submitted to the federal government. A day that had started full of tension ended with a framework for building the early childhood care and education system. Participants felt ownership. Most importantly, they now knew the coming community meetings would be fair and inclusive.

For Karen Gorton, from Metro Child Care Resource and Referral, the summit was "like a reunion....We had the common thread of care for children....We came together and said we can no longer be separate....We need to come together in order to be more effective."

Participation Becomes The Model

The participative methods that Oregon used for the child care plan provides a model for decision making in the childhood care and education community. Increasingly, diverse interest groups rely on this model to build common purpose. The people trained to facilitate for the Child Care Summit served as resources to extend the process to other settings. The participation process was the tool used to reach consensus on revised family day care rules; the state government used it to develop recommendations for reorganizing child care functions; and the Commission for Child Care completed its strategic plan with the help of a participative facilitator. Perhaps most importantly, local communities developed integrated plans for childhood care and education with the input of all the stakeholders. Dan Vizzini says:

> The participative process is a perfect fit in the child care community....We get consensus more efficiently and the meetings move more quickly...we've trained a generation of folks...Now there is a commitment to collaboration. There is pride in what we have done.

Importance of Legislative Leadership

Legislative leadership agreed to delay child care legislative action until the community planning process was complete, reflecting the high regard leadership held for community-based participatory planning. Such respect had not always been the case. State Senator Frank Roberts, first elected in 1975, remembered the "child care wars." Until his appointment to the Child Care Commission, he was skeptical that the early childhood care and education community would ever reach consensus. During this session, however, he literally risked his life to protect, not only the product, but the integrity of the planning process itself. Dan Vizzini, member of the Commission for Child Care, tells the story:

> It was in the last days of the legislative session. We were all hot and tired, things were pretty hectic. A powerful legislator broke rank and forced passage of his "pet project" to be funded with the child care funds. Advocates were furious because he hadn't participated at all in the planning, yet he came in at the last minute demanding funds. Frank [Senator Roberts] had watched the participatory process develop. He had gained an understanding and appreciation for diversity in perspectives. He drew on his 15 years of legislative experience and intervened successfully. A compromise was reached and the plan prevailed. Thanks to his efforts to preserve the integrity of the process, child care gained credibility. The day after the vote, Senator Roberts had a heart attack and open heart surgery. He survived to fight more political battles for child care.

In politics, as in life, however, winning a skirmish does not mean winning the war. Childhood care and education advocates recognized that the support achieved during this legislative session needed nurture and strength. Already thoughts were moving ahead to the next challenge to consensus for a unified vision. Their efforts were heartened by success stories.

Child Care: An Economic Issue

The situation is changing for parents like Margaret, the mother from Alsea, frustrated in her search for affordable child care. Help is also on the way to communities like Alsea. For the first time, the community recognized that child care is a real issue and decided to do something about it. Parents created a community development corporation and applied for funds from the state. The Forest Service donated an empty staff house for a child care group home for 12 children. The Child Care Resource and Referral agency recruited and trained a network of family-home child care providers to serve the more rural families. Now working parents did not need to take their children down winding mountain roads to the city for care. Parents could work without worry. Ann, the educator from Alsea, says proudly, "None of us could have done it alone. By working together we made a difference." Collaboration works for the children.

Child care providers benefit too, especially family child care providers. There are more than 15,000 family child care providers in Oregon, each caring for 4-6 children in his or her own home. Their backgrounds are as varied as their numbers are large. They may be women whose children have grown and left home, or parents choosing to care for other families' children while they stay home with their own. They are important small business people in Oregon communities, but in the past they were more likely to call themselves "sitters" than child care professionals. Marian Smith, a leader of the Children's Agenda observes:

> Family child care providers now know they are running a business. They have a profession; they provide a critical service to the community. That is a long way from "Yes, I'll watch your kids for you." Now the family care providers will drive across the state to attend meetings. They know they are important to families and to the child care system. They have a voice.

The 1993 legislative session threatened to undermine the solidarity and common purpose that had developed over the previous two years. Severe shortages in the state's General Fund raised red flags of budget cuts. Debate intensified over the delivery of services to children and families. Political leaders each advocated different approaches, believing his or her particular model was the best. Dell Ford, from Oregon's Department of Education's Head Start Collaboration Project, was afraid that the "day care wars" would break out again. Dell relates, "We could see fights breaking out between people who had just begun to build trust and work together. We had to do something to prevent that." They called another Childhood Care and Education Summit. In September, 1992, nearly two years after the first summit, Child Care Summit II took place at Linn-Benton Community College.

The diversity of participants reflected that of the first summit. They gathered to deepen the common vision for childhood care and education and to create the strategy needed to maintain unity for the 1993 legislative session.

It was a difficult legislative session: all programs and services faced large budget cuts. But by the end of the session, childhood care and education measures maintained funding levels and in some cases increased. Legislators approved some measures key to improving child care and throughout the legislative session, the early childhood care and education community stayed solid. Proclaiming a vision based on a common purpose and common values, advocates kept legislative attention positively focused.

Current Focus on Family Needs

The most exciting element in this story is that there is not an end, only another chapter. Child care providers, parents, community representatives, and advocates have learned how to work together and have developed skills to apply in new situations. Oregon is building a legacy of cooperation and collaboration, even through difficult times. Most importantly, though, these efforts are changing the lives of children and families.

One person whose life is better because of these efforts is Shanen, who was pregnant for the second time and in trouble with the law again. To buy drugs, she'd stolen from the store where she worked. This time, she chose inpatient drug therapy over prison. When she'd gone to jail before, her daughter had stayed with her parents, and had been abused by her grandfather. Shanen's drug treatment program now had child care, which meant that Shanen could take her daughter with her. Two months later, Shanen gave birth to David, the first baby born at the treatment center. He was drug-free. Since that time, Shanen has built a new life. She and her husband are drug-free, loving parents who are responsible members of society. The 70 drug-free babies born at the treatment center in the last 5 years have similar stories. Mothers receive caring support, and they no longer have to leave their children to get it.

Bobbie Weber, from The Family Resources Department at Linn-Benton Community College, has been active in Oregon's early childhood issues for 15 years. She attended both child care summits and felt they stood out as markers of the significant way interactions have changed in childhood care and education:

There is a growing understanding of what we all have in common. We have a real sense there is a "we" in what we do. We have a more detailed knowledge of the multiple agendas. We all see ourselves as interrelated. I wouldn't want a world in which all these parts were not there working together.

Today's situation in Oregon is a far cry from the days of the "day care wars." Slowly the negative trends are being reversed and the helpers are focusing on the needs of families instead of their own agendas. In Oregon, they use a slogan that states it best: "Childhood Care and Education Works, When We Work Together."

References

[1] Carnegie Corporation of New York. Starting Points: Meeting the Needs of Our Youngest Children (New York: Carnegie Corporation of New York, April, 1994).

[2] Oregon Commission for Child Care. Child Care in Oregon: Report to the Governor and Legislature-1990-91 (Portland, OR: Oregon Commission for Child Care, 1991).

[3] Klein, Abbie Gordon. The Debate over Child Care: 1969-1990 (Albany, NY: State University Of New York Press, 1992).

[4] Children First of Oregon. Measuring Our Commitment to Oregon's Children and Families (Portland, OR: Children First of Oregon, 1994).

[5] Oregon Commission for Child Care. Child Care in Oregon: Report to the Governor and Legislature-1991-92 (Portland, OR: Oregon Commission for Child Care, 1992.)

PARTNERS FOR IMPROVED NUTRITION AND HEALTH

COMMUNITY HEALTH ADVISORS

1992 Finalist ★ ★ ★ ★ ★ ★
FORD INNOVATIONS IN STATE AND LOCAL GOVERNMENTS

Chapter 18
Neighbor Helping Neighbor for Health Care

MICHELLE BRESSLER AND TERESA LINGAFELTER

*By recruiting the community's natural helpers, those
who already serve their community as trusted helpers
and advisors, and training them to enhance their
knowledge, skills, and understanding, Partners for
Improved Nutrition and Health (PINAH) and programs
like it count on the truism that homegrown solutions
are often the most long lasting. Instead of bringing in
staff to solve Humphreys County's problems and having
them work long and hard to build up trust and learn
the ins and outs of the community, PINAH tried another
approach. Why not train those who already know the
place and are in a pivotal position to help others?*

I t is not often that a small place makes big news. But a project born in
Humphreys County, Mississippi, has generated national press coverage, an award from the U.S. Secretary of Health and Human Services,
and a coveted finalist position in the 1992 Harvard/Ford Foundation
Innovations in Government contest. Humphreys County's journey to
national recognition began in a humble brick building in downtown
Belzoni, Mississippi. The pale blue plastic chairs of the waiting room of that
building were filled with witnesses to a quiet revolution. Alma Faye
Custom was waiting with her nephew to be seen by the staff at the

Humphreys County Health Department. They had signed in at 8:30 a.m. and here it was 10:00; they had yet to be called. Before 1989 she was just another client whose impatience could only be soothed by Cokes from the machine sitting in the lobby. Now she can wonder how such slow service can be improved. Now she is a community health advisor and although that position does not shorten her wait for care, it does increase the sense of ownership. No longer are the staff strangers; no longer is the system a confusing maze; no longer is she excluded from the problem of how to provide health services to a community with many needs and not enough resources. Now she is a part of the solution.

Neighbor Helping Neighbor: '90s Style

Partners for Improved Nutrition and Health (PINAH) enlisted the help of Ms. Custom and others like her to combat the many problems confronting people in the Mississippi Delta. PINAH was born as a unique partnership between the Mississippi State Department of Health, the Freedom From Hunger Foundation, and the Mississippi Cooperative Extension Service; they launched the Community Health Advisor program. But the truth is that the strategy employed is about as innovative as breathing. PINAH capitalized on the natural and enduring strength of Mississippi communities and built a program on the tradition of neighbor helping neighbor. Believing that every community contains the capacity for self-help, PINAH sought to elevate and honor the role of those in the community who are known and respected for their advice and assistance.

By recruiting the community's *natural helpers,* those who already serve their community as trusted helpers and advisors, and training them to enhance their knowledge, skills, and understanding, PINAH and programs like it count on the truism that homegrown solutions are often the most long lasting. Instead of bringing in staff to solve Humphreys County's problems and having them work long and hard to build up trust and learn the ins and outs of the community, PINAH tried another approach. Why not train those who already know the place and are in a pivotal position to help others?

The idea of training and supporting volunteers to promote health goals was based on experience with lay health advisor programs in India, China, Mexico, and elsewhere. In the third world context, the approach responded to a shortage of health professionals in the distant villages. Domestically the approach had been used to improve basic health information and skills in mainly rural communities.

Successes Built on Small Victories

PINAH organizers did not dream that their efforts could have an impact on race relations. Robert Lingafelter remembers, "Of course we all wanted that but didn't dare write it down as an objective because we felt we had little chance." But according to interviews conducted by an evaluation team, improvement in race relations was a direct, if unplanned, effect of the program. According to one town resident, "Since PINAH has been here, I have seen greater unity with people working together to try to improve their conditions." Another health advisor said:

> I think we are on the first leg of getting whites involved. Mrs. F has been working and she has been able to get some of her friends and especially her church to support us. When we had the fish fry, we had a very good turn-out, some very good support from the white community.

Besides the satisfaction of building bridges, PINAH has received positive attention from far and wide. In 1990, they received the U.S. Secretary of Health and Human Services recognition award. The next year the Mississippi state legislature dedicated a proclamation to the health advisors. The Health Advisor program achieved finalist status in the Harvard/Ford Foundation Innovations in State and Local Government competition in 1992. They were among the top 25 selected from over 1500 applications nationwide.

Women gathering to arrange silk flowers seldom signal significant change. But in a small Delta town, a white mayor working with a predominantly black group is a sign of transformation, especially considering the historical tensions in the relationship. In May of 1991, the partner foundation, Freedom From Hunger, held a board of directors meeting in the Delta to get acquainted with the PINAH story. Part of the stay included meeting with each health advisor group. A group in one town presented the results of its strategic plan for the next five years. Of course since this was a major event for a town of a few hundred people, the mayor was on hand to meet the visitors. She was present, too, when the chair outlined the plan to gain more satisfactory political leadership because of a lack of support. A few uneasy moments passed while everyone tried hard not to look to see the mayor's reaction. She then stood in front of the assembled bunch of health advisors and out-of-state guests, and affirmed her support for what the health advisors were doing. Confirming her interest in building relationships with the group, she offered to teach a flower arranging course when a few health advisors admired the Garden Club's display in the local library. About ten women gathered every Friday night that winter to share stories and learn about the art of displaying flowers. The Mayor later joined their efforts to organize a 4-H group for the youth.

As the incident with the mayor illustrates, the tightwire between political involvement and community action is very precarious. Few in the community oppose the health advisors' trying to improve the conditions that cause ill health. But when political action is used to move towards those ends, people get nervous. In a place where civil rights action created change and upset, any group which hints at political organizing risks losing widespread support.

Origins

In 1986 Alfio Rausa, M.D., health officer for a nine-county district for the Mississippi State Department of Health was at a crossroads. He had spent nearly 20 years of his life in public health in the Mississippi Delta. Conditions had improved a great deal over the years but troubling statistics made his district one of the worst in public health terms. Infant mortality was high, chronic diseases such as diabetes and heart conditions killed many people, and the rate of death from unintentional events was way out of proportion. Attempts to alleviate these conditions were bogged down by inadequate funding, lack of interagency coordination, insufficient outreach, and too much dependence on welfare programs. The legacy of troubled relations between the races meant a general atmosphere where it was a struggle for blacks and whites to trust each other and work together on community health problems. So when the Bronx, New York, native, Dr. Rausa, was asked about trying a new approach, his attitude was one of guarded enthusiasm: "It seems like everything has been tried here already, but I suppose it can't hurt."

Three Entities Join Forces

MISSISSIPPI
STATE DEPARTMENT OF
HEALTH

The State Department of Health, the Mississippi Cooperative Extension Service and the Freedom From Hunger Foundation of Davis, California, joined together to form PINAH. Their intention was to experiment with novel ways of solving community health problems by piloting a Community Health Advisor program in Humphreys County. The rural county was chosen for a number of reasons. The health statistics served as a warning that all was not well. While infant mortality is a very rare occurrence (an annual average of 33.2 babies out of 1000 did not survive their first year from 1984 to 1988 in Humphreys County), the statistic is like the canary in the coalmine. It signals an environment which if not healthy for the smallest among us, there must be something unhealthy for all of us. Humphreys County also had an Interagency Council, which meant there was a group already collaborating to improve services in the county. The combination of need and people willing to work to make things better made program planners focus on Humphreys County.

Below the Poverty Line

The county is home to just under 13,000 people, about half of whom live in the county seat of Belzoni. The remainder live either in the small towns of Isola, Louise, Midnight, Silver City, or out in the country. Although the county's economy has benefited from the development of catfish farming, Humphreys County remains one of poorest counties in the United States. While some conditions have improved, the fact remains that today more than one-third of all households live below the poverty line — roughly $14,000 a year for a family of four. In late 1986 people from various agencies and groups formed an interagency council. Responding to a statewide call for coordinated services, local agencies met and learned for the first time what other agencies were doing. By getting together, representatives from the county — and locally — Human Services and Health Departments, the state — Cooperative Extension Service, and the

Mental Health Department, the hospital, the home health agency, and others were able to untangle the web of all too often duplicated and unco-ordinated services. This group agreed to meet several times a year. They followed through this early commitment and became the first interracial group meeting voluntarily in the county. In early 1987 the PINAH partners approached the group about sponsoring the project in the county.

Project Aims

The PINAH partners explained that the project had three aims: to improve individuals' health promotion skills (counseling techniques, leader-ship skills), to improve inter-agency coordination, and to improve the com-munity's ability to identify and solve problems. The Council gave them the green light, and veteran consultants Teresa and Robert Lingafelter were hired to run the program. Some people questioned the hiring of people who had spent most of their recent years overseas. One member of the program's advisory board remembers thinking, "What does Jamaica have to do with Humphreys County and what do they know about Mississippi?" What they found to be true in Mississippi was the same principle they found around the world—that the more people participate in decision making about their lives, the better.

From the outset, participation was part of the game plan. The Interagency Council worked with the Lingafelters to identify neighbor-hoods in the county, highlight key health issues, come up with ways to identify natural helpers, and choose priority topics for health advisor training. The goal was to have each neighborhood name the people they relied on for help and advice and to include those people in the program. They also produced a countywide resource directory listing all agencies and services. The active role the council was asked to play was later seen as key to its feeling of ownership of the program, as well as contributing to a revitalization of the council itself.

At the same time, they began scouring the neighborhoods looking for the special people who fit the description of a natural helper. They went from door to door, noting on index cards the answers to the question, "Whom do people around here go to in times of trouble?" The people whose names were mentioned over and over were invited to a ten-week Community

Health Advisor training. They named preachers and teachers. They named Headstart workers and a funeral home director. They were mostly women, mostly in their 40s with families. One characteristic they all had in common was the trust of their neighbors.

Making Training Commitments

Potential health advisors going through the training were asked to promise two things: to attend every session and to share what they learned with their neighbors. Creating a long- term community development team was not an explicit goal. However at the final session of the training, the soon-to-be graduates looked around the room and said, "O.K., when are we going to meet and how much are our dues?" The experience of exploring problems and developing solutions together was contagious. Although some of the health advisors are more comfortable working in their own social networks at home, at work, and at church, some wanted to take on community-wide projects. The group decided to meet monthly to implement their plans. As one health advisor recalls:

> One of the things is the pulling together of the community to
> get things done. We were not going to get things done apart.
> The more of us that came together and shared ideas, the more
> we realized that the problems we were having are the same.
> We realized that we were going to get things done that way.

The training covered health, nutrition, and leadership skills. Resource speakers from the agencies came in to present the health and nutrition information. This let the health advisors get to know faces within the bureaucracies as well as let the agency know community residents as more than "clients." The resource speakers realized that they had allies in the community. Often these sessions became a forum for expressing concerns and clearing up misunderstandings. For example the common wisdom and practice about applying for food stamps was that people without income and thus no "proof of income" would be denied benefits. The health advisors in training sought to clarify this policy with the agency representative and were able to work out a better system in which people with no support at all could bring in a letter certifying that they were living with someone rent free and thus could receive the benefits to which they were certainly entitled.

The leadership part of the training challenged health advisors to begin thinking individually as well as together about the causes and potential solutions for health problems. They learned how to work as a team, tap into existing resources, lead workshops, as well as how to create and implement action plans.

Since the original health and nutrition training in Belzoni eight other groups of health advisors have been trained. During the first year of implementation, trainings were held in the Humphreys County towns of Isola and Louise. In 1990, Community Health Advisors wanted more to join their ranks so an additional training was held in Belzoni. Later that year, the state of Mississippi dedicated funds for PINAH's implementation. A community facilitator was hired. She received on-the-job training in Rosedale in Bolivar County where they trained the first health advisors outside of Humphreys

Community Health Advisor Sites

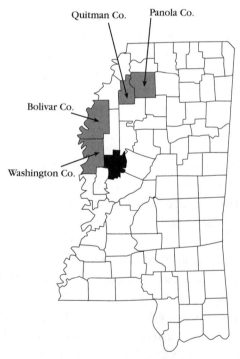

Map Source: "Community Health Advisors on the Move,"
Freedom from Hunger Foundation. 1991

County. She went on to train another group of health advisors in Leland in Washington County. A year later the state provided additional funds to hire a second facilitator to cover the adjoining 9-county district. In 1992 the Marks area in Quitman County was the site of a training while PINAH returned to train the first biracial group in Humphreys County. A group was later added in Panola County in the town of Sardis in 1993.

Health Advisor Initiatives

Experience showed that the work health advisors did could be divided into three categories: advice, assistance and action. Advice includes counseling and giving information. Assistance involves referrals to agency services, as well as direct service. Action is the organizing of communitywide action to deal with problems. The PINAH program aimed to strengthen all three levels. By including sound information in training, facilitators knew the content of advice was likely to improve. By providing information about agency services and introducing the agency providers, health advisors could give better assistance. And by bringing natural helpers together to explore community health issues and strategize solutions, PINAH was setting the stage for action.

Periodically health advisors were asked to report their helping activities of the past week as part of an evaluation of the pilot project stage. Early on, health advisors reported helping about three people a week. By the winter of 1992 each health advisor was helping seven people in a week on average. The surveys showed that health advisors help people in a wide variety of situations using a wide variety of skills from driving the church bus to finding shelter for a homeless teenage girl. The stories below are but a few of the helping activities reported by health advisors.

Providing Advice

One health advisor told this story in his report:

A college student had accidentally wrecked a friend's car. This brought about emotional problems as well as financial problems. It got so severe that the student felt she could not stay in school because of how she felt other students viewed her and because of the financial need to fix the car. She was torn mentally. I advised her not to withdraw, but to take some time, think things out, and answer the question, "Can I really afford not to stay in school and get an education?" After about a week she came back to school, worked out a financial plan, and now feels she made the right decision. Now she is one of the happiest students around.

At one point, the health advisors took the initiative to provide accurate advice about available services and organizations during a Community Services Information Campaign. The campaign was also designed to make people aware of the health advisors in their neighborhoods and how to contact them. The class of 1990 graduates who were from Belzoni and Isola, distributed 1200 lists of Community Services Hotlines at community events and door to door. These hotlines listed all important community phone numbers and services, making it easier for people to learn about services. During the neighborhood distribution, health advisors were able to assist people on-the-spot with questions about medications and referrals.

Offering Assistance

Health advisors also step in to provide services which make people's lives more manageable. For many health advisors "doing for others" is something their parents taught them. According to health advisor Sara Bush, "I've been doing so long I don't remember when I started." They know that even simple kindnesses can mean a difference in someone else's quality of life. Such was the case of a woman who had undergone surgery and was unable to hang out her laundry. The health advisor said, "I hung the clothes out and helped her fix her hair." Other times assistance has meant avoiding a potential life-long disability. A health advisor recalled:

> One of my neighbors came to see me last week. Her eight-month-old baby had been crying and then began running a high fever. The mother didn't know what to do. I talked with her about the various things that could be causing this and in the end we decided we needed to call the hospital. The hospital suggested we get the baby to a doctor right away. The mother had Medicaid but had no transportation.

I drove her and the baby the 15 miles to Belzoni where the doctor said the baby had a severe ear infection. He gave them some medicine and the baby is doing just fine now, but untreated such a severe ear infection could have caused partial or even complete loss of hearing.

Sharing Health Information

Health advisors use their knowledge and role in the community to exert a positive pressure for people to take care of themselves and seek the health care they need. Research has shown that most people consult their friends and family for health information. In the Mississippi Delta where regular contact with a health care professional is rare for low- income people, accurate advice from neighbors becomes even more valuable. They work one on one. For instance, as one person said, "A woman I know looks pregnant. I advised her to find out if she is, and to quit drinking in the meanwhile." But they also work to reach more people in groups by organizing health screenings, classes, and workshops.

Health advisors in Isola were concerned about the future of their community's children. So they organized a number of teen workshops and seminars. The teen workshop held in April, 1991 at the city hall had two goals: to provide accurate information about teen health issues and to engage the youth in a dialogue that would result in joint youth-adult problem solving. Thirty-five students; ages 8 to 17, attended the three-hour workshop which was facilitated by the Health Department and PINAH staff. The youth said they were grateful to have the chance to get accurate information about teen sexuality. They particularly appreciated the chance to discuss their ideas about preventing teen pregnancy. In the spring of 1994 PINAH's involvement with 4-H and Little League gave them another forum to share health information with the youth.

Health advisors also thought it important to bring information and screening to the community at large. As one of their first projects, the health advisors hosted health screenings during the heat of summer in 1989. Many other screenings have been held since. In collaboration with the Interagency Council they mobilized providers to offer blood pressure, blood sugar, height and weight, vision, and hearing tests. The most significant discovery was the large number of undiagnosed and untreated cases of high blood pressure in the county. One-half of those testing with high blood pressure had never been diagnosed before. In the small village of Silver City, a 41-year-old man came in with dangerously high pressure. He was sent immediately for medical attention. Health advisors were able to follow up with those diagnosed with hypertension and make sure they got proper treatment. One health advisor described the event:

> During the screening we discovered many people who were not taking their medication properly. We discovered a number of people who couldn't really read the instructions on their medication, but who didn't want people to know. We were able to help them work out a schedule for taking their medicine that they could understand and remember. We still need more screening so we can reach more people.

Community Action

During the training health advisors were asked to brainstorm the underlying causes for many of the county's health problems. They realized that certain problems like teen pregnancy and substance abuse were the result of a need for more community youth activities. This meant that the solution to health problems might involve things that are not medical at all, yet improved health does result.

As participants in the whole community, health advisors are involved in getting together Little League baseball teams, setting up flower arranging classes, and trying to get a school gym renovated. In Humphreys County, one of their initial efforts was a community clean up. The first one held in Belzoni broke new ground for cooperation and tonnage of trash gathered. The clean-up was scheduled for spring break and enlisted the help of over 200 adults and 100 youth. Residents not only beautified their own homes but also joined together to clean vacant lots and roadside areas. Approximately 50 extra truckloads of trash were taken to the landfill by the city trucks alone. As one community resident said:

> I've lived here for 20 years and have always wanted to do this. We just didn't believe that people would come out and work together, but now we've all seen what can be done with the cooperation of the whole community.

Who Are the Health Advisors

Although there is a story behind each and every health advisor, meet four of them here.

Alma Faye Custom of Isola was until recently employed by Jockey International as a seamstress. The recent closure of the factory has left her unemployed but not idle. She is active on the Helping Hands Board and as a 4-H Club volunteer leader. Since 1992 she has served Isola on the local board of aldermen.

Willie Tanner is the current chair of Helping Hands of Humphreys County, Inc. Father of two, he and his wife Deloris both serve the community as health advisors. He marks the time that he realized the importance of serving others to his days in the army in Vietnam. He returned to his hometown of Isola in 1972 and now spends his summers coaching Little League. Deloris Tanner was hooked into health advisor training when the health knowledge survey given in the first session made her realize that many of the answers she thought she knew were not accurate. She says helping others or "doing what you can when the time comes" is a skill that just grew up in her.

Pearl Scurlock and Pearl Carpenter are two health advisors each known to their communities simply as "Miss Pearl." They both are in their seventies. Ms. Scurlock has a reputation as a formidable do-gooder who gets action despite the rules. Although she does not drive, between the phone and friends, she "makes rounds" with elderly and shut-in residents of Marks. Rumor has it she called the ambulance when she heard a friend had been taken to the hospital. The ambulance picked her up and delivered her to the hospital door for visiting hours. She let the fire department take her home. Ms. Carpenter spent a good deal of her working life with the Headstart program. Her focus is on the children of Belzoni. She founded the Youth Helping Others Club. Although she doesn't drive either, her daily routine includes a spry walk to the Food Pantry where she serves as the coordinator.

The small disasters and emergencies that strike any community are compounded by poverty in Humphreys County. For many people being laid off or having a home destroyed by fire means a total depletion of resources. In these cases they turn to food stamps to feed their families. Unfortunately, one's stomach doesn't understand the time it takes for an agency to fill the need. To respond to this situation another initial project tackled by the health advisors was the organizing of the emergency Food Pantry. What started as a few packages of beans in a dark corner is now a large facility complete with freezers, shelves of staples, and a regular list of contributors. Fires, domestic situations, and illness bring young and old, black and white, into the Food Pantry for much needed assistance.

The establishment of the Food Pantry gives the Health Advisors in Humpreys County (who have incorporated themselves as a 501 (c) 3 nonprofit called Helping Hands of Humphreys County, Inc.) a place to meet as well as a physical presence in the community. The non-profit status enables the group to apply in its own name for funds and gives it official credibility when approaching donors. The whitewashed walls and plywood shelves of the Food Pantry are home to macaroni and frozen corn, as well as community action. Helping Hands is the source of sustenance for the hungry and a home for the health advisors set down a dirt driveway in the back of a brick building.

Impact on the Agency

While District Health Officer Rausa predicted that trying this new initiative couldn't hurt, the agencies involved found that the pains of adjustment did hurt. This PINAH approach of interagency collaboration and reliance on the community to generate answers required that agencies let go of their old ways and create "new ways of doing business." Dr Rausa remembers, "For all those years my way was to tell people what was wrong with them and how to fix it. If they didn't get better, it was probably their fault because either they didn't tell me right in the first place what the problem was, or they did not do what I said to cure it." This new approach meant giving some of the diagnosing and curing power back to the community. People were asked what they thought were the causes of their health problems and what should be done to solve them. Dr. Rausa was rejuvenated by the new possibilities created by involving the community in solving problems.

"Some people deal with their midlife crisis by buying a red sports car. I got lucky and happened on PINAH," he says today.

Certainly Health Department staff were aware as community residents that there were people in their midst who somehow were the glue that kept things together. But not until PINAH and the Health Advisor program came was there an official way to recognize these neighborhood resources, work with them, and celebrate them. Certain agencies appreciated the very grassroots the health advisors represented. The Mississippi Cooperative Extension Service and the Health Advisors worked together to reach the hard-to-reach who despite their needs do not always seek out services and programs. The joint effort has brought greater success.

Knowledge of how state and county offices work and who is supposed to get things done made health advisors aware of the power of information. As Bertha Thurman, health advisor, preacher, mother of seven, and foster mother to several more says, "We've got their number." Service providers know that they know and consequently, the wheels grind a little more quickly when a health advisor is on the line.

Challenges Beyond Health

In Humphreys County, Mississippi, the choice of health as a focus for community development and empowerment initiatives was taken consciously. Not only did the statistics of teen pregnancy and infant mortality justify an all-out effort to improve health, but organizers took the calculated risk that this was a "safe" issue to tackle that wouldn't be immediately associated with political or racial overtones. Indeed, whites and blacks alike could agree that health is a concern for everyone and something that they could join together in promoting. However, as veteran community organizer, Guy Steuart found, "Everything is health related." After a while, health advisors decided that certain obstacles to their community's health involved the way things were and that political action was a way to promote change.

In one instance, representation on the city council is limited to the incorporated city which does not include some majority black neighborhoods. Some health advisors thought that working for redistricting would help create better representation of their views about better housing. This proposed strategic direction was not taken lightly in the greater community; in a 1992 meeting when PINAH was working to set up another training with greater white involvement, a town official sounded a note of caution. He thought that as long as Helping Hands was going to be involved in politics, they were going to have a hard time involving white people. The debate over the definition of what is political and what is health seems to have touched a nerve. The challenge of moving towards real change, at the same time including as many people in the process, is still being resolved.

The Health Department took over the Health Advisor program officially in late 1993. The staff positions were moved to the corresponding State Department of Health offices and the PINAH office was closed. A new agency, Community Health Advisor Networks/Freedom From Hunger, was formed to support the Mississippi State Department of Health and surrounding states in the implementation of the Health Advisor program. The script for the response to this transition is still being written.

Undoubtedly, health advisors will continue helping their neighbors as they always have with the support of new-found allies in the agencies. The rebirth of the project as a regular Health Department program is a great achievement. Rarely is a public agency willing to commit to a program where community members set the agenda. However, in an environment where new issues are always pressing and resources being reallocated, there is a danger that the invisible but ever present nature of the health advisors' work will be taken for granted. The volunteers may have to struggle to be able to make their own decisions about community priorities.

And while health advisors are volunteers, their program requires money and management. Funds must be invested in supporting current health advisors by keeping them informed and energized, putting them in touch with resources and with each other, facilitating their activities, and providing them with ongoing training. But the challenge is worth it. The solutions to community problems lie within the community and do not come from on high. The experiment in the Mississippi Delta has shown that home-grown answers reached together in new partnerships are the ones that will endure after all federal and grant dollars go away. The desire for a better community exists in every place. As Herrestine Chambers a community health advisor said in her testimony before the Committee on Labor and Human Resources, United States Senate, on April 20, 1990:

We want you to know that you are not alone, and the Public Health Service and the State Health Departments are not alone in this struggle. There are people in every community in this nation who are concerned about the health of their community, and are looking for a way to do something about it. We are ready to join you, the health professionals and agencies, as partners for a healthy nation through healthy neighborhoods. It is important for policy makers to understand that local initiatives to the problems of poor health and poverty have the best chance of producing lasting solutions.

Chapter 19
Turning Neighborhood Energy Right Side Up

JOHN BURBIDGE

*The Youth Empowerment Project, along with the many
other innovative programs, has made Escondido a model
of community-based government. The combination of
widespread community involvement, public officials
working with citizens in a brokering role, and a
commitment to collaboration has become the
hallmark of the way Escondido does business.*

Escondido, California, is a city proud of its 100-year history. It is home
to some of California's founding families, Californianos, ranch owners
of Hispanic heritage who were already living there when California
was ceded to the United States from Mexico in 1848. This heritage
distinguishes it from many other California communities that have
acquired large Hispanic populations primarily through migration.
Escondido is also known for its reputation as a progressive and cohesive community, a well-deserved reputation due partly to the inclusive, community-
based approach to government taken by a number of its public officials. Many
of these officials have backgrounds in social service, public administration,

and organizational development. A cornerstone of Escondido's innovative approach to local government is what City Manager Douglas Clark calls its "brokering method of problem solving." Instead of providing a number of services itself, the city acts more like a real estate broker and plays the role of an intermediary. The city helps groups identify issues, brings the community together to discuss solutions, provides meeting space, and assists people in finding the resources to deliver the services. Says Clark:

> The cure for a lot of things we perceive as problems is not getting the city or the police to come in and fix them. We don't have any corner on the solutions. We need to give neighborhoods and families the autonomy and the means to do it themselves.

The roots of this approach go back about ten years and involve the Community Development Block Grants issued to local governments by the U.S. Department of Housing and Urban Development to support projects that benefit low- and middle-income groups. Instead of using its grants for public works, as many cities do, Escondido decided to devote the money entirely to social services, by disbursing the funds to empower community non-profit agencies. A number of these agencies occupy buildings the city leases to them for $1 a year, a deal which allows the agencies to put more money into service delivery rather than into building maintenance.

But, like any system, this too has its drawbacks, as Escondido discovered in the case of its child care services. City officials grew tired of all the child care organizations competing for block grants and decided it was time for a change. Clark continues:

> We referred to this competition as their annual guilt trip. Several years ago, we had $4 million dollars in requests and $1.2 million to give away. The agencies were asked to find a new, more collaborative approach to support child care programs. A voucher system was proposed. Now, organizations compete with each other to provide better services to their clients, rather than for a larger slice of the funding pie.

The brokering role the city has played in working with community agencies to deliver services is the backbone of Escondido's participatory style of government. In acknowledgment of its pioneering efforts,

Escondido was selected as one of 14 California cities to participate in the World Health Organization's Healthy Cities program. As City of Escondido Community Service Director, Jerry Van Leeuwen put it: "For us, Healthy Cities is a euphemism for participatory governance for community participation in problem solving. We are trying to elevate this approach in the city's priorities."

The Escondido Gang Project

Of the many programs which Escondido has devised to foster a healthy city, none has been as pivotal as the Escondido Gang Project. Escondido's proactive, community-based approach to city government was put to the test in mid-1991 when two gang-related killings took place — one, the murder of an 18-year old high school honor student and the other, the shooting of a five year-old boy waiting in a car for a pizza. Community reaction to these crimes was immediate. Some people tried to lay the blame for the incidents on the police department and city hall, but others decided it was time to come up with their own solutions to the problem of violence.

The Escondido Gang Project, which was just getting underway at the time, was an ideal vehicle for community involvement. The project, designed to engage a wide cross-section of the community in solving problems of gang violence, had been proposed by the Community Congress of San Diego, a lead agency in initiating community-based activities in the region. The Community Congress had obtained a two-year, $48,540 grant for the project from the federal Administration on Children, Youth, and Families Department of Health and Human Services.

Escondido's Gang Project built on a solid foundation. In 1989, the city had formed a Minority Roundtable of city and community officials to improve relations between ethnic communities and the police department. The Roundtable adopted a long-range community relations plan including a cultural awareness training program designed by the state law enforcement agency, and spearheaded by Escondido. Moreover, the police department had been working actively with gangs, both through a school-centered gang prevention education program and more directly in activities such as a police/gang softball game.

To launch the project, a diverse coalition of city departments, professional agencies, community groups, churches, schools, and individual citizens was formed. Manny Medrano, director of Cross-Cultural Services of the Counseling Crisis Services, Escondido Youth Encounter (EYE) and Jerry Van Leeuwen, community services director of the city of Escondido, were joint leaders of the project.

Ensuring broad-based community participation was key to the project success. To make sure this participation occurred, the coalition invited the Institute of Cultural Affairs (ICA), a not-for-profit organization working in community and organizational development, to join the coalition. The ICA trained a number of community people in its techniques of participation so they in turn could conduct community events where all participants were actively involved. Trainees learned how to elicit everyone's input in an open and nondefensive manner by having participants first write down their own thoughts on cards, then share them with a small group, and finally with the whole body. For many trainees like Gracie Castro, this way of leading meetings was a breath of fresh air. "When the cards went up on the board, we actually saw what everyone thought and said," she commented. "By the end of the meeting, we could see the results of our efforts. There was not the usual sense of boredom or wasting time."

The process began in the spring of 1991 with a series of six town meetings — four held in middle schools, one with youth members of the California Conservation Corps and another with gang members themselves. At the meetings, conducted in either English or Spanish, people were asked, "What can we do to create a safe and unified community?" Having the group take responsibility for creating and implementing solutions was a critical part of the method. People responded enthusiastically to the meetings. At the Spanish-speaking meeting at Grant Middle School, more than 50 people attended. Most stayed until 11:30 p.m. The later the meeting went on, the more engrossed people became. When food ran out, they sent out for tacos and juice, while they kept focused on the issues at hand. People spoke passionately of their concerns, especially the loss of traditional cultural values, poor communications between parents and youth, and the fear of attending school among Hispanic youth. As they worked through the evening and moved to decide what they could do about these issues, their excitement increased. Leticia Aroyo, principal of Felicita Elementary School, who facilitated this meeting, raved about what happened:

It was so revitalizing. New leaders emerged from that meeting, some with no education. But they were empowered. Parents started taking responsibility for things they wanted to organize, including a sports program, parent visitation days, and multicultural celebrations.

Following the six town meetings, an all-day community-wide meeting with simultaneous translation brought together the input from the individual meetings and created a strategic plan for the future of youth in Escondido. The meeting surpassed all expectations.

The diversity of participants alone made an impact on everyone. Parents, youth, police officers, former gang members, social workers, church leaders, and city officials for once were working for the same goal. "I didn't think I'd ever be in a meeting like that," said former drug addict and ex-gang member Mario Espinoza. "When the police chief came up to shake my hand and told me he liked what I said, I was amazed. That's never happened to me before in my life."

Nearly 80 people participated tirelessly throughout the morning and the afternoon. This meeting was different from anything they had ever attended. People really listened to one another, there was little of the usual finger-pointing, and everyone's ideas were incorporated into the proceedings. As they spelled out their vision for youth in Escondido, they saw a new picture of the community's future emerge. It included a Jobs for Youth work program, increased mentorships involving senior citizens and local business people, parenting classes, support groups, and positive recreational alternatives.

When asked what might block their vision from being realized, people dug deep to uncover root causes of the violence and disenchantment that characterize so many youth today. They pointed to the low priority placed on education, a sense of being ignored, scarcity of jobs for Hispanics, and poor communication within the Hispanic community.

They wrapped up the day by assigning taskforces to be responsible for implementing the strategic directions chosen. Some people agreed to work on building community awareness, others on activating the community. Among the myriad activities they planned were "Parent of the Month" awards, a semester of community service in high schools, and a town meeting to secure the commitment of the local business community to the project.

From Words to Action

Within a year after that community-wide meeting, the work of the those taskforces became obvious. Neighborhood Watch groups increased within the Latino community. Meetings with parents of gang members started to take place. A cultural awareness training program expanded its focus from city officials to the community at large, and the city council initiated community meetings at the neighborhood level.

At the same time, activities started by others in the community received new energy from the project and began to operate under its umbrella. One of these was the Understanding Culture Club (UCC), a youth group for those at risk to exposure from drugs and gangs. Although the UCC had been functioning about a year, it really took off after the town meeting with members of Escondido's rival Westside and Diablo gangs. At this town meeting, gang members voiced their concerns about the lack of places to hang out and things to do. The UCC seemed an ideal vehicle to address these issues, but it took time to begin to appeal to the young people themselves. Out of a total membership of nearly 60 youth, a core of 20-30 became involved on a regular basis.

UCC activities have included presentations, movies and videos on drug, alcohol, and AIDS issues; a twice monthly booth at the Escondido Farmers' Market; a monthly cleanup of a nearby lake; working with the Elks Lodge to serve breakfast to the elderly; Job Corp workshops, and more.

But of all these activities arising from the momentum created by the Escondido Gang Project, two were particularly significant. One was a conference of 150 parents of Hispanic school dropouts who came together to answer the questions: Why do Hispanics have the highest school dropout rate and what can we do about it? The conference revealed a number of factors contributing to the high drop-out rate:

- The dearth of positive role models of educated, successful Hispanics;
- The schism young Hispanics experience between the pride they are taught to have for their language and customs at home and the negative connotations these are often given in the wider society;
- The reinforcement of disempowering cultural stereotypes by the school system itself.

The other important event was a meeting with elected officials in Escondido held to strengthen their involvement in the project. City council members met with board members representing the sixteen elementary and five high schools in the city. As Medrano put it:

> We had gone to the city and to the community and asked what they could do. Now we flipped it and asked the same question of elected officials. They had a hard time with that at first because they were not used to being held accountable. But we didn't approach it in the usual negative fashion. We elicited their participation.

The result, according to Medrano, was a 100 percent buy-in. In a Memorandum of Understanding, officials of all three boards present committed staff to work with the Escondido Gang Project and to actively pursue joint funding between the school districts and the project. They suggested setting up a youth commission and youth recognition events. As Medrano summed up, "It is now hard to become an elected official in Escondido without being an advocate and supporter of the project."

As the project came to the end of its two-year federal grant, it had clearly won many supporters, both in Escondido and farther afield. One of these supporters was the city council. Although initially reluctant to fund the project further, the council changed its mind when a number of project participants wearing T-shirts proclaiming "Empowering Youth: The Escondido Gang Project" showed up at council meeting. The result? Strong endorsement of the project and a grant of $46,000 to the Escondido Youth Encounter organization, a lead agency for the Gang Project.

Another advocate for the project was former United States Senator John Seymour who proposed a $30 million investment in locally-based empowerment programs that help parents, schools, and communities fight gang activity and violence. Convinced that one of the most effective ways to fight "the gang culture" is to empower community-based initiatives at the grassroots level, Seymour was impressed with what Escondido had done. Addressing representatives of the project, he said:

> The best ideas don't always come from a think tank on the East Coast. You find them right here at the local level, where parents and youth, schools and law enforcement are all combining their efforts to make a difference in their community.

One way the Escondido experience is being shared with other communities is through a video made by Judith Belanger, a resident of Escondido's neighboring city of Carlsbad. Entitled "RAD 2000" (RAD = Rock After Drugs), this hour-long, award-winning video is targeted to youths aged 10-19. Designed in a talk-show format with MTV-style music, dance, and rap, it encourages self-esteem and social responsibility through one's own accomplishments. The video includes interviews with children involved in the Escondido project, then compares their responses to those of professionals who asked the same questions. Why are children killing one another? Why aren't more kids doing better in school? Who is selling weapons to children?

Belanger was surprised by the similarity in answers of the two groups. "They were amazingly in sync," she says. "Adults seem much more sensitive to where the kids are coming from than I imagined they would be." Belanger is using the video to catalyze public awareness and action concerning gang problems. In addition to distributing it through public access television and educational systems for national exposure, she hopes it will make an impact closer to home in San Diego's North County. "There's so much denial about the degree of gang activity in some communities," she says. "Perhaps this video will begin to open doors and allow the Escondido Gang Project to catalyze something in other nearby cities. They badly need it."

Beyond Programs: Addressing Root Causes

Two years into the Escondido Gang Project, organizers began to do some serious soul-searching about the effectiveness of their efforts. True, the project had catalyzed a number of programs as alternatives to gang activities, such as the UCC, a boxing club, apartment-based homework clubs, and the YMCA Pryde Program, which featured field trips, computer courses, substance abuse prevention training, and self-esteem enhancement. The project had also extended leadership to a much wider range of citizens than before, through the town meetings, ongoing taskforces, and increased activities.

But had it really addressed the root cause of violence in the community? Some, like Manuel Medrano, answered an honest 'no' to that nagging question. "If we had several shootings today, would it be because the Gang Project had failed? Or, because we haven't had them, can we say that it was successful, or was it because there were more police officers, or were we just plain lucky?" he asks.

Acknowledging this dilemma, organizers decided to shift the emphasis of the project from gangs to violence prevention, and from doing more programs to changing public policy. At the same time, they decided to give young people a greater say in project activities and attack the issue of youth violence from a public health perspective. To symbolize these changes, they renamed the project the "Escondido Youth Empowerment Project". Underscoring the need for changing policies, Medrano quoted a recent experience:

> We have a store in town whose video games attract lots of kids. Right across the street from the store there is a lot of gang graffiti. The problem is that it's a liquor store. What can we do to change policy so that liquor stores wouldn't be allowed to have video games that attract youth?

As a sign of support for this approach to solving community violence, the project was fortunate to receive a five-year, $775,000 grant from the California Wellness Foundation, as part of a statewide initiative aimed at preventing violence and promoting health and well-being in communities. With its track record and its highly collaborative approach, the Escondido Youth Empowerment Project was an ideal candidate for such a grant. It also received funding from two other private sources and from the City of Escondido.

Four interrelated components reflect the new focus of the Escondido Youth Empowerment Project:

- The Spirit of Escondido Youth Community Service Awards
- The Youth Empowerment Taskforce
- Community Collaboration (involving the ongoing Escondido Gang Taskforce)
- Palomar Hospital Violence Prevention Center.

While these components are distinct, they share a common intent to reduce and prevent youth violence in Escondido. Throughout the history of the project, participating members have displayed a variety of strong convictions, different approaches, and hidden agendas. These have ranged from Christian evangelists wanting to bring gang members to God, to irate apartment owners and managers wanting to limit damage to their property. But underneath these perspectives, everyone is clear on one reality. Local government policies need to create change through coordinated social action.

To this end, the project has set a number of policy objectives ranging from reducing youth's access to handguns, to establishing a code of practice for the news and entertainment industry's portrayal of youth and violent behavior. The latter seems particularly important. "We need to change the community's thinking about violence in general and the Hispanic community in particular," Medrano insists. "There often seems to be more violence on Spanish television than English."

While addressing policy matters is important, project members have also decided young people themselves need to be more active within the group. It is true that youths have participated from the initial town meetings to ongoing taskforces. But most of the time adults overshadow the young people's involvement. Now the project is turning its attention to those aged 24 or younger who are disproportionally represented both as perpetrators and victims of violence. "Traditionally, we have concentrated on those 18 and under," says Medrano. "But that eliminates a key group, those who dropped out of school at 15 or 16 and are still hanging around the streets with no job at 22 or 23. These are the guys we need to work with more."

With its change in name and shift in emphasis, the Escondido Youth Empowerment Project is embarking on a new phase. Its success in dealing with youth violence is difficult to gauge. If gang-related crime statistics are used as a measure, there is reason to be encouraged. Five gang-related deaths occurred in 1991, two in 1992, none in 1993, and none to May, 1994. The number of gang members in Escondido, considered to be around 350, has stabilized over the last couple of years. In many other communities, some nearby, the number has skyrocketed.

But according to former Police Chief Vince Jimno, the project has led to other residual benefits in the community, apart from its effect on gang behavior.

> We're seeing more openness from the community to law enforcement. There is less of, "'This is your job' and more of, 'What can we do to help?'" The community senses it has more control over its destiny and is responding accordingly. This kind of change of attitude is hard to quantify but you can feel it everywhere. The temperature is different here.

City Community Services Director, Jerry van Leeuwen, echoes a similar sentiment. "Although we have pursued a 'steer but not row' approach to government in Escondido for some time, the Youth Empowerment Project reinforced our belief in that approach and spurred on a number of other citizen-based initiatives as well."

Collaboration: Key to a Healthy City

In transforming the way it governs, the City of Escondido has come to embody the key elements of a new participatory mode of public service. It seeks broad-based citizen input in problem solving, acts as a broker with responsible community service agencies, and builds partnerships among all those involved in dealing with particular issues.

But if community participation in city government has become the way Escondido does business, collaboration has become its trademark. In 1993, the city council established collaboration, system integration, and prevention as the Community Development Block Grant priorities. That year, the city received only 27 proposals for funding, compared to 53 the year before. In Van Leeuwen's estimation, people see the value of collaboration and are acting accordingly.

A number of important programs illustrate Escondido's commitment to collaboration. One is the **Health Care and Community Services Project**. An outgrowth of the earlier Community Sobering Services, this project aims to reduce harm from substance abuse and increase public access to health care services. Instead of regarding drunkenness as a criminal offense, as is currently the case in California, the project treats it as a health issue. Granted, the county of San Diego offers an indirect incentive for this program by charging fees for each person booked on drunkenness charges. But it also makes plain good sense to provide more useful options rather than expensive and nonproductive protective custody in jail.

Collaboration in the Health Care and Community Services Project has happened first as a natural outgrowth of the need for agencies affected by public drunkenness to work together. These groups include the police department, the emergency department of the local hospital, and the publicly funded community health clinic. Second, collaboration has happened in relation to funding. Three local funding partners, the city of Escondido, the San Diego County Alcohol and Drug Services, and the Palomar and Pomerado Health Foundation together came up with over $600,000. This amount was matched by a $400,000 grant from the Robert Wood Johnson Foundation for a combined amount of $1.1 million.

According to Project Director Dennis Kelso, the Health Care and Community Service Project has saved the city the time and cost of two and one-half police officers on the street over the course of a year. Instead of paying to book inebriates into jail, Escondido has been able to leverage that money by expanding and integrating its health care services to assist people with drug and alcohol problems. Those abusers picked up by the police receive immediate assistance and direction to other services they may need, with transportation provided. In addition, health care patients are also screened for alcohol and drug related problems as part of an early intervention program to address concerns before they become more acute and more expensive to address. Says Kelso:

> Dealing with the 3-5% of the population who are alcohol and drug dependent is an important humanitarian response. However, most alcohol-related social problems involve light to moderate drinkers. Screening and inexpensive, brief interventions for nondependent drinkers with problems is a cost-effective community approach.

Another arena in which Escondido has demonstrated city-community collaboration is rental housing. Frustration among apartment owners, managers, and tenants over rising crime and violence peaked in the summer of 1992 when a local newspaper headline reported: FIG STREET — STREET OF SCREAMS. One apartment owner on this street, Gene Polley, had four of his tenants leave their apartments because of the violence.

Working with Jerry Van Leeuwen of the Escondido Community Services Department, Polley organized a meeting of owners and managers to address the situation. At this gathering many angry people engaged in active finger pointing, especially at the police and the city. Van Leeuwen, who moderated the meeting, sat and listened politely. Then he spoke. He put the ball right back in the owners' and managers' court. If they wouldn't rent to people who are likely to cause trouble, he said, they wouldn't have such a problem.

Out of this gathering, two grassroots organizations of apartment owners and managers emerged, **Neighborhood Empowerment Association (NEO)** and the **Neighborhood Owner Manager Association (NO MAS)**. Although they began as one organization, the group eventually split because of differences in approach and emphasis among members. Some wanted to focus on involving residents and others wanted to concentrate more on the owners and managers. However, most people agreed on one point. Concerned citizens, not the police, could make the greatest impact in dealing with community problems.

After just one year of operating, NEO piled up a number of accomplishments. Working with the police department and a local nonprofit organization, it devised a three-step process for apartment complexes to identify themselves as "drug-free zones."

- First, a complex must verify that at least 75% of its occupants support the program.
- Second, crime prevention officers and drug abuse prevention staff meet with the tenants to explain how to spot drug activities, drive away troublemakers, and develop neighborhood empowerment.
- Third, the tenants must sign an addendum to the rental agreement declaring they won't tolerate drugs. The property then receives signs announcing it as a "drug-free zone."

An offshoot of NEO is **RHITE —the Rental Housing Improvement Team of Escondido**. The city council was concerned about the deteriorating state of some of the rental housing stock in the city. First it tried to implement a mandatory inspection program, but apartment owners balked at picking up the $15 per unit tab. The council responded by challenging property owners and managers to come back with an alternate plan. They did. In early June, 1993, under the leadership of Rich Swanson, a group of property managers, owner managers, and concerned citizens proposed that they would be trained by the city as volunteer inspectors. They would inspect properties for code violations visible from the outside, such as improper storage of refuse containers, inoperative or abandoned vehicles, and broken windows. Aware of the need to respect the tenants' rights to privacy, they would not enter a unit, but would inspect by either driving or walking by. They would first try to rectify problems by talking with owners directly. Only if the owner failed to make corrections voluntarily would they turn the violation over to the city.

The council unanimously approved the plan in August, 1993. Volunteer training was held in October and inspections began in early November. By the end of six months, a team of 31 RHITE volunteers had inspected over 3200 units. They encountered 187 code violations, 90% of which people corrected voluntarily. Nearly four-fifths of the violations occurred in single family units and resulted from people's ignorance of city codes.

Gauging from the number of compliments RHITE received, most property owners support their efforts. The owners are grateful that volunteers have stepped in and made it unnecessary for the city to act in a mandatory capacity at a cost to themselves. In appreciation the city has donated $1500 to the group to buy a computer that will help streamline its operations. Other cities have begun to express interest in following Escondido's example.

At the same time as RHITE has been active, NO MAS, the other apartment owner/manager association led by Ray and Carmen Paez, has made a significant contribution to fighting crime. It has developed a Community Response Team of 20-30 men and women who will respond within five minutes to a call from the community for assistance. Often, these calls are to search for a lost child, but sometimes they are more dramatic.

A case in point is the call that came from an apartment manager, himself a member of NO MAS. One of his tenants had said she was being imprisoned in her unit by her husband, but when the manager tried to reach her, he was unable to do so. Not wanting to interfere in a domestic situation, he

City of Escondido

called on his colleagues at NO MAS for help. When a NO MAS team went to the apartment, they saw through the window a child with an empty bottle in one hand. In the other, he was holding another bottle full of rotten milk. Deciding the situation merited immediate action, and willing to risk a law suit for their action, the team broke into the apartment. They found the woman unconscious, and later discovered she was pregnant. The child had been defecating all over the place.

The NO MAS team called the police and fire departments, who took the woman to the hospital. She later recovered her health, and her husband was arrested and ordered to undergo therapy. Now they are both part of a resident's group helping other apartment renters in need. Building on this kind of success, NO MAS has expanded its activities to include the nearby communities of Vista, San Marcos, Fallbrook, and Oceanside.

Redefining the Public Sector's Role

The Youth Empowerment Project, along with the many other innovative programs, has made Escondido a model of community-based government. The combination of widespread community involvement, public officials working with citizens in a brokering role, and a commitment to collaboration has become the hallmark of the way Escondido does business.

Ask those involved in the many community-city partnerships, and they'll tell you they're continually learning as they go. But that is not surprising. On the contrary, it is at the very heart of what it is Escondido is trying to do to create a more open, inclusive, and people-centered style of government. Risking, learning and reinventing are what it's all about.

In the three years since I first visited Escondido, I have noticed a subtle but significant change in people's voices as they report what is happening in their community. In 1991, people were still reeling from the impact of the gang-related shootings that shook the foundations of their city. Today, there is a gentle confidence, if not a quiet pride, in telling what has been accomplished in Escondido. And there is good reason for such pride.

But in the final analysis, the real importance of Escondido's innovative projects may rest not in their accomplishments, as valuable as they are, but in the contribution they are making to redefining the role of the public sector. A new paradigm or understanding of public service is emerging today. A central feature of this paradigm is an ethic of inclusive responsibility for, and inclusive participation in, solving community and societal problems. At a point when people are yearning for new models of political, economic, and social development, Escondido's contribution could not be more timely.

MENTAL
HEALTH
ASSOCIATION
IN NEW YORK
STATE, INC.

Chapter 20
Empowering the Disempowered

IKE G. POWELL AND EDWARD KNIGHT, PH.D.

The stereotype of "once sick, always sick" is changing as more and more self-help is promoted and supported by the mental health system. Many recipients and professionals now believe that a person diagnosed with mental illness can lead a productive life. Clinical training programs are considering including recovery concepts and recipients in them. In New York State, the self-help movement has had a direct impact on the way the mental health system treats people diagnosed with mental illness. Although this change is beginning to affect the way some parts of society treat mental health, its greatest effect has been on the way people diagnosed as mentally ill see themselves.

Recipient Empowerment

Ms. G. lived in depression and fear, seldom leaving her small apartment in a Latino neighborhood of New York City. As a recipient of services from the New York state mental health system, she forced herself to make the weekly trip to the community mental health clinic. Her inability to speak English only added to her need to isolate herself. Her fear of traveling alone meant that her son had to skip school to accompany her to the clinic. He did this for seven years. But in March, 1992, Ms. G. became involved in a mental health self-help group that changed her life. Now, two years later, she needs no help in going to the clinic, and has developed friendships that get her out of her apartment. Also, she is taking English-as-a-Second-Language classes and feels a new strength and purpose in her life.

Until recently, recipient empowerment has been seen as a contradiction in terms by most mental health professionals, because empowered people feel *good* about themselves. They see themselves as worthwhile human beings. They are aware of their rights and are willing to speak out to protect those rights. They seek to get the best services for themselves and others. None of this fits the stereotypical picture of people diagnosed as mentally ill.

Dr. William A. Anthony, a leader in the field of psychiatric rehabilitation, writes,

> Until the late 1980s, the mindset was that people with severe mental illness would not recover, even though people were recovering. Now this thinking is changing, because consumers (of mental health services) and their families are asking if the disabling effects of severe mental illness are due to illness, or to the way the society treats people with mental illness, or to the way the mental health system itself treats people with mental illness.[1]

Traditionally, people have believed that those diagnosed with mental illness have impaired judgment, and do not understand their own needs and wants. Therefore, mental health care recipients have had little say about the kinds and quality of care they receive. This belief is changing in New York State. What catalyzed this change? It was the statewide self-help effort of the Mental Health Recipient Empowerment Project (MHREP). Dr. Richard Surles, Commissioner of the New York State Office of Mental Health, recently deemed it "…among the most important work that has been done in the New York mental health system in the past five years." The recipients in the 550 locally-operated, state-funded out-patient residence programs can attest to this positive change. Ms. G.'s participation in a self-help group may not have "cured" her, but it certainly lessened some of the disabling effects of her "illness".

The Power of Self-Help

MHREP is a program of the Mental Health Association in New York State, Inc. (MHANYS). MHANYS is a not-for-profit, statewide network of community-based mental health associations. The Empowerment Project seeks

How participants said they benefitted from participation in self-help activities.

90%	80%
• Increasing self-esteem	• Speaking in front of group
• Hope about the future	• Holding a job
• Connected to peers	• Staying out of hospital
• More assertive	**70%**
• Living more independently	-Better family ties
• Better problem solving	-More civic minded
• Sense of well-being	-Getting an education
• Getting along with others	**50%**
• Assuming responsibilities	-Stop abusing alcohol or drugs
• Power to make decisions	-Informed of rights
• Better listening skills	

Compiled by Office of Mental Health Bureau of Evaluation & Services Research Self-Help Study of Self-Help Group Leaders. Investigators: Sharon Carpinello, Ed.D., Edward L. Knight, Ph.D.

to enable recipients to be producers of mental health rather than consumers of mental health services. Throughout the state, the project encourages recipients to develop self-help locally. Self-help involves people who have had the common experience of being diagnosed with mental illness. Mental health care recipients voluntarily come together to help themselves and one another, in a trusting, open, and supportive environment. Self-help involves the ability to reach out, share experiences, and learn from one another. In self-help, no dichotomy exists between the helper and the "helpee." In self-help groups, the group makes its own decisions.

Edward L. Knight, Ph.D., has been MHREP project coordinator since its inception in 1988. Dr. Knight, himself a recipient of mental health services, is a strong proponent of self-help. A 1991 study, conducted by Dr. Sharon Carpinello and Dr. Knight, delineates the positive effects of self-help. The study included participants in self-help groups from across the state. It also combined focus-group interviews and key-informant interviews. More than one participant declared: "Self-help has given my whole life meaning...it has normalized my life." Recipients also talked about how they moved from dependency, self-destruction, or hopelessness to positive social identity.

As recipients talked about what self-help had done for them, common themes emerged. They saw themselves in a more positive light. They experienced a heightened sense of personal well-being and were more able to make decisions by themselves. They felt they were able to function better in society, and were less dependent on alcohol and drugs. Many were motivated to pursue educational goals and employment opportunities. All of these positive changes led to their having to return to the hospital less often[2].

In his first quarterly grant report to the Office of Mental Health, Dr. Knight stated: "...the key to organizing recipients of mental health services is the creation of a movement that fosters a social environment of self-help." Self-help works because it helps reduce the symptoms of mental illness as people come together to discuss their common concerns. This helps overcome the isolation that is so prevalent. Self-help also helps people move from the role of always being helped to the role of helping others. This gives them a sense that they have something worthwhile to contribute. Self-help group members share and learn from one another as equals who have had common experiences. Those who successfully cope serve as role models for people who cope less successfully. Self-help provides meaningful structure for people—not structure imposed from the outside by professionals, but one that is generated from the members themselves.

Mental health recipients have specific needs which self-help addresses. Dr. Knight bases his statewide organizing work on the three reasons why recipients have these needs. First, receiving a diagnosis of mental illness results in vulnerability. Secondly, the New York State mental health system is a monolith set up primarily to control behavior, not to treat illness. And last, nothing short of an empowered, trained statewide movement of recipients of services can have any impact on the mental health system.

Disempowerment

Being diagnosed as mentally ill alters a person's self-image and social image. When Ms. K. was first labeled "mentally ill," she saw herself as "flawed, hopeless, a failure, permanently defective." This is a common response. After many years of floundering in the system, Ms. K. became involved in self-help. She found out about her rights and began to teach others about theirs. Currently the director of a recipient-run organization advocating for both in-patient and out-patient rights, Ms. K. is very active in the statewide recipient empowerment movement.

Society, and the mental health system itself, regularly stigmatize people diagnosed as mentally ill. For instance, people diagnosed as mentally ill are aware of public stigma, because it is sensationalized by the media. They know they are seen as dangerous, unpredictable, unstable, and potentially violent people. This stigma causes them to lose or become disconnected from traditional support systems of family and friends, who often turn their backs, look the other way, or treat them like children. This loss of the opportunity for significant interaction with their loved ones can even lead to loss of housing, education, and employment, as well as access to financial resources. There is a general mood in society that "no one wants to be around the mentally ill."

Also, people diagnosed as mentally ill are aware that they are often seen as disabled. Neither society nor the professionals treating them expect them to do anything worthwhile. Based on the belief that the mentally ill can never really recover, the prevailing attitude is "take the medication and don't cause any problems." People describe the experience as feeling "written off" or "cast aside" by society. When Mr. G. was first committed to the hospital, his doctor told him, "You will have to give up your expectations of finishing college and getting a job. You will never be able to handle that much stress." Later, Mr. G. got involved in a recipient self-help project and began to represent other recipients on local boards and committees. Now he is on the staff of a local psychosocial club funded by the New York State Office of Mental Health and is successfully pursuing a degree in social work.

Many clients of the mental health system feel that the system focuses on illness and ignores clients' strengths. This focus tends to foster dependency. The system does not encourage clients to learn about their mental and emotional problems, or to take responsibility for their own recovery. The assumption is: you will have to trust the system to take care of you. People providing the services are often over-protective, tend to make decisions for their clients, and fail to acknowledge growth when it does occur. Mr. R. was told that he would never be able to leave the hospital: "You no longer have the strength to live in the outside world. Someone will have to take care of you for the rest of your life." He is currently out of the hospital and operates his own business. He credits his success to his participation in the self-help movement.

The issue of identity is perhaps the most important and the least concrete. People diagnosed as mentally ill often define themselves in terms of their "illness." Rather than having a diagnosis of mental illness, they see themselves as "mentally ill". This "mental illness," with all its negative connotations, becomes a way of life: it becomes their consuming identity. Physical pains, extreme emotions, attitudes, and moods are all seen, by the individual and other people, as a part of the "mental illness." Because of such a negative assumption, progressive mental health professionals do not ever use the terms mentally ill or mental illness.

Indeed, people diagnosed with mental illness often become unable to differentiate between what is healthy about their lives and what is "sick." When Mr. E. gets angry in the office, he initially views it as overreaction because of paranoia, rather than as the normal reaction to being aggravated by someone else. When he gets anxious before a speech, he thinks it is because he is frail and prone to panic attacks, rather than because anxiety is a normal response to giving a speech before a large audience. Through his involvement in self-help, he is learning from other recipients how to cope with symptoms of his diagnosis, and to distinguish them from "normal" feelings of anxiety and fear.

The disempowering nature of being diagnosed as mentally ill results in people who feel overwhelmed with isolation and hopelessness. What could induce more isolation and hopelessness than being at the end of a large, impersonal, and bureaucratic administration—a system that treats those it cares for as objects and numbers? What could increase that feeling more than having virtually no support from family or friends outside the system?

A Traditional State Mental Health System

When MHREP began in 1988, the mental health system was oriented toward hospital care and maintenance of individuals, rather than toward community care and recovery. The operating motif was: remove the person from society. Then place the patient in an environment with strong controls and minimal custodial care. It takes tens of thousands of people to maintain such a system.

The mental health system in New York State is indeed a large bureaucratic operation. In 1988, there were 33 state mental hospitals, with

20,502 in-patients, and 114 state-operated out-patient clinics. More than 31,500 people worked in the state hospitals and clinics. This does not include the people working in the state central office and those in the five regional offices. Nor does it include the number of people employed by the state-funded not-for-profit organizations that provide housing, day-treatment and other services at the community level. People whose work lives are invested in such a bureaucracy are very resistant to change—even threatened by it.

Under this system, people believed that persons diagnosed with mental illness would have an "illness" which would degenerate for the rest of their lives. Since people generally believed that patients who were discharged from the hospital would always have to return, community strategies aimed to maintain patients for as long as possible in the community between hospitalizations. Plans emphasized continuing day treatment programs rather than housing services. These programs amounted to "adult day care" that focused on simple crafts and adult daily-living skills. People assumed that programs based on teaching low-functioning skills, such as brushing teeth, combing hair, and taking showers were enough. However, people have learned that continuing day treatment programs tended to foster functioning at the level of the lowest common denominator.

People diagnosed as mentally ill were "treated" in custodial programs designed to fill their time and control their behavior without offering positive alternatives. The system cared for them, because the system believed that they could not take care of themselves, and would never be able to.

The new commissioner, Dr. Richard Surles, challenged this mindset. He asserted that people could recover if placed in the community and given the right supports. These supports included:

- housing with varying degrees of counselor supervision,
- psychiatric rehabilitation built around a patient's goals rather than around staff-imposed goals,
- intensive case management for the more "severely ill," to help them navigate the bureaucratic maze of community services, and
- promoting the concept of self-help among those diagnosed as mentally ill.

Many people thought the commissioner's notions would quickly die away because the average term for a commissioner of mental health is only

TIMELINE OF MAJOR EVENTS

	1988	1989	1990	1991	1992	1993	1994
RESULT	Initiate Self-help Movement	Consolidate Movement and Shift Emphasis to Projects			Develop Project Leadership Through Training and Technical Assistance		
ACTION	Recipient Town Meetings Recipients Only	Stigma Forums with Recipients & Family Members		Empowerment and Recovery Dialogues with Recipients and Professional Staff			
				Self-Directed Rehabilitation Workshops			
			Local Collaboration Project in Ten Counties				
		Statewide Recipient Conferences					

Recipient Town Meetings were conducted from October - December of 1988.
Stigma Forums were conducted from January - June of 1989.
Empowerment and Recovery Dialogues were conducted from June 1989 to the present.
The Local Collaboration Project ran from October 1990 until September 1993.
Self-Directed Rehabilitation Workshops were conducted from December 1990 to the present.
Statewide Recipient Conferences have been held every year beginning in 1989.

one and one-half years in the U.S. Only a few mental health advocates took him seriously, who themselves were fighting about priorities for using the limited community resources.

Emergence of a Movement

The Mental Patients Liberation Alliance (The Alliance) in Syracuse advocated against electroshock therapy and biopsychiatric drugs, and offered advocacy services and training. (A biopsychiatric drug is a drug that helps to regulate the flow of chemicals that help operate the brain and the central nervous system. They are extremely powerful and sometimes have debilitating side effects.) The Alliance viewed these drugs as "chemical straight jackets," used only to control and not to heal. In Hutchings Psychiatric Center, The Alliance advocated for people who were locked up, by informing them of their rights and pressing the hospital administration to guarantee those rights. The Alliance also trained others based on its work at Hutchings. It ran a drop-in center that housed one of the dozen or so self-help groups in the state. There were self-help groups in Buffalo, New York City, Poughkeepsie, and Ithaca. The only other incorporated group of clients in the state was Project Release in New York City. Their ideology was similar to that of The Alliance. All of these groups were initially suspicious of the new commissioner—he didn't seem staunchly against forced treatment and forced drugging, even though he was friendly to self-help.

Few professionals thought empowerment was possible. Most bought into the prevalent concept of "lock them up, medicate them, and hope that they will not cause any problems." While some saw Dr. Surles's ideas as threatening, most professionals did not view them as being seriously in danger of being implemented.

Knowing that the commissioner was friendly to self-help, Dr. Knight seized an opportunity to build a self-help movement. Such a movement might bring hope to a large number of people. Dr. Knight knew that, in order for the situation in New York to change, large numbers of people would have to be given a reason to hope, a means to overcome the isolation that dominated their lives, and a way to become actively engaged in running their daily lives.

Town Meetings for Empowerment

When he became the new director of the MHREP, Dr. Knight traveled around the state, holding town meetings. These meetings were for recipients only—a radical move in a system dominated by professionals. The focus questions were, What problems do you face before, during and after hospitalization? and, What can we do about these problems? The meetings were about two hours long and participatory in nature. Interestingly, in all meetings across the state, people recognized the same things as challenges:

- economic oppression
- disorganized and debilitating mental health system
- hospital abuse
- misuse of medication
- recipient population that did not experience itself as a community, with common values and goals
- treatment plans based on maintenance instead of recovery
- outpatient services that did not help people stay in the community
- negative public stigma

By discussing the second question eliciting solutions, people created a common agenda for action that was stated in the form of "New Directions," listed below:

- improved communication between staff and patients
- public education to reduce stigma
- better screening and training for staff
- a "Bill of Rights" for mental patients
- recipient-run treatment, housing, and socialization programs
- recipients hired to work in the system

In conjunction with the town meetings, Dr. Knight involved recipients from two existing recipient-run programs: Project SHARE in Philadelphia and Share Your Bounty in New York City. Project SHARE was a well-established organization delivering a variety of services in the Philadelphia area. Joe Rogers, executive director of Project SHARE, supported Dr. Knight's work, and he or his staff traveled with Dr. Knight on several occasions. Share Your Bounty was a new recipient-run organization providing food for the homeless in New York City. The executive director of Share Your Bounty, Edwin Montes, frequently traveled with Dr. Knight. Montes thought it was important for people to see and hear first-hand what recipients were doing, especially other recipients in New York State. Exposure to Share Your Bounty was crucial in this early phase. This helped overcome some of the stigma of buy-in and some of the recipients' disbelief.

Many participants in the town meetings realized that they were being taken seriously for the first time since they had been diagnosed. They were being told that they could think through their own problems and create solutions together. Ms. C. recalls her participation in her first town meeting. "I was being asked what I thought about my situation. This had never happened. I remember hearing myself talk and being pleased with what I was saying. I could think. Maybe I could act." This kind of experience helps people believe they can do something themselves and be effective.

Participants decided they could independently advocate against abuses. With scholarship funding from the MHREP, more people took advantage of the advocacy training offered by The Alliance in Syracuse. Recipients began to learn their rights and how to stand up for them. The fiercely independent attitude of The Alliance made this training especially valuable.

A group of recipients in Gowanda (in western New York State) received a grant from the state to run its own housing program. Thus, Housing Options, Inc., became one of the first recipient-run housing programs in the nation. The group worked with local landlords to overcome prejudice and secured safe and sanitary rental apartments that were acceptable to recipients. The $70,000 grant was for locating and providing housing for ten recipients. It provided housing for 20. Housing Options, Inc. currently assists over 150 people with housing services and has a budget of over $1,000,000.

Another group of recipients in Suffolk County (Long Island) came up with four "New Directions"—Educate Others, Educate Ourselves, Organize for Outreach and Organize to Protect our Rights. HALI, Inc. (Hands Across Long Island) is now the largest recipient-run organization in the state. Among its many activities, HALI operates 11 peer support groups and a drop-in center for socialization, publishes a monthly newsletter, and offers a variety of housing programs to 65-70 recipients.

Approximately 30 town meetings with over 400 participants took place between October and December, 1988. People were excited. For

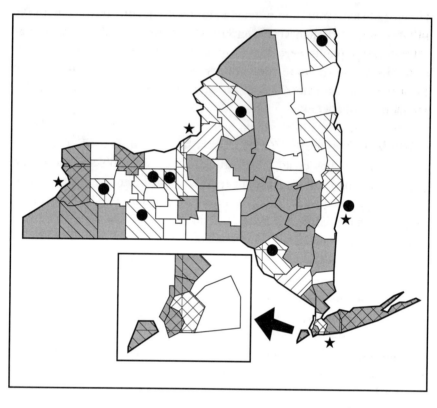

RECIPIENT TOWN MEETINGS

EMPOWERMENT AND RECOVERY DIALOGUES

SELF-DIRECTED REHABILITATION

LOCAL COLLABORATION PROJECTS

STIGMA FORUMS WITH FAMILY MEMBERS

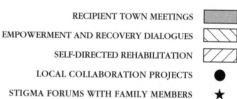

the first time, recipients came together in an organized manner across the state to share their concerns. Maybe they could do something about their situation. Hope was on the rise. Local self-support groups formed. Peers counseled each other. A sense of "common experiences and common concerns" started breaking down the walls of individual isolation. People began to speak out about their concerns. In 1989, the first statewide recipient conference was held. Over 130 recipients came together from all across New York State to hear what other recipients were doing in other states. In 1990, New York State recipients ran the statewide conference completely. They gave presentations. They ran workshops. They shared their learnings and successes. They argued about issues and priorities. And in doing so, they experienced a new sense of power, individually and as a group.

Stigma Forums with Family Members

The second wave of statewide meetings was with families and recipients. Called "Stigma Forums," these meetings focused on the powerful force of social stigma in the lives of recipients and their families. Stigma Forums were similar to town meetings except that families and recipients met together with no emphasis on planning for action. Instead, they discussed the questions, Where do you experience social stigma? and How are you affected by it? Consultants skilled in managing participatory meetings came in to help with these forums and to expand the work of MHREP. From the grassroots level, a consensus emerged that the mental health system itself was the most stigmatizing element in the lives of both the recipients and the family members. But no one felt able to act without first affecting the attitudes and actions of the treatment providers.

Dialogues for Empowerment

Now was the time to begin to move more directly on the mental health system itself. The system had engendered a sense of isolation, dependency, and hopelessness among the people it served. Dr. Knight knew that MHREP needed something more than town meetings and forums. In his first quarterly report, dated December, 1988, he wrote:

> ...we realized that one of the central blocks involved professional attitudes and frustrations....A Dialogue Day between professionals and recipients in some areas of the state may help overcome professional stereotypes and help overcome learned helplessness (on the part of recipients).

Dr. Knight hired Ike Powell, who had years of experience as a consultant, to help design and facilitate a more comprehensive curriculum of workshops and seminars. MHREP held more meetings across the state. This time professionals and recipients came together in a three-hour format called, "Dialogues for Empowerment." These dialogues focused on the questions, What was disempowering about being diagnosed mentally ill? and, What has empowered you? Two facilitators conducted the empowerment workshops: Ike Powell and a recipient of mental health services who was being trained as a consultant.

When the professionals and recipients in the workshop discussed their concerns as equals, both began to see each other in new ways. Professionals could see "clients" as articulate, thoughtful people who had insights about the services they were receiving—what was helpful and what was not. Recipients could see "staff" as caring, concerned people who often saw ways to deliver services better, but were controlled by guidelines, policies, and bureaucratic procedures that often did not make the client's welfare a priority. Most professionals who participated in the dialogues confirmed the earlier consensus that the mental health system itself was the most disempowering element. They saw it as a system that created dependence, was often abusive, and tended to focus more on controlling behavior than on achieving wellness.

Focus on Training

While the empowerment dialogues continued across the state, Ike Powell and Dr. Knight created other workshops and seminars to offer to the New York State community. "An Introduction to Self-Directed Rehabilitation" focused on taking more control of one's life through setting and achieving goals. "Recovery Dialogues" helped both recipients and staff to focus on what was helpful and what was not in the recovery process. Strategic Planning, Group Facilitation Training, and other special focus workshops helped prepare people for leadership roles in their local communities. As local recipients became more trained in organizing, facilitation, advocacy, and peer-support, more groups began to sponsor local recipient-run projects, such as drop-in centers, advocacy groups, housing alternatives, and employment skills training. These activities were funded by the New York State Office of Mental Health.

In 1990, New York State received a three-year grant from the National Institute of Mental Health to expand recipient leadership training into the rural and minority areas. Ten groups, each representing a county, received funding for three years. Their mission: to develop leadership skills around whatever project the recipients decided to initiate. Powell, selected to be the field consultant to this project, helped with organizing, training, and documenting. The Research Foundation for Mental Hygiene, Inc., selected both the target communities and the control communities. The groups sent out invitations to participate in the project, and held initial meetings in each county to explain the project and to answer questions.

Again, using participatory workshop methods, recipients, professionals, and families of recipient members met to decide projects for their respective counties. Recipients selected projects such as these:

- thrift stores
- computer skills programs
- drop-in centers
- monthly social and recreational events
- English-as-a-Second-Language classes
- advocacy centers

The recipients ran each project, with support from professionals and family members as needed. Recipients learned to maintain financial records, organize and facilitate meetings, work with community agencies, and advocate for their rights.

Benefits of Participation and Self-Help

In Dr. Knight's first quarterly report in 1988, he stated: "The key to creating a movement is creating a sense of community." But among recipients of mental health services, many things work against building community. For instance, recipients come from all educational levels and cultural backgrounds. (Ph.D.s as well as people who are skilled job holders receive mental health care.) Then, too, out of the cultural diversity of New York State, every group or subgroup in the population is represented. The emphasis on "expert opinion" in mental health care leaves recipients feeling that the mental problems they confront are ones with which only experts can deal. Traditionally, recipients have not even talked to each other about their emotional and mental problems, as if they needed to be certified to do so. There had been no place for recipients to gather, other than the hospital and out-patient clinics. And, even then, the stigma of mental illness often meant that recipients did not trust one another.

One benefit of both self-help and participation is that they create a common awareness about the situation. Coming together in town meetings, forums, and dialogues to discuss the common experiences of mental problems, treatment, abuse, and stigma was totally new for recipients. Participants in the workshops realized that other people felt the same way they did. For example, after being considered "delusional" or "liars," recipients who experienced physical abuse in the hospital could share with others who had similar experiences. This common awareness was especially evident when participants discussed what it was like to relate to a system that more often attempts to control rather than to treat. Such common awareness becomes the basis for community, which replaces the isolation that is so much a part of most recipients' lives.

As people became involved in activities that call for their input and opinions, they felt valued as human beings. In New York City, a group of Latino recipients decided to use some of their grant money to hire a person to teach them English. They advertised for the teacher, interviewed applicants, and negotiated schedule and salary terms with the selected teacher. Through their participation, they took responsibility for all aspects of the project. They began to see each other in a new light. Instead of individual clients coming to the clinic each day to see a professional, they became a group of people with common concerns who were willing to work together toward a common goal.

In Warsaw, New York, a group of recipients decided to use their money from an NIMH Systems Improvement Grant to set up and operate a thrift store. Because Warsaw is a rural community with no second-hand clothing store, the recipients saw this gap as opportunity to do something worthwhile and also possibly to change the community's image of those they considered to be "mentally ill." On their own, they searched for real estate space, negotiated with the property owner, arranged for utilities and phone installation, and did most of the physical renovation of the building. They realized that they could think through what was needed to initiate and establish a project: they could do things that "normal" people do.

In 1991, recipients began to work directly within the system. One of the most successful programs was the Peer Specialists program at Bronx Psychiatric Center. Funded through MHANYS, this program included Dr. Knight on the management team. Four recipients were hired to work as "assistants" to intensive case managers (ICMs), trained case managers carrying a small caseload of people who have been diagnosed more "seriously and persistently mentally ill." Regularly, ICMs must visit clients to teach them to function more effectively in the community. Peer specialists assist in many socialization activities, from taking the client shopping to educational or entertainment events. The clients seemed to relate in a special way to the peer specialists because of their common experiences, i.e., hospitalization, medication, social stigma, isolation, and hopelessness. The peer specialists saw themselves as valuable, significant human beings with something to share with others—because of their experience, rather than in spite of it.

Gradually, positive change began to spread in the state, independent of MHREP planning. Harlem Valley Psychiatric Center initiated a program to cover the cost for recipients to receive training in social casework, and then hired them as assistant case managers. Each of the five regions in New York has hired a recipient as the regional recipient affairs specialist. People are empowered when their past is seen as a time of valuable learnings rather than just shameful experiences.

Difficulties, Conflicts and Disagreements

Problems faced over the life of the project have been fairly constant, but have leveled off in intensity. Professional indifference or outright opposition has been the major obstacle. Professionals often fear all self-help is about "psychotics getting together and reinforcing each other's delusions and treatment resistance." In such cases, these professionals will not allow self-help to develop in those under their care. And in some cases, professionals have resented recipients "telling them how to run their programs."

Another significant problem is professional invasion of self-help, i.e., setting up professionally run groups and calling them self-help. This exercise is often hard to distinguish from genuine attempts of professionals to foster self-help. In many cases the professional never intends to let go of the group he or she formed. One hallmark of genuine self-help initiatives is that the professionals involved provide support but do not make decisions for the group. Also, genuine attempts to foster self-help always move to a letting-go stage.

Some professionals raised opposition when some recipients preferred a recipient-run self-help program to the program being offered by professionals. Since most professionally run programs are funded according to the number of participants, these professionals saw successful recipient-run programs as a financial threat.

Three to four years of "fighting for our rights" have left some recipients burnt-out and discouraged. Also, recipients who have preferred to let the system take care of them have resented other recipients rocking the boat. Then, too, recipient-run initiatives have often been managed by people with little organizational experience. Sometimes, this practice has led to poor financial management practices and accusations of mismanagement and fraud. Professionals have tended to take control when this happens. On the other hand, recipients have sometimes "thrown the baby out with the bath water" in their attempt to free themselves from professional controls. Also, some recipient power struggles have led to cases of mutual mistrust, anger, and hurt feelings.

Yet in spite of all of these difficulties, people's lives have changed, and the leadership of the state mental health system continues to support and encourage recipient self-help.

The Impact of the Self-Help Movement on the Mental Health System

Special Assistant to the Commissioner for Recipient Affairs, Darby Penny states,

> As state mental health agencies have increased their efforts to shift away from institutional care to community-based services in recent years, people who were once debilitated and dependent 'career mental patients' have become self-directed members of the community. As these people have begun to find their own voices, they have become increasingly outspoken about the harm that was done to them in institutions in the name of treatment, and the continuing harm done in community-based programs that operate with old institutional values[3].

In 1988, when the MHREP was initiated, about ten core groups were active in New York State. The Alliance in Syracuse was the strongest and had the longest history. It had then been offering advocacy training for over 15 years. Trained and awakened people were scattered across the state, but a large-scale movement had not emerged. By 1994, over 300 local core groups existed as well as 15 legally incorporated recipient-run not-for-profit organizations. Hundreds of recipients participated in housing, peer support counseling, case management, advocacy, and drop-in centers. In 1988, the number of patients hospitalized was 20,502, compared to 11,919 in 1993. In 1988, there were 16 state-operated out-patient residence programs, and 393 state-funded locally operated residence programs. In 1994 there were 37 state-operated programs and 550 locally operated, state-funded out-patient residence programs. Recipients successfully advocated for passing the Re-Investment Bill in the state legislature. This bill enables money to be shifted to community-support programs when hospitals are closed or downsized. Also, some professional programs are moving toward including self-help and real choice in programming.

Some professionals are seeking recipient input into the kinds of activities offered at clinics and continuing day treatment programs. Some professionally-run agencies are also making space in their facilities for recipient-run programs. Recipients are being requested to serve on state, county, and local advisory boards that oversee funding and determine policy.

In Retrospect

In its first five years, the Mental Health Recipient Empowerment project wakened individuals to its potential. The focus was on community education and outreach. MHREP stressed activities that enable broad-based participation in terms of rural, urban, geographical spread, various age groups, and all ethnic groups, to ensure that everyone felt a part of the movement. Not only was it important to reach out in a variety of ways, but also to offer a variety of ways for people to participate.

In the midst of broad-based participation, it was crucial to demonstrate to people what is possible. The locally operated, recipient-run services and programs caught the attention of key professionals in the state. They also gave hope to hundreds of recipients—hope that their efforts had produced some of the changes they sought. Housing Options, Inc. in Gowanda, PEOPLe, Inc. in Poughkeepsie, and HALI, Inc. on Long Island all demonstrated the power and potential of recipient participation for direct delivery of mental health services.

Not everyone has immediately jumped on the bandwagon of recipient empowerment and self-help. Tensions, conflicts, disagreements, and hard feelings sometimes developed between family members, professional providers, and recipients of services. Building the necessary support for the people and the activities of the movement often required having "friends in high places." To protect the movement, the groups found they must keep these key people informed.

Meanwhile, many good things continue to happen in the movement. People have been willing to explore all possibilities in order to find what will work. For instance, NIMH funded the Bronx Peer Specialists as a pilot program. Numerous "peer specialists" came to work in and receive funding from the Office of Mental Health. The peer specialist position is even recognized as a civil service category. Housing Options, Inc.'s success catalyzed numerous other recipient-run housing programs. PEOPLe, Inc.'s early work in peer support and counseling provided encouragement and training for other recipients. The Ithaca Mental Health Association received funding to establish a recipient-run crisis center. Perhaps this pilot program will catalyze other ways for people to get away from their current stressful situations and live in a recipient-supported environment instead of a locked hospital ward.

A key component to success was many people's determination to keep their success stories alive and well. Key phrases and symbols sustained and unified people's efforts. The mottoes, "Recipient Empowerment," "Choice Not Force," "We can speak for ourselves," "Advocacy," "Self-Directed Rehabilitation," and "Self-Help" motivated hundreds of recipients. Publicizing key events, individual successes, and group successes helped create an atmosphere of hope. When publicized, these successes became a part of everyone's story.

Where Do We Go From Here?

More professionals are beginning to value the recipients' contributions. Articles in professional journals acknowledge that recipients' contributions improve the quality of mental health services. Professionals visit recipient-run projects to see how they are different. The central office and the five regional offices hired recipients as special liaisons to the commissioners. Other recipients continue to be hired throughout the system.

In the words of Dr. Knight, "Nothing short of an empowered, trained, statewide movement of recipients of services can have any impact on the mental health system." Only this kind of movement can sustain the reason to hope, the sense of community, and the means for engagement that are so crucial to sustaining the current momentum.

People's lives have changed. Now those changed people must learn to work together over the long haul. For teamwork is the only way to change a bureaucratic system that is deeply rooted in years of tradition, rules, and regulations. But if the first years are any barometer of long-term success, New York's mental health care recipients are off to a healthy start.

References

[1]. Anthony, William A. *Western New York Mental Health World, Mental Health Associations of Western New York,* Vol. I, Issue 3, Summer 1993, Buffalo, New York.

[2]. Carpinello, Sharon E. A Qualitative Study of the Perceptions of the Meaning of Self-Help, Self-Help Group Processes and Outcomes, Bureau of Evaluation and Research, New York State Office of Mental Health, July 1991, pp. 2-3 of the Executive Summary.

[3]. Penny, Darby and David Hilton. Changing the Face of Mental Health Administration: Creating Offices of Consumer/Ex-Patient Affairs, draft of unpublished article, January 1994, pp. 1-2.

[4]. The Five Strategic Elements of Building a Movement are adapted from unpublished works by the Institute of Cultural Affairs.

AFTERWORD

THE HONORABLE BARBARA ROBERTS,
FORMER GOVERNOR OF OREGON

*We all know what the public is demanding from
government at all levels: that public employees work
smarter and work leaner, that we must do more with
fewer resources, and that we all must have the political
courage to stop doing things that are no longer
necessary or don't deliver results.*

Federal, state, and local government agencies have been aggressively changing the way they deliver services. Mostly, these changes come from our deep-seated desire to serve the citizens better. But also, they come from a demanding public who wants ever greater performance out of every tax dollar. Resulting from these citizen demands, a movement has been launched, and coined "reinventing government."

A central idea behind the reinvention movement and reflected in the stories in this book is that we have to know what we want before we can "invent" anything. We have to define our goals, set standards, and find ways to measure our program.

All too often in government, we forget that change and improvement aren't always synonymous. If our goals are undefined, if we have no realistic way to measure our success or failure, or no way to recognize the need to adjust our course midstream if we aren't measuring up, we won't "reinvent" anything. One of the most important challenges we face in communities throughout the nation is identifying the promising practices that can achieve measurable results while really making a difference.

For several years now, Oregon has worked on a process to ensure greater accountability. This innovative process began with the development of a strategic plan. With input from all sectors all across the state, we translated a vision into a series of measurable goals, which are being used now by local government, nonprofit organizations, the private sector, and grant-giving foundations in our state.

Our aim was to find ways to draw the entire state and all its citizens together towards a common purpose. We found that the more we used this approach, the more we recognized that to tackle the really challenging problems facing our state and our communities, we needed to work together, across all levels of government and every community sector. Improving outcomes for children, for example, requires the united action of families, schools, churches, social service agencies, and government. Improving competitiveness of industries requires not just effort from the private sector, but also quality education, and an advanced workforce, research facilities, and other public-sector products.

Also we learned from others' successes. As we developed new ways to run our programs, we put out requests for information to dozens of other states, gleaning ideas from chance encounters, pursuing every lead that promised an idea we could incorporate.

We learned that there must be a better way. In a time when we are working to streamline government and cut our costs, we shouldn't need to send our staff to dozens of conferences, looking for good ideas. We shouldn't need to struggle alone to reinvent governance, each in our own jurisdiction. And we certainly can't afford, state by state, city by city, agency by agency, to commission major studies to discover how other jurisdictions have achieved results.

This book will be a handy tool for those also committed to revitalizing their communities and their forms of governance. Stories like these need to be spread far and wide. They tell of communities and government agencies who worked together to create action plans that improved the way of doing things for everybody concerned. These success stories remind us that reinventing government is everyone's responsibility.

One of the most promising institutions I see for nurturing the reinvention movement is the Alliance for Redesigning Government. The Alliance is building a network of pioneers nationwide who are committed to improving the way we govern. Through a biweekly FAX newsletter, workbooks, and other avenues, it is connecting us all to leading ideas and initiatives. I encourage readers to seek out the Alliance.

Looking ahead, we see that one area deserving great attention is intergovernmental service delivery. We know at the state level that many of our dollars flow not to state-run programs, but to localities. We are trying to change the way those dollars are managed, by removing red tape and focusing more on results.

Similarly, the federal government needs to take a hard look at how federal dollars flow to state and local governments. There is wide agreement among all levels of government and political persuasions that the federal intergovernmental system is dysfunctional. There are too many funding categories, too much red tape, and too little focus on results.

The process we started in state government was never envisioned as a tool for state government alone. For instance, here in Oregon, we are working with the federal government to find a better way. We have proposed The Oregon Option, a special partnership and long-range demonstration project to redesign the intergovernmental system based on the principles advanced in the National Performance Review. This interagency, intergovernmental initiative would focus on outcomes and treat goals reached as the principal measure and benchmark of success. To help achieve results, we have asked the federal government to merge funding streams, create funding incentives that reward desirable results, and reduce micromanagement and wasteful paperwork.

We are delighted by the response. Federal, state, and local government officials have rolled up their sleeves to reexamine the basic assumptions we use to govern, and to apply new principles to achieve the results we all want. The most important benefit, and the ultimate test of The Oregon Option, will be results: higher numbers of healthy babies, lower rates of teen pregnancy, higher skill levels, higher wages, safer communities. In doing this, we hope to rebuild public confidence in government.

The Oregon Option and other such efforts will require a long-term, bipartisan commitment to succeed, and a fundamentally different way of thinking about the mission and structure of service systems at all levels of government. We know that change is not easy and will take years to complete. Yet, there is not a moment to delay.

The success stories in this anthology prove that we can improve the delivery of services. The articles in *Government Works* inspire me, and I hope they inspire you. They remind all of us that bold and visionary public leaders and attentive citizens throughout America are indeed making a big difference.